Tries in the Valleys

A History of Rugby League in

Edited by Peter Lush and Dave Farrar

"There are three things not discussed in polite society:
politics, religion... and Rugby League"

Twentieth Century Welsh Proverb

LONDON LEAGUE PUBLICATIONS LIMITED

Tries in the Valleys
A History of Rugby League in Wales

© Copyright the contributors. The moral right of the authors have been asserted.

Photographs may not be reproduced without permission. All photographs copyright to the photographer or provider of the photograph.

Typesetting and layout by Peter Lush, with assistance from Dave Farrar.

This book is sold subject to the condition that it shall not, by way of trade or otherwise, be lent, resold, hired out or otherwise circulated without the publisher's prior consent in any form of binding or cover other than that in which it is published and without a similar condition including this condition being imposed on the subsequent purchaser.

A CIP catalogue record for this book is available from the British Library.

First published in Great Britain in April 1998 by:
London League Publications Ltd, P.O. Box 10441, London E14 0SB

ISBN: 0-9526064-3-7

Cover design by: Stephen McCarthy Graphic Design
                          23, Carol Street, London NW1 0HT

Printed and bound by: Redwood Books, Trowbridge, Wiltshire.

Cover photos: Jonathan Davies: Graham Clay / *League Express*
                          1995 Wales World Cup Squad: Varley Picture Agency

Dedicated to all those who have attempted to develop Rugby League in Wales

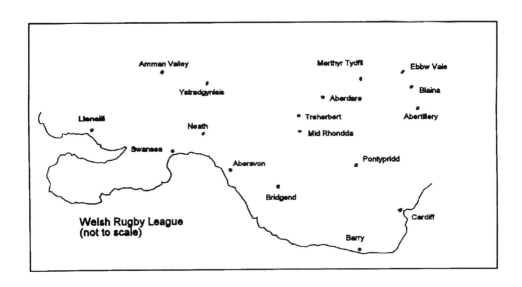

Foreword

The 1995 World Cup was fantastic for me and all the Welsh players. We had worked hard since 1989, had talked about this tournament and everything came together for us to reach the semi-final at Old Trafford.

How far Rugby League had got in Wales was shown by the support we took with us to Old Trafford. It was a great tournament, more so in Wales than many people realise. S4C (the Welsh Channel Four) showed our games live. The game against Western Samoa is still talked about - the atmosphere, the ferocity of the tackling, the skills and the passion of the Welsh boys.

Most of that team had played together in Rugby Union as well, and many of us were coming to the end of our careers. The team spirit was fantastic, both the players born and bred in Wales, and those who were born in Lancashire and Yorkshire, but qualified for the team through Welsh grandparents.

The semi-final was the end of my Rugby League career, because I was going back to South Wales to play Rugby Union for Cardiff, and I wouldn't have wanted to finish my Rugby League career in any other way.

I captained Wales at both Rugby Union and Rugby League. I was happy just to be able to play for Wales at both codes, and it was a great pleasure to be able to captain the sides. It was a fantastic honour for me, and I have great respect for the players in those sides.

When I left Wales in 1989, there was no Wales Rugby League team. Sometimes I felt like the Pied Piper, as other players then followed me up north. Sometimes the national team would struggle if we were short of players but, with our best side, we could give anyone a game. I would like to thank Clive Griffiths, Jim Mills and Mike Nicholas for the work they did in helping to build the Welsh team.

It was also a great honour for me to play for - and captain - the Great Britain Rugby League team.

I hope there is a good future for Rugby League in Wales. The development of the academy sides is very important. I believe that Rugby League and Rugby Union should stay as separate games. They are very different, with different skills, and it would be sad to lose one or the other. The games complement one another. Now players will have a chance to play both games professionally, which they did not have before, and that is very important. But I think that with Rugby Union going professional, less players will go north from Wales to play Rugby League. This won't weaken Rugby League, because only a small number of players have gone north recently. And I hope that the financial problems that both games face can be resolved.

I would like to thank Dougie Laughton for giving me the chance to play Rugby League, all the players I played with, and the clubs I played for in Great Britain and Australia. I hope all the readers enjoy this book, and appreciate the contribution Wales has made to Rugby League.

Jonathan Davies
March 1998

Preface

The question of developing outside of its traditional areas is one that has faced Rugby League since 1895. One of the key areas of potential development for the game has always been Wales.

Many famous players have 'gone north' from Wales to clubs in the north, making an enormous contribution to Rugby League. On the international stage, the Wales team has contributed much to the game. Their performance, and their supporters' enthusiasm at the famous match against Western Samoa in 1995 has become part of Rugby League folklore, and will not be forgotten by those privileged to be there. The battles of the Welsh team over the years, in particular those matches played in Wales, are covered by this book.

So why, despite various attempts over the years, has club Rugby League never become established in Wales? This is the other main area this book examines. One point worth remembering is that in all the attempts, there has never been a successful club side, playing at the top level, with adequate funding for marketing and development. In a nation where top class Rugby Union is the tradition, second class Rugby League has never succeeded.

The growth of the London Broncos shows what is possible for Wales. From crowds of a few hundred, playing in the second division, the Broncos now are a major force in Super League, attracting thousands to their matches. Such a development, we believe, is possible in South Wales. If Super League is to be more than the old First Division under a new title, development into new areas is crucial, and South Wales must be one of them.

We hope that Rugby League has a strong future in Wales, and that this book helps keep the idea of a Super League club in Wales on Rugby League's agenda for the future.

Peter Lush and Dave Farrar

Thanks

We would like to thank all the other writers, who gave advice and assistance well beyond their original remit. Most of the credit for the statistics must go to Robert Gate and John Coyle. We would also like to thank Gareth Harris for providing research material on the first attempt to set up a Northern Union club in Pontypridd, and Anthony Lewis for providing information about the Welsh League in the 1940s and early 1950s. They both showed that in the field of sports history, there are no barriers between the codes. Of course, any mistakes are our responsibility.

We would also like to thank Sandra for her hospitality and patience. Everyone who gave time to be interviewed enabled that part of the book to be written, and we are grateful for their co-operation and patience. People who subscribed to the book in advance showed faith in our ability to produce it, and provided important financial backing. The people listed below all helped with the book in different ways, and their support is appreciated.

Stuart Alexander
(Redwood Books)
Mike Bondy
Joan Coyle
Trevor Delaney
Harry Edgar and *Open Rugby*
Polly Goerres
Clive Griffiths
Les Hoole
John Jenkins

Peter John
Jean Jones
T. R. Jones
Vernon Jones
League Express
Sally Manders
Stephen McNulty
Phil Melling
Tim Moulding
Joyce O'Hare
Trevor Oldam

Dudley Stephen
Dawn Wicks
Staff at:
The National Library of Wales.
British Newspaper Library
Merthyr Tydfil Library
Pontypridd Library
Bridgend Library
Cardiff Central Library

About the authors

Tony Collins was a founder of the Rugby League Supporters' Association and is the author of *Rugby's Great Split: Class, Culture and the Origins of Rugby League Football*. A third-generation Hull KR supporter, he now works as the Rugby Football League's archivist in Leeds.

John Coyle was born in 1961 and lived in South Yorkshire for many years before moving to Solihull, where he now resides. John works in IT Recruitment, and has recently completed a Master of Arts Degree in Sport and Recreation at De Montfort University. His dissertation compared the expansion strategies pursued by the Football League and the Northern Union (Rugby League) prior to 1923. John is a member of the Association of Sports Historians and has contributed to a number of journals, fanzines and other publications. He is a long-suffering supporter of Doncaster Rovers and also follows the fortunes of Doncaster Dragons RLFC.

Dave Farrar has been watching Rugby League for more than 30 years. He was born in Salford, but did have a Welsh grandfather! He is a supporter of the London Broncos and co-author (with Peter Lush and Michael O'Hare) of *Touch and Go*; *I Wouldn't Start from Here*; *The Sin Bin*, (with Peter Hardy & Steve Spencer); *From Arundel to Zimbabwe* (with Peter Lush and Robin Osmond); and *The Right to Vote*, (with Yve Amor). Dave works as a manager in local government., and his boyhood heroes were David Evans, David Watkins and Maurice Richards.

Robert Gate is a life long follower of Halifax (that's just plain Halifax) RLFC, with a soft spot for Doncaster (that's just plain Donny), where he trained to become a teacher. In 1984 he foolishly decided to write about Rugby League for a living but has only half fulfilled that ambition. He certainly writes about Rugby League but as for making a living ... Sadly, recent years have seen him seriously afflicted by LFS (Lindsay Fatigue Syndrome). He hopes to get better soon but his doctor says he needs a change of climate.

Despite having written a two volume work on Welsh Rugby League players (*"Gone North" I* and *II* - stocks still available under the beds, in the garage, up in the loft), he is in no way Welsh. His wife, Myfanwy, at the other extreme, is Welsh-born and Welsh-speaking, but possesses neither a black hat nor a red shawl. They live in Ripponden in the far West Riding.

Peter Lush had a misspent youth playing and watching football. He was introduced to Rugby League by Dave Farrar when Fulham started in 1980. He did not then anticipate writing books about the game! He co-wrote *Touch and Go* with Dave Farrar and Michael O'Hare, and has developed an intimate relationship with England's motorway system while working on guidebooks for Rugby League and Cricket.

He has also written for *The Greatest Game* and *London Calling!* He is a season-ticket holder at the London Broncos and at West Ham United FC. When not involved in sport he works as a freelance housing and personnel consultant.

Michael O'Hare is the Production Editor for *New Scientist* magazine and has recently added writing for *The Guardian* and two startling appearances on TV sports shows to his portfolio, which includes work on *Autosport, Open Rugby* and *Touch & Go*, the forerunner to this volume. He enjoys, most of all, writing for *The Greatest Game!* fanzine and playing touch rugby in summer because the tackling doesn't hurt and he can drink beer outside afterwards. Sadly, he still supports Huddersfield RLFC and lives in Northwood, Middlesex but has, since his last book, married Sally. It hasn't changed either of them, but both their lives have subsequently been radically altered by a recent bereavement when Luther the goldfish died.

Huw Richards is the only Welsh contributor to this book, although there is a grain of truth in Dave Hadfield's allegation, in *XIII Winters*, that he "is from Bridgnorth in Shropshire but feels like he comes from Swansea because of the spelling of his first name". The happy timing of journalism training in Cardiff means that some of the Cardiff Dragons section was written from (hazy) first-hand recollection, although he was much more excited by Swansea City's only ever League Championship bid. He has written on Rugby League since 1983, contributing to the *Rugby Leaguer* and *League Express*, editing the Fulham RLFC programme in 1985-6 and writing chapters for *XIII Winters, Touch and Go* and the Rugby League Yearbook. He has been the *Financial Times* writer on both rugby codes since 1995 and is also author of *The Bloody Circus*, a history of the *Daily Herald* newspaper published in 1997.

Historical notes

Rule changes when the first clubs in Wales were starting

In *Code 13*, Trevor Delaney, stated "Some of the most radical experiments in the game's history were made from 1904 until 1908, and by the end of this period Northern Union legislators believed that the game as a spectacle had reached a peak". So the game in Wales was born at a time of change as the sport attempted to move away from its Union roots. Scrummaging was reduced and kicking had a lesser role with handling in the ascendancy.

Play the ball and ball-back: One of the most distinct features of today's game, the "play the ball" was introduced at the 1906 Northern Union AGM. It was different from today's game with the ball always heeled back to a colleague, because the tackled player could be surrounded by other players. The "ball-back" rule prevented kicking directly into touch from open play. If the ball did not bounce play was bought back to where it was kicked. This reduced the number of scrums and amount of touch kicking. These were major changes from Rugby Union.

Loose-heads: In 1907, one of the more defining rulings occurred with the defining of the scrummaging rules and the defending side being allowed the "loose-head" in all cases, before this apparently some sides packed all their players in the front row.

Tries are the aim not goals: At the 1908 AGM a fundamental change from the old rules of 1897 saw the object of the game being changed. In the old rule Law 1 (unchanged from Union) the emphasis had been on goal scoring. The rule was changed to "The object of the game shall be to cross an opponent's goal-line to score tries and kick the ball over the cross bar and over the posts".

(Based on an article in *Code 13* Number 9 by Trevor Delaney)

Football and Rugby

The Welsh Rugby Union was until 1934 called the Welsh Football Union, and therefore in the early chapters, the initials *WFU* are used. Association Football is generally referred to as *football* rather than soccer.

League Tables

Until 1930, the clubs in the Northern Rugby League did not all play each other, and the percentage of points won was used to calculate the final table.

Contents

Trevor Foster   Mike Nicholas
Clive Griffiths   George Nicholls
John Mantle   Danny and Kerry Sheehy
Phil Melling   Danny Sheehy (senior)
Jim Mills   Bobby Wanbon
Glyn Moses   David Watkins

Part One:

In the beginning

Chapter 1: The 1895 split and South Wales

"Why doesn't Wales play Rugby League?" This is a question often asked but rarely answered satisfactorily. Of course, Wales does play Rugby League, as this book proves, but those who ask the question are invariably referring to the Welsh nation as a whole.

After all, its national side has traditionally comprised miners, steelworkers and manual labourers, exactly the type of person who made Rugby League what it is in northern England. But it is not only the uninitiated who ask the question: many Rugby League followers feel that the Welsh are playing the wrong game - and certainly the pro-League comments of Jonathan Davies and Scott Gibbs following their returns from playing League to Union seem to confirm this suspicion. So why did the Welsh Football (Rugby) Union (WFU) maintain its allegiance to the English public school old boys who ran the Rugby Football Union (RFU) from 1895 up to the First World War, when the mould of British sport was being set?

Close bonds

The close bonds between rugby in the north of England and in South Wales were forged in the early 1880s, at the same time as the sport was beginning to find popularity among the working classes of the two regions. In 1884 Wakefield Trinity, then arguably the best side in the north, Batley, Dewsbury and Hull visited Cardiff, Llanelli, Neath and Newport. From then on, short tours by clubs became regular occurrences, especially at Christmas and Easter holiday times. Large crowds would greet the visitors, accompanied by outpourings of civic celebration.

Looking back on the 1880s, Llanelli forward Elias Jones recalled that: "Hull were especially popular visitors, and I remember that the horses were taken out of the brake in which they were to travel and the brake dragged to the Thomas Arms by the people who had gathered to welcome them. It was a remarkable sight, for many had secured cotton waste from the works and lit this to form a torchlight procession. Arriving at the Thomas Arms, there were scenes of great enthusiasm, and the Hull captain had to make a speech from the balcony."

These regular meetings not unsurprisingly led to the economically stronger Lancashire and Yorkshire clubs enviously eyeing the more outstanding of their Welsh opponents' players. Slowly but surely the trek of migrant rugby labourers began to tread a path from the valleys to the Pennines and its hinterlands.

The first reported Welsh player to 'go north' appears to have been international full back D.H. 'Harry' Bowen of Llanelli, who signed for Dewsbury in 1884. The following year Wales and Newport back James Bridie signed for Manningham. The first player to move north and make a real impact on the game was Wales and Cardiff half-back William 'Buller' Stadden who went to Dewsbury in September 1886.

In Lancashire, Oldham set the pace in bringing players up from the principality, the first being international three-quarter Bill McCutcheon who signed in 1888, swiftly followed by fellow international Dai Gwyn. McCutcheon later became a leading Rugby League referee and senior administrator with Oldham. Perhaps the most famous Welsh signings before the 1895 split were David and Evan James, who transferred from Swansea to Manchester's Broughton Rangers in 1892 for a reputed signing-on fee of

£250, contrary to Rugby Union's strict amateur laws.

The formation of the Northern Union (NU) in 1895 accelerated the flow of players from Wales to the north. For many NU supporters, the flood was too much - within a few months of the split, Wakefield Trinity were nicknamed the 'Tyko-Taffy Combination' because of the number of Welsh players in the side and in 1898 Huddersfield had seven Welshman in their team. It was also too much for the WFU, who sought to ban NU scouts from grounds and in one case struck off a referee whom they discovered had been scouting for a northern club. In 1899 the *Western Mail* reported that a Wigan scout was thrown into a river at Penarth to discourage his activities!

Yet Welsh Rugby Union was itself awash with accusations of player poaching and undercover professionalism. So widespread were payments to players in Wales that Bill McCutcheon remarked that it was often not wages but large signing-on fees which tempted players to go north. Some may even have been earning more as 'amateurs' than many NU 'professionals'. In 1901 Treherbert were accused of offering Pontypridd's Dawson £1 a week and in 1907 allegations were made that players were commonly paid between a sovereign and six shillings per match.

But the biggest controversy surrounded Welsh Rugby Union's greatest name, Arthur Gould. In honour of his achievements, a national testimonial was organised in 1896 which raised enough money to present him with the deeds to his house. The (English) RFU then declared Gould to be a professional and forbade its clubs and players from playing against him. In February 1897 the WFU withdrew from Rugby Union's International Board after it upheld the English ban. A split appeared imminent but by the start of the 1897-8 season a compromise was reached and the historic opportunity for the NU and the WFU to unite in a semi-professional British Rugby Union was lost.

Two factors stopped this happening: the cynicism of the RFU and the cravenness of the Welsh authorities. The 1895 split had been caused by the intransigence of the RFU towards payments to working class players. The clubs in the north of England had done everything possible to avoid a split; it was only when the RFU made it clear that they would expel the northern clubs one-by-one that self-preservation took over and the northerners formed their own union. Even then many of the NU's leaders hoped for a reconciliation. If the RFU had wanted to compromise, there would have been no NU.

But when it came to Wales, the RFU was prepared to compromise. A Welsh split would have been a massive blow to it and a huge boost for the NU. It would also mean the probable loss of the English west country because clubs there played most of their fixtures with Welsh sides. Despite spending the past decade pontificating about rigid adherence to amateurism, when it came to defending itself, principles went out of the window. The RFU rescinded its ban on Gould because, said RFU secretary Rowland Hill, it "was a question of expediency" as it would be "a serious strain on the loyalty of the West Country clubs". More openly, F.E. Smith, later Lord Birkenhead, the future Conservative cabinet minister, admitted in *The Times* that the RFU had compromised to "prevent the great accession of strength to the NU which would have followed had the Welsh Union been driven into their arms".

Not only was the RFU prepared to compromise, but the WFU was not prepared to split. Despite the fact that it rode the crest of the wave of national feeling sweeping Wales at that time, the WFU was neither separatist nor fundamentally opposed to rugby's *status quo*. Its 'nationalism' was part of its loyalty to the monarch, the British state and the Empire. Not for nothing did the Welsh national side's jerseys sport the three feathers emblem of the Prince of Wales and the motto *"Ich dien"* or "I serve". Indeed, many nationalists had little time for rugby: Lloyd George complained in the mid-1890s that the grip of "morbid footballism" was one of the factors stopping South Wales supporting his projected Welsh Liberal Party. And, as Welsh Rugby Union historian Gareth Williams has pointed out, "The WFU itself was guided by men like Sir John Llewellyn, Bart., H.S. Lyne and W.E. Rees, all three privately educated in England, Conservative in politics, Anglican in religion..." who shared the same background and prejudices of the English Rugby Union leadership. Given the opportunity to compromise with the RFU, the Welsh leadership was more than happy to comply.

On broader level, the Gould compromise also helped to legitimise the undercover payments made to working class players by the Welsh clubs. If its leadership was willing to endorse Gould's emoluments, it would also turn a blind eye to those of the sport's lesser lights, provided reasonable discretion was maintained. As if to prove the truth of Oscar Wilde's dictum that hypocrisy is the homage that vice pays to virtue, the Welsh authorities periodically carried out investigations into professionalism, but these were of minor players and clubs whose monetary dealings had become too obvious and threatened to embarrass the unspoken acceptance of payments. The WFU's refusal to pursue amateur purity was crucial in maintaining Rugby Union as a game for all classes in Wales and establishing it as the country's national game.

The 1905 triumph

The highpoint of Welsh rugby's claim to represent the Welsh nation came in 1905 when, alone among the four home nations of the British Empire, Wales triumphed 3-0 against the seemingly invincible touring New Zealand All Blacks. Yet although the New Zealand tour cemented the unity of Welsh nationalism and Rugby Union, it was also crucial to the growth of Rugby League. The huge profits of the tour were a key factor in the birth of Rugby League in New Zealand and Australia as players saw the possible rewards for their labours on the field.

In Wales, the pressure from players was lessened by semi-legitimate undercover payments and, unlike the situation down under, opportunities to go north. The impulse for the formation of Welsh NU clubs therefore came from entrepreneurial club officials. The announcement of the professional All Black Rugby League tour in March 1907 was the catalyst, bringing both hopes of a repeat of the commercial success of the 1905 Union tour and an international legitimacy to the NU. In May 1907 E.H. Rees, a former secretary of Aberdare RUFC, advertised in the *South Wales Daily News* asking for players to join a new NU club at Aberdare. Although Rees was implicated in a WFU inquiry into professionalism, his confident declaration that "the days of sham-amateurism are over" found a ready audience and plans for other Welsh NU clubs gathered pace.

However, the famous victory over the All Blacks was critical in establishing Rugby Union, in Gareth Williams's words, "as not merely a prominent constituent of Welsh popular culture but a pre-eminent expression of Welsh consciousness, a signifier of Welsh nationhood." To challenge Welsh Rugby Union now was to challenge Welsh national identity itself - it was almost an act of treason on the playing field. Predictably, the launch of League in Wales was portrayed by the WFU authorities as an affront to the nation. One WFU official claimed that "the quarters affected are not those in which the Welsh national sentiment is fairly reflected. The mining districts of the principality are the natural quarters for the development of the professional element, but these are not the localities whence the strength of Welsh international football is derived".

The new Welsh clubs were therefore seriously disadvantaged by their opposition to the national game. And, despite the wishes of its leadership and the reality of its situation, the NU was identified as a sport of the working class, independent of middle class control. The *Western Mail* noted that "to the colliers especially, the NU code, with its faster play, undoubtedly appeals".

Welsh NU clubs

The post-1905 period was one of growing class struggle, especially in South Wales. The Welsh NU clubs were based in areas at the centre of this upsurge: Aberdare had been a centre of working class militancy since the days of the Chartists and Tonypandy, home to Mid-Rhondda NU, was to become notorious in 1910 when Winston Churchill sent in troops to quell protesting miners. At best, the NU seemed to stand for the separation of the classes, and the Welsh middle classes who saw sport as a vehicle for social harmony, which was the explicit role of Rugby Union in Wales, were at best indifferent and at worst extremely hostile to the new sport.

Consequently the NU was unable to attract major Rugby Union clubs to its ranks, as it had hoped. For a senior Welsh side to cross the divide would have meant defying national sentiment, sporting respectability and middle class fear of workers' militancy. One may as well have also asked it to call for the overthrow of the King for all the likelihood there was of this happening.

For its part, the NU did nothing to encourage existing Rugby Union clubs to join it. In fact, it had a one-sided gentleman's agreement not to poach clubs from the RFU: "It is not the practice of the NU to canvas clubs to become members of the Union", its General Committee stated in 1909. This, however, did not stop the RFU making strenuous efforts to persuade Bradford to rejoin the 'shamateur' flock in 1906.

Bradford eventually switched to football to become Bradford Park Avenue, underlining the huge threat which that game posed for the NU, both in the north and in South Wales. In contrast to the NU, football provided a national sport where the civic pride of a town could be paraded and tested against clubs from towns throughout England and Wales. It had started to make inroads into South Wales at the same time as the NU and although it developed slowly in South Wales, by 1906 the Welsh FA had 74 affiliated clubs in the area, and this had risen to 262 in 1910.

Particular headway was made in the Cynon, Taff and Rhondda Valleys, areas which also encompassed most of the Welsh NU clubs. Other than its attractiveness as a sport, which because of the low standards of the Welsh sides was not always apparent, the NU had little to compare with the national competitions of football or the nationalist kudos of Rugby Union. With three sports competing for the winter affections, not to mention the cash, of the South Welsh public, the NU and its pioneering Welsh clubs were always going to have the hardest struggle for survival. The fortunes of each club are fully covered later in the book.

Chapter 2: First tries - Internationals in Wales 1908 to 1914

Expand or be damned. The first administrators of the Northern Union realised that motto applied to their sport more than any other. Confined, following the immediate years after its formation in 1895, to a few counties of England, it became clear that new clubs, players and revenue would be necessary if the new sport were to overcome its geographical limitations.

And the principality of Wales was an obvious target. Rugby was the national sporting pastime, yet the players and spectators in Wales had far more in common with their rugby playing cousins in the north of England than they did with that country's Rugby Football Union establishment whose intransigence and blinkered philosophy had led to the split of 1895. However, their allegiance, though tenuous, was to the latter.

Working class and low-incomed, the rugby people of Wales were seen as ideal fodder for the Northern Union (NU). Welsh players would be far more likely to accept cash for playing than the gentry and professional men of southern England, despite the secretary of the Welsh Football (Rugby) Union (WFU) of the day, Walter Rees, describing the new code as "the mongrel game".

The sport was rooted in Welsh communities, much like the industrial centres of Yorkshire and Lancashire and clubs and players in the principality, keen to supplement their income, would offer the NU a chance to break out of its narrow confines. Yet history has proved that to be only partially the case. Welsh players have adapted to Rugby League with style and vigour over the years, yet nearly all have had to travel north to display their talent as Wales has remained infertile soil for a lasting Rugby League club tradition.

But back in the first decade of the century the new code was convinced it could win over the hearts and minds of Welsh rugby. And so began almost a century of struggle by, first the NU, and then the Rugby Football League, to establish their sport in a part of the world that outwardly seemed ideal territory.

The story of these ventures is chronicled elsewhere in this book but the attempts to introduce the code into Wales also offered the sport another opportunity, one that would give it credibility in the eyes of outsiders: international competition.

If there was one glaring hole in the NU's armour it was the fact that the sport could not provide representative fixtures between nations. Any Welshman, New Zealander or Australian was unlikely to give up the chance of a national jersey to play a sport that would leave him ostracised by the Rugby Union authorities in his home country. Not only would he have no hope of representative honours, but he would be playing a game that had no certainty of survival. If the game died, thanks to the Union life-ban on League players, so did his hope of ever playing international rugby. The dawn of the Welsh influence in Rugby League, coupled with the arrival in Britain in 1907 of Albert Henry Baskerville's touring New Zealanders, changed all that.

Meaningful international competition was here to stay and, because of the regular supply of working class Welsh players travelling north to earn money playing Rugby League over the intervening decades, the Welsh national team has been, with a few notable breaks, a consistent thread in the story of international Rugby League. While Welsh leagues and club sides have come and gone, the numbers of Welshmen playing with northern Rugby League sides has meant that raising a high-quality XIII was rarely a problem. Indeed, the only substantial break in the story of the Welsh national Rugby League team came in the fifties and sixties when a dearth of high-quality players heading to League, the preference for a single Great Britain XIII and insularity on the part of northern administrators led to temporary suspension of the national squad.

In an attempt to address the early lack of international competition the NU had staged a somewhat cosmetic England versus Other Nationalities match at Wigan in 1904. The Other Nationalities team was composed almost entirely of Welsh players and triumphed 9-3 in game most notable for the fact that it was played with teams of 12 players. So perhaps it was fitting, yet surprising given the subsequent history of the sport, that Rugby League's first true international was staged in Wales.

First international

The New Athletic Grounds in Aberdare had the distinction on 1 January 1908 of seeing the New Zealand tourists lose 9-8 to a late Welsh try. Wales were the first winners of an international Rugby League match anywhere in the world. And it took place in Wales.

A. H. Baskerville was a postal employee from Wellington in New Zealand, a player and co-author of *Modern Rugby Football: New Zealand Methods*. He became intrigued by the new rules being introduced into rugby in the north of England and how they affected and improved play. Eager to learn, and in association with George W. Smith, a former Union All Black, he arranged a New Zealand tour to Britain to play the NU.

This was the tour party dubbed the "All Golds" by a critical press in New Zealand for their acceptance of payment to play the sport. So fearful were the squad of retribution from the NZRFU that their names were not released until just before departure for Britain and the NU were still unsure of which players were in the party until they disembarked at Folkestone. But, on arrival in Britain, they were rapturously received by the game's supporters, eager to see international competition. With the legendary Australian Dally Messenger, picked up by the tourists after calling at Sydney, now a part of the squad, the Kiwis won 19 out of their 35 matches under captain Hercules R. 'Bumper' Wright from Wellington, despite none of the players having played to the new rules before.

The party had been in Britain for three months prior to the opening international match and sufficient publicity had been generated to attract a crowd of around 17,000 to the New Athletic Grounds, a stadium to the south-east of the town owned by the Aberdare Athletic Association. The association had originally refused permission for NU rugby to be played there but relented when faced with the prospect of a large international crowd.

It is interesting to see how Aberdare came to be chosen for Rugby League's first international match for it was not a simple matter of putting a pin on a map. There were considered political decisions behind the town's selection.

The region, surrounded by the Rhondda and Merthyr valleys, had provided a large part of the team that had defeated the 1905 All Blacks Union team and local players, including powerful forward Dai Jones, were becoming targets of the newly professional northern clubs. Aberdare Rugby Union Club was becoming increasingly aware of the value of its players and it seems that, even without the influence of the NU, player payments and trade in players was an established feature of rugby in Wales. In 1907

Aberdare had complained that local rivals Merthyr Tydfil were enticing players over the mountain with money, fares and meals.

WFU Censure

Yet it was Union clubs in Aberdare who felt the hand of WFU censure when Aberaman (a suburb of Aberdare) were expelled from the WFU for offering payment to players and the WFU would not allow Tommy Arnold, a player who had recently arrived to live in the area, to play for Aberdare. The club was also refused a WFU grant while others were successful. Aberdare felt victimised and, with the people of South Wales so far removed from the Corinthian values of the RFU in its home counties surroundings, there were strong calls for cash remuneration for players finding it difficult to play rugby and work.

Not surprisingly, the NU were taking a close interest. *The Merthyr Express* wrote in June 1907: "Will Aberdare take the plunge... is there a probability of a NU club being started?". Apparently northern clubs had guaranteed Aberdare 24 fixtures plus £15 expenses per match for travelling north.

The growing interest in the new code was further heightened by the first indications that the NU would be prepared to sanction a match between the touring New Zealanders and a Welsh team in Aberdare, to bring attention to the sport and the proposed club. As the *Merthyr Express* said: "The team [New Zealand] is likely to be composed of many of the [Rugby Union] team who made the tour two years ago, and if they were to visit it would be a great draw".

The newspaper also pointed out that a NU team in South Wales was an obvious step because professionalism conclusively existed in the area.

However, initial interest was stymied, when the *Aberdare Leader* announced: "New club boycotted". The prospective club had applied to use the Aberdare Athletic Ground and had been turned down, notwithstanding the fact that there was no other application for its use. Yet in the next valley, the town of Merthyr was now gearing up to introduce a NU club. Getting wind of a revolt the WFU ordered an investigation into professionalism in both Aberdare and Merthyr, ostensibly based on allegations that Aberdare had rigged the deciding match of the Glamorgan League Championship against Treorchy by paying the Treorchy committee £15 to play an unregistered player - the argument being that if Aberdare lost they could still claim the match when the irregular player was pointed out.

It was then that Dai Jones, so successful in Wales's famous victory over the Union All Blacks, threw a spanner in the works. Aberdare cut his (unofficial) wages by half and he quit, choosing to return to his former club Treherbert. It was clear something had forced him to quit Aberdare, and the WFU, looking to make an example, banned Jones, seven other players and the Aberdare committee for life. Yet, suspiciously, the Merthyr Union club also being investigated, but gearing up for competition from the new NU club in their town, were allowed to go scot free.

The rugby people of Aberdare were angry at being ostracised. No rugby was being played in their town and their misery was compounded when Merthyr's NU team played against the touring Kiwis with former Aberdare players, including Jones, figuring prominently.

Their pride was damaged and Aberdare felt let down by those in charge of the game. Conditions were perfect for the NU to make its move, and rumours of an international fixture between Wales and New Zealand became reality. Aberdare would host the sport's first international game at the Athletic ground.

"Colonials' visit to Aberdare"

So it was with some expectation that the *South Wales Echo* wrote under the heading "Colonials' visit to Aberdare" that "the gathering of a large crowd at Aberdare to witness a match under NU rules was something new in the history of football in the principality. The crowd kept pouring in and the Welshmen who were led onto the field by Tom Llewellyn, their captain, looked exceedingly fit and they were accorded a rousing reception". So keen were the spectators to catch a glimpse of their new heroes that the crowd constantly encroached onto the pitch during play. The *Western Mail* reporter, 'Pendragon', told how "Inspector W. Nott and his men, by dint of strenuous efforts, were able to prevent the spectators from encroaching too closely".

The *Yorkshire Post* described the game as a "spectacular treat", despite the frosty surface. "Play was bright and fast with speedy running and good passing, just the sort of play the Welsh crowds revel in." Then as now. The paper went on to say that "during a game brimful of excitement there was no unseemly incident... nothing approaching undue roughness was noticed and... considering the bone in the ground and the strenuousness of the players, no serious injury occurred." The Kiwis were hoping to go one better than the Union All Blacks who had toured two years earlier and had suffered only one defeat to Wales in Cardiff.

On the morning of the match, however, it looked like their attempt at revenge might be delayed. The ground was solid with frost and the *Western Mail* said: "Despite the liberal application of rock salt, there were many patches of the field which were as hard as adamant, and risk of serious personal injury was involved in the resolution to play the game." But, with a large crowd expected and a show to put on, referee Mr Smith from Widnes and the teams elected to play. And a try five minutes from time fittingly scored by Welsh second row forward Dai Jones denied New Zealand any form of revenge.

'Muddied Oaf' of the *Aberdare Leader* reported that "the Welsh team entered the field to the strains of 'Hen Wlad fy Nhadau' by the Aberdare Town Band" followed by the New Zealanders performing the haka. With two such passionate nations the match was always going to be a tight struggle and Wales's single point victory was a hard-fought one. Although Wales looked certain to score international Rugby League's first try, Louis Treharne was called back for stepping into touch and from then on throughout the first half Messenger's tackling in the centres constantly denied them the chance to open up the game, although the *Yorkshire Post* said that "he did not appear the brilliant man he was at Merthyr", the *Western Mail* describing his play as "risky" and remarking that it was surprising that "he was not knocked out".

Yet it was the lone Australian who was instrumental in opening the scoring. His break gave Rowe the chance to free wingman Arthur Kelly with a clever crossfield kick. The Kiwi took his chance but Messenger failed to convert allowing local-born wingman Dai Thomas, then playing with Halifax, to level the scores, after he had been denied a fine opportunity only seconds earlier when loose-forward Howell Francis failed to release a try-scoring pass. Thomas took his chance well, according to the *South Wales Echo* his opportunity "would have been of no use but to a speedy player". George Thomas's conversion failed, leaving the scores tied at 3-3.

According to the *Echo*, the game opened up with tackling, passing and catching of a high standard and it was only a startling break from a loose ball that allowed New Zealand to break the deadlock and take the lead at half time. Messenger had already failed with a drop goal attempt that grazed the uprights when New Zealand picked up the loose ball and, with a bout of quick passing, freed stand-off Wynyard, one of two brothers on the Kiwi team. Messenger's kick was successful and the tourists led 8-3.

The best of the early exchanges in the second half fell to the Welsh and, after Treharne and Bert Jenkins had both gone close, Francis broke from a crush of players, superbly stepped through the defence and scored another unconverted try. Wales trailed by two points. It could have been more but for full-back Chick Jenkins's stout defence.

The home newspapers were full of praise for the Welsh. The *Yorkshire Post* selected Chick Jenkins and Johnny Thomas as "the pivots of the Welsh back play" with Jenkins "playing the game of his life" while the *Western Mail* picked Dai Thomas and Tom Llewellyn as the best of the threequarters. Indeed, there is no doubt that, as the game wore on, the Welsh became stronger and, although Thomas the Wigan scrum-half, repeatedly opened up the New Zealand defence, it seemed the visitors would hang on with some desperate defence until Jones scored the vital, and again unconverted, try. A strong forward rush freed the local boy allowing him the glory of securing the first win for the new Welsh team and the first winning try in a Rugby League international.

He was surely feted by his colleagues at the Boot Hotel reception later in the evening, despite Baskerville's contention that the New Zealanders had not played up to standard. It was an ironic tragedy that, having sown the seed of internationalism in Rugby League, Baskerville was never to return to New Zealand. He died of pneumonia in Brisbane on the return journey later that same year.

The NU, always quick to exploit new openings, was even proving media-friendly back in 1908, a function it is often criticised for not performing today. The *Western Mail* wrote: "The telegraphic and telephonic arrangements were excellent, and reflected great credit on the local staffs of the Post Office and National Telephone Company."

The match and the new code received popular acclaim, the *Western Mail* commenting that "the advancing popularity of rugby professionalism in Wales cannot be disputed. To colliers especially the NU code, with its faster play, unquestionably appeals." The *South Wales Echo* added that "the keenness of tackling was the most striking feature". The *Western Mail* truly went to town over the significance of the result: "New Year' Day in the year 1908 will rank as a red-letter day in the history of Welsh sport. On that date Wales gained her first victory under the laws which govern professional Rugby football in Great Britain. Cymric prestige in Rugby football was honourably maintained. Quite thrilled were the spectators when they saw the scarlet-clad warriors attacking in the old sweet way".

Yet the newspaper also had criticism. "The question might be asked, was the Welsh team that defeated the amateur All Blacks two years ago equal to either of Wednesday's sides? I am convinced that it was a good deal better, and would have beaten either team by a substantial score." The newspaper also concluded, contrary to other reports, that "play was not very pretty".

The *Yorkshire Post* noted that the Welsh forwards "excelled any amateur pack", adding that the NU officials "expressed themselves as delighted with the impression made upon the Welshmen, and assert that NU rules, and the payment of players will by this match gain such popularity in the Principality that next season there will be not two, but ten or a dozen clubs, sufficient to form a Welsh League".

The *Aberdare Leader* was also enthusiastic: "Those who witnessed the match... were given a good insight into the method of playing the game under NU rules. Personally, I admire the new method for it gives the spectator full value for his money. In truth it is a faster game than the old-fashioned amateur method." The writer saw an obvious route for the community to re-establish its wounded pride: "With the establishment of a NU club in Aberdare we might be able to uphold the proud prestige held by Aberdare in the sporting world."

The writer got his wish, Aberdare played in the Rugby League but, as with so many of the sport's more ambitious ventures, other matters closer to the northern clubs' hearts took precedence and the Welsh League clubs, despite perfect social conditions and local enthusiasm, stumbled out of existence through lack of official and playing support.

Clash against England

Yet before the new Welsh League teams even kicked off the NU were back. Nothing quickens the Welsh sporting pulse more than the prospect of a clash against England, especially when it comes to rugby. In line with its policy of taking the game to new areas the first Anglo-Welsh fixture was set for later that same season, as a follow-up to the Kiwi match. The Mid-Rhondda Social and Athletic Club at Pen-y-graig, Tonypandy was the host to the first of one of international Rugby League's more enduring fixtures on Easter Monday, 20 April, 1908.

As the *Western Mail* wrote: "It was in pursuance of an educational policy that the international was fixed for the Rhondda, where next season, it is confidently expected, at least two clubs who now play under the Welsh Union banner will join the NU. The success which has followed Merthyr and Ebbw Vale in their venture has led other organisations to consider the advisability of going over, and the formation of a Welsh NU League is practically a certainty."

However, the *South Wales Echo* offered only worried notes to its readers. Amid a report which actually published the wrong scoreline and at no point mentioned the Welsh victory, was the line: "today's encounter was looked upon as the 'thin end of the wedge' which leads to the establishment of teams under the new code". It also reported that a meeting of the NU before the game had attracted the interest of individuals wishing to form clubs in the Rhondda area.

And no doubt these pioneering delegates were even more encouraged when Wales ran out 35-18 winners against the English, scoring seven tries in the process. It took a superb second-half performance to secure the win because England had held the upper hand throughout the first 40 minutes. An early James Jolley penalty gave England the lead and it was the stand-off from Runcorn who instigated most of the adventurous early play by England which led to Birch of Leeds scoring a powerful forward's try which went unconverted.

Yet Wales levelled within minutes when wingman Louis Treharne of Wigan went in at the corner for the first of his two tries. It was a remarkable score after a move covering three-quarters of the field which, according to the *Western Mail*, sent the crowd "into ecstasies". The try was spectacularly converted from the touchline by Johnny Thomas at scrum-half. Thomas went on to convert all seven of Wales's tries, a remarkable achievement in addition to his inventive half-back play, and a Welsh record that stood until Jonathan Davies kicked eight goals against Papua New Guinea in 1991.

England reasserted their superiority with a try from forward Jack Spencer of Salford, converted by Jack Fish, the Warrington wingman, but Wales were always in the hunt and after Treharne followed up a towering kick to score beneath the posts the gap was closing. From the kick-off Welsh forward George Ruddick added a further try which gave Wales the lead for the first time. The *Western Mail* acclaimed Ruddick as the best of the Welsh pack alongside Dai Davies, Dai Jones and Oliver Burgham who were "ever in the van".

But the game was truly end-to-end and by half time the home team was behind once more, 15-18. Fish had scored two tries, one of them converted. The *Western Mail* wrote: "Up to half-time England fairly claimed an advantage that was rightly deserved, for better cohesion and combined play had been shown fore and aft."

However, the English would not score again as Wales took control in a second half that saw them score 20 points. The *Yorkshire Post*'s brief report said that "Wales opened the second half in determined style and that was obvious, for within five minutes of the restart they had scored to take the lead. Rhys Rees who, according to the *Western Mail*, "worked the scrums admirably", broke well to feed centres Phil Thomas and Jenkins who put Burgham of Ebbw Vale over for the half's first try. The Welsh backs began to run freely, a move in which every member of the division was involved resulted in Dai Thomas evading Fish and full-back Harry Taylor to score the fifth Welsh try.

England were constantly forced back towards their own line and saw little of possession. Their defending was valiant, but the Welsh were not to be denied two further scores by centre Bert Jenkins, the first of which involved clever handling by at least 12 players. In the end, 35-18 reflected Welsh dominance and made a big impression on the writer from the *Western Mail*, who wrote: "If first impressions count for aught, then the big majority of Rhondda Valley spectators who made their initial acquaintance with NU football must acclaim the game as played under the new regime with positive delight."

From a spectacular point of view, the encounter was a really superb exhibition between two well-matched sides, and at times reached a brilliance that was dazzling, whilst there was never a dull moment, and every movement sparkled. The rapidity, too, with which play was transferred from one end of the pitch to the other kept excitement up to concert pitch, and the highest tension prevailed throughout."

As already stated, the *Mail's* rival newspaper, the *South Wales Echo*, didn't even mention the Welsh victory in its brief report and even gave the wrong scoreline. It seemed far more concerned with the threat the match posed to the Union *status quo*.

Yet, while a crowd of 12,000 was attracted to the match, it was the only international to be played at Tonypandy, although the Athletic Grounds still exist on Primrose Street, with the pitch now surrounded by overgrown banking.

The international experiment in Wales had not yet finished, however, even though the Welsh NU clubs were beginning to falter. Attention switched to Ebbw Vale and the Bridgend Field ground, later to gain fame as Eugene Cross Park, home of the town's Union club and a venue for Glamorgan Cricket Club's county matches, and a Rugby League international in the 1980s.

The ground was chosen to host Wales's first international against Australia when the Kangaroos made their first tour in 1908-9, but the match was postponed because of snow and it was the English who were to be Wales's opponents at the new venue. A Welsh League XIII did eventually get to play Australia on that first tour and won 14-13 at The Amateur Ground, Merthyr Tydfil, but the game was not classed as a full international. Six thousand people saw a side solely selected from the Welsh clubs secure a notable victory. Eight players were from the Merthyr Tydfil club, three from Ebbw Vale, and Aberdare and Mid-Rhondda provided one each.

England defeated again

So, on 9 April 1910, a year after Australia had been set to play, Ebbw Vale received its first taste of international Rugby League when a meagre crowd of 4,000 saw Wales once again defeat England. They ran in nine tries in a stunning 39-18 victory.

The *Western Mail* was under the impression that the game was the fifth match between the two nations, mistakenly believing that the Aberdare game had not been contested by New Zealand. It was, however, the fourth meeting and England had by now gained some revenge for defeat at Tonypandy with victories at Broughton and Wakefield.

Yet, back on home soil, the Welsh were unstoppable. As the *Western Mail* reported "The sweeping victory... was even more decisive than the score would indicate". Once again, the Welsh were losing at the interval and it was through a dominant second half that victory was secured. "Wales were the best side in every department and phase of the game," wrote the *Mail*, "and Lomas, the crack Englishman [at centre], for once found his master in Chick Jenkins who skippered the Welsh side."

Weather conditions and the playing surface were ideal as the teams were led out, the English somewhat enigmatically - and arrogantly - selecting Rule Britannia as their national anthem. Perhaps spurred on by this the Welsh were ahead within a minute. Full-back Frank Young of Leeds cleared the ball which was misfielded by his English counterpart Jimmy Sharrock of Wigan. Welsh right wing Billy Williams scooped up the loose ball to score near the corner and give the Welsh a three-point lead.

The English immediately countered and, after Hunslet's Billy Batten (who later became a legend playing with Hull) had a try disallowed for a forward pass and some stout defending by Young, English pressure finally forced a try and "after a rattling bout of passing" Salford's centre Jimmy Lomas fed half-back Fred Smith of Hunslet who beat Young to score a converted try.

Wales's reply was positive but short-lived and the English stole a loose ball to break downfield. Young failed to gather and the English packed swooped to give the third of Hunslet's international trio, Billy Jukes, a try that was too far out for a successful conversion. The *Mail* reported that "the referee was loudly hooted for allowing the score, Jukes being clearly offside".

The Welsh counter-attack was swift with Chick and Bert Jenkins combining in the threequarters for the latter to score an unconverted try. The home side should have scored another through forward George Ruddick but he lacked pace when in the clear and also squandered a second when Williams knocked on. These chances were rued come the half-time break, because when Welsh forward Dai Galloway grubber kicked forward, Jim Leytham, the Wigan and England wing, picked up the loose ball and also kicked ahead.

The *Mail* insisted that English forward Billy Ward was offside but he was allowed to gather, run on and feed Jukes who notched his second score under the posts. Leytham converted to leave the score 13-6 at half time.

However, as the *Western Mail* reported: "after the interval... Welsh superiority was seen. The play during this half was mainly in the English 25, and the whites' defence was given plenty of work. Johnny Thomas, who played a magnificent game, and was easily the best man on the field, kept putting his threes in motion..."

This he did straight from the resumption and swift work by centre Jenkins saw Williams score a simple, unconverted touchdown. Thomas then scored himself, combining well with Williams, for Wales to take the lead. The try, beneath the posts, was goaled by full-back Young.

The English backs were tackling manfully but the Welsh were rampant and when Llew Llewellyn broke from a melee to score "play on the restart clearly indicated that England were a beaten side". Almost immediately Chick Jenkins scored a long-range try and then added another after smart footwork from himself and Thomas. At 29-13 the agony was not complete for the English. Further scores from Williams - who notched his hat-trick (Wales's first ever) - and Llewellyn followed, and a cheeky long range drop goal from Jenkins took the Welsh out to 39.

A late consolation try from Lomas did little to redress the balance and the Welsh clearly deserved their 39-18 victory having outscored England nine tries to four. The 1984 Wales versus England international at Ebbw Vale match programme described it as "The game all Welshmen dream about - the complete destruction of the English".

Yet the poor crowd was obviously spelling trouble for Welsh Rugby League. On the same day Treherbert were defeated 54-13 by Oldham, and much the same treatment was dealt out to all the Welsh clubs in the NU. Despite international success, without a sound base at club level, the game was going to struggle for support in Wales.

First English victory

Indeed, the next international at Ebbw Vale on 1 April 1911 was to be the last time the English would play in Wales until 1926. The Welsh were to play another international on home soil against the touring Kangaroos later that autumn, but the lack of a competitive home fixture against the English for another 15 years showed how momentum had been lost since 1908.

To make matters worse, the English scored their first victory on Welsh soil at Ebbw Vale, backing up the 39-13 victory they recorded earlier in the season at Coventry, another development venue. Harold Wagstaff, the Huddersfield centre, was outstanding for the English, fashioning most of their tries and the visitors went in at half time having scored four tries, Joe Miller of Wigan notching two from the wing, while half-back Fred Smith and Wagstaff himself got one apiece.

That the Welsh were still in touch at the break was down to the fact that none of the English tries were converted and that centre Bert Jenkins had scored another try for his country, this one converted by Johnny Thomas.

This time, however, Wales were not going to pull away in the second half. From their 12-5 interval lead the *South Wales Daily News* noted that "England had much the better of the concluding period." They certainly did. Two rapid tries from Bert Avery and

Billy Kitchen put them in the clear, with the latter being converted by Wagstaff. Local wingman Llew Llewellyn pulled back three points for the home side but England had the final say with two goals from centre Jimmy Lomas, one a long-range penalty, the other a conversion after Wagstaff's brilliance had led to him scoring late in the game.

At 27-8 defeat was emphatic for the Welsh who had been so dominant in previous home internationals against the English. "Welshmen listless" headlined the *News*, with the writer adding: "Taken altogether the game was most disappointing, and was not by any means up to international standard. It entirely lacked those fine brilliant movements which one expects to see in NU games. It was more of a scrambling game than a scientific exposition."

The newspaper admitted that "The Welshmen were clearly beaten by a more clever side, who were able to combine much better than the representatives of the Leek". The *News* blamed the forwards for losing too much possession and denying the skilful backs any running opportunities, and full-back Chick Jenkins of Ebbw Vale for not giving an "exhibition equal to what he has given at club matches". In contrast the paper was full of praise for the whole English back division ably led by Wagstaff.

Perhaps of more concern to the NU was the headline "Poor gate at Ebbw Vale". Only 4,000 turned out for the game which probably went a long way to explaining the demise of the fixture, alongside the recent departure from the NU of Welsh clubs Merthyr Tydfil, Aberdare, Barry, Mid-Rhondda and Treherbert. The Ebbw Vale club struggled on until 1912.

Australian victory

Nonetheless, or perhaps because of the club's efforts to remain afloat, the final international of the period was played at Ebbw Vale on 7 October 1911. The touring Kangaroos were the visitors and the crowd delighted in a 10-try exhibition, as Australia won 28-20. Will Davies, playing on the left wing for Wales, scored four, the only player to score so many in an international and still be on the losing side.

These were the second Kangaroos who had arrived only three weeks earlier in Plymouth bringing with them a real live Wallaby - apparently a Kangaroo was too big to be shipped out. With five New Zealanders in the party they were officially billed as Australasia and were, surprisingly, without Dally Messenger who, recently married, had opted to stay at home.

The tests against Britain - which were won 2-0, marking the Kangaroos' first series victory - were played in the development areas of London, Edinburgh and Birmingham so it was only right that the Welsh, with teams already having played NU rules, should be awarded a fixture.

That the home team did not win should not detract from what was a fine spectacle, attended by 7,000 spectators. The Australians were superb but were well-matched by their losing opponents. The *Athletic News* wrote: "[the] success has been attained in such a manner which suggests that soon the tourists will be regarded as well nigh invincible". Yet it also pointed out that for "sixty minutes Wales were the superior side".

It was the Australians who scored first, after only four minutes, centre Vivian Farnsworth fashioned a simple try which Arthur 'Bolla' Francis, one of the New Zealanders, converted. A Welsh penalty for obstruction reduced the gap and inspired the home team. Strong pressure on the Australian line led to a second penalty from Johnny Thomas which left the Australians defending a single point lead.

Yet, against the run of play, the visitors broke downfield. Francis, having a strong game in the forwards, made the opening and fed the supporting Bob Craig who touched down for the converted try. Wales continued to pressurise, however, and Australian full-back Chook Fraser's high kick was charged down and chased by Davies who scored the first of his four tries in the corner. Thomas's conversion attempt struck the upright.

The end-to-end nature of the match did not abate. Farnsworth fooled the Welsh defence who, expecting him to kick allowed him to break loose. He passed to fellow centre Herb Gilbert who fed wingman Albert Broomham. Smart interpassing between the two wrong-footed the Welsh cover and the winger who, according to the *Yorkshire Post* "absolutely refused to be tackled", scored the Kangaroos' third try. Farnsworth's conversion gave the tourists a 15-7 lead.

By the interval, though, Wales had reduced the gap. Thomas's third penalty was followed by a fine combination between the stand-off, his scrum-half Tommy Grey and Bert Jenkins, the centre. Between them they fashioned an opening for Davies to score his second. Amazingly, Thomas's conversion attempt again hit the posts leaving Wales three points in arrears at the break.

The Welsh squandered simple chances at the start of the second half that were to cost them dear. Thomas missed a simple penalty and Jenkins knocked-on with the line at his mercy. Yet it was the home team that opened the second-half scoring. Scrum-half Grey fed Thomas who jinked through weak defence to open the field for the three-quarters. Jenkins made good distance and allowed Davies to complete his hat-trick. Although the kick was a difficult one, Thomas landed it and Wales led by two, *Athletic News* noting that "for some minutes the spectators demonstrated in characteristic style".

However, the celebrations were to be halted by Australian forward Tedda Courtney. Following dogged forward play taking the visitors right up to the Welsh line, Broomham scooped up the ball to Courtney who flung himself over the line, close enough to the posts for Francis to goal. Wales were not finished and once again Grey and Jenkins were instrumental in freeing Davies for his record-breaking try.

At 20-20 there was everything to play for but, sadly for the locals, it was the Australians who finished the stronger. Francis, running powerfully until the end, broke through the Welsh defence to pass to the supporting Craig who secured his second try. Although injured in the move, Francis notched his fifth goal. The Welsh were still within a score but never looked like troubling the tourists again. It was Farnsworth, supported by Charlie Russell, who scored a second try to put the match out of reach at 28-20.

Nonetheless the game was a fine exhibition of NU rugby. The Welsh played with tremendous spirit, only fading in the final 10 minutes. As is often the case, Australia took the opportunities they were handed and made the opposition pay. The *Athletic News* paid "tribute to the brilliant finish of the Australians as it is in these fateful moments that games are won and lost".

The *News* also paid tribute to the Welsh forwards who tied up the game in the middle of the field and denied Australia the opportunity to move the ball as they had been so keen to do on earlier matches in the tour. The writer singled out Welsh half-back Thomas for special praise saying he "bewildered" his opponents and played with "enthusiasm. Rarely has the Wigan half-back given a more finished display". Bert

Jenkins was also singled out for praise as was his namesake at full-back 'Chick', who improved considerably on his performance earlier in the year against England. And Davies was commended for his finishing which kept Wales in contention for so long.

Despite New Zealander Frank Woodward being overshadowed at half-back - he was a replacement for the injured Bill Farnsworth (brother of Vivian) - the critics singled out the Australian three-quarter line as being the mainstay behind the tourists' success. Centres Vivian Farnsworth and Bert Gilbert had strong, skilful games in attack and the young full-back Fraser "was capital... using splendid judgement".

The praise for the match did not come from *Athletic News* alone. The *Yorkshire Post* wrote: "One could not have wished for a game more exciting or more full of thrills... The Welshmen were not inferior in any one position, although they had only themselves to blame for the defeat, inasmuch as their defence crumbled when it should essentially have been at its best." The *Post* was critical of Farnsworth, however, stating that "he will need to better control his temper on the field or he will certainly not be well received in England". Despite Farnsworth's temper the writer still saw fit to call the match "one of the best and most open games ever seen in Monmouthshire".

Yet it was to be the last international played in Wales for 10 years. A match against England had been scheduled for March 30 1912 but the demise of professional Rugby League and a coal strike which led to a disruption of rail services meant that preparations never got off the ground. In January 1912, Wales lost to England at Oldham. Two further defeats in England against the old enemy followed, including one at Plymouth, before the First World War brought an end to international matches.

Despite the success of the international matches the demise of club Rugby League in Wales coupled with the safety valve of professionalism in the north of England for any Welshmen who seriously wished to earn a living playing rugby, meant that any NU foothold, club or international, in Wales was certain to be short-lived. It is possible and - certainly a recurring argument over the years - that the onset of professional rugby in the north saved the Welsh Rugby Union from having to embrace professionalism and face ostracism from the other Rugby Unions. Instead of having to confront a clamour of support for broken-time payments from the Welsh working class rugby communities, the players who were good enough to earn a living from the game travelled north to play for Rugby League clubs, leaving a lobby much weakened by their absence back in Wales.

Chapter 3: The early Northern Union clubs

The five years from 1907 to 1912 provided the biggest base, in terms of professional clubs, that Rugby League has ever had in Wales. However, many of these clubs had a weak structure and the top Welsh players continued to join clubs in the north. This chapter concentrates mainly on Merthyr Tydfil, one of the longest lasting clubs, in more detail than the other clubs because their experience probably best reflects the problems that all the teams encountered.

Apart from the clubs covered below, there were also attempts to set up a Northern Union team in Pontypridd in 1908, which is covered in a later chapter.

As well as competing in the Northern Rugby League, the Welsh clubs also contested the Welsh League as a separate competition during some seasons. The figures given for league results and places only cover the Northern Rugby League matches.

Merthyr Tydfil: 1907 to 1911

The Merthyr Tydfil story really began on 16 December 1905, with Wales's historic Rugby Union victory over the All-Blacks. Merthyr Tydfil's leading rugby club, Merthyr Alexandra, exploited the enthusiasm roused by the national triumph to enjoy its best ever season in 1906-7. This good news was rather overshadowed at the club's AGM in July 1907 by E.H. Rees, who alleged that W.T. Jones, the Merthyr secretary, had demanded £7 5s to bring his team to Aberdare in April 1907. He also alleged that two players had received 24 shillings and 12 shillings per match respectively for playing for Merthyr. These allegations prompted an official inquiry by the Welsh Rugby Union (WFU).

Rees had also announced plans to form a Northern Union (NU) club at Aberdare. Whether he had talked to members of the Merthyr club is unclear, but at the AGM Charles Leonard proposed "that we adopt professionalism" in order to escape from the hypocrisy of "bogus amateurism". Seconding, Mr Harris pointed out that the WFU inquiry was likely to expel the club, and anyway "pure amateurism was an impossibility and the Committee knew it". However, an amendment which favoured the club remaining amateur was passed overwhelmingly, so Merthyr Alexandra did not defect. Nevertheless, a week after the AGM it was reported that fixtures had been arranged, players signed on and guarantors found for a new "professional rugby club".

In July 1907 the new side joined both the NU and the Northern Rugby League (NRL). They began the 1907-8 season with two heavy losses: the first a 6-25 defeat by Oldham, who ran in seven tries, the second, at Wakefield by 8-35.

The cause was not helped by the report of the WFU's enquiry which concluded about Merthyr Alexandra, "although not satisfied that the laws against professionalism have been adhered to as closely as might be wished, no proof adduced of the actual breach of such rules". The WFU's whitewash was designed to prevent the defections to the professional ranks which would inevitably follow if suspensions were imposed.

The NU club's first win came in November 1907, defeating Runcorn 15-13 and by early 1908 a creditable 13-9 victory over high-flying Hunslet brought the comment that "as they gradually become familiar with NU methods, they are likely to develop into a useful team".

Although 52 full WFU international players turned professional between 1895 and

1923, only one joined a Welsh side. Dai 'Tarw' Jones, a forward who had appeared for Wales in the victory over the 1905 All Blacks, signed for Merthyr in October 1907. Because he was one of the few players permanently suspended by the WFU enquiry "for receiving money consideration for playing football", he had little to lose by throwing in his lot with Merthyr. Three other suspended players, T. Arnold, Dai Thomas and Rees Rees, none of them internationals, also joined. This highlighted a problem which was to dog Merthyr and the other Welsh sides: their inability to attract star names. Most of the club's early signings were ex-Alexandra players, but the real star of Merthyr Rugby, Chris Williams, first reserve for the national Union XV in 1906-7, refused to sign.

Although a disappointing crowd of between 2,000 and 3,000 had attended Merthyr's first NRL match, this was attributed to inclement weather and high admission prices. Matters did improve for Broughton Rangers's visit a few weeks later, the crowd being more than 4,000. The crowd for the fixture against the New Zealand tourists in November 1907, estimated at between 8,000 and 12,000, was also encouraging.

This suggested there was a market for top-class professional rugby, and the high point for the club perhaps came in January 1908 when Huddersfield's visit attracted more than 3,000 spectators. The game between the Swansea and Merthyr Union clubs on the same day only drew about 600 people. However, in March 1908, the referee at the game against Rochdale Hornets reported that he had been 'molested' by spectators, and Merthyr's College Field ground was suspended for two weeks. Despite this Merthyr's first season was reckoned to be a success, even though they took only eight victories from 30 NRL matches and they also reached the third round of the Challenge Cup before losing 2-8 at Leigh. Merthyr finished 23rd out of 27 clubs. Their league record was:

Played	Won	Drawn	Lost	For	Against	Points	Percentage
30	8	1	21	229	400	17	28.33

In 1908, Merthyr appeared to have pulled off the star signing they required when the great Duncan McGregor, a New Zealand tourist in both rugby codes, joined the club. Sadly, he injured his ankle on his debut at Batley and afterwards did not play frequently. Thereafter, the club recruited local amateurs and survivors from the wreckage of other Welsh sides. The only notable signing was Tom Thomas, who was secured from Wigan for £60, a sum which the club treasurer, J.B. Evans, claimed came from his own pocket.

The following season, 1908-9 saw Merthyr finishing eighth of 31 clubs in the NRL with 11 wins from 18 matches. However, all but two of those wins came against Welsh sides, and despite their high placing in the NRL, Merthyr finished well behind Ebbw Vale in the short-lived Welsh League. They defeated Barrow 15-12 in September and recorded even more creditable results with a 3-3 draw against Huddersfield, a rare away win, 9-5, in the return at Barrow, and a 15-13 win in February 1909 over the touring Australians, before 4,000 people. For 1908-9 attendances averaged 3,000, with 4,000 watching Huddersfield in November, and at least 5,000 for the December visit of Ebbw Vale. Their final league record was:

Played	Won	Drawn	Lost	For	Against	Points	Percentage
18	11	1	6	184	156	23	63.88

At the same time, Merthyr began to find that its better players were tempted north. York signed Smith and the prolific winger Cowmeadow in December 1909, and further into the future, forward Dan Lewis on the eve of the 1910-11 season. Subsequently Swinton moved in for Dai Davies, capped five times for the Wales NU side, plus full-back Palmer Griffiths.

1909-10 saw a marked fall in attendances. A change of grounds, from the centrally-situated College Field to Rhydycar, on the outskirts of town, probably did not help but, by now, local people were taking an increasing interest in the affairs of the Merthyr Town Association club. Despite the change of venue, crowds continued to be boisterous - in January 1910, following a 3-9 defeat by Dewsbury, the referee, Mr Tonge of Swinton, who had sent off the home forward, Dan Lewis, was pelted with "clods and clinker" by spectators, sustaining a cut head. The Rhydycar Ground was suspended for four weeks.

The club treasurer, J.B. Evans, was also suspended because he refused to pay the referee's expenses, even though he claimed the club had no money.

In their final two seasons, Merthyr won only seven of 39 NRL matches and suffered some heavy reverses, especially on their visits to the North. Even when they did win, their matches were reckoned to offer a poor spectacle. In 1909-10, their only wins came over Treherbert and Warrington, and Merthyr finished 27th out of 28 clubs. Fellow Welsh strugglers Treherbert finished bottom. The final league record for Merthyr's worst season was:

Played	Won	Drawn	Lost	For	Against	Points	Percentage
21	2	1	18	94	354	5	11.90

In October 1910, a 13-70 defeat at Hull KR saw the team "cut a ridiculous figure" and club officials "realised that if they were to retain public support the tide of defeat would have to be stemmed". It was to an extent, with home wins over Barrow, Bradford Northern, Salford, Keighley and Ebbw Vale following, but by then the end was nigh. This final season saw some small attendances along with the disappointing results. Even the wins at home were watched by small gatherings and, although the final home game against Ebbw Vale was witnessed by a crowd of around 4,000, the visitors were well represented. The club's final game came at Coventry on Saturday 31 December 1910, when Merthyr were defeated 18-3 in a Challenge Cup qualifying game. The season's final record showed an improvement on the previous dismal campaign, with a climb of one place in the final table to 26th, but it was not enough to save the club.

Played	Won	Drawn	Lost	For	Against	Points	Percentage
18	5	0	13	90	335	10	27.77

Merthyr's demise was hastened by poor administration and the overall weakness of club administration was a serious hindrance to the progress of the NU in Wales. As *Athletic News* commented, "the average Welsh club official... displays a woeful lack of business instinct". This barb was probably aimed at the three other Welsh clubs which collapsed after the 1908-9 season, but Merthyr also displayed some serious weaknesses.

A hint of the trouble ahead had appeared in December 1909 when "as usual, several of the selected players failed to turn up" for a match against Treherbert. Soon after,

Merthyr were "only indifferently represented" in a 67-0 rout at Wigan, and these comments suggest that perhaps players were unsure of being paid. Certainly, no limited company was formed and there was confusion about who officially employed the players. More light was shed on the shambolic administration of the club by a hearing before Merthyr County Court in December 1910. Messrs Ellison & Co had taken action against the 25 members of the Merthyr Tydfil club for recovery of £10 17s 6d in respect of hire of turnstiles. The judge asked Mr Lewis, the club secretary, who was running the club, and he replied that he did not know.

Further details of the shambles emerged following the club's sudden demise in January 1911. Following the Challenge Cup defeat at Coventry the *Merthyr Express* interviewed former club treasurer, J.B. Evans, who pointed to internal problems. During the first season, he said, the club had been backed by two bonds, one of £200, another of £560, but losses were still incurred. In their second season the club lost £250, making total losses since formation of £473, and it was decided to float the club as a company but, while directors were appointed, no flotation took place.

The position became more confused still when the owners of the Rhydycar Ground refused to let the land to the club itself, but were prepared to do so to a syndicate of seven individuals. This syndicate then sub-let the ground to the club, but subsequently the syndicate found themselves subject to legal actions launched against the club for non-payment of bills. As a member of the syndicate, Evans had demanded the gate receipts from the final home game, apparently to ensure the players were paid. However, because he and his fellow syndicate members had received no rent for the season he "reluctantly accepted" that the club had "ceased to exist".

Association football

The chief beneficiary of the club's collapse was football. One of the successes of Merthyr Tydfil NUFC was in effectively seeing off the opposition provided by the Union code. The WFU Secretary, Walter Rees, had promised a fightback against "this mongrel game", with the leading South Welsh clubs such as Cardiff and Swansea playing matches in "the hills". However, within two years it was "taken for granted" that there would be no Rugby Union club in Merthyr for 1909-10. Nevertheless, the NU club was unable to gain possession of the amateurs' old home, Penydarren Park, a centrally-located and well-appointed ground owned by a local syndicate. The Union club did eventually vacate Penydarren which became home to Merthyr Town AFC, and in July 1909 the NU club put a bid before the Park syndicate to share it with the Association side. However, the syndicate would not let the ground to the Northern Unionists, despite having earlier invited them to submit a bid.

Instead, the club reached agreement with Crawshay Brothers for the use of a field adjacent to Rhydycar Road. The agreement for the new venue, the Rhydycar Ground, was only reached in July 1909, so it was quite some achievement that it was ready for Merthyr's first NRL engagement that season against Hull which attracted a 1,500 crowd, on 4 September 1909. Rhydycar remained Merthyr's home until December 1910, when the aforementioned dispute between the club and the syndicate who had leased the ground on its behalf precipitated Merthyr Tydfil's rapid demise.

If Merthyr Tydfil was not large enough to support two senior rugby clubs, neither was it able to support two codes of football, and the rise of Merthyr Town AFC hammered a large nail into the NU club's coffin. However, back in 1906, "Merthyr soccer was on a very pedestrian plane". Even as late as 1908 a Wales versus Ireland soccer international at Aberdare was regarded as "dull" in comparison to the "sparkling" NU match which had preceded it. Yet that same year, a meeting was held to form an Association Football club in Merthyr, which included "several gentlemen formerly connected with the amateur rugby club... though the soccer club is to be run on professional lines". The football club gained sole tenancy of Penydarren Park, and in March 1909 a "large crowd" saw the club reach the final of the South Wales and Monmouthshire FA Cup. Merthyr Town lost the final, but a few weeks later the visit of Manchester City for a friendly drew 7,000 to Penydarren.

In 1909-10 Merthyr Town took a huge step onto the national stage by joining both the Southern League and the Western League. Like Rugby Union, football allowed the town to be represented on a national stage, whereas Merthyr Tydfil NUFC represented a regional game which, after the summer of 1909, had contracted severely in Wales. At first, NU crowds appeared to hold up, 3,000 watching the game with Treherbert, while only 800 saw Merthyr Town defeat Radstock at football. However, on Boxing Day only 3,000 saw the Welsh League match with Ebbw Vale, while 8,000 were at Penydarren to see Town play Treharris. The same football opponents drew 6,000 for a Welsh FA Cup tie, while at Rhydycar, Merthyr were losing an NRL game against Dewsbury with 1,500 spectators. The football club were eventually to join the Football League in 1920.

It was also apparent at the time that attitudes in the NU did little for the long-term survival of the Merthyr NU club. Initially there was an undoubted keenness to promote the Welsh clubs. In June 1907 the *Merthyr Express* reported that prominent NU officials "are delighted at the prospect of having fixtures with South Wales clubs". Bill McCutcheon, an NU official, wrote to E.H. Rees promising that "if you decide to go on with the project... the whole Union will back you all it can to provide a counter-attraction to the Welsh (Rugby) Union". One unnamed club secretary thought "all our clubs will be prepared to lend a helping hand" and said that at least a dozen clubs would guarantee the proposed Welsh sides fixtures.

It was also hoped that players who had gone north but subsequently returned to Wales could sign for the new clubs without a transfer fee. However, one unnamed secretary could not say that his club would give all its old Welsh players free transfers as "there is one man down there who cost us £60: it would hardly be reasonable to expect us to give him a free transfer". On the question of travel expenses to subsidise trips north, he felt sure "some of the wealthy clubs would stump up, but, I am afraid we cannot". This attitude, with northern clubs putting their own short-term interests ahead of the game's development, was one reason why the NU failed to expand.

The dilemma for the NU was that it was expensive and inconvenient for northern clubs to play in Wales but it was essential if the game was to thrive there. It is perhaps unsurprising that clubs like Merthyr came to be regarded as a drain on resources. The trip to Merthyr was described as "a fag and a worry", and their visits north were seen to draw small crowds. The collapse of the Welsh League forced an increasingly unwilling group of clubs to travel to Wales and, following Merthyr's demise in 1911, their chief concerns appeared to be that those who had travelled to Wales to play Merthyr should be compensated for the loss of the return fixture.

Merthyr Tydfil also came into conflict with the NU over player registration. Paddison, who had joined from Merthyr Alexandra and appeared in Merthyr's first match, was banned for a month after Salford complained that he had already signed forms for them. In 1909, Merthyr planned to sign Tom Thomas, a Welsh player who had failed to settle in Wigan. The Lancashire club put a price of £60 on his head, which Merthyr raised, with much difficulty. The northern clubs' demand for transfer fees for players who were apparently of little future use to them may have made sound business sense, but it did nothing to help the game in Wales.

The failure of Merthyr Tydfil NUFC was perhaps inevitable, given the origins of the club. The club was an opportunistic venture, hoping to capitalise on the problems of the WFU and the local Rugby Union club. But without a tradition of support, it never attracted the star players, nor did it achieve the playing success, which might have encouraged local people to attend games in large numbers.

That was achieved by the town's football club, from 1909 an increasingly significant force within Merthyr's sporting community. Merthyr Tydfil NUFC's administration and structure were shambolic, and by 1910 no-one really appeared to be running the club, while its reliance on unsecured loans helped to precipitate its rapid demise. Nevertheless, apart from in the earliest days, Merthyr received little assistance from NU officials, while northern clubs and the sporting press there became increasingly hostile to a club viewed as a drain on resources and of limited interest to northern spectators. By the end, there was little support in Wales or in northern England.

Ebbw Vale: 1907-1912

On 15 July 1907 at the Bridge End Hotel, Ebbw Vale, Mr William Evans, secretary of the Ebbw Vale Rugby club, announced the formation of an NU club "in the face of bogus amateurism in the Monmouthshire League". Evans had already met the NU Committee and won guarantees of £10 expenses for each match played in the north for the first season. The Bridge End Field, the Rugby Union club's home, had been secured because Mr. Jones, the owner, "had no objection to an amateur or professional club having the field".

On 26 July 1907 the AGM of Ebbw Vale Rugby Club voted 63-20 to adopt professionalism, and on 16 August the Ebbw Vale Rugby Football Club Company Ltd was formed with capital of £250 in 10s shares, with Evans as secretary. The club, players and officials were all suspended permanently by the WFU. To assist, the NU stated that "no men from South Wales, for the present... will be allowed to go north until they have been refused places in the Ebbw Vale or Merthyr teams". Despite this, a week later the Tredegar player, P.S. Greaney, signed for Leeds for £75 down, £2 a week wages and a job at £2 a week.

Ebbw Vale's first Northern Rugby League fixture was on 7 September 1907, when they lost 3-26 to Keighley at Lawkholme Lane, Evans scoring their only try. *Athletic News* felt the contest had been an unequal one only because the "Welshmen had not had a full team practice under the new rules". On 19 October the home game with Swinton was watched by a crowd of around 2,000 who saw a 10-2 home victory, while the 8-33 loss to Halifax on 18 January 1908 was watched by around 4,000. In February a 5-10 defeat by Barrow at home was watched by a similar crowd. Wins were secured against

Swinton, Merthyr, Hull, Leeds, Dewsbury and Keighley, and the team finished 26th out of 27 clubs. Their final league record was:

Played	Won	Drawn	Lost	For	Against	Points	Percentage
30	6	2	22	153	426	14	23.33

Despite this poor record, Ebbw Vale was re-elected for 1908-9. The six Welsh clubs then competing were promised at least four home and away matches with northern sides, as well as playing each other home and away in both the NRL and the new Welsh League. The clubs were to receive £5 each time they travelled north, a reduction from the previous season's grant of £10 per trip. Vale did much better in 1908-9, though they were helped by playing many games against the new Welsh sides. On 28 November they recorded their ninth successive win in all competitions when beating Treherbert 16-2 after winning Northern Rugby League games against Welsh opponents six times, plus victories against Bramley and Rochdale.

On 12 December they visited Merthyr, losing 2-12 but taking many followers. As the *Merthyr Express* reported when Ebbw Vale entered the field "the cheer which greeted them indicated that they had brought a considerable number of supporters with them..." The return game, at Bridge End Field on Boxing Day was marked by "stirring scenes" and "great enthusiasm" which would "live long in the memories of the thousands of spectators". Some sources reckoned the crowd was 8,000 for a match which Merthyr won 4-0. On the other side of the coin, Barry's failure to turn up for the game on Christmas Day cost Ebbw Vale an estimated £80 to £90 in receipts. A more positive note came in holding the Australian tourists to a narrow 8-9 defeat, with 5,000 people attending a Monday afternoon fixture on 18 January.

Ebbw Vale became Welsh champions that season, having beaten Merthyr twice in the Welsh League, and they celebrated with a 20-0 win over a Welsh League XIII. The season's gate receipts had been a highly respectable £1,159 12s 2d. The chief blemish on the season was the famous 2-7 defeat at amateurs Beverley in the Challenge Cup on 27 February 1909. *Athletic News* described the match as a "Welsh disaster". Nearly 3,000 people saw Ebbw Vale lead at half-time through a Llewellyn drop goal. But Beverley's strength in the forwards paid off in the second half. A converted try and a drop goal in the final 15 minutes secured the Welsh side's infamous fate. Ebbw Vale were the last professional club beaten by amateurs in the Challenge Cup until the 1990s, when Beverley again beat professional opponents, winning 27-4 at Highfield in 1995.

Ebbw Vale finished 14th out of 31 clubs, with a final record of:

Played	Won	Drawn	Lost	For	Against	Points	Percentage
24	12	1	11	249	269	25	52.08

1909-10: Clash with Merthyr

For 1909-10, Ebbw Vale AFC were allowed to use Bridge End Field when not required for NU fixtures, a sign again of the rise of football. In September, Challenge Cup holders Wakefield Trinity's visit produced "one of the largest crowds seen at an ordinary league match", but the home side lost 0-10. Yet the players were still performing well against

Ebbw Vale NUFC circa 1908-9. 'Chick' Jenkins seated centre, Jack Foley
(Welsh NU international) second player from right on back. Photo courtesy Robert Gate.

OLDHAM F. C.
Official Programme.

OLDHAM v. EBBW VALE
AT
WATERSHEDDINGS, OLDHAM.
Saturday, October 1st, 1910.

(Oldham programme courtesy Mike Turner)

Athletic News's view of Ebbw Vale's defeat at Warrington January 1910

Welsh opposition. In November Ebbw Vale versus Merthyr attracted "the best gate of the season", Vale winning 11-5. On Boxing Day 3,000 saw Vale win 6-3 at Merthyr in the Welsh League.

Challenge Cup

In February 1910, came the "long awaited" Challenge Cup Tie at Merthyr, watched by a crowd of 4,000. Ebbw Vale won 12-7, giving them an away tie at Huddersfield, and they produced the shock of the round, if not the season, by winning 8-3. The attendance was 10,000 and the *Athletic News* sang Vale's praises: "NU club football in South Wales has, with one exception, made little progress. That exception is Ebbw Vale, and Saturday's great victory will tend to further encourage the officials".

Vale were drawn at home to Salford in the quarter-finals, but elected to give up home advantage, presumably for financial reasons, and lost 2-8. However, they clinched the Welsh League title again when they beat Merthyr 29-5 on a Wednesday afternoon in March, watched by a crowd of 4,000 and they completed the season with a 20-8 home win over Broughton Rangers. The club reported a profit of £81 on the season, while their football neighbours were wound up after a poor season. This was in sharp contrast to the position in Merthyr, where the football club was gaining greater prominence than the NU side. Ebbw Vale's final position in the league was 17th out of 28 clubs, with a record of:

Played	Won	Drawn	Lost	For	Against	Points	Percentage
24	9	2	13	156	211	20	41.66

One positive note for the club was the selection of centre T.E. "Chick" Jenkins for the Great Britain tour of Australia and New Zealand. He played 10 games on tour, scoring three tries and four goals.

In 1910-11, Vale achieved only one win from the first seven games, a 16-7 win over Rochdale Hornets, before managing successive home wins over Runcorn 14-3 and Swinton 8-2. On Boxing Day 1910 Ebbw Vale beat Merthyr 23-5 and Merthyr won the return 2-0. Both games attracted good attendances, but with Merthyr's demise they were to be the last fixtures between the clubs. Ebbw Vale then entered a slump, and did not win again until the final game of the season.

On 7 January 1911 they lost 2-6 at home to Hull and the referee was booed off the pitch after he failed to award Vale a penalty try. Worse was to follow two weeks later, as they lost 10-11 at home to Coventry and the club subsequently failed to score a try in eight successive games. In the final match of 1910-11, they beat York 14-6. The club finished 25th out of 28 with nine wins. Llew Llewellyn finished as the 12th highest try scorer in Rugby League that season with 24, a considerable achievement in a struggling team. The team's final league record was:

Played	Won	Drawn	Lost	For	Against	Points	Percentage
30	9	0	21	178	297	18	30.00

The 1911-12 season was to be Ebbw Vale's last. They opened it with a 10-37 defeat at home to Huddersfield. Wigan, Swinton and St Helens were all beaten at home, but the team failed to win any match on their travels.

Two of the club's players, Jenkins and Llewellyn were selected for a Wales and West of England side who took Rugby League on a rare visit to Bristol. Staged at Bristol City FC's Ashton Gate ground, a Wednesday afternoon crowd of 1,000 on 20 December saw the Australian tourists win 23-3.

In April, Vale played at Halifax and Hull KR and were only able to field 12 men in each game. Because Llewellyn was hurt at Halifax, they had to borrow Watson, a Hull KR reserve, for the second game. Both matches were lost, but Vale did go out with a bang, beating York 17-0 on 20 April 1912. They finished 25th out of 27 clubs, and only won four league games. Their final record was:

Played	Won	Drawn	Lost	For	Against	Points	Percentage
30	4	3	23	168	520	11	18.33

In August 1912 Llew Llewellyn moved on to Wigan and W. Higgins to Hull. The *Merthyr Express* was concerned that Ebbw Vale might not be able to start the coming season because of the unsatisfactory state of club finances, yet conceded that "the attractiveness of the NU style of play seems to have enamoured the people of the hills". *Athletic News* doubted whether Ebbw Vale would complete their fixtures and "many clubs would not mourn if the trips to Monmouthshire were knocked on the head".

Despite this, Ebbw Vale were expected to open their programme at Huddersfield on 7 September 1912. However, two days before this date it was announced that they would not appear and that Vale had resigned from the League. Thus did the NU's first great Welsh experiment in club Rugby League end.

Aberdare: 1908-9

Because E.H. Rees, former secretary of the Aberdare Rugby Union club, was the man who blew the whistle on 'shamateurism' in the WFU, it seemed likely that Aberdare would see the first of the professional sides in Wales. However, Aberdare failed to secure the necessary financial backing and, more to the point, at this time failed to obtain the use of Aberdare's Ynys Field. Because this was the only suitable ground in the town, the enterprise had to be put on hold.

On New Year's Day 1908 the Ynys Field, later renamed the Athletic Ground, was hired by the NU for the Wales versus New Zealand international and a crowd of around 15,000 paid £560 to see Wales win 9-8. Now aware of the commercial potential of NU football, a group of "tradesmen and sportsmen" met in Aberdare in March 1908 to guarantee the sum of £150 for the formation of a NU club. They must have been further encouraged when, following the suspension of Merthyr Tydfil's College Field, the Merthyr versus Wigan game was played at Ynys Field. The game attracted a crowd of 6,000, many of whom must have been impressed by the "sparkling play".

The prime mover behind the Aberdare club was Llewellyn Deere, a native of nearby Mountain Ash who had gone north in 1900 to join Huddersfield, reportedly for a signing-on fee of £150. In 1908, Deere became landlord of Aberdare's Locomotive Inn, and he set to work forming a club. A limited company was created with share capital of £500 in £1 shares. Deere was secretary and Ted Ruther became chairman. The directors included a brewer, a fruit merchant, two innkeepers, a fish merchant, a grocer and a builders' merchant, the qualification for directorship being £5 in ordinary shares. On 21 July 1908 Deere attended a Northern Rugby League Committee meeting and Aberdare and Barry were admitted. There were now enough Welsh clubs to form a Welsh League. The NU had presented the League with a cup, value 50 guineas, for the Welsh champions.

The long-awaited debut took place on Saturday 5 September 1908, when Wigan were the visitors and 3,000 spectators came to Ynys Field. Wigan were "far and away too clever for the home men" and Aberdare "evidenced a decided weakness in their application of the rules". Wigan won 56-0, scoring 12 tries.

This unhappy baptism was followed by two defeats, the second a 0-8 loss at Treherbert. Worse, their 5-13 home reverse to Treherbert was watched by a meagre crowd. At kick-off there were fewer than 300 present, in stark contrast to the crowds being attracted by "the soccerites" who played on the same ground. The visit of Wakefield Trinity on 17 October 1908 drew a "larger crowd than usual" and the home side was not flattered by a 0-26 scoreline. But then they gained revenge over Treherbert, winning a Welsh League game 20-8.

On 9 November, the Australian tourists attracted a 5,000 crowd on a Monday afternoon but the tourists scored nine tries in their 37-10 victory.

This was followed by a thumping first, and only, Northern Rugby League victory over Barry, by 43-5. The *Aberdare and Mountain Ash Weekly Post* felt that this victory would lead to a "greater share of patronage" and "infuse vigour and determination" into the team.

The next match saw Merthyr Tydfil visit and Aberdare did well to go down only 9-12. There was a large contingent of visiting supporters and, after the sending-off of a Merthyr forward, the visitors barracked the referee and later burst onto the field.

Aberdare had some consolation when Will Hopkins was chosen for Wales against England in the match at Broughton on 28 December 1908, although England won 31-7. However, he was absent as Aberdare lost 5-23 at Merthyr on Boxing Day. Indeed, Aberdare's next win did not come until February 1909, when they secured a "thumping" 19-2 success at Barry in the Welsh League. This was Aberdare's first and only away win in any competition. Sadly, it was business as usual a week later when visitors York won the final NRL game to be played by Aberdare at Ynys Field, by 16-5.

On 13 March 1909 Aberdare played their final NRL game, losing 18-45 to St Helens in a match played at College Field, Merthyr in an attempt to attract a larger crowd. Sadly, there was "very little interest" in the game. Towards the end of the match Whittle scored Aberdare's final try in the NRL, converted by Rees. Thereafter, Aberdare played only Welsh League games, losing 5-30 at Ebbw Vale, 0-14 at home to Mid-Rhondda and finally 5-14 at home to Ebbw Vale on Tuesday 13 April 1909. They should have visited Wakefield, but the Wakefield committee refused a £15 advance to meet travel costs, believing the gate receipts would not cover the expenses, and the game never took place. Aberdare finished bottom of 31 clubs in the NRL, with a league record of:

Played	Won	Draw	Lost	For	Against	Points	Percentage
17	1	0	16	134	406	2	5.88

So the Ebbw Vale game proved to be the last for Aberdare. *Athletic News* described

Aberdare, Mid-Rhondda, Barry and Treherbert as "ignominious failures in the playing and financial senses, and the latter sense alone appealed to the founders". The Northern Rugby League passed a by-law that clubs in arrears with subscriptions, fines or debts would be named defaulters and banned from next season's competition and Barry and Aberdare were both cited thus. On 8 July 1909 Aberdare told the League that it expected to meet its obligations, but two days later the club reported "unexpected difficulties" relating to its ground and effectively resigned from the League. And there ended Aberdare NUFC.

Barry: 1908-9

According to Rugby League historian Trevor Delaney, the idea of an NU club in Barry had been first mooted in 1906, but they had problems securing a ground. However, in April 1908 the *Barry Herald* reported that Barry was "going strong for a NU club". A meeting at the Windsor Hotel, presided over by Mr. J. White, had been successful and he reported to an NU meeting at Merthyr Tydfil that a ground was available and that a company was to be formed. In August the *Herald* predicted that "Barry will loom large in the football world" with the Australians and "crack NU Rugby teams from the North of England" expected to visit.

The local Trinity Street ground had been enclosed for use by the club, Fred Kirby had been appointed captain and the club colours would be the same as Cardiff Rugby Union Club. A company had been formed at Barry with capital of £250 in 10s shares. The first subscribers were all local men including an auctioneer, an engineer, a foreman, two joiners, a clerk and a cycle maker. The minimum cash subscription was 50s and qualification for the board of directors was £5. The Barry Railway Company offered 'special facilities' for those travelling to matches from the Rhondda Valley and Cardiff.

Barry's first NU game was at home to Treherbert on 5 September 1908. The match took place "in the presence of a large crowd" and was kicked-off by Councillor W.J. Williams, JP, a ship owner and chairman of Barry District Council. Johnny Williams scored the first try for the visitors, beating Dow to the ball, but Treherbert lost Harris through injury and Barry got on top. Kirby equalised in the second half and then Tresize set up Christopherson for the winning try, the final score being 6-3.

A week later, Barry travelled to Keighley, leaving Barry by train at 5.00 am and arriving at Leeds at 1.30 pm, and Keighley at 2.30 pm. Unsurprisingly after such a tiring journey, Barry went down 0-31. Their next home game, against Leeds (lost 3-17) was watched by around 2,000 people, but thereafter crowds declined. In October, Barry lost a poor game 3-12 to Ebbw Vale, and it was reported that "for disciplinary purposes" the club had replaced three of the original selection. Their second NRL win followed when they defeated Aberdare 13-5. However, a week later a depleted team lost 0-37 at Ebbw Vale and then a "very weak team" lost 6-31 at Widnes.

Worse was to follow on 31 October 1908 when Oldham came to Trinity Street and won 54-0 in front of "probably the best gate of the season". A week later Barry were able to field only 11 men at Merthyr, Rufus Davies, "the enthusiastic secretary", having to play full-back. In the circumstances a 7-21 reverse was no disgrace. Barry suffered a further defeat when visitors Mid-Rhondda won 6-5 at Trinity Street. Aberdare then avenged their loss at Barry when "a rather weak team" lost 5-43 at Ynys Field. In

December, Treherbert too, gained revenge winning 11-5. Barry had to strengthen the team and obtained several new players leading to victory at home to Aberdare 9-5 in a Challenge Cup qualifying tie at Trinity Street.

However, on Boxing Day, Barry's hopes of progress in the Cup ended with a 0-2 defeat at Trinity Street against Mid-Rhondda. A day earlier, Barry had upset Ebbw Vale by failing to turn up for a Welsh League fixture. In January they were defeated 46-0 by Oldham, 27-2 by Merthyr and 16-6 by Mid-Rhondda.

They did no better in the Welsh League, with successive home losses to Merthyr Tydfil, Mid-Rhondda and Aberdare. The last NRL game played at Trinity Street, on 20 February 1909, brought a rare victory over Widnes. New recruit, half-back Dicky David, had played for Cardiff and Wigan and in expectation of seeing him "a good crowd assembled" but David wired to say he could not appear due to "business". Nevertheless, Barry won 12-6 after trailing 2-6 at half-time. This was Barry's first and only win over a northern team.

Barry's last NRL game came at Headingley in March where they lost 0-56 to Leeds with a "depleted" team. Their final game came on 10 April 1909, a Welsh League encounter with Ebbw Vale at Bridge End Field, which they lost 0-38. Another Welsh League fixture was cancelled because they were unable to raise a side. They finished 29th out of 31 clubs in the NRL, with a final league record of:

Played	Won	Drawn	Lost	For	Against	Points	Percentage
18	3	0	15	76	445	6	16.66

In June 1909 they were named by the League as "defaulters". On 12 July 1909 *Athletic News* reported that "Barry has failed to fulfil the conditions laid down by the Committee" of the NRL and were "practically expelled". It is noticeable that the *Barry Herald* had ceased to cover the club's activities very much after Christmas, giving up totally after the Widnes match. Perhaps their brief only extended to reporting on winners.

Mid-Rhondda: 1908-9

The full name of the club was the Mid-Rhondda Social and Athletic Club. Their headquarters was the Cross Keys Hotel, Tonypandy and their ground was the Athletic Ground. In April 1908 this venue had staged the first Wales versus England international, which Wales won 35-18 and was watched by a crowd estimated at 12,000.

Mid-Rhondda Athletic Grounds, TONYPANDY.

Great Northern Union Football Match !

AUSTRALIA
(1st Match of the Tour) v.
MID-RHONDDA ATHLETIC
On the above Grounds,
On Saturday October 3rd, 1908.

Gates open at 2.30. Kick off 3.30.
Admission—1/- each. Grand Stand, 1/- extra.
Enclosure, 6d. extra.

On 30 June 1908 Mid-Rhondda were elected to the Northern Rugby League and their debut came on Saturday 5 September 1908 when they hosted Bradford Northern in front of a crowd of around 2,000. Fearnley, an ex-Cardiff Rugby Union player, scored a try for the home side, which he converted, but tries by Mitchell and Mann and a goal by Wilson, sealed Bradford's 15-5 win. Two weeks later, the first Rhondda derby, against Treherbert, was played at Tonypandy, but the home side suffered a 3-5 reverse.

The Australians opened their tour at Mid-Rhondda, and not surprisingly won 20-6, after leading 18-0 at half time, Wrentmore and Dai Thomas scoring second half tries for Mid-Rhondda. A crowd of 7,500 attended, with gate receipts of £140. The immortal Dally Messenger scored two tries and four goals for the Australians.

In October, 2,000 spectators saw Mid-Rhondda beat Merthyr 7-3, and they enjoyed success against other Welsh sides, beating Aberdare 12-2 and winning 6-5 at Barry in November 1908. December and January were also good months for the Rhondda men, who again beat both Aberdare and Barry. They also went to Barry in the Challenge Cup, and a 2-0 victory was rewarded with a visit to Hunslet. However, the legendary Billy Batten scored four tries for the Parksiders who ran out 25-5 victors. Although only securing five wins and a draw in the NRL, the Tonypandy side was seldom outclassed. In February 1909 they lost 7-16 at Swinton and 7-15 at Hull KR. They finished the season with a flourish, a "good attendance" seeing them beat Salford 11-9 at Tonypandy. They then won a Welsh League fixture at Merthyr 10-3, and completed a double, beating the same opponents 5-2 at home. The team finished 24th out of 31 clubs with a final league record of:

Played	Won	Drawn	Lost	For	Against	Points	Percentage
18	5	1	12	111	214	11	30.55

However, low attendances meant that the club's officials were not satisfied with the financial rewards of the NU game. In April 1909 the final of the South Wales and Monmouthshire Association Football Cup was played at the Athletic Ground between Merthyr Town and Ton Pentre. The match, which Ton Pentre won 2-0, was watched by a crowd of 8,000. After the game, Mr Griffiths, Chairman of the Mid-Rhondda NU Committee announced that "they were going to have a soccer team at Tonypandy next season. He had been a great supporter of amateur rugby and NUism but the financial position had not realised expectations. They were going to fall away from NUism as they could see that soccer was the coming game".

In July 1909 it was reported that Mid-Rhondda and neighbours Treherbert were not being included in the Challenge Cup draw, because they were in arrears to the NU on 30 June. Later in the same month, it was reported that they had withdrawn from the NRL, and, as predicted, an Association side appeared at the Athletic Ground, under the Mid-Rhondda banner, from 1909-10 onwards.

Treherbert: 1908 to 1910

Treherbert and District Northern Union Club Ltd was formed in April 1908 with capital of £500. Their ground was the Athletic Ground, Treherbert, formerly home to a Rugby Union club, and their headquarters was the Dunraven Hotel. Treherbert were admitted to the NU in June 1908 along with near-neighbours Mid-Rhondda and their first game was a 3-6 defeat at Barry.

Treherbert's first home game in the NRL was on 12 September 1908, when they lost 6-27 to Halifax. This game "proved a great attraction" but the visitors were too strong and outscored Treherbert by seven tries to two. A week later, though, Treherbert secured their first league points, winning 5-3 at neighbours Mid-Rhondda. They then completed a rapid double over Aberdare, winning 8-0 at home and 13-5 away, but went down at home to Runcorn and Leigh in quick succession. Later that month Treherbert also lost 2-16 at Ebbw Vale.

December saw Treherbert clinch a fourth NRL win, again over Welsh opposition, Barry being defeated 11-5 and, later that month, a 4,000 crowd for a Thursday afternoon match against the Australian tourists saw a narrow defeat 3-6, by one try to two.

In January 1909 they lost 8-24 at Runcorn, despite tries by Hanford and Griffiths, and worse followed with a 0-25 rout at Dewsbury. In February Treherbert lost 0-10 at home to Merthyr and two new players, Bob Williams and H. Harding had been expected to turn out but, although "their forms had been filled out", for some reason they had been destroyed.

A month later, a 13-3 victory over Merthyr was described as "one of the greatest surprises of the football season". The final home game of the season, a Welsh League contest with Mid-Rhondda, ended in controversy when the referee walked off some minutes before the official end, in protest at both teams' rough play. Two men had already been sent off in a game which Treherbert lost 7-15.

They finished the 1908-9 season 28th of 31 clubs, with a league record of:

Played	Won	Drawn	Lost	For	Against	Points	Percentage
18	4	1	13	81	212	9	25.00

In 1909-10 Treherbert failed to manage a win in the Northern Rugby League. They opened the season with a 10-22 defeat at home to Hull KR, then went down to both Ebbw Vale and Merthyr. In October, their visit to Keighley saw them "bewildered by the passing of the home men", and they lost 3-20. A visit from Huddersfield in November 1909 produced a 27-3 trouncing. Perhaps the closest they came to win was in December 1909 when they lost 3-6 to Keighley at home. There was, however, a poor attendance, many team changes at the last moment and the club secretary, Mr H.R. Jones, resigned. The only consolation came when David Galloway, a 22-year-old forward was selected for Wales against England at Wakefield on 4 December.

In February 1910 Treherbert lost 5-7 to Merthyr in a Welsh League fixture, their final home game. On the following Monday they failed to appear for a Welsh League game at Ebbw Vale. Subsequently they failed to fulfil a fixture at Hull KR, the home side arranging a friendly with the newly formed Coventry club instead. Coventry had also clashed with the Rugby Union authorities over allegations of professionalism, and played for three seasons in the Northern Union, ironically replacing Treherbert.

Treherbert's final match was on 17 April 1910, when they lost 13-54 to league leaders Oldham at Watersheddings, Treherbert being described as "pathetic". In June, at the NRL's AGM at the George Hotel, Huddersfield, the NU secretary, Joseph Platt "pointed out that the Treherbert club were defaulters and that although they had been assisted by other clubs they had failed to fulfil their fixture list and were therefore... not eligible for re-election". Their place was awarded to Coventry, and the bottom three clubs, Merthyr, Bramley and Barrow, were all re-elected. They were the only Welsh club to play a complete season without a league win. Their final sorry record was:

Played	Won	Drawn	Lost	For	Against	Points	Percentage
12	0	0	12	55	289	0	0.00

Why the clubs failed

Faced with unremitting hostility, nationalist and class prejudice and the rise of football, it was perhaps inevitable that the breakthrough of 1907 ended in failure. The Welsh NU clubs were weak organisations, unable to match the signing-on fees paid by northern sides and poorly financed. They appeared unbusiness-like, and, it was remarked that their "affairs are conducted in an easy-going fashion". For Welsh players, local NU clubs were a poor alternative to their richer cousins up north. The great Ben Gronow turned down Ebbw Vale's offer of £25 and a job, yet later signed for Huddersfield for £125. The only Welsh Rugby Union international who signed for a Welsh NU club was Merthyr's Dai 'Tarw' Jones.

Nevertheless, the NU did little to help them overcome such obstacles. The NU had initially allowed a travel subsidy of £10 to Merthyr Tydfil and Ebbw Vale each time they played in the north. But after the election of the other four clubs the subsidy was reduced to £5 and remained at this level despite the newcomers' problems.

Worst of all, the Welsh sides had to contend with uncaring attitudes from the north. One writer commented that "if the game there [South Wales] cannot be made self-supporting, clubs in the north should not be taxed to make good its weakness". When Ebbw Vale appeared likely to fold in 1912, *Athletic News* felt that "many clubs would not mourn if trips to Monmouthshire were knocked on the head". As throughout Rugby League's history, member clubs' self-interest overrode the desire for expansion.

In reality, the NU had no expansion strategy. New sides were formed by local entrepreneurs or club officials tired of covert professionalism. Such clubs were given senior status with few questions asked, yet were expected to stand on their own feet and provide proper competition for their rivals. And once in the senior ranks, the new clubs were competitors for scarce resources and if outside the NU heartland also imposed additional travel costs. This is not to say that the NU did not try to promote the code outside the north. In 1907-8 two of the three internationals against the New Zealand tourists were played outside the north, at Stamford Bridge, Chelsea, and at Cheltenham. Insofar as it had one, the NU's real "expansion strategy" was aimed at giving a regional sport national prominence - not at establishing viable clubs across Britain.

Not for the last time in its history, Rugby League found its progress in Edwardian Wales blocked by a social hostility beyond its control and the parochial short-sightedness of its clubs which its leaders showed little desire to control. And yet, despite such failure, the dream of establishing Rugby League as a major Welsh sport continued to burn brightly in the hearts of its supporters.

Part Two:

Between the wars

Chapter 4: From Pontypridd to European Champions
- international matches between the wars

International Rugby League had not gone for good when it departed from Ebbw Vale in 1911. The horror of the First World War precluded any meaningful international competition until after 1918 and granted, it took the return of the Australians in 1921 for the Northern Union (NU) to consider a tour match in Wales once more but, with Welshmen still turning in numbers to play the northern code, a viable international team was always waiting to be assembled.

Under the circumstances, it was a brave venture to take the game to Wales. The NU had not attempted any expansionist moves for some time and the game was possibly in one of its most insular phases. The 1921 Kangaroos were the first to play all their tests against Great Britain in the north, going down 6-0 in the Ashes decider at Salford.

Australians in Pontypridd

The Australians arrived in Pontypridd on 10 December, still level in the Ashes series after losing at Leeds but taking a 16-2 victory at the Boulevard. The local media was keen to see how the code from the north of England had progressed since its last visits a decade earlier and the people of South Wales also turned out in force, enticed by special third class trains and cheap fares on the Taff Vale Railway (as long as no luggage was taken). Taff Vale Park, despite its lack of basic facilities, managed to cram in 11,000 spectators to see the home team lose 21-16 to the powerful tourists. The venue was then home to the famous Welsh Powderhall professional sprint race and to Pontypridd Dragons football club of the Southern League but it was the first outing there for the NU.

The day was wet but coverage in the local press and elsewhere was comprehensive and most of it very positive if lacking a little in geographical and ethnological knowledge, the *Rhondda Leader*'s feature writer describing the Australians' "war-chant" as a "strange, guttural song in some Maori dialect".

However, this was the writer who also said "when the Australasian backs set to work I thought the four winds had been let loose. Blinkhorn and Horder moved like quicksilver. No pressman is supposed to feel excited. It is part of his trade to kill emotions. But it was no good. Whenever Burge broke through, or when Blinkhorn shot with arrowlike speed straight for the goal, I forgot everything and yelled." He did also add that "Northern Union rules do not give to the game that breathless vigour I had thought to see." Apparently the writer was hoping to see longer scrummages, line-outs and "continual touch-finding", the very activities the NU had sought to eradicate.

The *Yorkshire Post* thought the crowd was a fair one considering the 2 shillings entrance fee, the high unemployment in the region and the continuous drizzle that fell throughout the day. The writer also thought that the Welsh were unlucky to lose but failed to take all the chances that came their way. He also criticised the tourists for continual obstruction and offside which he felt marred an otherwise entertaining game.

It was a match in which the Welsh were always struggling to make up lost ground although they did hold the lead briefly. It was the visitors who scored first after 5 minutes when, from a scrum, Frank Burge fed Jimmy Craig with a simple scoring opportunity. Wales suffered a setback when stand-off Johnny Rogers of Huddersfield was injured and his debilitation left Wales without a key playmaker in the centre of the field. So it was that Australia were able to score a second unconverted try after coming close on a number of occasions. This time the fine tackling of Jim Sullivan at full-back was unable to stop Australian wing Cec Blinkhorn and the visitors had a 6-point lead.

Wales then entered their best phase of the game. Continual pressure saw centre Tommy Howley break through to score beneath the posts ensuring a simple conversion for Ben Gronow. Gronow's kicking gave Wales the lead shortly afterwards when he landed a long-distance penalty for obstruction. The match looked to be swinging the way of the home side until just before the break. Two swift converted tries, the first by Burge, the second by prodigious wingman Harold Horder, showed up Welsh defensive frailty and left the Australians 16-7 to the good at half time. The *Rhondda Leader* admitted that "the Welsh players did not tackle well".

Early Welsh pressure after the interval (The *Rhondda Leader*'s man put it down to the "lemons") produced a string of missed chances and penalties, only one of which was converted by Sullivan. For much of the second half Australia were on the defensive, rarely breaking towards the Welsh line but their defence was solid enough to restrict Wales to a further Gronow penalty and one from Sullivan before the tourists clinched the match. There was "more than a suspicion of forward passing," wrote the *Yorkshire Post*, "before Burge got the ball, and finished a hurricane rush by flinging himself over the line near the posts, for Thompson to add the goal".

Wales were to score a late try when the injured Rogers had recovered to dummy the defence from a scrum. The kick was a difficult one but Gronow landed it and Wales lost by five points, 21-16. Despite their constant pressure on the tourists they failed to take many chances and Australia, perhaps, deserved their victory for their stout defence.

One thing was certain, the *Rhondda Leader* writer did not care for some individuals in the crowd. "One man roared; 'Bring him down, the -------.' I have since been told that these noisy men are Bristolians and Forest of Dean immigrants. I am sure, I hope so."

His countryman 'Observer' at the *Western Mail* looked instead to the pitch to make his critical assessment. "It was, undoubtedly, a brilliant and exhilarating exhibition," he wrote, but he saw the players, rather than the NU rules as the explanation for the high standard. "Such clever exponents of back play as the Australasians would, in a Rugby Union game, have produced equally as satisfactory football."

'Observer' commented further on NU rules: "Generally they strive to attain continuity of play, to give incentive to attack. Those who have been unutterably bored by the endless and aimless kicking to touch indulged in by amateur [Rugby Union] players warmly approved of the NU prohibition of kicking out of play except under certain circumstances." Surprisingly, the writer could not see the advantage of line-out abolition or the play-the-ball as a means of restarting the game.

Of the teams, the *Western Mail* was full of praise. 'Observer' described the Australian back play and handling as "scintillating" but noted that the Welsh forwards were able to monopolise play, especially in the second half, singling out George Oliver, Edgar Morgan and Tom Woods for special praise. The writer was also full of admiration for Welsh full-back Jim Sullivan and, of the tourists, "none caught the eye more than Latta and Burge".

The *Yorkshire Post* also noted that the Welsh forwards dominated and suggested that Great Britain should take heed as the third test approached and prepare for "scrummaging, wheeling and quick footwork". As in the *Western Mail*, the writer was critical of the Welsh backs for not taking their chances, but lay much of the blame at the feet of the Australians because of their "inexcusable acts of obstruction... which marred the game. It was apparent that the resources of law-breakers are not exhausted".

Yet the lasting impression of the game was a positive one. The *Rhondda Leader* wrote: "There were moments of fine play. Spirit and zest were there in abundance, and the game was kept open and fast."

The venture was a success and interest in Rugby League appeared to be strong in Wales. Yet the NU was still tentative. It was another five years before the English brought their national team, once again to Taff Vale Park in Pontypridd, to give the Welsh public another taste of international League. Apparently the authorities took a lot of persuasion despite the fact that the Welsh had played nine matches against their traditional rivals in England between 1912 and 1925. They had won only one of these games, 13-2 at Wigan in 1923, but the scorelines suggested that there was little difference between the teams and home advantage could prove to be the deciding factor in a Welsh resurgence.

Despite this NU reluctance, the Welsh public were ready to support League in numbers. As Gareth Williams and David Smith wrote in their history of Welsh Rugby Union, *Fields of Praise*: "Throughout the twenties the dour nature of much club play, and the not unconnected dull spectacle presented by the constantly unenterprising and unsuccessful Welsh international sides, contrasted unfavourably with the attractive handling skills of professional Rugby."

Players such as Jim Sullivan made the trip north at a young age depriving Union of some of its finest talent. Welshmen had heard of their exploits in the northern code and, disappointed at the dull Union fare on offer in their homeland, were taking an interest in their former heroes.

Record crowd

The NU clearly had no need for concern, which was shown when it finally agreed to stage a match in Pontypridd on Monday, April 12 1926. A staggering 23,000, a record for a Rugby League match in Wales, turned out to see a 30-22 English victory in a fabulous match at the much-improved Taff Vale Park. The stadium was now capable of holding up to 40,000 and had a fine playing surface which no doubt contributed to the exhilarating game.

"Bewildering speed of Rugby League 'national" announced the *South Wales Echo*. But not everybody was impressed. Amazingly, the *Western Mail* complained that "Kicking [was] sacrificed for passing". Generally, however, media and public impressions were favourable.

The *Yorkshire Post* wrote that the game was "bright" but perhaps "if anything, too much on the exhibition side". But, it added, "the speed of the game impressed all". The referee, the Reverend Frank Chambers who was to commentate for BBC radio on the first Challenge Cup Final at Wembley in 1929, allowed the game to flow and its pace was certainly relentless as the Welsh began with a flurry. Frank Evans, Wales's Swinton winger, broke infield and fed his centre, the supporting Mel Rosser. Jim Sullivan failed to convert the try.

With attack clearly dominating over defence, play swept from end to end, offering numerous openings and it didn't take long for England to level the scores. Charlie Carr, the Barrow centre, scrambled over for a try and was followed soon after by Frank Gallagher, the forward backing up well after Jonty Parkin broke from the scrum. Billy Burgess struck the crossbar with the conversion but the ball crept over and England held an 8-3 lead. This became 11-3 only minutes later when Bob Taylor of Hull was fed by wingman Billy Bentham and burst through some weak Welsh tackling.

The home team struck back with possibly the game's finest try. Intricate and constant passing opened up a gap for Jim Bacon, the left winger from Leeds. He still had to create an opening and, with strength and a wicked side-step he defied the cover to score. Sullivan's goal reduced the English lead to three points.

The Welsh crowd, perhaps restrained by the fact that their countrymen were all from clubs in the north of England, were initially and untypically reticent but the Welsh fightback prompted a surge of enthusiasm and English tries from Sid Rix and a second for Taylor - this one goaled by Burgess - prompted booing around the ground. Conversely, resounding cheers followed Edgar Morgan's converted try just before half time which left Wales trailing by only six, 13-19.

Unfortunately for the home team, and in the days before substitutes, centre Joe Jones of Leeds was unable to restart the second half, his injury sustained when attempting to stop Gallagher's try. Dai Rees, the Halifax forward, was also limping badly. He played on but it was destined to be an uphill struggle for Wales. Nonetheless they opened the second-half scoring when Ike Fowler made an opening and fed Jim Sullivan. The gap was down to three points but it was nearest the Welsh got.

With Wales no doubt hampered by a lack of defensive players the English began to dominate. Three quick tries scored by Burgess (this after a superb passing movement), Bentham and Carr took the game out of reach and, although England relaxed a little, to allow Evans and Fowler to score for the Welsh, the final score was 30-22 to the visitors. The English outscored their opponents by eight tries to six but the goal kicking was poor, with Burgess landing only three for England and Sullivan replying with just two.

Of the English, the *Yorkshire Post* chose to praise Parkin who used the ball provided by his forwards to good effect along with Gallagher and Burgess whose passing and support play created many openings. The writer suggested that the Welsh defeat was a result of poor tackling and was "amazed" at the number of times their defence fell for the dummy. The *South Wales Echo* described Parkin as "the inspiring force, and far and away the greatest attacker".

From a propaganda viewpoint there was no doubting the success of the match. In purely commercial terms it raised a handy £2,306, but as a springboard for a relaunch of Rugby League in Wales, it also offered much. As the *South Wales Echo* wrote: "Rugby League football has many thousands of admirers in the North of England and in some of our Colonies... and, quite irrespective of the merits of the rival Rugby games, one is bound to acknowledge that the interest was well deserved." Even as long ago as 1926 the writer felt it necessary to note what many Rugby League followers have constantly tried to insist between the two codes of the sport - that they are, essentially, different games. "The points of contrast were more marked than those lending themselves to comparison."

The author did, however, write that the game seemed much faster than the Union code he was used to: "the speed, both with the forwards and the backs, was extraordinary, and the passing was not only accurate, but was bewildering in its swiftness." Yet just as his counterpart at the *Western Mail* had suggested, the *South Wales Echo* journalist thought that perhaps there was too much passing, and not enough kicking. He was also, perhaps justifiably, disappointed at the standard of defence.

After his criticism of the excessive passing the *Western Mail* writer, in contradictory fashion, was quick to note that "it was positively refreshing to find that the ball was only kicked nine times in the first half". In praising the game, he wondered how the contemporary Welsh Union team "would have done in the international matches during the past couple of years had some of the professional backs been available. The lightning rapidity of the passes... the ignoring of the kick, and several other things impressed, and at times I wished for what appeared the better type of Rugby."

But his overtures stopped there. "Then I saw the faults of Rugby League football," he wrote. The League game has often been noted for its sturdy defence and robust tackling. However, at Pontypridd that afternoon, this was clearly not the case. Maybe it was a one-off aberration creating a game of astounding defensive frailty, but all reports of the game were very critical of the standard of tackling including the *Mail*. "Tackling was unknown to the majority of the 26 players," it said. Strange that this is an argument now more frequently aimed at Rugby Union.

But most post-match criticism was good. The *Echo* was full of praise for the attacking abilities of both teams and commented on how the speed and ability of former Welsh Union players had improved immeasurably. It was also quick to point out how the full-backs were used in attack as well as defence: "a revelation" to those only used to defensive, kicking full-backs.

Wales versus England at Pontypridd 12 April 1926.
Back row: Mr E. Osborne & Mr J.F. Whittaker
Standing: H. Rees (reserve), D. Edwards (reserve), F.L. Roffey, E. Morgan, Rev F.H. Chambers (referee), W. Hodder, J. Thompson, Mr J. Leake & Mr W.M. Gabbatt
Sitting: B. Phillips, J. Jones, I. Fowler, D. Rees, J. Bacon. In front: F. Evans & W. 'Billo' Rees.
Photo courtesy Robert Gate

Most of the newspapers also chose to cover the after-match dinner, for it was here that the RFL announced their intention to bring the sport to Wales "if there was a serious demand for it," according to Edmund Osborne, vice-chairman of the Rugby League Council. Tom Mallet of the Welsh Rugby League Commission proposed the toast of "the Rugby game", and added that the day had produced magnificent football and he would like to see the Rugby League and the Rugby Union knitted together as one. Mr Osborne concurred, adding that the people of South Wales were "becoming broadminded" and were "at least all true sportsmen". What the Welsh thought of this backhanded compliment is not recorded.

The RFL was keen to say that it was an honest organisation, paying men openly for playing Rugby with no underhand methods. The day's referee, the Reverend Chambers, said "that although some people condemned the Rugby League because they paid men for loss of time for playing football, he thought there was a much bigger wrong in expecting a married man to lose a day's work and deprive his family of a day's wages".

And the RFL appeared to make it obvious that they wanted to foster Rugby League in South Wales. As Mr Osborne said: "If the Rugby League came to Wales it would be a successful venture." Maybe Mr Osborne would have been proved right but, once again, ultimately not enough support and time was forthcoming.

Yet the Welsh were keen to see League at the highest level. Writing in *Fields of Praise* Gareth Williams and David Smith noted: "The spectators at Taff Vale Park were enthralled by the fast, open play." On the back of the staggering success of the two Pontypridd international matches a professional club was set up in the town to play in the 1926-27 Rugby League season.

Kiwi visitors

Pontypridd hosted a third international at Taff Vale Park. On 4 December 1926 the Kiwi tourists came to Pontypridd and, once again showing the immense popularity for top-class Rugby League in the region, 18,000 turned out to see Wales victorious 34-8. In the tests against Great Britain, the New Zealanders were to lose all three and the tour, as far as the visitors were concerned, was a failure.

It was the first time since the inaugural visit of 1907-8 that the Kiwis had been seen on British shores and a players' strike (resulting in *sine die* bans for many tourists) plus the heavy defeats suffered, meant that New Zealand would wait another 13 years before returning to the northern hemisphere. Nonetheless, international matches were still a big drawcard in Wales, especially as the home team included Jim Sullivan who starred for Britain in the test series, and was seemingly scoring at will. The 18,000 attendance was the highest of the tour and the Kiwis returned to play Pontypridd on Christmas Day, with an 18-7 victory for the tourists.

On announcement of the fixture the local community took the chance to show their hospitable character and enthusiasm for high-class sport. John Leake, a key mover in Rugby League in Wales and then chairman of Pontypridd RLFC wrote to Pontypridd Council suggesting the Kiwis should be afforded a civic reception. The *Pontypridd Observer* reported that the council "referred the matter to the clerk and chairman".

The referral was obviously approved for the *Observer* reported a few days later that the New Zealanders "would be entertained to tea and to the evening performance at the cinema. On Saturday morning it was proposed to give the visitors a charabanc tour and if the Great Western Colliery was working they might like to visit it [or] the Power Station at Upper Boat. They would proceed from Upper Boat to Cilfynydd and the team were desirous of placing a wreath at the foot of the war memorial".

One of the local councillors told the visitors that "if you ask Mr Evan Williams perhaps he will let you go down Dan's Pit but you will have to go down one at a time". The tourists' response was unrecorded. As a result of their efforts in entertaining the visitors, the council members thought it only fair that they should grant themselves free entrance to the match. No holds were barred in attempting to create a carnival spirit for the game. In a country noted for its abstinence it is interesting to discover that nine local pubs were allowed time extensions to their licences to accommodate and refresh the visiting crowds on condition that sandwiches were provided as well.

The match saw the Kiwis totally outclassed by a magnificent Welsh team. The *Yorkshire Post* described the victory of "inestimable value" to Rugby League and the Pontypridd club in particular. Sadly international success did not translate to club level.

There was, however, no doubting Welsh superiority that day although New Zealand put up stout opposition during lengthy periods of the game. Lost opportunities cost them dear, though, and the handling in their backs was questionable. Thus the *Western Mail* headlined its report "New Zealanders outclassed". Once again the *Mail* sent a Rugby Union writer to the match who remarked critically and probably to the puzzlement of readers that "the rules have been so obviously made for the spectator". He added, "there were still many good points. [The] Rugby [is] much faster than the amateurs play and is replete with spectacular incidents".

The writer also described the Kiwis as "the weakest colonial team which has visited us. . . the home country scoring tries with ridiculous ease". This was probably unfair on both the visitors and the home team. Wales were in fine form that day and their finishing was clinical. Jack Gore of Salford who scored two tries, plus his forward partners Wilf Hodder, Frank Stephens and George Oliver were, according to the *Yorkshire Post*, the bedrock on which the Welsh backs built their lead, while Eddie Caswell and Billo Rees as half-backs repeatedly created openings for the three-quarters, allowing wingman Frank Evans of Swinton to score a hat-trick.

Yet it was Jim Sullivan, the Wigan full-back, who caught the eye once again. The *Mail* had four paragraphs headed "the greatness of Sullivan" and went on to praise him in no uncertain terms for his attacking and defensive skills and his "dangerous policies which paid". Of course, the writer had to add that he was stolen in one of the north's "periodic raids" on Welsh clubs. This was an argument often used by Union writers in the succeeding years, ignoring the fact that firstly, Sullivan and others of his like signed for League clubs of their own free will and, secondly, they often signed when only teenagers and became the great players they did because of immersion in the skills and techniques of League. Who knows what players such as Sullivan would have become had they stayed in Wales? It cannot be assumed their success would have been assured.

Evans opened the scoring for Wales with his first touchdown but, shortly afterwards, New Zealand took the lead for the only time when Benny Davidson worked an opening for Delgrosso to notch a converted try. It did not last long. Sullivan landed a colossal drop goal from halfway to level the scores and then Wales took control. "The Welsh backs were handling in bewildering fashion," said the *Mail*, and Gore scored his

43

first, to be followed by Evans. With only one of the tries converted, Wales held a 13-5 half-time lead.

It was soon extended. Sullivan landed a penalty and Gore took a simple pass to score his second try. Evans's hat-trick was completed with ease. New Zealand briefly threatened a comeback with Thomas's try but the Welsh then dominated the remainder of the game. Danny Hurcombe scored a Sullivan-converted try, followed by neat work leading to a score by Caswell. Then the Wigan full-back scored the try of the match - "a masterpiece" in the words of the *Western Mail*. The forwards won good ball near the halfway line and Sullivan hit the back-line at pace coming onto a well-weighted pass from Caswell. He had some defence to beat but made it to the line without a finger touching him. According to the *Yorkshire Post* "the crowd went mad with delight". Billy Rhodes, one of four Pontypridd players in the team, converted, for a final score of 34-8.

It was a fine Welsh win although the newspapers tended to dwell on the paucity of opposition. Of the New Zealand backs only Davidson and Gregory, Sullivan's opposite number, emerged with reputations intact. All the Welsh back division received praise especially Evans and centre Hurcombe who "displayed any amount of dash".

The *Western Mail* concluded that: "There were a good many Rugby Union supporters among the spectators and I do not think they were altogether satisfied with what they saw, for despite the fact that there were many fine movements, there was always something lacking. The game, delightfully open as it was, could not rouse people like an amateur encounter can." This is a continual gripe from Union observers down the years. Rugby League, they often concede is a faster, open, more skilful and spectacular game, yet they often feel it lacks a *je ne sais quoi*. They are, of course, entitled to that view, but as this never appears to include anything other than a yearning for more kicking and set scrummages, it is probably little more than unfamiliarity with the rules, abilities and tactics of League and its players.

Indeed, the *Mail* writer added that the crowd was subdued. "I think the truth is that few of the people present had a grasp of the rules," he wrote. "Thus... there were many occasions [when] the spectators were mystified by the rulings of the referee."

Despite this, crowds for the two international matches in 1926 were excellent and added to the sense of gloom when the Pontypridd club was disbanded in the autumn of 1927. At the post-New Zealand match reception the chairman of the local Rugby League committee Mr J.E. Brooks accepted the congratulations of the Kiwi management who predicted that the game had a strong future in South Wales and the Kiwis were praised in return for their sportsmanship in defeat. Brooks suggested that League "had made a huge step forward" with local dignitaries attending and implored the directors of the local club to reduce attendance fees so more people could attend matches.

He even suggested local tradesmen should send a regular cheque every six months to Pontypridd RLFC to boost the sport because it attracted such good trade to the town when big matches were played. It seemed the audience for League existed, yet despite all the rhetoric it would remain one that was unfulfilled.

Of course, there were still enough Welshmen taking up offers from League clubs to sustain a Welsh international XIII, but only once between the New Zealand match and 1935, when the vital introduction of France to international Rugby League made a European Championship viable, did Wales meet their regular opposition, England, on home soil. All five away matches in this intervening period were lost to England.

England come to Cardiff

For the sole home game, between 1926 and 1935, played at Cardiff on 14 November 1928, the Welsh were expected to fare much better. Sadly, after holding their own during a close first period, the Welsh succumbed 39-15 to a second-half English rampage which, unfortunately, did not aid the cause for regular internationals in the principality.

Nonetheless, the match saw some fine play. "Spectacular Rugby" headlined the *South Wales Echo*. And, once more, a good crowd was there to witness the game, some estimates of the attendance being as high as 25,000, although 10,000 seems more likely. The *Western Mail* wrote: "That representative Rugby League matches have the power of drawing large crowds in Wales was made abundantly clear."

The game was staged at what was then known as the 'Welsh White City', properly called the Sloper Road Greyhound Stadium and situated near to Ninian Park football ground. The ground was proposed as the home for the Cardiff club that was accepted into the League in 1928, but never took up its place.

Sloper Road had an capacity of 70,000 and was only demolished in 1984 to make way for a housing development. The match was Cardiff's first League international and "it must be regarded as having been a decided success", said the *Mail*. Yet the newspaper remarked that there were "differences of opinion as to the character and effect of the actual play. Those who are wedded to amateur Rugby can never watch a Rugby League match without thinking of the features which it lacks when contrasted with the amateur game". The *Mail*'s editorial line clearly remained steadfast.

According to the *Yorkshire Post*, there were three decisive factors in the Welsh defeat: their backs lacked pace, their positional play was poor and their forwards failed to control the scrummages. The writer also felt that the Welsh backs were too small and therefore unable to defend against the powerful running of the English which, combined with their ball-handling ability, proved too difficult to hold.

Eleven of the English team were Lions tourists and this obvious advantage, coupled with the team play their experiences together engendered, was always going to be a decisive factor. It was this sense of teamwork that set the English off to the best possible start. Even before the Welsh had established any pattern of play they found themselves two Jonty Parkin-converted tries down. Sloppy passing by the Welsh saw English centre Charlie Carr of Barrow scoop up the ball and find St Helens winger Alf Frodsham who, avoiding the cover, ran half the length of the field to score beneath the posts. In the following minute scrum-half Parkin of Wakefield opened up play for Carr and his centre partner Billy Dingsdale. They fed Alf Ellaby, Saints' flying winger, and his immaculate body swerve flummoxed Jim Sullivan, once again playing full-back for Wales, to allow a simple score.

In fact Ellaby won most of the post-match plaudits. The *Yorkshire Post* wrote: "there was no player more distinguished... [his] swerve and side-step left the Welsh crowd - and Sullivan - gasping." The *Western Mail* also praised him, with the heading "Ellaby a great player" and adding "it was Ellaby who really made England's line the power it was. Ring [his Welsh counterpart] was a nonentity when it came to stopping Ellaby who would be certain of a place in any national side. He was a great player."

Yet, in the first half, the Welsh came back well. Centre Tom Parker broke from inside his own half supported by Johnny Ring of Wigan who scored a Sullivan-converted try. Wales would have soon been level had Sullivan managed to convert Dai Jenkins's try in the corner but his long-distance penalty shortly afterwards made amends and Wales were on level terms at 10-10. And it wasn't long before they were in the lead, Sullivan and centre George Lewis combining to give Maidment an opening which the full-back converted. Frodsham pulled back three points with a try in the corner but, at the break, the Welsh led 15-13 and a home victory seemed possible.

Hopes were dashed in the first minute after the break, however. A gap opened up in the Welsh defence for Dingsdale to score a converted try and from then on it was all England. Ellaby was the next to score after a scramble on the Welsh line and full-back Jim Brough - who was to captain the Lions in 1936 in Australia - landed the touchline conversion and it was Ellaby who added the next, perhaps the game's best try, when he sprinted more than half the length of the pitch to score beneath the posts only for Parkin to miss the simple kick. The half-back made amends shortly afterwards when he raced clear from his own half to add another try. Dingsdale did much the same towards the end of the match when he added his second score and, with the home crowd drifting back to the railway station, Brough finished off a fine passing movement to complete the scoring. Parkin's conversions left England with a victory of 39-15, with nine tries in the process.

It was, in the end, a comprehensive victory and while Wales, according to the *Yorkshire Post*, "had their inspired moments" they looked a beaten team in the second half. Welsh players singled out for praise were Emlyn Gwynne, the winger from Swansea, who had signed for Hull and Sullivan, although the *Post* conceded that, on the day, the great man was outplayed by his opposite number Brough. Dai Jenkins was the only forward worthy of praise, according to the *Western Mail*, which was very critical of the home players, although the writer, being a Union man, was always going to compare the team unfavourably with its Union counterpart.

Nonetheless, the newspaper conceded that "the work of the winning team was delightfully polished and spectacular. Swiftness of thought and action were the hand-maidens of fleetness of foot... one had to distribute one's admiration between the gloriously elusive swerve and the perfect combined work. The blend and understanding in England's attacking line reached a stage which has rarely been approached in Rugby or Rugby League football." Would such elegant prose appear in a newspaper report today.

The writer thought the Welsh were their own worst enemy. He considered their attacking play to be almost as good as England's but letting the ball run free at vital moments, while woeful in defence, lacking "the stamina required to subdue an attack".

While the game was truly spectacular in the amount of tries run in, especially for that era, the *Yorkshire Post* felt that the crowd "would have preferred to see more keenness in defence" and became "disillusioned" when a Welsh defeat became certain. The *Post* journalist concluded by asking: "What impression did the game leave on the Welsh crowd? Is Rugby League football likely to be established in Wales? These questions remain to be answered." As indeed they still do.

While Wales continued to play away internationals in England during the following years, it wasn't until the emergence of France as a third genuine European Rugby League power in the thirties that League internationals were a viable proposition in Wales once again. The RFL considered matches in Wales to be a non-starter without the regular fixtures of a competitive professional club presence in the principality. Sustained interest and growth in the sport was their aim and, while hit-and-run internationals provided short-term success, their organisation and execution did not merit the time and money spent on what was only short-lived propaganda.

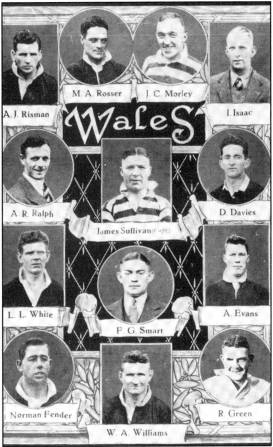

Wales team against Australia at Wembley 1933. Wales lost 19-51.
Photo Roger Davies, courtesy Phil Melling

France arrive

The arrival of the French prompted a change in thinking, however. A triangular European competition was now a genuine possibility and with three nations, England, Wales and France, both guaranteed two international fixtures under such a format, each could play one at home and one away. The Welsh were to be treated to international Rugby League once again.

Rugby League was born in France in the early 1930s. Union had long been a populist sport in the country, in much the same way as it had been in Wales, with football often forced into second place and the French national team was often successful against the home nations. But trouble was brewing. In 1931, the home Unions got wind of the fact that some French clubs were paying their players. This, coupled with increasing success and violence in international matches over the home nations, was enough for the British Isles to ostracise the French, bar them from the five nations championship and ban clubs from touring.

It was a heaven-sent opportunity for Rugby League. In a meeting in Paris in 1932 between John Wilson, the RFL secretary and a former Olympic cyclist, and Victor Breyer, editor of *L'Echo Des Sports,* a French newspaper, Wilson suggested to Breyer that the cycling stadiums of France could also be used to play Rugby League now that the French Union had been shunned by the British Isles. Breyer, whose newspaper was involved in a circulation war over rival *L'Equipe*, based ostensibly on the popularity of cycling in France, saw an opportunity to be involved in a new, crowd-pulling sport and agreed to publish articles on the new game with a view to playing an exhibition match in Paris between the Australian tourists of 1933 and a British XIII.

This was the Australian side that had taken on and beaten the Welsh at Wembley 51-19 earlier in the tour after also beating them at the same stadium in 1930, 26-10. While the Welsh had wanted home fixtures, clashes with international Union matches and the belief by the RFL that expansion would be better served by games in London meant that England remained the territory in which Wales played the majority of their matches.

But now the French were coming. While *L'Equipe* opposed the new sport from the outset and created obstacles to the staging of the match in Paris, Breyer managed to secure the Stade Pershing for the game on 31 December 1933. Australia destroyed England 63-13, scoring 15 tries. More importantly though, a member of the 5,000 strong crowd was a young player, Jean Galia, a Catalan from Perpignan. Galia had been banned from Union for allegedly offering money to Catalan players to join his club in Villeneuve.

Because Galia denied the claims and was thoroughly disgruntled with French Union, he was looking for a way to restart his playing career and, as a successful entrepreneur, to open up business opportunities into the bargain. Rugby League was the ideal avenue for this pioneer and, at Breyer's behest, he left Paris to head for the French Rugby heartlands of the south to recruit a 13-a-side squad to tour England.

The tour, in March 1934, was a resounding success despite the French being new to the game and regular internationals between the three European nations were started immediately, as much to encourage the French development as to take internationals back to Wales, but home matches for NU Welshmen were once again a possibility.

European Championship

Their opening international against the French *treizistes*, was in Bordeaux on the first day of 1935. The French took their first international victory 18-11 and prepared to play the return fixture at Llanelli on 23 November that year, the first international in Wales for seven years, and the first match of that season's European Championship with home and away games for each nation.

The previous season had seen a makeshift championship that involved two away games for Wales. They lost the match in Bordeaux and also lost in Liverpool to England, 24-11, in a competition that gave France two home games and England the title on points difference after their 15-15 draw with France in Paris.

Llanelli's Stebonheath ground witnessed two records that afternoon in late 1935. The crowd of 25,000 was a record for a Rugby League international in Wales and the emphatic 41-7 victory for the home team was its highest ever victory. The Welsh scored 11 tries (landing only four conversions) and 'Nomad's' report in the *Llanelly Mercury*

[sic] was headlined "France trounced by Wales - Huge crowd at Rugby League international".

Using the English spelling of his town's name the writer continued: "Those responsible for the promotion of the event must have felt satisfied. People poured into the town from all directions, by rail, bus and car, indeed the number of cars must have constituted a record. It is evident that Llanelly is an admirable centre for the holding of important sporting events," he concluded, blowing his home town's trumpet.

The speech by the Mayor of Llanelli, Alderman Tom Charles, at the civic reception afforded the French team on the evening before the game, reflected on the co-operation between Britain and France during the First World War. Of course, neither group knew that co-operation would be called on again so soon in 1939. The French, for their part, replied that Wales was famous for its sportsmanship "but its hospitality, if possible, excelled even that".

The French consul, Monsieur Brun, was present on behalf of the French government who, at this stage, were obviously taking the new Rugby code very seriously, as was Victor Breyer who, of course, had much invested in the French game.

The following day's game was well covered by the local media and the *Llanelly Mercury* continued to be impressed. "it was a brilliant exhibition of handling," wrote 'Nomad'. "The manner in which the players 'juggled' with the ball was amazing." The writer also talked of "terrific pace", "bewildering rapidity" and "speed and anticipation", yet he admitted that because the game was foreign to him, he was inclined to be biased against it. "I confess I was disappointed," he added. "In the Rugby League game, speed has been made a fetish, to the detriment of other equally interesting aspects of Rugger. I am all for back play, but at Stebonheath there were thirteen backs on either side."

This argument in favour of Union's scrums, lineouts, mauls, rucks and frequent kicking is still used today. "One sighed for a real old-fashioned tussle for the ball, with the steam rising from the scrum," lamented 'Nomad'. He did qualify his argument with the point that, in Rugby Union, "the player who kicks is eulogised more than he who prefers to use his hands".

But enough of journalists' opinions - of more relevance was the performance of the French team new to the sport. They had performed well in their early games but were to find the finesse and might of the Welsh on home soil a different proposition. Immediately in possession after the kick-off, Welsh pressure told when scrum-half Billy Watkins scooped up a loose ball near the French line to take a lead his team never relinquished. This was the only try from loose play, the remainder were all the result of passing movements or good positional and kicking play.

Jim Sullivan goaled Watkins's effort but failed to improve Alan Edwards's try in the corner five minutes later. By now the French were finding their feet and Max Rousie, Roger Claudel and Georges Lavielle all went close, as did Rousie with a long-range penalty attempt.

Both sides were showing inventiveness and fast, open play but, when the Welsh scored their third try after fine handling on the right led to loose-forward Ossie Griffiths of St Helens receiving a simple scoring pass, it seemed there would only be one winner.

True, the French pulled points back when a powerful, galloping run by Rousie led to him converting his own try out on the left, but Wales soon redressed the balance when Griffiths scored his second. By the interval a fumble by French full-back Henri Mounes directly in front of his own posts had given a simple opportunity for Iorwerth Isaac of Leeds to score a Sullivan-converted try, leaving the half-time score at 19-5.

There was more trouble for the French defence immediately after the restart. Sullivan, from a scrum well inside the Welsh half, drew the French cover and fed wingman Jack Morley who scampered 40 yards to score an unconverted try. He was pursued all the way by French winger Andre Cussac who, the *Yorkshire Post* noted, "played in shoes".

The next try was described by the *South Wales Echo* as "the best incident of the match". From a scrum 20 yards from the French line, rapid passing saw the ball moved along the Welsh back line, before an inside pass sent Watkins heading for the posts. The French defence moved in but Gus Risman, backing up well, took the sharp reverse pass to score a try by the posts which Sullivan converted.

Wales were now well in command and Isaac's superb solo effort was followed by further tries from Risman and Dennis Madden, the surprise choice at centre, and a member of the short-lived London professional team Acton and Willesden. The only French reply was a Rousie penalty goal which was matched with a similar effort from Risman and it was left for the Welsh to avenge their defeat in Bordeaux with a late try from Morley.

Record victory

The result was certainly more than the Welsh had hoped for. They were dominant in all aspects of the game against a highly rated French squad. The *Western Mail* wrote that "Wales won through their superior handling and greater polish about their attacking movements", although the *Yorkshire Post* put success down to the power of the Welsh forward play, especially Griffiths and his team-mate Hal Jones of Keighley, who drove the French "to a bewildered defence in which they paid heavily for tackling weaknesses and faulty positional play". The French had "definite limitations" concluded the *Post*.

Of course, the French were lacking the inspiration of Galia who was unable to play and they seemed a different proposition without him, lost in attack and weak in defence. Of the few who did impress, the *Western Mail* selected try-scorer Rousie as "France's shining light". The forwards, however, were ineffectual and half-backs Etienne Cougnenc and Joseph Carrere, outplayed by their Welsh counterparts. Clearly the talented French team did not travel well.

Yet the Welsh were so strong that day that the *Yorkshire Post* suggested that they could have easily defeated England, with wingers Morley and Edwards and captain and full-back Sullivan all showing form. Once again the Wigan star impressed all onlookers with his speed and dexterity.

The crowd was far in excess of that the organisers had hoped for and receipts totalled £1,100, a return unexpected prior to the game. But the spectators, while enjoying the home victory, were apparently disappointed that they did not see a closer, better-contested match. And, according to the *Yorkshire Post*, the Welsh supporters could not get used to Rugby League's play-the-ball rule. In a sub-section of the newspaper's report entitled "Play the ball puzzle", the writer says that "there was a time when it created laughter". The *Llanelly Mercury*, however, praised the game for its good spirit and clean nature, bemoaning the fact that club Union in the area had degenerated "into a frenzy" and was "unnecessarily vigorous". It argued that the RL international "if it did nothing else, showed us that [Union] could be made brighter and cleaner". It was a decent tribute to the League code and the organisers who decided to play the match in Wales.

It was to be a fine year for the Welsh in the European Championship. They took advantage of their winning start and although on 16 February England beat France 25-7 in Paris, the Welsh had already secured the title against England at Craven Park, Hull. A close 17-14 victory meant that Wales were the first champions of the competition played on a home and away basis.

Champions

Capitalising on the success of this first proper tournament, the European Championship became a regular event before the outbreak of the Second World War and Wales was to have its fair share of home fixtures and success. As Gareth Williams and David Smith noted in *Fields of Praise*: "The Rugby League had re-activated its campaign in South Wales. The number and quality of Welsh players in the Rugby League ensured that Wales won the RL [European] Championship for three successive seasons, 1936-37-38."

Indeed it was a golden era for Wales, their most successful ever in terms of competitions won. The following season's championship played in late 1936 and early 1937 saw them take the title again. England once again beat France, this time 23-9 at Halifax in April, but this game was purely to settle second place, Wales had already secured the title by beating France 9-3 in Paris in December. Prior to this match their campaign had got off to a winning start with the visit of England to Taff Vale Park, Pontypridd on 7 November.

Sea of mud

This was the last Rugby League game to be played at Taff Vale Park, although the pitch still exists, and stages school sports. The match attracted the lowest crowd for an international there. Due in the main to dreadful weather conditions which led to local Union games being postponed, only 12,000 hardy souls turned out to see a dour encounter but one in which the Welsh secured a vital 3-2 victory.

Once again the locals had honoured the arrival of their guests with a civic reception attended by the head of Pontypridd Council, Mr Jack Jones JP, and a carnival atmosphere presented itself on the morning of the game in clear weather. However, in the hour before kick-off a torrential downpour reduced the field to a sea of mud.

The strong English team, expected to avenge the previous season's defeat, were unable to show their ability and Wales took full advantage. The conditions certainly seemed to deflate the English as the game kicked off in conditions described by the *Yorkshire Post* as "as dismal as can be imagined".

Wales were quickly on top of the game, Billy Watkins dribbling the ball into the English half but the situation was saved by one of England's few outstanding players that day, Billy Belshaw, the full-back from Liverpool Stanley. For the early part of the match though, the pattern was set. Constant Welsh pressure on the English line was repelled but the English never looked like getting the better of the home team. However, it seemed that they might reach half time without conceding any points, especially when Welsh full-back Jim Sullivan hit the post with a simple penalty when England were caught offside.

As the rain intensified and conditions became even worse, the game dissolved into a tedious forward struggle, despite the efforts of Emlyn Jenkins at stand-off and the ever keen Gus Risman at centre. Play was scrappy and, although it looked like Wales had scored when wingman Alan Edwards of Salford followed up a kick, the ball had gone dead. Yet, shortly before half-time the breakthrough came. Edwards scooped up a low pass from centre George Gummer and scrambled over in the corner. Under the circumstances it was impossible for Sullivan to convert the try.

Wales seemed to relax a little and although they held their 3-0 lead until half time England began to exert pressure on the Welsh line leading to the home team conceding a number of simple penalty attempts, all of which Martin Hodgson, the English forward, failed to convert.

After the interval, England returned with only 12 players, centre Billy Stott being sidelined with an ankle injury, yet it was the English who notched the first (and only) points of the second half. Hodgson finally made a penalty kick count and there was only one point in it. Although it was the English who were chasing the game Wales continued to dominate attack and Jenkins, Alec Givvons of Oldham and Gummer all went desperately close for the home team. Givvons was one of the many black players who grew up in the Tiger Bay area and went on to represent Wales.

The *Yorkshire Post* reported that England "never really had a chance even though they were only a point behind for the last 40 minutes". When Harry Beverley, the English loose-forward, left the pack to replace Stott in the back line the Welsh "commanded the scrummage and... the Welsh halves, were given more rope".

Edwards, Risman and Gummer were all singled out for praise for the home team, but the terrible conditions mitigated against any of the players being able to open the game up. Most of the journalists present singled out the full-backs, who had more space in which to run and kick, as the outstanding players of the game, particularly Englishman Belshaw who played even better than the renowned Sullivan. The *Yorkshire Post* wrote "it is probable that this Pontypridd international will be remembered by the brilliance of the full-back work. Belshaw made only one handling slip. And that with the odds against the taker of the ball every time".

Yet the Englishman ended up on the losing side in the match that effectively decided the European Championship. Indeed it was another success for Rugby League in Wales and not only in terms of the championship result. The *Yorkshire Post* wrote that "the Rugby League council had reason to feel that they had triumphed over the worst of conditions and that they had staged another memorable international in the Principality.

"The receipts were £650, the game very thrilling and good enough to hold the attention of loyal Welshmen right to the end." The international game was truly enjoying a great period of success in Wales. Indeed moves were made to play a Wales versus Australia international at Taff Vale in February 1938 but the plans did not come to fruition and the following season's European Championship was the next international action Welsh spectators would see.

Results had already gone Wales's way by the time France arrived at Stebonheath Park, Llanelli on 2 April 1938. They had defeated England in January at Odsal in the Championship opener 7- 6. It was a closely fought game and it could have gone either way but two Sullivan goals and a solitary try by Cliff Evans saw the Welsh gain a vital victory. The result of the second match also went the way of the Welsh with England beating France in Paris on 20 March by 17-15, leaving Wales requiring only a draw to take their third successive title.

Wales did better than that, winning 18-2 and maintaining a 100 per cent record in the championship. The *Yorkshire Post* had already predicted in its preview that "The odds are on [Wales] keeping their grip on [the championship] this season", although it didn't expect a runaway victory such as when Wales played France at Llanelli two seasons previously. "The French have learnt much since that disastrous day," it wrote. "Their scrummaging powers have stiffened, they have strengthened considerably their defence, and they have improved their attack."

The newspaper also bemoaned the fact that the international match "weakens several of the Northern Rugby League clubs who are concerned in the race for the top four positions, and it does look as though the Rugby League Council will have to give attention in the very near future to the preparation of a plan which will prevent international fixtures from interfering with vitally important League games." The insular practice of club officials feeling that their matches are more important than international football, the pinnacle of any sport, obviously has a long history.

Fortunately the weather was a great deal better than for the previous year's international game and 20,000 turned out to witness what many regarded as a game that did not live up to its billing. The *Western Mail and South Wales News* wrote that: "From a spectacular point of view the match was disappointing, and the tameness of the play... was really surprising. In fact it offered a strong contrast to an ordinary Welsh Rugby Union club match... the vast crowd was left unmoved."

Of course, both that newspaper and the *Llanelly Mercury* sent their Rugby Union reporters to the match. The *Mercury's* 'Nomad' was keen to dispel any attractions the League code might have . "Would the Rugby League game oust the Rugby Union game in South Wales?" he asked. "The atmosphere one finds [at a Union game] was markedly absent. This may be attributed to a feeling that this was not Rugger as we know it in Wales, it was something alien. Fast though the game is, and spectacular as is some of the tackling, the game is not full-blooded like the Rugby Union game. And one missed the swirling hurly-burly of two good solid packs. One missed the lineout. The Rugby League code tried to improve the older code. Now their players deliberately go against the spirit of a rule. The result of this [is] a tiresome slowing down of the play." Union writers often allude to their sport's technical aspects. This one was obviously a devotee.

However, most witnesses felt that Wales deserved their victory. The *Mail* wrote "they were superior in every department," though it added as a qualifier "the handling left much to be desired. There were many dropped passes." The *Yorkshire Post* added that although the Welsh crowd "were unfamiliar with Rugby League methods, enthusiasm ran high on the limited occasions on which the Welsh backs brought off rounds of passing." This is in marked contrast to the *Llanelly Mercury's* report.

Yet the French put up a strong early showing and it was not until their left wing Henri Sanz left the field with a broken nose that Wales began to totally dominate. The French were accused of kicking too often, Max Rousie of Roanne, the captain, especially prominent, and throwing away possession with the effect that their backs never truly had a running chance. The French defence was roundly praised for stern tackling but their chances of dominating were greatly reduced thanks to their tactics on attack, especially in the second half, when they kicked into a stiff breeze.

The first half was closely contested though and Wales only led 3-2 at the interval, Dennis Madden's unconverted try being pulled back by a penalty from Rousie. But the second half belonged to the home team. The *Guardian* selected Gus Risman, Alan Edwards and Jim Sullivan as the outstanding players and it was the famous full-back who slipped through after a pass from Dai Jenkins to score the first try in the second half. Des Case, the Bradford Northern winger, crossed after good work by the forwards and Edwards wound up the scoring with a fine individual effort. Sullivan converted on each occasion, his third kick being his 100th goal of the season, the 17th year in succession he had achieved the feat. The *Mail* wrote that "the Welsh full-back and captain was perfect in all that he did".

Most writers felt that the French defence had stiffened considerably, until it tired with Sanz's absence, with Rousie being outstanding. "The French were real triers," wrote the *Mercury*, but it preferred to concentrate on where the Welsh succeeded and, more frequently in its opinion, failed. "The better heeling of the Welsh pack was not fully utilised," was one of the complaints. There were many others. "Jenkins did not possess an impeccable service... his inaccurate and delayed passes placed his partner at a disadvantage." "There was much automatic running and very little straight running." "Since it was the general view that [Alec] Givvons [the Oldham forward] was outstandingly good, this view is certainly controversial. I feel that [Givvons should have been] content to act as an extra back."... "combined movements of Rugby League seem to offer little chance of absolute success."... "The Welsh forwards were a bit too robust in their methods. I must say I thought the referee very lenient." The list of criticisms seemed almost endless but not surprisingly ended with the rejoinder "My knowledge of the finer points of the Rugby League game is very limited." The writer still felt he had plenty to say if that was the case.

In fact, one of the few times he chose to bestow praise was on "Oliver Morris, the Llanelly boy, at stand-off half for Wales... a speedy and elusive runner". But this seemed to be because "I drew the attention of the Llanelly club to Morris, then a youngster with promise". But, sadly, even his ability to pass well had apparently been stifled by playing Rugby League.

However, the *Llanelly Mercury* was not deterred from visiting the following season when Wales opened the defence of their title against England at the same venue. This first match of the last European Championship before the start of the Second World War was played on 5 November 1938 and, although it saw Wales take a seventh successive victory in the championship, they were to lose their title later in the season. On 25 February at St Helens, England went down 9-23 to France leaving the clash between France and Wales in Bordeaux on 6 April - the last international match before the war - as the title decider. On home soil the French claimed their first European crown 16-10 and Wales's run of success was ended.

England beaten at Llanelli

The Llanelli match back in November, though, had seen Wales continue where they left off the previous season. Another large crowd, 17,000, turned out to see the game, despite gloomy conditions and although many were from the north of England "many people travelled from the different parts of Wales to see former Welsh club players who are now 'stars' of Rugby League". Oliver Morris was unable to play in the game so local interest settled on Emlyn Hughes, the former Llanelli forward, then playing with Huddersfield.

According to the *Mercury*: "The game proved more interesting than the previous Wales v. France games at Stebonheath, the opposing side being more evenly matched." No doubt the writer would have to rethink his assessment when France took the title later in the year. Yet all was going well for the Welsh in November. As the *Yorkshire Post* noted "The Welshmen in the Rugby League find rare inspiration when they play in their own country in these days." A 17-9 victory was proof of that, made all the more remarkable because Wales played with only 12 men in the second half when forward Harold Thomas of Salford (and formerly of Neath) sustained a fractured pelvis.

It seems that once again Wales were worthy of the victory and, despite the heavy fog that shrouded the ground, the crowd was treated to an entertaining open spectacle. The first half was dominated by the home team with England looking ragged and lost. English full-back Billy Belshaw missed the first attempt at goal when his early penalty sailed just wide and that was the nearest the visitors came to scoring in the first period. Almost immediately from the restart Salford's Gus Risman, playing centre, dribbled the ball into the English half and, from a powerful push in the scrum, the Welsh forwards won possession leaving Alan Edwards a simple chance to score in the corner. Jim Sullivan's conversion was a towering effort in the dismal conditions.

The Welsh pressure was relentless and seemingly unaffected by the greasy conditions. Sullivan, playing in his 18th season, increased their lead with another long-distance goal from a penalty, but another try was always on the cards. Hughes combined with Edwards in the Welsh half to set wingman Des Case clear with three-quarters of the pitch to cover. The English defence failed to get near him and his fine try was once again converted by the Welsh captain leaving Wales with a useful 12-0 half-time lead. But with the unfortunate Thomas picking up his injury just before the break they would have to play the remaining 40 minutes with only 12 players.

Wales versus England at Llanelli 5 November 1938
Photo courtesy Robert Gate

At first it seemed that England would make their advantage tell. They produced sustained pressure on the Welsh line and went close more than once, yet it was Wales who came up with the first score of the second period and it was a truly magnificent try, well-described by the *Western Mail*: "Whitcombe fielded a high kick from Belshaw between the English 25 and halfway line. He cut straight through towards the posts and when challenged by Belshaw flung out a wide pass to Jenkins who, lurching forward, caught the ball in his stride. Jenkins, quick as a flash, passed on to Risman, who had the defence well beaten for one of the best tries imaginable." The *South Wales Football Echo* described the effort as "glorious".

Sullivan's failed kick meant that there was a glimmer of hope for England when Belshaw landed a simple penalty from in front of the posts. His attempt earlier in the half was ruined when the wind continually blew the ball over and he ended up opting to kick for touch as the crowd became impatient, but his first successful penalty was soon cancelled out by a neat drop goal from Risman.

Belshaw added a further penalty for the English but their late flurry, including a converted try from Tommy Shannon, the Widnes stand-off, was too late and succeeded only in making the 17-9 scoreline a little more respectable.

The *Western Mail* paid due tribute to Sullivan, however. "Sullivan was a great factor in the game," it wrote. "His kicking has never been surpassed, and apart from landing three goals, two of which were kicked from wide angles, he opened out the play in brilliant style." It was a terrible shame that the Second World War was to put paid to his career for Wales which saw him amass a record 26 caps, 60 goals and 129 points.

Other Welsh stars that day included Risman, Edwards, Case and Hughes who were all superior to their opposite numbers. "Wales deserved their victory, being the faster and cleverer side," wrote the *Echo*. "Considering the wretched conditions, play was fast, and the crowd were loud in their appreciation of the brilliant movements."

More plaudits for the Welsh came from the *Western Mail*: "Backs and forwards joined in delightful handling movements with lightning speed and precision." The *Mail*, though, was also full of admiration for the English defence which "offered stern resistance and tackled with great deadliness". Jim Croston of Castleford and Shannon, the English try scorer, were particularly singled out. The *Llanelly Mercury* too was more impressed, commenting that: "The tackling was generally deadly, and the speed with which the passing movements were carried out was a tribute to the players' fine condition. While everyone enjoyed the game, local opinion continues to be divided on the respective merits of the two codes. But that is the sort of argument to which there can be no answer. There can only be agreement to differ. All agree, however, it was a very fine struggle between two good sides, resulting in a spectacle that was well worth seeing."

Rugby League had made its game faster, more exhilarating and more skilful than Union since the breakaway in 1895. Yet more than 40 years on, and with war set to call a halt to any plans League had of developing the game further in Wales, it seemed that Rugby Union was as entrenched as ever in the sporting consciousness of Wales. The attitude of the Rugby Union writers appeared to be the attitude of most people in positions of influence in Welsh rugby. League was better in many respects, yet they still preferred Union. We can only speculate as to whether this was the view of the average Welsh rugby spectator, but the war put paid to any hope of testing the waters further. Rugby League would have to wait six long years to find out more.

Chapter 5: Pontypridd RLFC 1926-27

The 1926 General Strike and its aftermath - a bitter seven month miners' strike - left the South Wales economy was in a state of crisis, with coal and steel production falling. The widespread unemployment in Wales, that grew from 13% in December 1925 to 23% two years later, was overwhelmingly concentrated in the industrial areas of the south. Pontypridd, according to the history of the Labour Party and Trades Council for the town, "was in the thick of the fight" of both the General Strike and the miners' strike.

This was the background to Rugby League's only professional club between the wars in South Wales - Pontypridd RLFC.

Pontypridd, 12 miles north-west of Cardiff, had already staged an international in 1921 against Australia. The game had been so exciting, it was reported, that "constant demands have been made for another match of a similar category". It was the success of the Wales versus England match in April 1926 at the town's Taff Vale Park stadium that led a group of local businessmen, including former members of Pontypridd RUFC, to form a club and apply to the Rugby League for membership.

Most of the Rugby League Council had attended the 1926 international match, and were "well satisfied" with the enthusiastic response to the sport. The 3,000 seats were sold out before the game, and the match yielded receipts of £2,301 19s.

Athletic News's intrepid reporter 'Forward' reported that "optimism was prevalent" at the official dinner after the game and Mr Osborne, soon to be elected chairman of the Rugby League Council, said that the League would give every encouragement to clubs in South Wales.

In June, the Pontypridd club was accepted for membership of the Lancashire section of the League. They had secured Taff Vale Park, described as a "first class" venue as their home ground. The previous occupants, the Southern League soccer club, the Pontypridd Dragons, had finished one from the bottom of the Welsh section of the Southern League and collapsed. The capacity of the ground then was at least 30,000. Today the ground stages school athletics and Rugby Union, with no sign of the stands and terraces of the 1920s.

The new club was promised assistance with players. There was speculation that other Welsh clubs were interested in joining the Rugby League, with the possibility of a stand-alone Welsh League being raised. All the new club's funding came from the directors and *Athletic News* was assured that none had come from the Rugby League.

Incidentally, the other new 'expansion' club accepted for League membership at this time was Castleford - right in the game's heartlands. The two new clubs would have contrasting fortunes.

1907: The first attempt

The 1926 club was not the first attempt to set up a Rugby League club in the town. In 1907, the local Rugby Union club were playing at Ynysangharad Park, but fell out with the manager of the local chainworks, who owned the park.

They decided to move back to Taff Vale Park, which they had built in 1890, but since left. Several members of the club were unhappy with this move, and meetings were held to discuss starting a Northern Union team. They felt that Ynysangharad Park, in the centre of town, was a more viable venue than Taff Vale Park, a mile from the centre.

The promoters of the new club visited Merthyr and Aberdare to see the Northern Union game in action. A committee was formed, with a resolution to start a Northern Union club being moved by a former captain of the Rugby Union club. However, realising the dangers of this new venture, the Rugby Union club resolved their differences with the owners of Ynysangharad Park, and moved back there. This effectively destroyed any hope the Northern Union club had of getting off the ground. The exact reason for this is unknown, but it could have been that the Northern Unionists felt Taff Vale Park, now the only available ground, was considered to be too far from the town centre.

So in 1926, despite the economic background, which was affecting all sport in South Wales, perhaps the choice of Pontypridd for League's new venture was not such a bad one. The two internationals staged in the town, in 1921 and in 1926 had been well supported, the local soccer club had collapsed and the local Rugby Union club were at a low ebb. They were attracting crowds of 200, and opened the season with debts of £230. Appealing for help and better fixtures to the Welsh Rugby Union, they were faced instead with an investigation into their committee, and in particular their secretary. He had been accused of "extremism" by a policeman playing for the team but, in fact, was only a Labour supporter and member of the Miners' Federation.

The arrival of the new Rugby League club was clearly causing considerable interest in the town. During a debate in the local council about the terms to be charged to the Rugby Union club for their pitch, one of the councillors claimed that they would be "up against it" with the launch of the Rugby League club.

The competition and, at times, bitter rivalry between the two codes was an ongoing issue for the next two years, as it had been since the 1895 split. Tom Mallett, a former Welsh Rugby Union referee, and member of the Rugby League's Welsh Commission, optimistically argued for a *rapprochement* between Union and League. He regretted how the "autocratic regime of the Rugby Union has already divided the empire into two codes". He said the two games should work in a united system.

His appeals for unity were met with increased hostility from the 'amateurs' of the Welsh Rugby Union. One "prominent" member of the Welsh Rugby Union denounced those starting Rugby League as "agitators". He said the support for the game came from "a few persons acting as commercial travellers trying to persuade sportsmen that their goods are best".

Optimistic opening

Nonetheless, the season opened optimistically. The first trial match, a week before Challenge Cup finalists Oldham were due at Taff Vale Park, was described in the local paper as "one of the most exhilarating games seen on this ground for a long time", and the crowd was "filled with delight".

As with later Welsh clubs, the players were a combination of signings from Rugby Union and Welsh players who had "gone north" to clubs in Lancashire and Yorkshire, and were now returning to this new club in the valleys.

One of the best known was Jerry Shea, who came out of retirement to become player-coach. In 1920 he had scored 16 points for the Welsh Rugby Union side in a famous 19-5 victory against England. He had then turned professional with Wigan in

1921, for £700. He played for Wigan until 1924, scoring 27 tries in 85 games and won international honours for the Welsh Rugby League side. He had also been a professional boxer, once fighting Ted "Kid" Lewis in a non-title fight. In 1920, the Scottish RU had threatened to cancel their match with Wales if Shea played, because of his professional boxing activities. He was also appointed as a member of the club's match day committee.

At full back, W.H. Price was signed from Swinton, the Challenge Cup holders. On the wing was W.R. 'Buller' Loveluck, from Hull, who had been a reserve for the Wales Rugby Union team when he played for Mountain Ash RUFC. His team-mate George Oliver, was a valuable signing for the Pontypridd pack and W.H. Rhodes was signed from Rugby Union. In 1924-5, he had scored 55 tries for Blaenavon, and joined from Pontypool RUFC, although he would soon be transferred to Warrington. Bryn Williams and J. Grant were signed from Leeds. Of the 22 players listed in the club's squad in *Athletic News* at the start of the season, only five had professional Rugby League experience

One of them, Bryn Williams, capped for Wales at both codes, had gone north in 1920, but had returned home to Llanelli, having played a few games for Leeds in the 1925-6 season. He played one game for Pontypridd, against Leigh on 25 September, before retiring. In 1977, he received his cap from the Welsh RU, 57 years after playing for his country. It had been withheld because of his League connections.

Seven of the team that faced Oldham were playing their first competitive Rugby League game. 'Forward' reported in *Athletic News* that there was promise of better results "when inexperienced players become more familiar with the altered rules of the code". Despite the "unmatched determination of the new players to overcome difficulties and open out the game in the approved spectacular style", Oldham won 33-15 in front of 10,000 fans. James, Fowler and Garside scored tries for Pontypridd, Shea adding three goals. The teams for this historic match were:

Pontypridd: Price; Fowler, Shea, Rhodes, Loveluck; James, Garside; Grant, Green, Oliver, Davies, Hellings and Harris.

Oldham: Knapman; Corsi, Holliday, Biggs, Rix; Johnson, Hesketh; Read, Lister, Marlor, Wallace, Baker and Brough.

Pontypridd's inexperience saw a further four defeats before the first win, against Widnes at Taff Vale Park. Coming from behind, the team used "aggressive tactics", and won a "well-merited" victory. Shea scored a try and three goals.

Although further defeats followed, the team was establishing itself. At Wigan's Central Park, "the spectators cheered the fine work of the Pontypridd players", who "exploited passing movements with great skill". But Wigan, with Welsh legend Jim Sullivan at full-back, won 23-15.

At Swinton the following week, the crowd "cheered the Welshmen for their plucky display". This was followed by defeat by a single point at home to Leeds, described in *Athletic News* as a "moral victory". This margin was reversed soon after with an 11-10 triumph over Rochdale at Taff Vale Park. Jerry Shea was still the team's star, but the forwards were becoming more accustomed to Rugby League play, and Fairfax was becoming a key member of the team at stand-off.

Local development was not being neglected, with two junior teams being formed. These players did not sign professional forms, with "their desire only being to play the Rugby League game for the love of it". There were also attempts to form junior teams in the Rhondda and Merthyr valleys. Spreading the word included a friendly played against Halifax at Llanelli, the Yorkshiremen winning 26-8.

It seemed that the sport was becoming more widely accepted with even the local newspapers drawing a distinction between the codes. The *Glamorgan County Times* was now heading its Rugby Union reports "Under Old Rules".

A rare (even for those more low scoring times) 0-0 draw at Wigan Highfield, despite the Pontypridd forwards playing with "wonderful dash", was followed by a victory against the same opponents at Taff Vale Park the next week. After 12 league fixtures, three had been won with one draw.

The pioneering work continued, with a midweek match at the Mid-Rhondda Athletic Ground, which saw Pontypridd beat a team of "players who had assisted English Rugby League clubs" 56-6.

The next match at Taff Vale Park was the highlight of the season, with Wales taking on the New Zealand tourists. Full details can be found elsewhere in this book, but the tourists returned to take on Pontypridd on Christmas Day, winning 17-8, although the match was not as well attended as the international. The Pontypridd team "put up a surprisingly good fight... and in open stages had decidedly the better of play".

The *Pontypridd Observer*, which rarely covered Rugby League, now said the game had received a fair trial, and "the bulk of the criticism is in its favour, it is... faster and more open... this sustains interest to the final whistle and the glorious struggles for supremacy seen on Taff Vale Park this season have been greatly appreciated".

The Rugby League was looking for new areas to develop professional clubs at this time. Attempts were made in Llanelli and Port Talbot which fell through. In Newport, a group trying to start a Rugby League club identified a piece of land as a possible ground. Suddenly, from a very low valuation, the price was raised so it was beyond them. But it was reported that the land was under water for much of the winter, so "perhaps it was just as well".

New Year victory

The new year opened with victory over Barrow, helped by two drop goals, a "beautiful" one by Shea and a "marvellous" one by full-back Roberts from near the half-way line.

Further defeats followed, with Rhodes, who had played for Pontypridd earlier in the season before being transferred, starring for Warrington at Taff Vale Park against his former club. This match, a narrow 13-8 defeat was reported as "sensational play", with both packs laying "themselves out resolutely to scrummage", and the backs displaying "wonderful accuracy in handling and great thirst". But the run of defeats was leaving the team near the bottom of the league and the Challenge Cup offered no relief, a 23-2 defeat at Widnes ending the club's run at the first hurdle.

Despite the team's series of defeats, the Rugby League Council was "highly pleased" with progress in South Wales. There was speculation about a club in Swansea, and the Welsh Commission was advocating a Glamorgan and Monmouthshire team being included in the County Championship for the 1927-8 season. A further sign of expansion was the formation of a Welsh Rugby League Referees Society.

At the end of February, the Welsh Commission announced that an amateur Junior Welsh League Championship would be held in 1927-8. The Welsh Rugby Union responded to this by proclaiming that even players who played Rugby League as amateurs would be banned from Rugby Union. A confident John Leake, chairman of the Welsh Commission, said that "we shall build up some great clubs in Wales, worthy of the great Welsh Rugby tradition, and we shall then retain in Wales the best players who are now going north. That is the aim".

Back at Pontypridd, a "magnificent" second half display against Hull at Taff Vale Park ended a run of six defeats, with Mills's "powerfulness and cleverness", and Jerry Shea proving "a tonic of strength" bringing a 10 point victory . This was ample revenge for a 26-0 defeat a couple of days before. This match was the first time the team had failed to score apart from the scoreless draw with Wigan Highfield.

A "fine display" against Salford bought a 13-5 triumph at Taff Vale Park, winger Loveluck running through the Salford defence to score. But then the run of defeats continued, the only other win being against Batley in the final home game.

Yet the club had continued to promote the game in South Wales. A second team played regularly, opponents including sides representing the Warrington and District League and the Leeds and District League. At local level there was encouragement too. In April, Tom Mallett, Secretary of the Welsh Commission, asked for an extension to the season so a cup competition for 14 amateur teams could be completed. Apparently, one club had recruited 44 players.

As with many teams in their first season, especially at the time of a one division League, Pontypridd had faced an uphill task. However, the biggest score they conceded was only 35, at St Helens in October, and 13 of their 24 defeats had been by less than 10 points. But crowds had declined, partly reflecting the economic situation, and partly because of the team's lack of success. They finished 27th out of 29 teams but the other newcomers, Castleford, finished bottom. However, Castleford would go onto better things. Pontypridd's final record was:

Played	Won	Drawn	Lost	For	Against	Points	Percentage
32	7	1	24	223	447	15	23.43

Left-winger Loveluck finished top scorer with 10 tries, followed by Rhodes and Fairfax with five each. Jerry Shea was top goal scorer with 18 goals.

The 'battle' of Ebbw Vale

The last couple of months of the season had seen a further degeneration in the relationship between Rugby League and Rugby Union in Wales, with the 'battle' of Ebbw Vale.

The Rugby League had been invited to play a match at the Ebbw Vale Welfare Ground, home of the local Rugby Union club, to help raise funds to pay for the town's War Memorial. The Welsh Rugby Union's policy was to suspend any club that allowed professional Rugby to be played on their ground. Yet the local Union club did not own the Welfare Ground and the question of whether to allow Rugby League to use the venue went to a vote. If the Rugby Union club lost the vote at the Welfare Committee that controlled the ground, would the club be suspended by the Rugby Union?

Athletic News reported that the Rugby Union club were "agitated" and the Welsh Rugby Union "watchful and conservative". It spoke of a "war between amateur and professional Rugby forces developing in South Wales".

Soon the reports were being headed "Wales at War". The Rugby League was seeking new clubs to join a Welsh Section of the Rugby League. Meanwhile, the Welsh Rugby Union had confirmed that they would ban any rugby ground that staged a professional match and then the League match got the go-ahead. So Ebbw Vale would face being suspended unless they could find a new ground.

The Rugby League selected teams to represent Glamorganshire and Monmouthshire to play in the game on 2 May. Five Pontypridd players were chosen, along with other leading Welsh players from northern clubs.

The tension between the two codes heightened with more reports at the end of April that D.T. Harris, former Swansea RU and Wigan Rugby League player, was attempting to form a Rugby League team in Swansea.

The Rugby League did play their match, but the Rugby Union seem to have realised the powerlessness of Ebbw Vale RUFC's position, as they continued to play at the Welfare ground, but there was obviously an even greater degeneration in the two codes' relationship. Ironically, in the 1980s, now renamed Eugene Cross Park, the ground again staged Rugby League, with a Cardiff Blue Dragons match and a Wales versus England international played there.

Despite the still humble size of Rugby League in Wales, (one professional club and some amateur teams), *Athletic News* reported in May 1927, under the headline "Rugby SOS", that the inroads of Rugby League were "of a serious character and in some districts, at least, jeopardise the future of amateur football". It was being suggested that the Rugby Union form a Welsh amateur league "to introduce the competitive spirit into the game in the hope that this will rekindle interest". It was clear that Union feared the presence of League.

1927-8: The second season

In June, proposals to form a senior league competition within Rugby Union in Wales were rejected by the Welsh Rugby Union. The advocates of the league pointed out that the Rugby League had received 14 applications for membership (to play in an amateur league) and that if Rugby League became established in Wales, it would spread to the west of England. The advocate of the scheme, a Mr Ewin from Paignton, in south-west England, said that clubs should leave the Rugby Union and form a new amateur federation, playing under laws similar to Rugby League, but "keep quite distinct and apart from the professional Rugby League".

The tension between the codes was increased when Tom Mallett accused senior Welsh Rugby Union clubs of using players who had played in trials for northern Rugby League clubs and subsequently not signed for them. His accusations were supported by the Welsh Commission's John Leake. Needless to say, their accusations were denied by the Welsh Rugby Union. However, they had accepted the word of one player that he had not played in a trial match, but then investigated his movements over three years and found he had played in a trial game. He was suspended from Rugby Union *sine die*, showing that Tom Mallett was correct.

The debate continued, but it is significant that Mallett admitted that Rugby Union was not the only obstacle. The Welsh Commission's efforts are "not looked upon with any great favour by many of the Rugby League Council, and the Welsh section have a very hard fight in front of them".

On the playing side, 25 players were signed for Pontypridd's second season, with only two, Shea and Fairfax, having experience with northern-based Rugby League clubs. Twenty-two players had come from Welsh Rugby Union clubs, with one, Dai Thomas, being recruited from Rugby Union in Torquay. However, the standard of play at the public trial was described as "promising", with several players showing "excellent form".

There was concern at the Rugby League club when it was reported that Taff Vale Park had been leased to a greyhound racing syndicate, but it was confirmed later that it would definitely be available for Rugby League.

The season started with a 17-0 defeat at Leigh, with *Athletic News* reporting that Leigh needed to improve. Morgan and Shea were missing from the Welsh side, resulting in their play being "disorganised". The first home match saw a 7-11 defeat against Bradford Northern, with Shea playing at full-back. The next week, opponents Wigan Highfield won their first match of the season against the struggling Welsh side, 20-7. Another defeat, at home to Rochdale, followed. Pontypridd were said to "have much to learn in the matter of successful tactics" and relied too much on "forceful methods", and too little on "scientific development of attacks". Despite this, Shea's tackling, fielding and kicking were "superb".

'Buller' Loveluck marked his return to the side with two tries at Castleford, but could not prevent a 26-6 defeat, although the Welshmen played the second half a man short due to injury. But Loveluck was missing, along with Jerry Shea the next week at St Helens Recs, and a 40-0 defeat resulted, with the Welsh side's play being described as "stereotyped". The *Glamorgan County Times* described the opposition as St Helens Reserves, unintentionally reflecting their position in the town.

The first win came on 8 October against Barrow, although it was before a crowd of less than 1,000. In a "thoroughly deserved" 13-7 victory, Pontypridd "proved a really good side", with former Welsh Rugby Union international, Oldham Rugby League and Swansea Town football player, Ben Beynon making his debut at stand-off. The forwards were now becoming more accustomed to Rugby League, and had learnt "good scrummaging and quick heeling".

However, Pontypridd's future was suddenly cast into doubt. Only, two weeks later, the club would play its final game which, as with the first at Taff Vale Park, was against Oldham. After leading early on, the Pontypridd side went down 5-14, Loveluck scoring the last try, and Beynon adding a drop goal. The receipts were only £24.

Three days later, on October 25, the Pontypridd club resigned from the League. Their record, which was deleted from the League table, was:

Played	Won	Drawn	Lost	For	Against	Points	Percentage
8	1	0	7	48	149	2	12.5

But what had caused such a rapid and catastrophic demise? In September, as mentioned earlier, it had been reported that the future of the club was in jeopardy because the Greyhound Racing Association had purchased Taff Vale Park. A deputation from the Rugby League visited London to see if an agreement could be made for the club to continue to use the ground after the end of the year, when the RL's agreement expired.

However, although uncertainty over the future of Taff Vale Park was a factor in the club's decision to resign, it appears that economic problems were the main cause. The *Glamorgan County Times* said that support had "owing to the conditions in the mining industry, been very disappointing".

John Leake denied this, however, and said that the club resigned from the Rugby League because of isolation from the other teams, and was quite solvent. He said that the League had decided that it was wiser for the Pontypridd to strengthen the Glamorgan senior and junior leagues, by joining them. He added that the club's resignation from the Rugby Football League, "far from being a death blow, begins the missionary work", and that plans were being made to enter two teams in the Glamorgan League.

However, a report in *Athletic News* the following week said that "Trade depression [i.e. unemployment] was mainly responsible for the disappointing takings at home matches". The report spoke of the "impossibility of balancing receipts and expenditure at Taff Vale Park". The final accounts showed a loss of £1,393, including £730 owed to the Rugby League Council, with assets of only £75.

It pointed out that the team in the first season was comprised mainly of players released by other clubs and in the second season the concentration on local players had seen the release of these more skilful and experienced players. The report concluded that "Rugby League football in South Wales, to be a paying proposition, must be attractive and capable of holding its own in the serious competition with other codes for public patronage". The representative matches had been successful because of the players being "skilled craftsmen". These comments could apply to any of the attempts to establish a successful club Rugby League side in South Wales. A successful team, with players of high quality, playing high quality opposition, is necessary. Second class fare will not sell.

Despite the collapse of the Pontypridd club, a Cardiff club applied for membership of the Rugby League a week after Pontypridd's resignation. They planned to play at the new Sloper Road Greyhound Stadium, near the centre of Cardiff. In December, a Special Meeting of the clubs accepted their membership for the 1928-9 season.

However, in May, doubts were expressed about whether the club would take up their place, and in June this was confirmed. Ironically, Carlisle City were elected to play in 1928-9. Had Cardiff joined, the two expansion clubs joining that season would have been the same as in 1981-2, when Cardiff Blue Dragons and Carlisle joined the League.

Taff Vale Park staged two matches for the Glamorgan and Monmouthshire side, and in 1936 staged another Rugby League international. The amateur leagues continued until at least April 1930, when Graigwen beat Treforest to win the Pontypridd Rugby League Challenge Cup. But as these leagues collapsed, the players were accepted back into Rugby Union. Wales would go through the depression of the 1930s and a world war before club Rugby League would again be seen there.

Chapter 6: Glamorgan and Monmouthshire 1927-1931

Just as the Pontypridd club was coming to the end of its short period of membership of the Rugby League, a new form of representative Rugby League arrived in Wales. A Glamorgan and Monmouthshire side entered the County Championship.

The County Championship was formed in 1895, with the formation of the Northern Union. The original entrants were Lancashire, Yorkshire and Cheshire, with Cumberland joining in 1898. Cheshire's last season was 1904-5.

Players were eligible to play for the county of their birth, or the county where they first played professional Rugby League. So the Glamorgan and Monmouthshire side was often potentially nearly as strong as the full Welsh international side. However, initially it was decided that players from Carmathen were not eligible, so players such as Frank Evans and Billo Rees could not play.

1927-8: The first season

The new county's first match was at Hunslet against Yorkshire on Monday 26 September 1927. The team's shirts were white with broad red stripes, and their badge combined Glamorgan's chevrons and the crown of Henry of Monmouth.

Fairfax and Green of Pontypridd were the only Welsh-based players selected, the rest coming from northern clubs. A 20-12 defeat was, on paper, a respectable result for the new county, with tries for the Welshmen from Ring and Flynn, with Jim Sullivan adding three goals. However, much had been expected of the Welshmen, because they had a side packed with internationals. Also, Yorkshire had played much of the game with 12 men, Askin being taken to hospital with a bad cut.

The new team's home debut was at Pontypridd's Taff Vale Park, on 15 October, against Cumberland. The Welsh Commission selectors made three changes from the team that lost at Hunslet.

The Welsh side made a disastrous start, conceding two tries in the first eight minutes. *Athletic News* put this down to "moderate understanding" between the Welsh half-backs. Their hopes of recovery from this start were hit by an injury to centre Melville Rosser, who had to leave the field after half an hour.

Although the Welsh side staged a "rousing finish", which kept the result in doubt until the end, they owed much to Sullivan's "resourceful defensive play". Maidment and Ring scored tries for Glamorgan and Monmouthshire, with Sullivan again adding three goals. But Cumberland were successful on their first trip to Wales by 18-12.

An even tougher test awaited Glamorgan and Monmouthshire on 12 November, when county champions Lancashire were the visitors to Taff Vale Park. Although the Lancashire side almost had a "monopoly" of possession, their passing was so poor that they did not score a try until two minutes from time. Williams and Higgs had already set up a try for Ring for the Welshmen, and Parker added a second. A Sullivan goal had given the home side an 8-4 half-time lead. Two further Sullivan goals, one from the touchline, made the game safe for the Welsh side, before Frodsham scored for Lancashire. Gowers failed to convert, so Glamorgan and Monmouthshire won 12-7, to finish second in the final championship table behind Cumberland.

1928-9: Tough start

A visit to 1926-7 champions Cumberland was a tough start to the following season's competition. The Welsh side had widened their selection criteria, because Billo Rees was now selected, although according to reports, he had an "off day". The Welshmen attracted more than 5,000 people to Whitehaven for the match which, according to the *Western Mail* "was a wonderful tussle between Cumberland's wrestling giants and the light Welsh threequarters".

Despite Jim Sullivan scoring a "glorious" try and adding the goal, the Cumbrians won 15-5. The *Western Mail* summed up the game as a clash of "brawn versus brain".

Six weeks later, at the beginning of December, the Welshmen faced another tough away match, against Lancashire at Leigh, with 8,000 people turning out to see a Lancashire side described as "practically an All-England team". Four tries in the first half gave Lancashire a 14-0 half-time lead. The second half saw Glamorgan and Monmouthshire "at their best... when they worthily attempted to imitate the standard of their opponents, without, however, attaining the same standard". Their efforts produced tries from Ring and Walker, and two penalty goals from Sullivan, but Lancashire added a further three tries to win 25-10.

The final match of the season saw the Glamorgan and Monmouthshire side make their debut in Cardiff on 15 April 1929 against Yorkshire. A 6.15 pm mid-week kick-off attracted a good crowd to the Sloper Road Greyhound Stadium. The home team included 10 Welsh internationals, while Yorkshire fielded six English internationals.

According to 'Old Stager' of the *Western Mail*, their Rugby Union reporter, "the pleasure of once more seeing so many outstanding Welsh amateur Rugby players of other days in action again in another capacity was therefore tinged with regret". He said they were good individually, but missed "the blend and certainty of action which is reserved for those who have been nurtured in Rugby League football".

Once again, the Welsh side's northern opponents had an advantage in the pack. The visitors established a 12-point lead, and although the home side fought back to 15-15, Yorkshire ran out winners by 22-17, despite losing full-back Jenney through injury. The *Western Mail* said that the Welsh side's brightest work came from the backs. Ring's try came from "a perfect round of passing" and Sullivan "dodged his way practically through the whole of the Yorkshire team" for his try. White added a third try, and Sullivan kicked four goals, but it was not quite enough.

1929-30: Kangaroos' visit

The most prestigious match to be played by the Glamorgan and Monmouthshire side attracted one of their smallest crowds. The Australian tourists were the visitors to Sloper Road on 11 December 1929. But the game was played on a Wednesday afternoon, and only 2,500 came to see the Kangaroos' only visit to Wales on that tour. 'Old Stager' covered the match for the *Western Mail*. Headlined "Colonials a Great Team", he said the tourists played "delightfully bright, open and clever football".

However, despite playing into a gale force wind in the first half, the Welsh side's defence was described as "weak", while their attack was "poor". Yet Sullivan was "as good as ever", and Melville Rosser "made a couple of good runs".

Glamorgan and Monmouthshire versus Australia in 1929. Photo courtesy Robert Gate

One of the crowd's biggest problems was identifying the scorers of the Australians' tries, as the numbers on their shirts were "urgently in need of renewal". Rosser scored the Welshmen's solitary try and Sullivan added three goals. A 9-39 defeat was the biggest in Glamorgan and Monmouthshire's short history. But the Australian side contained 10 players who had played in their 31-8 triumph over Great Britain at Hull in October, so maybe the result should be viewed in context.

Ten days later, the Welshmen resumed their County Championship fixtures, taking on Cumberland at Sloper Road. Around 2,000 people saw a game with "many exhilarating passing movements". But Glamorgan and Monmouthshire's backs could not take their chances, and Cumberland won 14-6. Frank Evans and Williams scored tries in the first half for the home team, which ended with the northerners holding a narrow 7-6 lead. But the Welshmen could not add to their score, and Holding's two goals and a try by Reed gave Cumberland their victory.

Tries from Melville Rosser, Johnny Ring and Les White, with two goals from Sullivan gave Glamorgan and Monmouthshire an excellent victory over Yorkshire at Hunslet in February. But they could not repeat this form at Warrington two months later and 9,000 people saw Lancashire triumph 29-3. The *Western Mail* described this as "a very poor show". Despite Evan Williams at stand-off being described as "a poor connecting line", he scored the Welsh side's only try.

1930-31: Final season

It was a sign of the game's weakness in Wales itself that all Glamorgan and Monmouthshire's matches this season were played in the north of England on their opponents' grounds. Ironically, it was their best season in the championship.

The campaign opened with a 14-10 victory against the current champions Lancashire at Salford on 22 November. *Athletic News* reported the victory as "unexpected but thoroughly deserved after a contest rich with spectacular merit considering the weather and ground conditions".

Loose-forward Maidment gave the Welshmen an early lead when he scored after 13 minutes from a 5-yard scrum. Sullivan kicked the goal. A penalty and a try awarded for obstruction, duly converted by Dingsdale, gave the home side the lead, but then a Sullivan penalty bought the score back to 7-7. Woods then scored in the corner to give the home side a 10-7 lead at the break. The second half saw the Welshmen "much more businesslike and determined", and Salford's Gus Risman created a try for Williams. Two further penalty goals from Sullivan gave the Welshmen a well-earned victory. The visitors' backs had played with more cohesion than the home side, and at half-back Meek played well at stand-off in the absence of Billo Rees. The "compactness" of the Welsh scrummaging was a notable feature of their game.

The next challenge for the Welshmen came at Whitehaven on 21 March. Glamorgan and Monmouthshire won their first victory against Cumberland, who were to end the season with three defeats from their three games. Five goals from Jim Sullivan gave the Welsh side a 19-12 victory. Most of the Glamorgan and Monmouthshire team had played in an international against England the previous Wednesday and this showed as they tired in the second half. But they had built up a 17-point lead, and the Cumbrians could not recover. Sullivan had given the Welsh side a quick lead with a penalty after two minutes. Then Morgan punted through for Lloyd to score, Sullivan converting for a 7-0 lead. Jenkins then added a further try, Sullivan again converting to increase the lead to 12-0. Cumberland missed two chances through "indifferent finishing", but Risman, showing "promising form" at centre set up a second try for Jenkins. Sullivan again added the goal. As the Welsh side tired, the home side converted two penalties, and then Southward scored their first try. A further penalty from Sullivan ensured the Welsh side's victory. A last minute Cumberland try by Lister did not affect the final result.

So the final match of the County Championship season would decide the destination of the championship, because both Glamorgan and Monmouthshire and Yorkshire had won their first two games. Glamorgan and Monmouthshire travelled to Halifax's Thrum Hall ground on 15 April. A small crowd of 1,500 yielded receipts of only £88.

The Welsh side started well and, playing against the wind, ran up a lead of 10 points in the first 17 minutes. Thompson and Risman had scored the tries, Sullivan adding a goal. Their backs, according to the *Yorkshire Post*, had "more promise... than in the Yorkshire rearguard", and the forwards were "getting a fair share of the ball". But then the Welsh side's scrum-half Thomas suffered a serious knee injury, and had to be taken to hospital. In the days before substitutes, this was a serious blow. Moving a player out of the pack, combined with losing Thomas's effective play, saw the Welsh side lose their lead in the 18 minutes between his injury and half time.

Although a Sullivan penalty bought the teams level after half time, from then on the Yorkshire side dominated the game, and went on to win 33-12. This was to be the Welsh team's last county match.

The costs of running the Welsh county side had been paid by the Rugby League. The lack of a base for the game in Wales was probably the main reason for ending their involvement in the championship. Ironically, this was their most successful season, finishing runners-up with two wins from the three matches against their northern opponents. The team had shown there was life outside the traditional counties, but, like so many such experiments, it was short-lived.

Part Three:

The post war boom

Chapter 7: Internationals in Wales 1945 to 1953

The Second World War brought an abrupt end to Welsh success in European international matches. War-time internationals were played against England but none took place in Wales. Wales notched a single victory in the first of six charity matches which raised money from the Red Cross but three of the other results went England's way with two matches drawn, amazingly both by the same score of 9-9.

The war also saw Rugby Union lift its hypocritical and ludicrous barriers on Rugby League players playing their game, with the effect that two similar charity matches were staged between League and Union players (to Union rules of course). The League side contained many Welshmen who had switched pre-war to League clubs, including the likes of Trevor Foster of Bradford Northern, Les White of Hunslet, and Roy Francis, who was to carve out a career as both player and coach at the very highest levels of Rugby League. No doubt these players with Union experience were instrumental in seeing the League XV win both matches.

Following the cessation of hostilities the Rugby League authorities were keen to reintroduce the European Championship, both to capitalise on its pre-war success and to cash in on the post-war boom in attendances at spectator sports. A war-weary public was turning out in great numbers at sporting events having been denied the opportunity for so long. The RFL quickly needed a venue for home matches for the Welsh national team.

Surprisingly, the stadium selected was St Helen's, one of Union's sacred grounds and now home to Swansea RUFC. During the war the original Swansea club had ceased to exist and the lease on the ground had passed to the local council. Rugby Union wartime internationals between Wales and England had been played at St Helen's and these had pitched the best in both codes together on the same field. Welsh supporters had become used to seeing Rugby League players (albeit playing Union rules). Come peace-time, the council had no qualms over hiring out the stadium to anybody willing to pay and so it was that, amazingly, Rugby League began to be played at one of the Welsh RFU's international venues. In each of the four seasons following the end of the war England met Wales at Swansea.

The match against England on 24 November 1945, Wales's first post-war international, was the first of 11 to be played at St Helen's. Thanks to the aforementioned crowd boom, it immediately set an attendance record for an international in Wales with 30,000, paying more than £4,000, turning out to watch an 11-3 home victory - the crowd record still stands today.

This was also the opening match of the resurrected European Championship and it gave Wales a winning start. Remarkably though, they were to finish bottom of that season's table as the English went on to record victory over France 16-6 at Swinton in February while Wales, needing only to draw in Bordeaux in March, lost 19-7. The title, with all teams level on 2 points and England and France matched on points difference, went to England by virtue of their success over France.

But, for the large crowd at Swansea in November 1945, it appeared that the Welsh were all set to continue their European dominance. With the aftermath of the war still affecting everyday life it seemed initially as though Wales were going to lose five of their first choice players who were still on active service on the continent. In the event, both sides turned out at full strength on "perfect turf, and drew encouragement from a red-ribboned crowd which made, with song and cheers and the inevitable attempt to hoist the leek to the crossbar before the kick-off, the international setting the traditional one".

The *Yorkshire Post* felt, though, that the standard of play did not match the occasion. Defence and excitement were there aplenty but "play rarely ran smoothly". Yet the game began with a flurry. Wales missed an early penalty but immediately afterwards took the lead with a try from Ike Owens. Welsh full-back Joe Jones of Barrow who had already diffused a high bomb in the first minute and had a fine game throughout, set up the scoring position by linking with the attacking line and feeding Gus Risman who put Owens over. Risman was still the fine player he had been before the war and was an obvious choice for captain when the Lions headed for the Antipodes on their 1946 Ashes-winning tour. He was the second Welshman to captain a Rugby League touring squad, following Jim Sullivan in 1932.

However, in this match it seemed he might rue the missed conversion because, within a minute, England were level. Their forwards took play into the Welsh half and Bob Nicholson of Huddersfield burrowed over. It was "the sort of try looked for from a sturdy Cumbrian" wrote the *Yorkshire Post*. Ernest Ward of Bradford missed the kick.

The Welsh attack, according to the *South Wales Echo*, "executed several brilliant passing movements," one of which led to Gareth Price, the Leeds centre, grabbing the first of his two tries after smart interpassing with Owens. Risman added the conversion to leave Wales leading 8-3 at half time.

By now the English were hampered by the withdrawal of the injured Fred Higgins and were always going to struggle defensively as they tired in the second half. Wingman Albert Johnson of Warrington was also playing with an injured shoulder, constantly leaving the pitch for attention, and Wales had little difficulty in coping with a blunt English attack.

The crowd were now well behind the home team and keen to see stand-off Willy Davies, then with Bradford but formerly a Welsh Union international star, perform the heroics they were used to seeing in a Union shirt. It was Davies who paved the way for Price's second try and the one that clinched the match for Wales. A smart round of passing in the threequarters led to Price finding a gap in the corner and his score took Wales out to 11-3, although Risman was again unsuccessful with the kick.

It was a fine start to the Welsh post-war campaign. Yet, while the crowd went home happy, the *Yorkshire Post* described aspects of the match as "moderate". The passing was considered "slow and flat. The scrummaging was uneasy and a vast amount of time was spent on the ground." Of the beaten English only Martin Ryan, the full-back from Wigan was deemed a success and he was credited with keeping the scoreline down to a respectable total.

But the European title was not to come Wales's way that year, nor indeed the next season when, for the first time each team played four fixtures, the competition having been expanded to home and away matches between each nation.

1946-7: Bright start

Wales started brightly enough in October 1946 when, with tries from Reg Lloyd, Bill Davies and Roy Francis, they beat England 13-10 at Swinton. Their second match was also against England on 16 November. The return match at Swansea, though, was not to go Wales's way. England took a 19-5 victory and, when England went on to defeat France both home and away while Wales could only win their home fixture against the French, England became the first European champions under the new format.

In November, however, Wales sat on top of the table and a crowd of 25,000 expectant home supporters turned up in Swansea to see them take on England. That they went away disappointed owed much to the superb display by the visitors whom Ike Owens, the Leeds forward, described in the *Yorkshire Post* as "the best he had ever played against". Referee Paul Cowell also added his praise saying they were "the best England team I can remember". And the English had to be good to beat a strong Welsh team for the first time in Wales since 1928.

There was confusion before kick off with both public and press desperate to get a good view and the *South Wales Evening Post* was very critical of the media arrangements. "There was chaos at the back of the grandstand a few minutes before the Rugby League international match started. About 40 pressmen, many from Yorkshire and Lancashire, and some of them with typewriters, took up the Press accommodation as their right. They did not know, because of a misunderstanding, all these seats had been sold to the public and when the command came that they must move out there was nowhere for them to go. [The] English journalists were very indignant. When the game ended Mr Griff Owen who had made the local arrangements, offered his sincerest apologies." The writer told us "It was my worst experience at an international match and I have had some pretty bad ones. This sort of thing must not be allowed to happen when the Rugby League stages a match between Wales and France in the New Year." Of course, had the public been ejected to make way for the journalists, we might not have heard so much about the situation.

Despite their difficulties, the reporters were on hand to relay the story of the match. And they were all most impressed by the performances the English left-wing duo Albert Johnson, who notched a hat-trick of tries, and Johnny Lawrenson, who with two tries and two goals, scored the remainder of his team's points.

According to Alfred Drewry in the *Yorkshire Post*: "The switch of Ernest Ward from full back to centre not only provided the back division with a master link, but also resulted in Lawrenson playing better than he has ever done before in representative football." Bill Hudson, the Batley forward, and half-backs Willie Horne of Barrow and Wigan's Tommy Bradshaw were instrumental in opening up the game. Joe Egan's dominance in the scrums meant the English had the ball for long periods.

The Welsh too, had their moments, in what was truly a fine spectacle. "There was more incident, more whole-hearted endeavour, and more quickness of movement," than in the corresponding fixture 12 months ago, according to the *Evening Post*. But Welsh captain Trevor Foster's team was ultimately "outpaced and outplayed". Of the Welsh players, Mel Meek at hooker (who lost 85 per cent of the scrums) and Willy Davies "suffered in comparison" to their English counterparts. Ike Owens and centre Bill Davies of Huddersfield were the only Welshmen selected as outstanding in a game dominated by the opposition.

The Welsh right wing, Arthur Bassett of Halifax, had a torrid time facing up to Lawrenson and Johnson and his sparkling reputation was left in tatters as England, scoring all their points on his wing, were 14-5 up at half time. Lawrenson scored the first two tries, both created by Johnson, one he converted himself. Then from two long-range kicks by Ward, Johnson followed up well to score. The Welsh reply came late in the half when scrum-half Dai Jenkins of Leeds skipped through poor tackling after he supported an Owens break, to score a Bill Davies-converted try.

England had done enough in the first half to ensure victory and scored only once more in the second. It was, however, the game's best try following "sparkling passing" by the threequarters. Lawrenson's penalty gave a final scoreline of 19-5.

So convincing was the English performance that the *Yorkshire Post* suggested that the meeting of the English selectors to pick their team to play France in Bordeaux would be "one of the shortest on record. If Ryan is fit they can do no other but choose the same team in its entirety."

The Welsh press was still drawing comparisons between League and the game it was more used to, even after years of regular international games. "Definitely it was faster," wrote the *Evening Post*, "but the absence of the line-out and the lack of 'devil' forward were things we regretted. There was a lot of bunching and some of those short, sharp passes, looked to some of us to be forward."

These criticisms did not deter the crowds and, for the visit of France in the second home game of the championship on 12 April 1947, 20,000 turned up at St Helen's. And, although they were to be satisfied with a home win, the French put up a storming finish to a match in which they almost snatched victory in the final 15 minutes. However Wales's dominance during the early part of the game, with centres Gareth Price and Norman Harris particularly prominent, was probably enough to justify a Welsh victory.

Still, 'Pendragon' of the *South Wales Evening Post*, was impressed with both the visitors and the game itself. In a piece entitled "Rugby League 'national full of surprises", he wrote: "[France] revealed such surprising stamina that they could have drawn if Lespes's try, the last to be scored, had been rounded off by a successful goal kick. "The Frenchmen seemed to last the cracking pace better than their opponents. They fought back with a tenacity which was inspired."

Wales versus France at Swansea 12 April 1947. Photo courtesy Robert Gate

Many of the French players caught 'Pendragon's' eye, especially full-back Puig-Aubert of Carcassonne. "[He] was a full-back of high capacity, one who could do more with the ball than merely kick it. In the Rugby League game full-backs do a lot of running, and the Frenchman, as well as his opposite number W. T. Davies, often gained big stretches of ground... though it was Puig-Aubert who impressed most." Forwards Gaston Calixte and Elie Brousse also came in for praise following their powerful running displays ("in spite of their weight, they ran like greyhounds"), but the French were also chided for their impetuosity and over-eagerness as typified by Ode Lespes as he scored his try. He "made the kind of leap which one expects from a hurdler" just before scoring.

Ultimately it was the kicking of Bill Davies that won the match for the home team. Both sides scored three tries but Davies outscored Puig-Aubert by four kicks to three, his first after 12 minutes giving Wales the early lead. This was extended when Oldham centre Harris plunged over for an unconverted try but Puig-Aubert pegged the lead back to 5-2 with a penalty.

France were to prove powerful in the forwards but the Welsh defence seemed able to contain them, especially in the first half, and it was the home team which added further points through a second penalty goal and an unconverted try from Emlyn Walters. Smart interpassing from centres Price and Harris put the Bradford Northern wingman over in the corner.

Wales's 10-2 half-time lead became 15-2 when Davies converted Dickie Williams's try which had been created by an elusive piece of running. From then on, however, Wales were on the back foot. At last the powerful French forward play reaped dividends and centre Jo Maso and Brousse of Perpignan scored. Both were converted by Puig-Aubert and the French were only three points behind.

Wales's only respite came in the form of a penalty from Davies. Yet, the two points were to prove decisive for, in the final seconds, when superb back play and rapid passing saw Lespes over for his try in the corner, Puig-Aubert placed the conversion attempt tantalisingly wide.

The whole of the Welsh team came in for praise after the 17-15 victory with, in addition to the two centres, Davies at full-back and Walters on the wing being the pick of the backs, Walters chosen "for his determined bursts and sturdy tackling". The former Swansea Union player Doug Phillips, then playing with Belle Vue Rangers, was the pick of the forwards.

Once again Welsh journalists were impressed by the fluidity and speed of the game. "All the way through pace was the keynote. In a game abounding in rapid changes of scene one never knew what was going to happen next."

A microcosm for the story of international Rugby League in Wales perhaps? Certainly it has run an unsteady course of hits and misses but the post-war period was one of relative stability, with a regular season of international competition holding sway until the dawn of the fifties.

1947-8: The Kiwis arrive

Consequently the Welsh national team was now considered a worthy opponent for international tourists. The first post-war arrivals were the 1947 New Zealanders who became the first to adopt 'The Kiwis' as an official name, although they had been referred to by the moniker in the past.

Their three-match test series against Great Britain was a close affair with the first match at Headingley seeing the home nation squeeze home by a single point 11-10, despite Wigan hooker Joe Egan being dominant in the scrums for the Lions. Of course scrums dominated in this era - Egan also winning them 44-12 in the second test at Swinton. Yet, despite this superiority, the New Zealanders levelled the series by winning 10-7 following a stunning try by forward Chang Newton. In the decider at Odsal, however, the Lions inspired by Welshman Roy Francis's two-try test debut, came good winning 25-9 to take the series.

Between the first and second tests the Kiwis had sojourned in Swansea to play the Welsh for only the third time on 18 October 1947 before another impressive crowd of 18,283. They were a fortunate audience because although the *South Wales Evening Post* decreed the home team "were outplayed", they witnessed a truly enthralling match whose fortunes twisted and turned throughout. The *Post* did admit that the match was one of "the most spectacular games of this type at St Helen's since Rugby League football was introduced there."

And the writer was surely correct. The New Zealanders constantly fought back from the edge of defeat with full-back Warwick Clarke in outstanding attacking form. Once again the tourists were defeated in the scrum but in open play their forwards, especially Travers Hardwick who notched a hat-trick, were dominant.

Wales began strongly but, somewhat against the run of play, the Kiwis scored the opening try, Les Pye touching down after 15 minutes. With Clarke's conversion being successful, the tourists held a five-point advantage. Yet the Welsh stormed back, picking up 15 points without reply. The first came from impressive wingman Reg Lloyd of Castleford who tended to see far more of the ball than Bradford Northern's Emlyn Walters on the opposite flank. Lloyd's try was the best of the game with Joe Jones, the full-back and Dickie Williams of Leeds, deputising at stand-off for the injured Willie Davies, interpassing to completely flummox the defence before putting their winger over.

Ted Ward's conversion was successful, as were two further attempts following tries from Williams and Ike Owens. Tellingly, however, the home team could not hold onto its 15-5 lead as the interval approached. Hardwick's powerful running brought him two of his tries, both converted by Clarke, and the Welsh saw a winning position vanish. The *Post* wrote of the first period: "an orgy of scoring was indulged in, a distinguishing feature being the accuracy of the goalkicking. A division of 30 points in the first half gave eloquent expression to the rapidity with which the lead was lost and recovered."

And worse was to follow for the Welsh. John 'Nippy' Forrest scored the opening try of the second half for the visitors which, although not converted, gave the Kiwis an 18-15 lead. Demoralised as the Welsh were, with such an open game in progress there was always going to be the opportunity to snatch victory. With only 10 minutes remaining, it seemed as thought they had done this when Ward broke through the Kiwi defence to score and convert his own try.

The home crowd now expected victory but, amazingly, it was not to be. Ten points in 10 minutes saw a dejected Wales throw away a winning position. Tries from Hardwick and Jack Newton plus one conversion and a penalty from Clarke gave the visitors a 28-20 victory in a breathless finish. "[The Welsh] lasting powers dwindled," wrote 'Pendragon' of the *Post*, "but above all they found themselves outmanoeuvred by better tacticians." This seems a fair assessment of the game and, while the audience went home disappointed by the failure of the home team, "there was long-distance running to inspire the big crowd to volumes of impartial cheering when, sometimes, nearly the whole length of the field was recovered by the defending side".

The weakness of the Welsh defending under pressure did not augur well for the continuation of that season's European Championship which had begun back in September with a 10-8 victory over England at Wigan, Les Thomas scoring both Welsh tries. The week after Wales had lost to New Zealand the English beat France 20-15 at Huddersfield and a Welsh defeat in Bordeaux in November by 29-21, left all three nations equal with one win each.

Thus the match against England in Swansea on 6 December took on great significance. Sadly for the home team, the defensive frailties exposed by the New Zealanders continued to plague them and England took a decisive step towards the European Championship by winning 18-7. Rising star Roy Francis was selected on the right wing for Wales that day, even though he had already played against the Welsh for England at Swansea in one of the war-time services internationals. The Army's qualifications' rules being more a case of play for the country you are selected for rather than the country of your birth.

Yet even the talented wing could do nothing to redress the balance on a day when the English threequarters dominated before a disappointing crowd of only 10,000. Bad weather certainly did not help the organisers nor the standard of play and, with Wales succumbing easily, it was a poor day for League in the principality.

Perhaps in more ways than one, for the *South Wales Evening Post* noted the story of one of the first instances of crowd disturbance at a League match when, returning from the game, obviously in a state of disappointment, William Arthurs, a labourer from Swansea, was arrested for being drunk and disorderly and fined £1 for smashing the window of a bus. Apparently, when asked to plead in court, he could not because he said he had been drunk and could recall nothing.

If he had been able to he would have remembered that the English forwards, with hooker Joe Egan out-striking his rival Mel Meek of Halifax, won most of the ball and with full-back Martin Ryan of Wigan hitting the attacking line at speed, the Welsh were outplayed in the backs.

It was Ryan who created the opening for England to open the scoring when he put right-wing Albert Bowers of Hull through a gap on halfway for the best try of the game. Bowers notched another before the break and with Willie Horne landing one of the conversions and a second goal from a penalty, England were already on their way at 10-2 - the only Welsh reply coming from a Ted Ward penalty.

Wales were expected to put up a better show with stand-off Dickie Williams (a future Lions captain), scrum-half Dai Jenkins and loose-forward Ike Owens all coming from the Leeds club. But the English, with Horne playing a strong defensive role, never allowed them to run the game as predicted.

It was not until late in the day that Trevor Foster scored Wales's only try, converted by Ward, following a fine cross kick by Castleford's Reg Lloyd, the only Welsh back to enhance his reputation. But by this time the English had taken their score out to 18 with tries from Ernie Ashcroft of Wigan and Russ Pepperell of Huddersfield, Harold Palin of Warrington landing one of the conversions.

Alfred Drewry, writing in the *Yorkshire Post*, said that "the Rugby League selectors have reason to be fairly well pleased with the result of the international match at Swansea which was more important as a trial for the third test against New Zealand than it was as a championship game.

"[The English] were better served in practically every position on the field. Ryan whose choice for England was widely criticised laid irrefutable claims to the full back position." Drewry also went on to praise Ashcroft and Pepperell in the centres, noting that Horne's inventive play at stand-off linked with them "perfectly". Drewry saw an all-English test line-up for the deciding match against the Kiwis, with only Francis or Lloyd breaking the stranglehold. Francis did make the team and scored two tries in the British victory as noted earlier.

France at Swansea

England would go on to win the European title that season in the final match in Marseille in April where they defeated France 25-10 in what had become the deciding game after the French had travelled to Swansea on 20 March 1948 and handed out yet another defeat to the beleaguered Welsh national team. A crowd of only 6,500 turned up to see the French win 20-12 as a Welsh team that had once been the sporting pride of the post-war nation seemed to be struggling to compete with its peers.

Nonetheless the Welsh could always be counted on to put up a fine struggle and many Welshmen in the crowd felt their defeat owed more to the decisions of the French referee, Monsieur Pascal, than to failings on the part of the home side. The referee from Toulouse certainly awarded a succession of penalties to the visitors but the dominant and effective French forwards built a platform from which France emerged worthy winners.

The Manchester *Guardian* paid tribute to Gabriel Berthomieu and Gaston Calixte as the architects of the French forward assault while both that newspaper and the *South Wales Evening Post* were full of praise for Rene Duffort, an "efficient scrum half" and two-try winger Ode Lespes "not only the fastest but the best of all the wings".

Wales only had themselves to blame for the early French lead that left them constantly chasing the game. Roy Francis on the Welsh right wing failed to gather a rolling ball in the fifth minute and Lespes pounced to notch his first. Indeed the *Post* described the Welsh wings as "shadows of their former selves, their weakness thrown into bold relief by the speed and determination of Lespes". The French wing's second came from swift back play and, with full-back Jean Barreteau landing one of the conversions, France at 8-0 up should have held a commanding lead at half time, such was their dominance.

Yet slack defence allowed Gareth Price of Leeds in after a "passing movement in which half-a-dozen players handled", this after Alan Edwards had had a claim for a try disallowed. With Ted Ward landing the conversion and then a simple penalty Wales, despite being outplayed, found themselves only one point in arrears at the interval.

Amazingly, and much against the run of play, the Welsh briefly snatched the lead shortly after the break. The *Post* described Trevor Foster's score as "a purely individual effort... the most impressive try of the afternoon, for Foster ran 60 yards to get it, outpacing two opponents who were hot at his heels, one of them throwing himself headlong in a despairing effort to get to grips with the Welsh forward's legs." Ward's conversion was successful and Wales led 12-8.

Once again, though, defensive frailty was to be the downfall of the home team. Within minutes the French regained the lead when Andre Beraud of Marseille dived through an opening, Barreteau adding the conversion and, although they didn't add to their score until the last minute, Wales had no answer to their opponents' rock solid defence. Centre Paul Dejean's converted try was the final act in the match and the 20-12 scoreline was no more than the French deserved.

'Pengradon' of the *Post* felt that much of the blame lay with stand-off Willie Davies who, on the infrequent occasions when the Welsh forwards won possession "seemed anxious to get rid of the ball as soon as he had it. Certainly this was not the Willie Davies we used to know". Outright criticism of Rugby League had waned in recent reports as the writers learnt more about the game. But comments such as this remained frequent - many players were considered as inferior to their former selves once they had switched from Union - this despite Davies creating the opening for Price's try.

'Pendragon' also criticised the referee who "came here with the reputation of being very sparing with his whistle, yet I doubt whether anyone has blown oftener in a Swansea game". Of his penalty decisions 'Pendragon' wrote: "It seemed unjust that Wales should have been saddled with so great a proportion of the blame."

But it would also be unjust to say that the referee was responsible for the Welsh defeat. The team had been struggling for some time and many of the players were reaching the veteran stage. Their worsening performances were shown by the decline in attendance figures for internationals. Although the following season was to see the visit of the first Australian touring team since the war, local supporters and Rugby League critics alike realised that the Welsh would have to improve enormously for the momentum to be maintained and for the home team to provide more than cosmetic opposition for the tourists.

1948-9: The Kangaroos

Prior to the arrival of the Kangaroos, however, the Welsh had the chance to form some cohesion and regain much of their lost confidence with the start of the 1948-9 European Championship. Following the previous season's poor performances it was vital that they redeemed themselves and attempted to build a better team before the tourists arrived at Swansea in November. Matches away to England and at home to France were to be their testing ground.

The match against England at Wigan in September was lost 11-5 and, under increasing pressure to get their European campaign back on the rails as well as prepare for the Australian match, the Welsh faced a strong French XIII at Swansea on 23 October in the second match of the European Championship. Sadly for the home spectators the French took a close but deserved victory, the *Guardian* putting victory down to France taking their scoring opportunities better than the Welsh.

What was also a shame for the Rugby League authorities was that the game was tight and defensive with little open play and many of the crowd of just over 12,000 had left before the final whistle, ironically missing Wales's best period of the match.

The *Sporting Chronicle* wrote that the international selectors had been given "little guide towards the choice of their team for the second Test with Australia at Swinton", with few of the Welsh players rising above club standard. That was certainly true of Castleford's front-row forward Del Harris who was sent off just before the interval for striking, the first Welsh international to be dismissed. The *Chronicle* journalist Bryn James thought this a major contributory factor in the Welsh defeat but to be fair the French showed more ability than the home side, despite losing heavily in the scrums. The loss of so much possession was countered by solid defensive work and it wasn't until late in the game that Wales were able to unlock the French stranglehold.

The Welsh team was roundly criticised with only centre Ted Ward's powerful running and Harry Royal, the Dewsbury scrum-half (playing his first Welsh international after a 12-year career), receiving praise. Ike Owens was ineffectual at loose-forward and the backs missed Skidmore, the Castleford centre, who had to withdraw with fibrositis.

However, there was no mistaking who the star of the French team was. Puig-Aubert, the flamboyant full-back, was everywhere "cool in defence, flashing suddenly into attack and fielding safely". The *South Wales Evening Post* said: "the Frenchmen owed their success to the ingenuity and forcefulness of their diminutive full-back, Puig-Aubert, who persisted in mingling happily with his threequarters, obviously enjoying himself immensely."

The full-back, who is still a Rugby League legend today, in no small part because of his exploits on the 1951 French tour to Australia when France scored an unexpected 2-1 series victory, had already landed a penalty when Harris was sent off. With Welsh tackling beginning to become weak and ineffective and Ward failing to take a couple of decent scoring opportunities, Pierre Taillantou, the visitors' stand-off, broke through to score the game's first try. Puig-Aubert added the conversion and Wales were facing a 7-0 deficit at half time.

In the second half, French passing and defence were excellent and, going into the final 10 minutes, the visitors had increased their lead to 12-4, loose-forward Raoul Perez scoring a converted try, with the only Welsh response being two penalties from Ward. The final moments of the match were easily the most exciting as Wales rallied and almost snatched a victory against the run of play. It might have been an unjust and unlikely comeback but, after Howes of Wakefield had notched a Ward-converted try to leave the score at 9-12, left-winger Alan Edwards dropped a long pass in acres of space and then his right-wing counterpart Steve Llewellyn fumbled with the line open.

However, at 12-9 to the French most observers felt justice had been done, the *Post* writer 'Columbus' ascribing defeat to the instability of the Welsh defence, a problem that was clearly taking some time to correct. The writer also returned, even after years of regular League internationals in Wales, to the old fallback position of Union writers by comparing his game with League. Not surprisingly, considering his allegiance and the defeat of his home nation, he wasn't impressed. "Although the professional system is reputed to be faster and more entertaining than the Welsh Union game, I have seen many first-class clubs play equally well and handle the ball quicker and with more dexterity." It was possible, that in this instance with regard to his countrymen, that he was correct.

As Bryn Williams wrote: "Wales will have to find a stronger side if defeat is to be avoided when the Australians go to Swansea next month." And, with worrying overtones for the future of the Welsh national side, he added: "the numbers of outstanding Welshmen coming into the game are falling off."

In an interesting article for the November 1948 edition of *Rugby League Review*,

Eddie Waring, the famous BBC commentator, then a print journalist, took up a similar theme. "Rugby League in Wales - What are our plans?" he wrote. "It was unfortunate that the Wales vs Scotland association football match was played at Cardiff on the same date," he noted, echoing regular criticism then and now, of bad strategic planning by the authorities, but he was even more critical of the Welsh team itself. "I have not seen a weaker Welsh side. One thing is certain, the Rugby League officials are going to have to decide whether they are desirous of continuing matches in Swansea. Because it is the Australians who will provide the next opposition... every effort must be made to see that no spectator is lost to the code. It is up to the teams but more so to the RL officials to present the match in its most attractive form."

Waring argued that the team's results were suffering because there was little honour in playing for their national side any more. The sport treated Welsh international matches as secondary to playing for Great Britain against touring teams and the Welsh players only took up the option of playing for their country so they could visit their relatives back home. This may or may not have been true but to be fair to most of the players who have pulled on a red Welsh jersey whatever their sport, commitment has usually been the one factor that has not been absent.

Waring was also unsure of the game's dedication to the region. "Just why are Rugby League matches played in Wales? It cannot be to make money. Therefore I can only assume the powers that be really hope one day we shall obtain a foothold in Wales with Rugby League. It is time a policy was decided upon and a statement made of the future the Rugby Football League plans to have in South Wales." How often do we hear similar pleas today?

With two defeats in two games the Welsh European challenge was effectively over. Although the following year they were to defeat England in Swansea in a game that showed the team still had talent, a further defeat 11-0 in Marseille in April was to leave them at the bottom of the championship table and France, who beat them twice, at the top, claiming the European title after swapping victories with England.

Australia in Swansea

So, it was with some trepidation that Wales faced up to Australia on 20 November 1948. By now the International Board had come into existence. It was founded in Bordeaux on 25 January 1948 with France, Australia, New Zealand and Great Britain as members and the Kangaroos were making the first tour under its auspices. They were expected to bring a powerful team yet there was some cause for Welsh hope because early tour matches indicated that Colin Maxwell's 1948 Kangaroos were proving to be something of a disappointment. Although the first test against Great Britain in October at Headingley proved to be a real humdinger watched by nearly 37,000, the Australians had gone down 23-21 with Welshman Trevor Foster getting two tries and it was the nearest they came to test victory. The second test at Swinton in early November had produced an easy British victory, 16-7, and, by the time the Kangaroos came to Swansea, the series (which was to be a whitewash with a 23-9 loss at Odsal in January) was lost.

Sadly for the Welsh there were early withdrawals from the squad. Dickie Williams, the Leeds stand-off had picked up a groin injury playing against Dewsbury the previous week while Trevor Foster, the Great Britain forward, had hurt his back in the second test and had spent some time in hospital. It was the third Welsh match in row that Foster had been forced to miss. However, journalist Bob Pemberton thought that Len Constance and George Parsons (both of St Helens), drawn in to replace Foster and Williams, were able replacements while hooker Frank Osmond from Swinton, would be able to outstrike Kevin Schubert to give the home team much-needed possession. The same writer felt that the tourists had been mediocre so far with poor "team work and tactics".

But the Kangaroos had problems too. Alf Gibbs, the front-row forward had needed five stitches in a knee wound sustained at Workington, while tour captain Colin Maxwell was laid up in bed with flu. Fortunately for the tourists star player Clive Churchill was fit to play at full-back and scrum-half Bruce Hopkins, who had made a big name for himself on the tour, was available after injury.

The 1948 Kangaroos were also the first to play in Wales for more than 25 years, and were the first Australian Rugby League team to play at Swansea.

The home side realised the importance a win would mean to the game in the region and gave their all against a very fit team. Indeed, the match proved to be the proverbial game of two halves as Wales had the upper hand in the first period - despite losing 7-0 at the break - and the Australians piled on the pressure in the second. "Youth won match for Australians," headlined 'Pendragon' in the *South Wales Evening Post*, and it was correct. Fitness took its toll in the second half and even though the tourists relaxed allowing Wales to rally at the end they still emerged 12-5 winners.

'Pendragon' told us that "the Welshmen flattered to deceive. For 30 minutes they appeared to hold the upper hand, then they went all to pieces." The Welsh backs failed to take the opportunities that a lot of forward possession had gained them with reserve stand-off Constance often hesitant. Yet *Sporting Chronicle* writer Bryn James felt that the Welsh were a match for their opponents and, in the first half, should have taken their opportunities to make the game secure. As it was, the Australians were allowed to take a lead into the interval that was against the run of play. "The Kangaroos were not brilliant, but they made more than the Welshmen did of chances," he wrote.

The *Post* said "when the Australians opened the scoring with a Jack Horrigan penalty goal, they did not deserve to be in the lead." But by the time Dutchy Holland dived over for a try just before half time which was then converted by Hopkins they were beginning to get the upper hand. Horrigan was firing well at centre and Churchill was at his best at full-back and, as the second half got underway, Australian fitness told. After Pat McMahon, the Australian right wing had gone close, his centre Johnny Hawke put

Wales versus Australia at Swansea 20 November 1948. Photo courtesy Robert Gate

them further ahead with a fine try as the Kangaroo backs broke downfield, and with Hopkins adding a goal, a 12-0 lead seemed invincible, especially against a tiring Welsh pack. From then on, until the final moments, Australia controlled the game. Gareth Price's try for the home team, after good work by Constance, came far too late for a recovery. Though Ted Ward scored the goal from the touchline, the Welsh were left to rue a 12-5 scoreline that could so easily have been reversed.

Both sides were praised for their defence with wingman Dennis Boocker, the only Australian-born Welshman to represent Wales, and Kangaroo centre Hawke being particularly outstanding. The *Post* felt that Boocker had played himself into contention for Great Britain in the third test. However, most journalists picked out full-back Joe Jones as Wales's best player in the match. 'Pendragon' wrote: "He did some spectacular running-in to meet the ball in flight and his tackling undoubtedly saved Wales from a heavier defeat. The only time he could be faulted was when he was sold a dummy by N. J. Hawke when the latter scored Australia's second half try."

Perhaps of even more concern than the result to the Rugby League authorities however, was the fact that the gate of 9,224 only raised £1,350. After the Australians had taken their contracted 65 per cent cut, the match had been a loss-maker. The League's secretary, Bill Fallowfield, had already appealed to the Welsh public to tell him why attendances at internationals in Swansea had swung into sharp decline. Four questions were asked in the match programme: Is it that soccer is taking the place of rugby at Swansea? Are you tired of Rugby League games at Swansea? Are the Welsh teams not good enough? Is there anything wrong with Rugby League football?

Unfortunately, the answers to these questions, if any were received at Rugby League Headquarters, are not recorded but, with Wales already effectively out of contention for the European Championship, their remaining home fixture that season against England was always going to struggle to draw a crowd.

England defeated

In the event, the 9,553 who did turn up witnessed a fine Welsh performance as they defeated England 14-10 and effectively ensured that the French, not the English, would be the season's champions. Surprisingly, considering the RFL's wavering commitment to internationals in Wales as attendances declined, the authorities were planning a final attempt to establish club Rugby League in Wales with a Welsh League kicking off in autumn 1949. The decision came after the England international, when St Helens and RL champions Huddersfield made a brief tour of the principality. A gate of 29,000 at their deciding match of three at Abertillery convinced League officials that the popularity of the sport, especially at club level, had not waned. Tour referee Mr Phillips claimed that "despite the hostility here and there, the teams were given a great reception".

It seemed that the poor performances of the Welsh national team had been the main cause for the slump in international attendances and club rugby was still a major draw. The fact that all international games were being played at the same venue may also have been contributory.

A League of eight teams in Wales was set to kick off in late 1949 and in support the Rugby League authorities aimed to take international games away from Swansea to promote the sport to a wider audience.

But for the moment, the contract with Swansea was binding, and Wales met England as scheduled on 5 February 1949, some weeks before Huddersfield and St Helens would make their successful promotional tour. The 14-10 Welsh victory, which ended a losing streak of five matches, in this excellent game went some way to convincing the authorities that the two northern clubs should pay a visit as they noted how the crowd responded when the quality of play was good.

And a fine victory it was for Wales against a very strong English team. Wales were fielding three new caps (a total of 27 players having been used in the four internationals that had been played that season) with Billy Banks of Huddersfield at scrum-half, Arthur Daniels of Halifax on the right wing and Eynon Hawkins of Salford in the front row. With criticism of poor feeding of the backline a constant comment over the previous few matches it was the introduction of Banks that finally saw the true potential of Wales's threequarters unleashed.

"Wales find right blend at last," wrote Bryn James. England were fielding 11 test players and the result caused great surprise, the *South Wales Evening Post* writing: "Form turned a somersault when Wales defeated England in what was acclaimed as the best game of the kind seen here since St Helen's became available for professional football. It was a fast moving picture with interest at fever heat because until the last whistle the result was in doubt." Wales deserved the victory but Martin Ryan, the English full-back was having an outstanding match before he dislocated his shoulder just before half time as he dived on a loose ball at the feet of Welsh forward Doug Phillips. There is little doubt that the English suffered as a result because he had been linking well with centre and captain Ernest Ward and his wingman Stan McCormick of St Helens who, after Ryan's departure, often found himself isolated.

The key to the Welsh victory, however, was their improved play around the scrum base prompted by Banks. Dickie Williams of Leeds proved a capable stand-off and loose-forward Ike Owens, now with Huddersfield, finally produced the performance for Wales that he had been giving at club level.

Wales were scintillating in the first half, attacking the English line constantly. Their first score came from a clever round of passing when Arthur Daniels of Halifax dived over on 25 minutes. Ted Ward kicked the conversion. But fears that the Welsh would run out of steam as they did against Australia after Ernest Ward landed an English penalty and wing Johnny Lawrenson scored a converted try, proved unfounded as Ryan left the field and Lawrenson moved to full-back. Ted Ward's first penalty kept the scores level at half time, 7-7, and Wales maintained their momentum in the second period.

Ted Ward kicked Wales back into the lead soon after the break and the against-the-odds victory was secured when Owens and Mel Meek combined to put Phillips over on the hour. England pulled points back with McCormick's try but, with the two Wards swapping goal kicks, the Welsh advantage was held to give them a fine 14-10 victory.

Owens had been outstanding and he, Ted Ward and Joe Jones were the only three players to appear in all of Wales's international matches so far that season. Jones in particular lived up to his reputation as an attacking full-back but was also superb in defence as the English led by forwards Jim Featherstone and Bob Nicholson mounted attack after attack. Indeed Featherstone impressed 'Pendragon' of the *Post* who wrote: "In Featherstone England had an outstanding second-row forward who showed all the skill of a threequarter".

For Wales it was a great shame that such a fine performance had come too late to save their season. But in many ways Wales were still fulfilling their role as missionaries when, in losing their last match of the year in Marseilles, they were watched by a crowd of nearly 30,000.

In an attempt to bring this kind of attendance back to internationals in Wales the Rugby League authorities made two significant changes to the schedule for the following season. A new team was added to the European Championship itinerary and Wales were to play some home games at Abertillery where the promotional match involving Huddersfield and St Helens had proved so successful.

Promotion of the new Welsh club league was also at the front of the minds of the administrators when they announced the alterations. However, in retrospect, as far as international rugby was concerned, the changes were only ever going to be cosmetic.

The new Other Nationalities team was a response first to the fact that only three nations were contesting the European Championship and second to give the growing numbers of fine players in the RFL who were unable, because of their country of birth, to play for any of the existing nations, some representative rugby. The team was first created in the 1904-5 season when it met England in an attempt to give Rugby League players international competition, before the first New Zealand tourists were assembled, and then comprised mainly Welshmen but the team had played only sporadically since. Many of the players, including Australia's Brian Bevan and Lionel Cooper and Scot Dave Valentine who was later to captain the British Lions to World Cup success, were already stars in Britain, thrilling crowds in club rugby. The authorities hoped their presence would boost attendances if they were combined into a single international team.

1949-50: Crowds fall

Although the European Championship was still drawing big crowds in the North, this was not the case in Wales. Many fans saw the exercise as a transparent attempt to increase the number of international teams. When the 1949-50 season's International Championship got underway with four teams playing each other only once, the attendance at Wales's opening fixture at Abertillery against the Other Nationalities was a mere 2,000 spectators.

The Park ground belonged to the local council and was the home venue of Abertillery RUFC. A local councillor had already been banned by the Welsh Rugby Union for allowing the RFL to use the stadium but he had clearly been enticed by the £500 on offer from the League authorities for use of the ground. The RFL were in many ways unlucky with the choice of Abertillery on the date they selected for terrible weather was to ensue, but they were enthusiastic for the fixture to take place following on from the massive crowd for the St Helens versus Huddersfield fixture there.

However, perhaps they could have seen that Welsh internationals fielding what had become to be regarded as a losing team against a cosmetic international side would not prove as popular. Crowds had already been low for the newly-introduced Welsh League, and the omens were not good. What the authorities couldn't have allowed for was the driving, ice-cold rain and lightning that met the teams on 22 October 1949 which no doubt drastically reduced the size of the attendance, bearing in mind that there was only cover for a mere 650. In the end the RFL had to settle for a loss of £439.

At one point it appeared that the match might be postponed as both captains pleaded with referee, Charles Appleton, to abandon the game, but fearful of calling off a game that would be difficult to reschedule, he insisted it took place.

The Welsh put up a good fight against the powerful Other Nationalities squad and the correspondent of the *Western Mail* thought "Wales was slightly unfortunate to lose for the team attacked for two-thirds of the game and at times only desperate tackling prevented them from scoring." But hold firm the Other Nationalities' defence did and it wasn't until the final seconds when a superb solo effort from Jack Davies saw him weave his way over to score near the posts that Wales finally broke through. His own conversion took Wales to within a point of their opponents but it was not enough. The Other Nationalities had already scored two unconverted tries and sneaked home 6-5.

The conditions were truly awful and The *Mail* described them in poetic style. "The match was fought out in a Wagnerian setting - how well is the Abertillery Park suited for the operatic stage, with its mountains rolling down to the evergreen pitch. Lightning spotlighted the first kick of the match and the thunder and rushing mountain streams provided the 'applause'. Under the circumstances the match was a well-contested affair and the players never forgot the first essential of the League game - open football. The handling, especially in the first half, was amazing. From a 'gate' point of view the game was a 'flop', from a propaganda angle of how to handle a greasy ball it was a success."

Trevor Foster was again outstanding for Wales. His leadership ensured the Welsh dominated the forward play but outside Billy Banks and Jack Davies at half-backs, the Other Nationalities proved too strong in the threequarters and it was here that the game was won. Cooper and Bevan were two of the world's outstanding wingmen and they provided the scoring platform for the Other Nationalities success.

With Valentine and Arthur Clues moving the ball quickly wide after only six minutes Bevan caught the Welsh flat-footed when he received a long pass and he made it to the corner for an unconverted try. For more than an hour the Welsh tried in vain to cancel out the deficit. With eight minutes remaining Sid Williams at full-back failed to clear a kick and Cooper, following up well, scooped up the ball and went in at the corner to give the Other Nationalities a 6-point lead. The Welsh comeback was once again too little too late.

France beaten

Only three weeks later the Welsh were due back at Swansea for the next fixture in the European Championship. The visit of the French drew 4,749, losing £200 in the process, and it was clear the city's potential as an international venue had waned. Only one more match in this period would be played there when Wales met the Other Nationalities in 1951. Although the Welsh team continued to compete, the decision would soon be taken that all its 'home' matches would be in the north of England.

For the moment though, the Welsh were still playing in their home country and on 12 November 1949 they had a chance to avenge a double defeat by the French the previous season. Cardiff's Glyn Morgan's selection in the key position of scrum-half showed just what potential there was in Wales for Rugby League and what might have been achieved with greater resources and commitment. Sadly, when the Welsh League finished in 1955 only a handful of colleagues had followed him into the national team.

Yet Morgan played a key role that day in a fine Welsh performance as they took their first victory of the season winning 16-8 against the European champions. Once again the Welsh left it late but this time their finishing surge was enough to bring them victory. For with only 15 minutes remaining the Welsh were trailing 8-3. 'Pendragon' of the *South Wales Evening Post* was present once again and wrote: "During 20 minutes packed with dynamite Wales shook the French defence to its foundations."

The French, who had controlled play well until that late stage, were suddenly put under immense pressure and then, reported the Manchester *Guardian*, "the old French failings asserted themselves - over elaboration in running and passing and a lack of steadiness at crucial moments". This - coupled with a sudden downpour and a loss of indiscipline in the French ranks, completely altered the direction of the game. The referee constantly had to warn the French players during the final few minutes and any hope of them retrieving the match was gone as late Welsh scores took the game out of reach.

The French arrived expecting their success of the previous season to be repeated. But a more determined Welsh team was prepared to take the game to their opponents and when at half time the French lost their captain and centre Paul Dejean with a broken nose, they were always going to be up against it. Even before Dejean's departure the French were struggling to come to terms with Wales. The *Post* noted that "contrary to expectations the Frenchmen showed no superiority in pace, nor were they the equals of their opponents in constructive skill."

Indeed, the Welsh should have led by more than 3-0 at half time. They had the wind at their backs and the threequarters saw a lot of the ball. Yet the passing often went astray and too many offences were committed in the scrum which gave the French some respite. The only score came in the 15th minute, after Puig-Aubert, the French full-back, had already missed three penalty attempts, when Ralph Morgan of Swinton, his Welsh opposite number, struck a post from a penalty. The ball rebounded into Welsh possession and a quick play sent the ball left to Les Williams who scrambled over in the corner.

The kick was missed and the French held out until half time. Indeed they might have levelled the score before then when forwards Ulysse Negrier and Rene Duffort made penetrating runs. Gaston Comes, the best of the French backs, nearly completed a length of the field try before being brought down by full-back Morgan.

Morgan, the Welsh captain, was never as spectacular as Puig-Aubert but his defence was rock solid, as was that of the Frenchmen until the last quarter.

When Dejean did not appear for the second half the signs for a Welsh victory seemed hopeful. Yet, inexplicably, the visitors played much of their best rugby with 12 men and early in the second period had cancelled out Wales's early lead. Comes nearly broke the Welsh line, being stopped only a few yards short, but Duffort took the attack forward, dummied the defence and sent wingman Raymond Contrastin over on the left. There was no conversion but, only minutes later, Comes was again making good ground to feed prop Andre Beraud who put Ode Lespes through a gap. Puig-Aubert converted and the Welsh suddenly found themselves chasing the game at 8-3.

Then came the rain. The Welsh forwards responded well to the change of conditions with Frank Osmond, Bryn Goldswain and Elwyn Gwyther "proceeding to hammer and harass the hitherto sound French defence; even Puig-Aubert who had been a tower of strength became disturbed." Sadly for the game the French were forced to resort to indiscipline in an attempt to halt the Welsh momentum and 'Pendragon' wrote: "there were incidents of which the crowd showed their disapproval by 'booing'". Osmond was carried off after a blow to the head and Gwyther was injured in a tackle but played on. Yet the ferocity of the play only seemed to inspire the Welsh. When prop Tom Danter of Hull broke through the French line and whipped the ball to Arthur Daniels of Halifax the wingman came inside to score a tremendous try between the posts, Morgan converting to level the scores.

The Welsh forwards were now in fine form and threatened to score at every play-the-ball. With minutes remaining Gwyther took on a huge pack of French defenders but strength and determination saw him clamber over the line to put the Welsh three ahead. Victory was secured in the final minute when the French fumbled a pass and Glyn Morgan scooped up the loose ball to score a converted try. A final score of 16-8 marked a remarkable comeback by the Welsh with many players outstanding including Penclawdd-born Gwyther. Both wingmen, Dennis Boocker and Daniels, also caused the French problems with their strong running out wide.

Unfortunately for the Welsh this fine performance did not mark a renaissance in their international fortunes and it was to be three seasons later, in October 1952, when they next took victory in the re-christened International Championship. Sadly, by then they would be playing all their 'home' matches in England. The remainder of the 1949-50 season saw the English win in Bordeaux in December and the Other Nationalities lose in Marseilles 8-3 to leave England requiring a victory over Wales at Wigan to overtake the Other Nationalities at the top of the championship table. When they duly defeated the Welsh in front of 27,500 England were crowned champions for the fourth time in five years and the Welsh, with a solitary victory, were stranded in third place.

Calls were growing for the Welsh national team to play all its matches in the north of England. Crowds in Wales had dwindled, yet nearly 30,000 had turned out to see them play England at Wigan. The waning support from the north for any projects in Wales was shown when, in February 1950, only Harry Hornby of the RFL's liaison committee bothered to travel to attend the Welsh Commission for one of their scheduled meetings. Writing in the *Rugby League Gazette* in April 1950 'Cambrian' said: "Welshmen are now anxious to hear news from the North but in the meantime the Welsh Commission are

Wales versus England at Wigan 1 March 1950. Back: Goldswain, Llewellyn, Osmond, Hawkins, Danter, Mahoney. Sitting: Howes, D.R. Morgan, Foster, Daniels, L. Williams. Kneeling: R. Williams, Banks. Photo courtesy Robert Gate

going ahead with their own plans and are confident that Rugby League has come to stay in Wales." Circumstances would prove otherwise but enthusiasm was still present as 'Cambrian' pleaded: "an imaginative lead from the North now could very well set Wales alight with the flame of Rugby League next season. I sincerely hope the Rugby League Council will not fail to seize its chance." He could have been writing in the 1990s.

1950-51: Italians on tour

Yet Wales was still regarded by some in authority as a catalyst for expansion of the game. When the news arrived in Britain of an Italian Rugby League team keen to tour, a Welsh match was immediately added to the itinerary.

Dissatisfaction among Rugby Union players in Italy had come to a head in Turin where local players revolted and took up the alternative code. They had as their coach Dennis Chappell, a former Wakefield player, who had stayed in Italy following the war and they were captained by Vincenzo Bertolotto who had six Union caps. League was to endure a brief existence in Italy - including a second UK tour in 1954 - as funds for the project from the existing League nations were minimal, but the tour that took place in the 1950-51 season brightened up the grim-looking development situation in Wales.

All Italy's games on that first tour were lost and, although the Italian match played at Bridgend was not a full international (it was contested against a South Wales XIII) it is indicative of the RFL's hit-and-miss policy as far as the Welsh national team was concerned. On the one hand there were constant calls for a cessation of international games in Wales, yet the newly emergent Italians were offered a fixture there at a time when the international game was at its lowest ebb in the principality.

The match, played on 2 September 1950 at the Brewery Field lost £40 and was played out in front of only 2,500 spectators. The Brewery Field was the traditional home of Bridgend RUFC but in 1949 the club lost its lease to the Welsh Rugby League Commission, who secured the ground for three years to allow the Welsh League's Bridgend Rugby League team to play there.

In the event, South Wales defeated the naive Italians 29-11 with Les Lewis of Ystradgynlais and Roy Lambert of Castleford both notching hat-tricks. The Italians tried hard but had little experience and they left Wales never to play there again.

Much the same appeared to be the case with Wales's own national team. Only three more home matches would be played there in the near future, plus a Wales versus British Empire game. For nearly 20 years, the country would not see its team play on home soil.

Vincent Firth, writing in *Rugby League Review*, summed up the attitude of many when he said: "It is gratifying to learn that it has at long last been realised that the playing of 'home' Welsh international matches in Wales is a shameful waste of time and money, and that these games will in future be played in the North. The next question is 'If Wales is to be scrapped as an unsuitable venue, why not go the whole hog and leave Wembley?' By this time even the most obtuse should have realised that there is no hope of converting the South to Rugby League. We [should] take steps to bring the Challenge Cup Final back to the North." Would that Mr Firth could see the London Broncos club of today. What is most disappointing about his comments on Wales (and indeed the south of England) is that they would not seem out of place now. Short-termism is a long-running concept in Rugby League circles.

On the Welsh League front the 1950-51 season initially looked promising. Cardiff aimed to make this season their last in the Welsh League and hoped that the year would gauge their chances of competing in the full RFL competition the following year - an ambition they achieved despite losing to many of their Welsh League counterparts - and in some quarters it was felt that the Welsh League might still be a viable competition as a feeder league for the northern Rugby League.

The first of the three remaining genuine home international fixtures came in the month immediately following the Italian tour game as the International Championship for season 1950-51 kicked off. However, if Wales had still harboured any hopes of reviving their fortunes and convincing the Rugby League authorities that their team was worth serious investment this campaign must have come as a serious blow to them. They lost all their matches, starting with a 22-4 defeat against England in Abertillery on 14 October 1950.

Unfortunately for Wales, who actually put in a good all-round performance, they suffered from the loss of influential scrum-half Billy Banks after only 15 minutes with a facial injury which had to be treated in hospital. This meant that the English had more space and the Welsh had lost a key playmaker.

The ability of the Welsh in defeat can be seen by the *Yorkshire Post*'s eulogy which stated that: "Wales will never lose with greater honour than they did at Abertillery". At half time the home team were still in the game, trailing only 9-4 after stout defensive work had restricted the English to a solitary try from Tommy Bradshaw, the Wigan scrum-half. Ernest Ward, playing at full-back for the English, landed the conversion and two difficult penalties (the *Western Mail* described him as "a brilliant player") while Bryn Goldswain, the Welsh forward playing with Oldham, replied with two goals.

Early in the second half the Welsh showed little sign of wilting with only 12 players on the field and, with Dickie Williams playing as a makeshift scrum-half making "glorious bursts from the base of the pack, distributing the ball quickly and well", the Welsh had a fine third quarter, subjecting the English to strong pressure. Unfortunately for Wales, according to the *Rugby League Gazette*, Williams was not as effective as he would have been at stand-off. "It was a pity for Wales that Dickie Williams was denied the opportunity of operating at stand-off half where his undoubted skill and speedy penetration would have made the game a classic."

Unfortunately the sustained Welsh attack yielded no points. In a rare break, it was the English who scored the first points of the second half when Johnny Lawrenson, the Workington winger, crashed over in the corner seven minutes after the restart to make the score 12-4.

Still the Welsh, showing "traditional fire and vigour", kept the English penned back until only three minutes remained and the home team were clearly tiring, allowing Jack Broome of Wigan and Harry Street at loose-forward, to add to England's tally. Ward converted both tries to leave the Welsh on the end of a lopsided 22-4 scoreline.

Other than the obvious numerical advantage, England's victory was probably achieved through hooker Joe Egan's dominance of the scrums, giving the visitors much-needed possession during long periods in their own half. Thanks to this, the *Western Mail* reported that "England [had] more cohesion."

Yet many Welsh players had outstanding games including Hunslet's Jack Evans at full-back, Don Gullick, the St Helens centre, and the only Welsh club player Roy

Lambert of Neath. "His powerful, speedy bursts up the wing required all the weight of the England right flank defence to stop him."

Of the game itself 'Cambrian' wrote in the *Rugby League Gazette*: "The International at Abertillery was not as successful as one would have wished. Even so, a crowd of about 10,000 [it was later confirmed as 8,000] attended and the opportunity was there to convert many of them to our code. The game, however, was not a classic of Rugby League Football and quite a number I should imagine were not wholly convinced. There was some fine football, of course, but not nearly enough from a game of so much propaganda importance."

Other Nationalities return

And there was no disguising that the Welsh had lost another important match on home soil - they were going to have to wait until March of the following year before they would get a chance to redeem themselves against the Other Nationalities at Swansea. In the interim the northern RL authorities were become ever more edgy about Welsh involvement and the future for the game in the region. As 'Cambrian' wrote in the *Rugby League Gazette* in late October 1950 "Welshmen are disappointed about fixtures with Northern sides. It seems the clubs are not anxious to increase their already heavy fixture lists." The promotional games that the Welsh hoped northern clubs would play in the country to promote their league and the sport were not forthcoming.

By the time of the next Welsh home game England had beaten the French 14-9 in Leeds and France had defeated Other Nationalities 16-3 in Bordeaux, to leave England atop the table and both the Welsh and the Other Nationalities looking for their first win when they met at St Helen's in Swansea on 31 March 1951. Astoundingly, this match was the best game of that season's International Championship. The shame was that only 5,000 turned up to see it.

It was, as Robert Gate later described it: "A 12-try extravaganza of open rugby and an international match to rank with the very best in history." The *Yorkshire Post* described it as "One of those delightful games in which every player had at least one moment of glory in this stimulating show of brilliant running and handling."

It had all looked very different in the days leading up to the game, as the *Rugby League Review* wrote: "Which team has proved the biggest disappointment these last few seasons? The answer to that question is the collection of overseas stars labelled Other Nationalities. When they were reintroduced into the International Tournament it was generally accepted that they would sweep all before them. Such has not proved to be the case, however." The writer still assumed they would beat Wales though and he was proved right - but only just.

Alfred Drewry also previewed the match in the *Yorkshire Post* and said that the game would not attract much attention because it came after a tough Easter club programme. Once again, it seems that international matches were relegated to second place. He went on to lament that the next match in the championship between England and Other Nationalities would also prove unpopular because it came after the Challenge Cup semi-finals and two days after vital league championship matches. He bemoaned the fact that players had to leave their clubs to play "Cinderella" internationals.

All this negative publicity plus the fact that the Other Nationalities had to reorganise their forwards by bringing in the untried Johnny Mudge of Workington and Bob Robson, a Scot (partnering his countryman Dave Valentine of Huddersfield), from Salford pointed towards a game that would not provide great entertainment. Drewry suggested that the lack of strong forwards would mean the fine Other Nationalities threequarters would not see adequate possession. All the predictions, fortunately, proved to be wrong.

John Christopher in the *South Wales Evening Post* wrote: "Professional rugby in South Wales was given a great boost at St Helen's, when Wales played a star-studded Other Nationalities team, because no one could wish for a finer exhibition of handling and tactical brilliance.

"Whatever other difference there may be between professional and amateur exponents of the game there is one which is outstanding. The dexterity and accuracy of the ball-play easily surpasses that of the amateur code, and this match has done more for the cause of the League game than any premeditated canvassing."

It was a fine testimony to an excellent match which saw 12 tries but which Wales lost 27-21. At half time the Other Nationalities led by 11-10 although the Manchester *Guardian* questioned the legality of Peter Henderson's try when he appeared to lose the ball as he grounded it. Wales had fought well to keep in the hunt. The star of their excellent threequarter line was Terry Cook whose fine tackles on the left wing halted the running of his more famous opposite number, Brian Bevan.

Indeed Cook's two Jack Evans-converted tries kept the Welsh in the game after Ike Proctor, Trevor Allan, and Henderson had notched their tries for the Other Nationalities before half time with one converted by full-back Bert Cook of Leeds. Excellent tackling by both teams had kept the scores close and right through the second half the result remained in doubt.

With 10 minutes remaining two more Welsh tries by Mel Ford of Aberavon (the only Welsh club player in the team) and Don Gullick of St Helens had cancelled out a converted try by flying Australian Lionel Cooper and the match was poised at 16-16.

Welshmen Billy Banks, Del Harris and Gullick tried all they knew to carve openings in the opposition but it was Arthur Clues who broke the deadlock with a fine effort as time was running out. A penalty by Bert Cook and another try by Bevan, who finally escaped the clutches of Terry Cook, took the game out of Wales's reach. Although Hunslet loose-forward Granville James pulled points back for Wales with an Evans-converted try, centre Tony Paskins added the final points with a try for the Other Nationalities in what had become a breathless and free-scoring final 10 minutes.

It had been a thrilling game and John Christopher was quick to praise the work of Terry Cook who "made a name for himself in his first League international. His opponent Brian Bevan lived up to his reputation as the finest wing in the game, but Cook did more. He completely subdued Bevan."

Christopher also picked out Ray Cale as a powerhouse in the Welsh forwards for his "flashes of brilliance" and Les Williams, Billy Banks and Dickie Williams for their experience and maturity. For the Other Nationalities Henderson, Allan and Paskins were singled out for their winning contributions, even though Paskins was to be dropped from the team for the next match against England for not showing "a proper appreciation of Brian Bevan's capabilities".

Writing in the week after the game, the *Yorkshire Post*, under the headline "Brilliant propaganda" commented that: "If there is any life at all in the Rugby League movement in Wales, the patient should soon be sitting up and taking nourishment after this stimulating propaganda show."

Yet, sadly, the crowd had only been a miserly 5,000 and, once more, Wales had ended up on the losing side. In fact, for the first time since the war they would not win a single game that season, going on to lose their final championship match 28-13 to France in Marseilles which handed the French the title after England had crashed 35-10 at Wigan to an ever-improving Other Nationalities.

The Welsh even lost their other minor fixture when they played the British Empire at Stebonheath Park, Llanelli on 19 May as part of the Festival of Britain celebrations. This match too was hailed by those there as great propaganda for the game with the *Llanelly Mercury* writing: "It gave the impression that ordinary Rugby Union club training must be farcical. The players tore into each other like tigers on defence and on attack were jet-propelled."

The crowd of 6,500 saw their team lose 29-16 with Les Williams giving a particularly good display in the centre.

1951-2

But, as stated earlier, time was running out for international League in Wales. The final match of this era to be played on Welsh soil took place at Abertillery on 1 December 1951 before a crowd of only 3,386 (although, interestingly, many press reports estimate a crowd of 10,000). The Welsh had already lost the championship opener 35-11 to England at Knowsley Road and following another Welsh defeat to the Other Nationalities the arguments in favour of returning Welsh 'home' matches to the north of England (where crowds for internationals were still strong) became a clamour and, consequently, it would be a full 24 years before the national team would return to the principality.

The game was up for Wales as early as the first minute of this final match at Abertillery. Australian Brian Bevan was back to his best for the Other Nationalities and his scything run from halfway in the first 60 seconds set the tone of the match. His stunning try was converted by Huddersfield's Pat Devery and Wales were left chasing the game. As the *Western Mail* wrote: "The Other Nationalities were far superior to the Welshmen. They showed better team work, greater speed and more thrust. There was no fire in the Welsh pack."

The writer also complained of a lack of traditional "hywl" from the crowd and perhaps it was this, more than anything else, that led to the demise of Welsh Rugby League in the 1950s. Compare this with the immediate post-war situation and crowds that regularly topped 30,000. Then, as now, many supporters go to experience a special atmosphere, especially at international matches. In a crowd of around 3,000 this will always be sorely missed.

Cardiff winger

Milson Hunt, the 22-year-old Cardiff club winger, had a fine debut. He was the one outstanding Welshman in the team as he successfully opposed Huddersfield star Lionel Cooper and it was Hunt who scored Wales's first try in the eighth minute. The kick was unsuccessful and by half time the Other Nationalities had restored their lead with a try from Devery.

Wales had their strongest period early in the second half when Dickie Williams at stand-off, despite a leg injury, found gaps for big forward Doug Phillips to run into, but their pressure did not pay dividends as both Bevan and Devery made their try tally a brace and Cooper and Tony Paskins (restored to his centre berth) both scored one try. Fortunately for Wales Harry Bath of Warrington could only convert one of the tries.

The Welsh rally came late in the game. After Ted Ward had landed a fine 50-yard penalty attempt, Dickie Williams and his namesake Les scored tries, the latter creating a fine opening. But at 22-11 the Welsh were well beaten.

Dave Valentine, Arthur Clues and Bath were all powerful in the pack and the threequarter line was always penetrative. Billy Banks and Dickie Williams tried hard in the half-backs for the Welsh but only Phillips reacted to their prompting in the forwards. Jack Evans, the Welsh full-back naturally had a busy game but coped well, despite the opposition notching six tries.

But, as it was, Les Williams was to score the last international try on Welsh soil for nearly a quarter of a century. The Welsh were set to meet New Zealand at Bradford only one week later (a match they lost 15-3) - even though the Kiwis had played in Wales against the Cardiff club team - and it was in England that the Welsh team would domicile until its demise in 1953-54. The remaining match of that season for the Welsh was in Bordeaux and France again clinched the title with a 20-12 success after earlier beating England 42-13 in Marseille. The French had lost to Other Nationalities whom the English defeated but still took the title on points difference.

Even though Wales took part in two more championships before the national team was finally disbanded, winning two matches in 1952-53 over France and the Other Nationalities and finishing second to England in the table, all the matches were lost in 1953-54. Ironically Wales's final game of this period was a fine match in Marseille in December 1953 in front of 25,000 people in which they lost by just one point in 45.

The championship was suspended in 1954 because the nations were taking part in the first Rugby League World Cup in France. Wales and England were playing as a combined Great Britain team (ironically captained by Scot Dave Valentine of the Other Nationalities) and, against all the odds won the competition with an under-strength team by defeating France in the final in Paris.

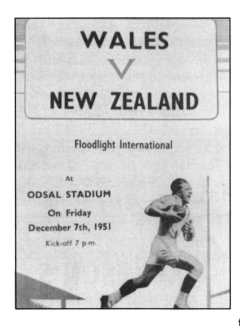

Wales versus New Zealand programme
at Bradford 7 December 1951.
Photo Peter Lush

The following season's International Championship was to be the last of the era and Wales did not take part as the Other Nationalities, containing a number of Welsh players such as Billy Boston and Billy Banks, took the title. The previous season had also seen the demise of the Welsh League along with the national team and the future seemed very bleak indeed for the sport in Wales.

A number of factors had led to the end of the post-war Welsh international experiment and all played a major contribution in seeing Rugby League retreat back into its northern heartlands.

A relative dearth of quality Welsh players coming into the game (with notable exceptions such as Billy Boston and Lewis Jones) thanks to post-war prosperity in Britain and, after the advent of the Welsh League, threats from the Welsh Rugby Football Union of life bans for players taking up League contracts made players wary of signing up to a sport with an uncertain future in their region. This certainly meant that the Welsh might not be competitive against their English and French counterparts, but in actual fact there were always enough players still turning to Rugby League to field a decent team that could compete on its day.

The success of Great Britain in the 1954 World Cup also contributed to the demise of the Welsh national team. France was a very competitive League nation at the time and the RFL reasoned that regular test matches played by the new world champions Great Britain against the runners-up France were potential moneyspinners. A crowd of more than 30,000 had watched the World Cup Final, a figure far higher than crowds for Welsh internationals. The administration had been looking for a means to end the Welsh experiment which was costing the RFL a lot of money (albeit arguably well spent if a long-term plan was in operation) and the prospect of annual Great Britain versus France tests allowed them to do this without alienating Welsh players of international quality.

The early 1950s had exposed the difficulty of generating Welsh interest in the sport, especially international matches, without delving too deeply into the RFL pocket. In the post-war boom years crowds would turn out for any sporting event. But, as the 1950s approached, the public could afford to be more selective with its entertainment and, if promotion of a sporting event was not made a priority, it would suffer.

Many northern Rugby League people saw the monetary support of international matches - to say nothing of the Welsh League - as an unnecessary burden on a sport that was deeply entrenched in northern communities and they were not prepared to spend their club's money on touring Wales with exhibition matches or supporting international matches from which they could see no obvious, short-term gain. This is a problem that has obviously dogged Rugby League throughout its history and could still be seen in the late 1990s with the inability of the RFL Council to agree on a structure that allowed for clubs like Paris and South Wales to have a share of the Super League financial cake, even though the admission of such teams to the top level of the game would bring untold benefits to a sport still regarded as essentially a northern one.

"Entrenchment"

This attitude was summed up in an article entitled "Entrenchment" in *Rugby League Review* in February 1952 in which it was pointed out that when Bradford Northern played the Kiwis at Odsal 29,072 people turned up. When Wales played New Zealand at the same venue there were only 8,568. The logic ran that clubs in the north were better supported than Welsh international teams and international matches involving Wales only cost the RFL money. In effect, it was telling us that many of the people who support Rugby League then as now are parochial in their outlook towards teams and countries other than their own. The article went on to argue that Welsh international matches only swelled "the already huge debit account on RL football in Wales".

The writer also considered promotional matches in London to be a waste of time and money and that touring teams should be encouraged not to play there by making them pay for any losses incurred in such matches. "In vulgar parlance the Rugby League Council was 'left to hold the baby,' while the 'propagandists' added another nice sum to their swag bags." Opinion, according to the writer, was definitely in favour of retreating to the heartlands and he appeared heartily pleased that no member of the Rugby League Council had attended the press lunch called by the 1951 Kiwis in London before they left for France. All matches should return to the north where they could make a profit, we were told, with no more expenditure on the "scandalous South Wales Bubble".

There was no mistaking the message. According to *Rugby League Review*, "Retrenchment" should be "the watchword for the future".

Chapter 8: Cardiff 1951-2 and the Welsh League

If the social and economic context of the Pontypridd bid in the 1920s had made it an almost certain failure, the next attempt to make professional Rugby League work in Wales was launched in more promising conditions.

If ever a time was propitious for professional sport, it was the years immediately following the Second World War. Demand for entertainment - fuelled by six years of war and the deprivations of the period immediately afterwards - reached unprecedented levels. Total Football League attendances peaked at more than 40 million in the late 1940s - around double the number going to games half a century later. Average attendances in football's Second Division were higher than those attracted by Premiership clubs in the late 1990s. And more than 158,000 people attended the Headingley Test Match against Donald Bradman's 1948 Australian cricket tourists.

Rugby League shared in the prosperity. Football's attendance peak in 1948-9 coincided with League's as a total of 6.86 million paid to pass through the turnstiles of the 29 clubs then competing, an average of more than 13,000 per match. In the 1990s total attendances, even before the Super League reorganisation greatly reduced the number of matches, were around a quarter of that. The achievement of a single club, Bradford Bulls, in surpassing the 1948-9 whole league average attendance, was rightly regarded as remarkable.

Big matches pulled in giant audiences. The 102,000 plus-and-counting invasion of the 1954 Challenge Cup Final replay at Odsal, brilliantly chronicled in Robert Gate's *There Were A Lot More Than That*, came a little later. But the end of the 1940s saw attendances like the 75,194 at Maine Road, Manchester who saw the 1949 Championship final, in which Huddersfield beat Warrington 13-12.

Mass enthusiasm brought prosperity which was reflected in fast-growing transfer fees for star players. The pre-war transfer record of £1,450 paid by Warrington for Liverpool Stanley full-back Billy Belshaw in 1937-8 was beaten in the first season after the war, as Dewsbury paid Huddersfield £1,650 for their Welsh full-back or centre Bill Davies. There had only been seven hikes in the record between 1901, when Jim Lomas went from Bramley to Salford for £100, and the start of the Second World War.

The four years after the Davies deal were to bring eight new marks, with the record finally coming to rest at £5,000 after the 1950-1 season, shared by hooker Joe Egan's move to Leigh from Wigan and the Cherry and Whites' acquisition of Harry Street from Dewsbury.

Expansion

The favourable circumstances were also reflected in the game's most successful British expansion outside what we now know as the M62 corridor. Cumbria's grassroots strength, outside Barrow, had only previously been reflected in the short careers of Millom (1899 to 1906) and Carlisle (10 matches in 1928). But the end of the war brought the admission of Workington Town. They were instantly competitive - winning 16 games out of 36 in their first season, then establishing themselves as a fixture in the top half of the table. Within five years, inspired by the apparently indestructible Welshman Gus Risman, they were a power in the game - winning the championship in

1951, then the Challenge Cup in 1952, when Risman was 41. Whitehaven, who joined the League in 1948, were less successful, but established themselves as a respectable mid-table club.

Two other new clubs joined in the decade after the war - Doncaster in 1951 and Blackpool Borough in 1954. If both were recruits to the game's perpetual strugglers, they still contrived to survive longer than any club from outside the borders of Yorkshire, Lancashire, Cumbria and Cheshire has yet managed. There was one casualty in this period - founder members and 1902 Championship and Challenge Cup double winners Belle Vue Rangers (Broughton Rangers until 1946) went out of business after losing their ground in 1955.

But this was a rare period in which the game's development ledger was undoubtedly in the black. During it, though, thoughts inevitably turned again to Wales. Welsh players continued to play a prominent role at the game's highest levels - with Risman's feats for Salford and Workington matched by those of Trevor Foster and Willie Davies in Bradford Northern's greatest ever period.

Post-war Wales was more prosperous than it had been for a good 30 years. Historian Kenneth Morgan records that "For the vast bulk of the people, the period from 1945 to 1951 was a time of great hope and progress, with rapidly rising living standards". Welsh economic output would rise by 23 per cent between 1948 and 1954, against 18 per cent for Britain as a whole.

Attendances for Welsh sport reflected post-war hunger for entertainment, renewed prosperity and the success of some of its teams. Glamorgan won their first county cricket championship in 1948, and matches against touring teams at St Helen's, Swansea regularly pulled in crowds of more than 50,000 over three days.

Cardiff in particular enjoyed a period of great sporting prosperity. Cardiff City FC, a Third Division club when peacetime football began in 1946, were in the First Division by 1952, attracting a Second Division crowd of more than 57,000 for the first post-war derby against Swansea Town in 1949-50. Cardiff RFC enjoyed a spell during which they justified the label of *The Greatest* so modestly bestowed in their centenary history. They topped the *Western Mail* unofficial Rugby Union club championship four times in the first nine post-war seasons, providing up to 10 of the Welsh XV and pulling in crowds of 30,000 or more to the Arms Park.

Welsh Commission

The Rugby League's Welsh Commission, still in existence as a remnant of the ambitions of the 1920s, could hardly be expected to pass up the opportunity provided by conditions like these. Further encouragement came from the local response to the renewal of League internationals in Wales after the war.

St Helen's, Swansea would remain a regular venue for Union internationals until 1954, but its town council owners were - as they would be again in the 1970s - quite happy to entertain the rival code. The first post-war international, an 11-3 defeat of England in November 1945, left spectators more accustomed to the sedate safety-first game played by Union full-backs gasping at the audacious running of Gus Risman and pulled in a crowd of 30,000. Good attendances at a further eight internationals in the next four seasons encouraged the belief that time was right for another assault on Wales.

Harold Stacey

A fresh campaign was launched in February 1949 in terms which historians Gareth Williams and Dai Smith point out in their history of Rugby Union in Wales, *Fields of Praise* "rang with military symbolism". Harold Stacey, the Neath-based organiser of Welsh Rugby League, warned in early 1949 that "From Neath... cohorts are to go out into every town and village in Wales preaching the League game...in an honest endeavour to raise the standard of Rugby Football in South Wales and regain some of the past glories of the game... Nothing will prevent us...even if it takes up to fifteen years, we are coming into Wales".

The three matches played in May by St Helens and champions Huddersfield was the final testing of the water for the Rugby League. Huddersfield took the series by two matches to one, but far more important was the evidence of attendances - 5,000 at Pontardulais, double that at Bridgend and finally no less than 29,000 at Abertillery.

But even before that final match offered apparently conclusive proof of the game's potential appeal in Wales, the League had been convinced. On 18 May, the day of the Bridgend match, a League delegation including chairman Tom Brown, secretary Bill Fallowfield and several Rugby League Council members, met the Welsh Commission in Neath. The League promised £1,000 to support the game in Wales, and added that "Application for further financial assistance would probably be favourably received".

A local press account of the match at Bridgend underlined the task facing the Welsh Commission. This was long before television coverage had made League at least broadly familiar to audiences outside the game's heartlands. Eddie Waring was still League's best known print journalist rather than a much-imitated and debated broadcaster. And television sets were anyway very rare in South Wales.

The reporter and spectators inevitably saw League through Union-accustomed eyes. The writer reported that "Most of the spectators were ignorant of the League code rules, but were able to follow the game with ease owing to the commentary given by the chairman of the St Helens club.

"Naturally the feature which impressed everyone was that the ball was in sight all the time. Scrums were quick and heeling seemed quicker than is usual in Union games, and, of course, there were fewer scrums. When a man is tackled the other players are not allowed to crowd around and go into a loose maul, but the player with the ball in his possession is allowed to get up and heel the ball back to his threes. This greatly speeded up the game, but the standard of tackling seemed rather poor, most of the players going high all the time and it often took two or three men to bring one down".

Trevor Foster told a post-match meeting: "I think handling and rucking is better than getting into a loose maul, as so often happens in Welsh Rugby. You in Wales have rugby in your blood. You are rugby minded here and it is up to you to decide which code provides the best spectacle. We think League is best."

The reporter's assessment was calm and judicious: "Many people came out of curiosity and to give the new game a chance of showing what it could do. The real test will come when local League games are playing at Bridgend. The partisan spirit will then be present, and a fair comparison can be drawn between attendances at home games of local League and Union matches".

The partisan spirit did not have to wait for the following season to emerge. The Welsh Rugby Union made it clear from the start that it regarded the new League venture as a threat. The Welsh Rugby Union secretary responded to Stacey's early 1949 rhetoric by saying that "My Union intend to fight the challenge of the Rugby League, and support those clubs wherever they may be in Wales who are threatened with opposition".

William Hodges, a member of the Abertillery District Council - hosts for the exhibition League match in May 1949 - was suspended from his position as an official of the Blaenau Gwent Rugby Union club. This was in spite of his protestations that the local community had gained £500 from the match and his club's view that the punishment was harsh and unjust.

Rowe Harding, among the most influential figures on the Welsh Rugby Union, would tell the 1950 Annual General Meeting that "The Rugby League is only an infant, but it wants strangling". Those with long memories possibly recalled that this was the same Rowe Harding who had once scandalised Union opinion by proclaiming of the Cambridge University teams he played in from 1925 to 1928 that "We played Rugby, talked Rugby, thought Rugby and dreamed Rugby. For one term we were professional gladiators, devoting all our time and energies to winning the Varsity match".

But there were more substantial reasons than mere class prejudice to explain Welsh Union's hostility to League. Phil Melling has described Wales's cumulative loss of Union talent to the north, particularly in the hungry inter-war years, as one of the greatest migrations of sporting talent in history. Robert Gate records that 70 full internationals 'went north' between 1919 and 1939, a total which leading Union historian Gareth Williams calculates equates to no fewer than 900 first-class players making the move during the same period. Wales's failure to win a Triple Crown between 1911 and 1952 was hardly coincidental.

True, the bans the WRU imposed were a consequence of Union's restrictive attitude. But it was hardly surprising that the clubs and supporters of Welsh Union should see League, rather than their Union's regulations, as a predator.

As a consequence, finding somewhere suitable to play would be one of the greatest problems facing the nascent Welsh Rugby League. The Cardiff and Neath clubs were unable initially to play in the communities that gave them their name. Llanelli's apparent advantage of a plutocratic backer who owned a 27 acre site known as Penygaer Fields and hoped to build a stadium for them was negated by opposition from the local council - first because it had an alternative use for the land and wished to purchase it itself and subsequently due to resident opposition to dual use with speedway. *Rugby League Gazette* recorded that legal fees for the two inquiries had cost League more than £1,000. The price in lost time, energy and enthusiasm is not recorded.

Bridgend

The club in Bridgend was luckier. But its success both reinforced Union views that League was a predator which was to be resisted at all costs, and ensured that this period of League development would leave at least one mark on Welsh rugby folk legend. If it is remembered for anything, it is exiling Bridgend Rugby Union club from their Brewery

Field ground for eight years.

This, ironically, was the ground that had hoisted notices in the 1920s proclaiming that Rugby League scouts would not be admitted. And it was not the first time that Bridgend RUFC, who first played there in 1912, had lost the site. In 1928 it had been outbid by a greyhound racing promoter, but the local football club had conveniently folded at the same moment, allowing the Union team to move across town until the Brewery Field fell vacant again in 1935.

The lease, previously set at £156 per annum, was up in 1949. Bridgend RUFC bid £500, but the new Rugby League club outbid them by £100. The news was handed to Bridgend RUFC secretary Durbar Lawrie as he left the Welsh Rugby Union's 1949 AGM in late May 1949. A dispute over the ownership of the goalposts on the site was settled by *force majeure* by a late-night raiding party of unionists, who carried them off to their new council-provided ground.*

Welsh League

Life was never to be simple for the new league - *Rugby League Gazette* columnist 'Cambrian' would report in September 1949 that northern enthusiasts "cannot visualise the obstacles and antagonism that this group of Rugby League enthusiasts has met". But in the same article he could also note that February's aspiration had become August's reality, with the opening match played at Brewery Field on 20 August, where Cardiff beat Bridgend 45-10.

The first league matches were played three weeks later, on 10 September. The results were Amman Valley 5, Cardiff 34; Llanelli 49, Aberavon 5; Bridgend 7, Ystradgynlais 23; Neath 19, Welsh Dragons 16. The Dragons had been formed by the Welsh Commission after a Pontardulais club withdrew without playing a match. The Dragons certainly did not last the season, but a table published in November 1949 shows they played, and lost heavily, at least two more games.

The teams were inevitably a mixed bag. Northern watchers at the Bridgend opener concluded that Cardiff would be unbeatable because of a wealth of ex-northern talent. At least half a dozen of the team had professional experience including the player-coach Idwal Davies, previously of Leeds. Davies had played centre for Wales against England at Union while still with Swansea in 1939. Joining Leeds within weeks, he was not given his cap by the Welsh Rugby Union until the mid-1970s.

Most of the other clubs had a sprinkling of League players who had returned to Wales. As we have seen vast numbers had gone north in the 1930s and the war had interrupted many professional careers, giving players little reason to stay in Lancashire or Yorkshire. Aberavon's ex-pros included Danny Sheehy, formerly of Dewsbury and Keighley, whose family remain a force in Welsh Rugby League to this day. Bridgend, however, was reported as being "almost wholly Rugby Union men" with the exception of their captain Ivor Bennett, who had previously played for Warrington.

The League faced a battle from the start. 'Cambrian' reported in November 1949 that "It costs a lot of money to get a team on the field and considerably more to provide

---

* In 1985, on a quiet Sunday, in a similar situation, Fulham Rugby League supporters removed the posts from their former home of Craven Cottage, and carried them down the river bank to their new home at Chiswick.

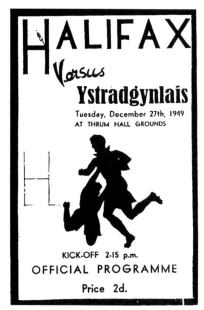

HALIFAX
Versus
Ystradgynlais
Tuesday, December 27th, 1949
AT THRUM HALL GROUNDS

KICK-OFF 2·15 p.m.
OFFICIAL PROGRAMME
Price 2d.

the field". Help came from Northern clubs willing either to travel to Wales for friendlies - Hull beat Cardiff 27-17 at Abertillery while Widnes beat a Welsh XIII 9-6 at Bridgend - or to entertain them in the north, where more than 12,000 saw Warrington beat Cardiff 35-10 on 27 December, the same day as 6,000 watched Halifax beat Ystradgynlais 33-6 at Thrum Hall. Welsh players were reported to have offered to play these matches without pay if it helped get the clubs off the ground.

But the key would inevitably be the ability of the new league to attract fans to its own fixtures. In November 'Cambrian' admitted that they had so far not been very good - the 5,000 for Cardiff v Llanelli at Pontypool, a location testifying to Cardiff's difficulty in getting a ground, much the best with most crowds nearer 2,000. By the standards of the 1980s these would have been decent attendances, but by those of the 1940s they certainly were not. The crowd for Neath versus Aberavon on December 17 - a mere 45 - would not have been acceptable under any circumstances, inadequate grounds and freezing weather notwithstanding.

The great success in this respect was Ystradgynlais, a Swansea valley village which was much the smallest community represented in the competition. Their team was entirely made up of ex-Union players. But unlike the majority of the other teams, they had no direct first-class Union competition and appear to have made a rapid impact on their community. 'Cambrian' reported regular attendances of well over 2,000 in spite of a ground with no spectator cover, not a recommended deficiency in South Wales: "It is boasted of them that more people watch Rugby League football than the whole population of the village". A strong women's committee was a particular feature.

Ystradgynlais emerged as the surprise team of the league - "The team of the year" in 'Cambrian's' view. Champions Cardiff and Llanelli finished above them in the league, well ahead of the rest of the competition. But Ystradgynlais won the cup, defeating Cardiff at Llanelli.

Bridgend had their moments, taking their revenge for that August hammering by becoming the first Welsh side to defeat Cardiff. And there was a fresh positive development in early 1950 with the formation of a club in Blaina, Monmouthshire under the leadership of Bill Gore, a hooker who had been capped three times as a Union player in 1947, and then briefly joined Warrington.

It was evident that there were quality players in the new league. Cardiff scrum-half Glyn Morgan was chosen to play for Wales against France in November. But the Welsh faced the same difficulty as all development areas - the very best players want

WOODLANDS FIELD, YSTRADGYNLAIS
FRIDAY, MAY 19, 1950

Widnes
v.
Ystradgynlais & Neath
Combined XIII

Kick-off - 6.30 p.m.

Official Programme · 1d   No. 930

C. D. LAKE Proprietor: James Lewis
YSTRADGYNLAIS
Newsagent and Tobacconist
Please order now for Meccanno Sets and Hornsby Trains

Widnes on tour in 1950

to test themselves against the very best. Cardiff were to lose three players to the northern clubs in early 1950.

And that second-class status applied to more than just relationships with the established powers of the north. By April 1950 'Cambrian' was calling for Welsh clubs to be admitted to the senior Rugby League. While spectators who had been to League games appreciated the code and its rules: "It's only human for the average person to go and watch first-class Rugby Union clubs playing on decent grounds in preference to watching second-class Rugby League clubs playing on open fields", and pointing to the fact that the Welsh Rugby League was pulling in larger attendances than second-class Union in Wales: "That I assure you, is the growing need among the spectators down here - first-class Rugby League on first class grounds - and the sooner it comes the better". The end-of-season tours by clubs such as Keighley, Featherstone and Widnes helped bring top class clubs to the valleys, but were no substitute for Welsh clubs participating in the Rugby League itself.

The Welsh Commission agreed with 'Cambrian', adopting the policy of "First-Class Rugby League for Wales". The decision was made to bid for two entries - Cardiff from East Wales, Llanelli for the West. On 1 May 1950, their applications were submitted to the Rugby League, and a three-hour meeting decided that they should be admitted from June 1951, subject to their having adequate grounds. 'Cambrian' reported that some Welsh opinion was disappointed, feeling that the game could not survive another season of second-class competition. His own view was that it was the right decision, giving the clubs the chance to organise properly - and in particular to ensure that they had adequate grounds, before taking on the challenge of senior competition.

The second season began in September 1950 with the same eight teams - Blaina now admitted as full members - that had finished the previous season. Idwal Davies, operating from a base in Llanelli, had been appointed Welsh organiser. He worked hard at trying to establish new clubs, with public meetings held in Skewen (including a film show of Rugby League matches), Glynneath and Pontardulais during the season.

The regular league season was preceded by two representative matches. A trip north

Ystradgynlais RLFC 1949-50. "Everyone a convert from the Union code and now enjoying their football more than ever! One of the best team in the Welsh League with a good chance to represent Wales in the Cup". (Signed H.C. Stacey). Photo courtesy Robert Gate

to Wigan was an unhappy experience, with the Welsh XIII going down 74-29 and an 8,000 crowd disappointing the organisers - although several Welsh players who had not previously seen Rugby League at its best were reported to be enthused by the way Wigan had played. A few days later an Italian touring team - Wales was not the only area where League was trying to expand in this period - were beaten 29-11, with Neath winger Roy Lambert confirming the good impression he had made at Wigan with a hat-trick. Lambert was to join Dewsbury before the end of November.

1950-51

The 1950-51 season was to a great extent overlain by the prospect of Welsh clubs entering senior competition in the following season. Ystradgynlais had another excellent year, retaining the cup by defeating Bridgend in the final and finishing second in the league. They also found time to help a Rugby League region at an even earlier stage of development, the south of England, by playing Slough in November - offering them half the gate money and scoring more than 50 points against them.

But attention will inevitably have focused on the two aspirants to senior status. In late December 1950 *News Chronicle* League correspondent Tom Longworth speculated in *Rugby League Gazette* that neither Llanelli nor Cardiff would make it to the starting line "for some time to come". He was right about Llanelli, wrong about Cardiff.

Unfortunately the playing indications are that the wrong club made it to senior status. Llanelli won their opening match 36-11 at Bridgend and dominated the league season, with their failure in the Welsh Cup semi-final against Ystradgynlais the only real blot. As well as winning the league, they qualified for the Rugby League Challenge Cup, defeating Ystradgynlais in the final qualifier. They went down 62-14 over two legs to Barrow, a respectable display against a team who would go all the way to Wembley that season. Exactly at what point Llanelli's bid for senior status went down or was rejected is unclear. A report at the end of 1951 quoted in Geoffrey Moorhouse's *A People's Game* refers to their chief backer, Alby Evans, being ill and taking no further interest in the club, and to a lack of funds, yet also credits them with possession of an adequate ground.

(Cartoon from *Rugby League Gazette*)

Cardiff's season was discouraging from the start. 'Cambrian' said rather alarmingly that "little has been heard of Cardiff and not much is known of the team" before their opening match, and a 26-9 defeat by Neath was not calculated to encourage, while Bridgend knocked them out of the Welsh Cup. 'Cambrian' felt that they had not been the same since losing three of their best players to the North during the previous season. But better news was forthcoming off the field, with plans for the 30,000 capacity Penarth Road Stadium, their intended home, accepted by Speedway's ruling body in December. 'Cambrian' as ever remained optimistic: "To me it seems ludicrous that people consider that Cardiff, with the greatest Rugby Union team in the country, could not raise an average RL team". The chance for his faith to be tested was confirmed on 30 April 1951, when Cardiff were finally elected as members of the Rugby League alongside Doncaster.

Cardiff enter the League

When the new season started those high hopes were rapidly dashed. Cardiff's first week as a League club was hardly disgraceful despite them failing to win. They finished with three defeats away to Hull Kingston Rovers then at home to Widnes and Hull. There were indications that they lacked the physical strength and staying power necessary for senior League, falling away after half time both in the 39-13 debut defeat at Hull Kingston Rovers and the 27-10 loss to Widnes on their home debut. Wing Milson Hunt made a great impression in all three matches. The *Western Mail* reporter cheerfully concluded that Cardiff had "justified their election" against Widnes and "did better" in the 31-10 home loss to Hull, destined to finish third at the end of the season.

But warning signs were already there. A crowd of 2,500 for the Widnes game had fallen to 1,500 for the visit of Hull - far from adequate for a professional club during this period. While none of the matches had been a massacre, they were still conceding points at an average of more than 30 per game - a high score in the 1950s.

The *Western Mail* noted that they had fielded three different hookers in their first three matches, symptomatic of the instability of the team as a whole. A fourth hooker would appear in the following match, and a fifth two games later. Of the team who faced Hull KR only the half-backs Pugh and Bennett remained in the same positions for the Widnes match, with six new faces introduced. Thirty-two different players were to appear in the first five matches, with shirt numbers 4, 5, 8 and 10 changing hands for every game.

It is perhaps little wonder that the roof fell in with a vengeance in the next two matches. First came a visit to Central Park, with Wigan enjoying perhaps their greatest period before the 1980s. Wigan had just won the Challenge Cup - and that was the only trophy they were not to take in 1951-2 as they captured both Lancashire trophies and the Championship. Cardiff, with 11 changes, five of them positional, from the team who had lost at home to Hull, went down 72-5.

Even worse was to come at home to Barrow on 8 September. Barrow would contribute three players to the Great Britain team who beat Australia in the following season. If not in Wigan's class, they were a good side. But they had taken two matches to run up 62 points in their cup-tie against Welsh League Llanelli the season before, held to a respectable 23-9 in West Wales.

On this visit to Wales they took only 80 minutes to run up 66 points to Cardiff's 13. It was, the *Western Mail* reported: "A true reflection of the play". Barrow had even eased up in the second half, but "could not fail to score for the tackling of the Cardiff backs was woefully weak".

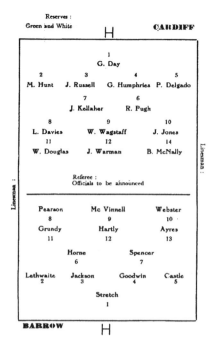

1
G. Day

2   3   4   5
M. Hunt   J. Russell   G. Humphries   P. Delgado

7   6
J. Kellaher   R. Pugh

8   9   10
L. Davies   W. Wagstaff   J. Jones

11   12   14
W. Douglas   J. Warman   B. McNally

Referee :
Officials to be announced

Pearson   Mc Vinnell   Webster
8   9   10

Grundy   Hartly   Ayres
11   12   13

Horne   Spencer
6   7

Lathwaite   Jackson   Goodwin   Castle
2   3   4   5

Stretch
1

BARROW   H

Cardiff versus Barrow programme teams, including Great Britain star Willie Horne at stand-off for Barrow. He scored 12 goals in Barrow's victory - for many years a club record

Cardiff 1951-2, at Belle Vue 6 October 1951. Back: R. Thomas, Gibson, Campbell, Proctor, Bennett, Rosser, Douglas. Sitting: O'Brien, Meadows, McNally, Hunt, Hughes. Kneeling: Pugh, M. Thomas. Photo courtesy Robert Gate.

Stand-off Willie Horne claimed 24 points from 12 goals while Jim Lewthwaite, on one wing, claimed five tries and Frank Castle, on the other, three.

Worst of all perhaps, was the attendance, reported as a mere 200, while the city's Rugby Union club was pulling in 22,000 for the visit of Swansea.

Defeat followed defeat through September, although the scores were a little less spectacular - indeed they finished the month with a respectable display away to champions Workington Town, going down only 30-8 and leading the *Western Mail* reporter, most likely a Cumbria-based agency man, to comment that they had "nothing to reproach themselves for". But they still had no points and had broken the pledge made on leaving the Welsh League, that they would continue to run a second team in competition. It had been withdrawn in late September.

Something clearly had to be done. Perhaps it was the next match, against Belle Vue Rangers, that gave the Rugby League the idea. Cardiff maintained their relative improvement, leading by eight points in as many minutes before going down 25-14. But the distinctive aspect of this game was the number of Welshmen on the field - 20 in all, with the home club fielding seven.

A reminder of the extent of Welsh talent in League was timely. Back as far as the Barrow game, the *Western Mail* had argued that the Cardiff club needed new players if it was to be viable. Now the Rugby League acted on this viewpoint. James Hilton, the chairman of the League management committee, visited Cardiff together with Wigan representative Tom Hesketh, to look into the state of the club. They affirmed their commitment to the club: "Cardiff Rugby League club will definitely carry on... there is no intention... to cancel their membership at the end of the present season", and announced that Welsh former League players who had returned to Wales would be allowed to play for Cardiff without a fee having to be paid to their former clubs.

The *Western Mail* listed 10 notable players who came into this category. Over the next few weeks most would indeed be recruited by Cardiff, notably goal-kicking former Great Britain captain and centre or forward Ted Ward, who became player coach. He joined the club from Oldham, and was described by Robert Gate in *Code 13* as "one of the true stars of the game from 1945 to 1950". He was an excellent signing, who scored 34 goals and four tries for the struggling Welsh club.

Other signings included former Salford full-back Glyn Moses, Leeds loose-forward Les Thomas and Batley hooker Cliff Carter. Nine new players in all were recruited in a matter of weeks.

Critics noticed an immediate improvement, particularly in the pack. The first victory was recorded, at the 13th attempt, on 27 October as York went down 12-6 to a Cardiff team inspired by Les Thomas, "playing superior football and with a fervour that surprised even their most ardent supporters".

But hopes that a permanent turnaround might be inspired by the new recruits were rapidly dashed. After Moses had played three impressive matches Salford refused him permission to play further because they wanted a transfer fee for him. He would not play again for Cardiff, but was signed by Jim Sullivan for St Helens from Salford in 1952. He went on to play for Great Britain, and to tour Australia twice.

There was also a creditable display against the New Zealand tourists, who were held to 18-10 in front of a 2,000 crowd at Penarth Road on a Wednesday afternoon. But this attendance was put into context by the 40,000 crowd who three days later watched

THE STADIUM
Penarth Road, CARDIFF
RUGBY LEAGUE

Wednesday, Dec. 12th
Kick-off at 2.15 p.m.

**NEW
ZEALAND**
versus
CARDIFF

Programmes - - Sixpence

Printed by Storey Bros., Neath

Swansea play the South African Union tourists.

There were no more wins until Christmas Day, when fellow strugglers Liverpool City were seen off 11-0 away. But at least the massacres had stopped. Leigh, who finished seventh were twice run close, and champions Workington Town held to a respectable 18-8 at Penarth Road.

If the figures quoted by the *Western Mail* are to be believed, attendances at Penarth Road oscillated between 200 and 1,700 - presumably in relation to other attractions offered locally, because one of the lowest attendances was for the visit of champions Workington Town complete with Welsh legend Gus Risman. The crowd was given as 212 - and this presumably includes the Workington players, who paid their admission fees as a gesture of goodwill. An attendance of around 250 against Wakefield Trinity generated receipts of £12, not even enough to pay the referee and touch-judges.

Survival

The club could not possibly survive on such attendances. While it was not directly stated that there was no other way to ensure its continuation, the Rugby League's decision to guarantee Cardiff for the rest of the season has to be seen in these terms.

The *Rugby League Review Annual* for 1952 would refer to the withdrawal of the club's financial backer at this point in the season. *Rugby League Review* columnist Vincent Firth, evidently the archetype of those who see no point in expansion beyond what is now called the M62 corridor - later in the season he would call for the abandonment of Wembley as the Challenge Cup Final venue - argued with much spleen that the RL "should pull out of Wales completely and not continue to throw good money after bad... the North has for too long been the milch cow of the Welsh Valleys".

Firth's knowledge of Welsh geography was deficient - Cardiff is on a coastal plain. But maybe he had a point. The last few months of Cardiff's season were a depressing struggle with few redeeming features. There were three more wins after that Christmas defeat of struggling Liverpool City - against Rochdale, City again and then Bramley. Cardiff were part of League history when Bradford Northern staged the first League match under lights, going down 38-5 in front of 16,000 spectators. Hunt was capped for Wales against Other Nationalities, giving them further representative honours.

Bradford Northern versus Cardiff
12 January 1952
under floodlights.

Final match

The end came at home to Wigan on 26 April 1952, but not at Penarth Road. The Maindy

Stadium was adopted for the day, and 1,450 people saw a side containing only three survivors from the team who had set out so hopefully eight months and a few days earlier - Hunt, half-back Pugh and prop Gibson - go down 59-14 to Wigan.

They didn't actually finish bottom. Coming bottom took some doing in the 1948 to 1954 period when Liverpool City, with 45 points from 216 games, were putting together a record six consecutive wooden spoons. The double over City saved Cardiff at least from that ignominy. But the final Wigan romp took Cardiff's points against total into four figures. They were the only team to concede more than 1,000 points in more than half a century between the Liverpool City team of 1906-7, whose 30 straight defeats and points difference of 76 for and 1,398 against make them unchallengeably the worst senior team in history, and the Doncaster team of 1959-60. Their final league record was:

Played	Won	Drawn	Lost	For	Against	Points	Position
36	5	0	31	342	1,024	10	30th

But such a record, combined with atrocious attendances and untenable finances, made their survival impossible. Within two days of the Wigan match, on 28 April, Cardiff had resigned from the Rugby League.

Firth, in another bilious column, accused the Welsh of being bad losers who "prefer an inferior brand of rugby to enable them to win". Rugby League accounts showed that payments to Cardiff had been £2,324, which an outraged leader column in *Rugby League Review* reckoned equated to a total loss of about twice as much over three seasons of Welsh development: "And what have we to show for this staggering expenditure? NOTHING - JUST NOTHING. What a pity the Rugby Football League's auditors have no power to surcharge the Council members for this amount".

The RFL annual meeting was told that Cardiff's real loss, once the share of pools and other income was taken into account, was £866. The 1952 *Rugby League Review Annual* said the Welsh development was "doomed from the beginning" and the RL Annual Report referred to "a very dismal record, attracting very little public interest".

J.R. Jones, argued in the *Rugby Leaguer*, that: "The sponsors of Rugby League in Wales have been attempting the impossible. They have in plain language demanded of the Welshmen that they renounce the habits of a lifetime, forget the fruits of accumulated experience and that they forsake all the pride and tradition engendered by close on a century of Rugby Union football, and accept instead a version of Rugby football which cuts across and outraged their every concept of the game - and all this overnight."

Cardiff were readmitted to the Welsh League which staggered on for another three seasons until the end of 1954-5. Graham Morris argues that their failure had destroyed the Welsh League's sense of purpose. It would be more than a quarter of a century before professional League returned to Wales as part of a league competition.

Postscript

Professional club Rugby League made a short-lived return to South Wales at the end of the 1958-9 season. A Midlands businessman promoted the games, and according to newspaper reports lost a great deal of money. On Whit Monday, St Helens beat a Welsh

XIII 44-28 at Llanelli, 3,593 attended the 'missionary' game, with Stan Owen scoring 10 points for the Welsh side.

Two days later, 1,250 spectators saw St Helens triumph again, 35-19 at Pontypool. The final match took place at Cardiff's Maindy Stadium, the venue for the 1951-2 Cardiff club's last match. This time 3,217 fans saw St Helens win 47-31. The game may have lost money for the promoters, but it did give the Welsh public a rare chance to see Billy Boston's "wonderful running", as he scored two of the Welsh tries.

Part Four:

The modern era

Chapter 9: International matches in the modern era

Welshmen continued to head north to earn money openly for playing rugby throughout the two-decade absence of international Rugby League from their homeland in the fifties and sixties and players the calibre of Lewis Jones, Billy Boston (who was never capped for Wales at Union or League), David Watkins, John Mantle and Clive Sullivan, all enriched their careers and the sport with Great Britain test appearances. Yet, save for three unofficial matches by Welsh XIIIs in France in 1955, 1959 and 1963, all lost, the Welsh international team was never considered a serious proposition.

But then television took an interest in Rugby League. The game was seen as a decent and cheap space-filler for sports programmes and, in the late 1960s, both the RFL and TV saw an excuse to revive the three-cornered European Championship. The Welsh team competed in its first full international matches for 15 years but sadly the view still prevailed that Welsh home games would take place in the north of England and Welsh rugby supporters were denied, for the short duration of the unpopular European competition, the possibility of seeing their former heroes back on home soil.

Yet, as Robert Gate pointed out in *Open Rugby* magazine, the competitiveness of any such tournament is undermined if one team is denied home fixtures. He wrote that "the record [of Wales] for games played in the principality is much better than their overall record" and said that, at home, they had won more games than they had lost against all opposition except Australia. "The argument for allowing Wales to play their home games in the land of their fathers is strengthened when their away record against England is considered." Wales had only ever won six matches there despite playing more than 30. Yet still home matches were denied to the Welsh players and public.

As a taster to the launch of the European Championship, Wales played both England and France away during the 1968-69 season and experienced a successful return to the international stage when, on 7 November 1968 they beat England at Salford 24-17 with a team that contained the likes of Clive Sullivan (soon to be a Lions captain), David Watkins, Kel Coslett and Colin Dixon. Later that season, in March, they travelled to Paris where they lost to France 17-13 with Gordon Lewis of Leigh scoring two tries.

The following season's European Championship proved to be a frustrating one for the Welsh team as they were beaten twice at Headingley by the English 40-23 and 26-7 yet they went on to defeat France at Perpignan 15-11 after losing 8-2 at Salford. The victory in France handed the English the title - they had lost and drawn with the French but ended up champions on points difference - and also spawned one of international Rugby League's nastier incidents when the referee for the Perpignan match, Dickie Thomas, was attacked by irate French supporters. Violence aside, the tournament had not raised sufficient interest and, with the 1970 and 1972 World Cups looming - the latter during which, of course, British captain and Welsh wingman Clive Sullivan played a legendary role by scoring a crucial length-of-the-field try in the final - the Euro competition was shelved once again.

It would be five more years before the Welsh national side would take to the field but, when they did, it would be as part of one of the International Board's more ambitious projects. The 1975 World Championship was the first to see five nations competing for the crown as Great Britain was divided into separate English and Welsh teams. Although the British were set to oppose the dilution of their challenge it was clear that the French proposal to the International Board was likely to be supported by Australia and New Zealand and the British were forced to accept the compromise.

However, the number of Welshmen coming into Rugby League, as economic conditions worsened in Britain, had increased to such a level that the new administration at the Rugby Football League, headed by David Oxley, was prepared to contemplate the proposal. Ever the internationalist, Oxley, who replaced the autocratic Bill Fallowfield as secretary, considered a Welsh squad had a viable competitive future. Players who were to play a big part in British Rugby League in the seventies and eighties such as David Watkins, Tony Fisher, the Bradford Northern hooker, the infamous prop Jim Mills and top-try scorer Roy Mathias, had all made the switch to League and at last Wales were deemed strong enough (and marketable enough) to compete in their own right. Such a division at World Cup level would not be seen again until 1995.

Prior to the start of this new competition and to give the newly revived international teams of England and Wales much needed competition, the triangular series of matches between the three European League-playing nations was reintroduced and played in early 1975, just before the World Cup began in March. In January the English beat France at Perpignan and when Wales went on to lose 12-8 to England at Salford on 25 February it became clear that their match nine days earlier at Swansea against France had been the wooden spoon decider. Yet it was, in retrospect, an historic event for the Welsh international Rugby League team was once more deemed fit to be presented to its home nation.

Return home

On 16 February 1975 Wales played an international at home for the first time since December 1951 - 14 matches and nearly 24 years had passed. And people were pretty keen to see their former heroes who had headed to the north of England. The crush on the turnstiles at the St Helen's ground was such that they had to be opened to let the crowd in and an estimated 15,000 lined the terraces. And they were not to be disappointed. A 21-8 Welsh win was sealed after a stunning second- half performance saw them turn a 2-3 deficit into victory with Colin Dixon and Jim Mills unstoppable in the forwards.

Estimating the crowd at a little higher than the official figure, a contemporary newspaper report announced that: "More than 20,000 fans flocked to Swansea to give a magnificent welcome home to the Welsh team and leave Rugby League officials shaking their heads in disbelief. It is nearly 25 years since the League staged an international in Wales but plans are already going ahead to play one of the World Championship matches at Swansea in October. So many fans were queuing up outside the St Helen's ground that overworked officials opened the gates and let in around 3,000 supporters 15 minutes after the start and they weren't disappointed."

The *South Wales Echo* continued the upbeat mood. It quoted a "delighted" David Oxley as saying: "The response of the Welsh public to this match has been fantastic. We are absolutely thrilled, not only with the attendance - but also with the fervour of the crowd." It was Oxley who had given the order to allow people in for free, reasoning that those people still outside would be deprived of seeing a match and might not come back in the future.

Welsh skipper, David Watkins, declared: "We can hardly wait to come back. It was a very emotional occasion and many of us were on the verge of tears."

Perhaps the emotion overtook the Welsh players as they struggled to perform well in the first half, Kel Coslett's penalty for the home team being bettered by a Victor Serrano penalty and a Jean-Marie Imbert drop goal (now worth only a single point) as the Welsh trailed 2-3. But from then on it was all plain sailing for the Welsh. Watkins landed the equalising drop goal shortly after the break and four minutes later centre David Willicombe opened up the defence to feed his winger Roy Mathias and Wales, with Coslett converting from the touchline, led 8-3.

Tony Fisher, playing a fine game at hooker, flicked out a splendid short pass for John Bevan to score on the left wing and, only seconds later, Jim Mills broke through three tackles to score a great solo try, Coslett's conversion giving the Welsh a 16-3 lead.

A French revival which led to a 30-yard sprint for the line by stand-off Michel Moliner and conversion by Victor Serrano was nipped in the bud by Bevan's second try, Coslett's goal giving Wales a popular and emphatic 21-8 victory.

Indeed the only words of caution came from the *South Wales Echo* which had obviously sent its Union writer to the match. He spoke to a Welsh Union official who suggested that: "Rugby League will never be a threat to Rugby Union in Wales. The pattern of play is too predictable, too monotonous. Although it was worth £1 to watch, I found myself missing the rucks, mauls and line-outs. People didn't come to see Rugby League, they came to see David Watkins and John Bevan."

The writer agreed but did add that "as long as there are personality players like these the Welsh Rugby League team will always draw a good crowd." With the World Championship fast approaching it was to be hoped that he would be proved correct.

World Championship

When the World Championship finally got underway the Welsh appointed Les Pearce, then with Leigh, as coach for the competition after he had already coached Wales in the two matches against France and England. Former second-row forward Pearce had turned professional with Halifax in 1949 and had been an international Union trialist while playing with Swansea. It was a fine squad he had at his disposal for the eight matches his side would play but, unfortunately for the team, the long-winded World Championship of 1975 was probably not the ideal stage on which to make a global debut.

While the 20-match format gave Wales their first opportunity to play matches outside Europe it was, as Keith Macklin describes it in *The Story of Rugby League*: "a bewildering and long-drawn-out hotchpotch of fixtures, and crowds varied between 33,858 for Australia versus England at Sydney to 1,581 at Bordeaux for France against England. The long series of international matches stretched at intervals over nine months and parts of two seasons. It was unwieldy and did not inspire great enthusiasm." And, with all the nations losing somewhere in the region of £10,000 each it was, therefore, hardly the stage that Wales needed to relaunch an international future.

Welsh success was made doubly difficult when they learned that, unlike the other four nations, two of their 'home' games would be played outside Wales. Their last match of the tournament was a 23-2 victory against France at Salford but, even more ludicrous, their opening 'home' fixture was against England in Brisbane! This was the fourth match of the tournament - Wales had already lost to France in Toulouse in March (only days after completing the European Championship campaign against the same nation), England had beaten France at Headingley and Australia had beaten New Zealand in Brisbane - but, ironically, Wales's 'home' match in Brisbane was to have a great bearing on the championship for they defeated England on 10 June 1975 12-7 with tries from Clive Sullivan and David Treasure of Oldham. Although the match was marred by brawling, it was a victory that Welsh League supporters and players still recall today. When the final table was drawn up in November of that year the Australians topped it by a single point leaving the runners-up England to regret the Brisbane defeat.

Only four days after the match against England the Welsh were due in Sydney to play Australia. A crowd of 25,386 saw the green and golds, with legends such as Graeme Langlands, Bob Fulton and Tommy Raudonikis all scoring tries, take victory by 30-13 in a match which saw a total of 14 goals landed by David Watkins and Mick Cronin.

Wales's next outing came two weeks later as they moved on to Auckland to take on the Kiwis. In addition to their international commitments they had also scored victories in tour matches against Ipswich (in Brisbane), and Wellington, West Coast and Canterbury. And, after the New Zealand World Championship match, they stayed on to lose to Auckland and defeat the New Zealand Maoris.

The match against the New Zealanders was another close affair but five goals from Warren Collicoat saw the Kiwis home 13-8 even though the Welsh scored two tries to the home team's one.

Yet further defeat was to follow when the competition returned to the northern hemisphere in September. The English avenged their Brisbane setback at Warrington, beating Wales 22-16 and next up were the Australians. David Oxley had been as good as his word and Wales were given the chance to perform in front of their own public as the World Championship table-topping Kangaroos arrived in Europe to complete their fixtures in England and France as well as the principality. Although they were to lose to England at Headingley in November by 16-13, their crushing 41-2 success over France in Perpignan the previous month would ensure that they became world champions as England rued the defeat to the Welsh in Brisbane.

The 1975 Wales World Championship squad. Photo courtesy *Open Rugby*

116

But on 19 October, the Australians arrived in Swansea, still needing to beat Wales to keep their championship hopes intact. This was the Australian team captained by the rugged Queenslander Arthur Beetson and it contained stars of the Sydney competition such as wing Ian Schubert and goal-kicking master Mick Cronin.

Glyn Turner was the man picked by the *South Wales Echo* as the likely Welsh hero. He had only recently left Ebbw Vale Union club to play for Hull Kingston Rovers and was returning to Wales to play stand-off (or fly-half as the newspaper put it) for his country. "I never expected to play in Wales again," he told the *Echo*, revealing the hostility still reserved in Union circles in Wales for those who chose to make an honest living from their talent.

But with coach trips organised from all over the country Turner was looking forward to seeing a big crowd at the match. "I think Wales are in with a good chance of winning," he added optimistically. "Tomorrow's match means a tremendous amount to me and all the Welsh boys," he concluded, underlining the difference playing on home soil makes to players of any nationality.

Captain David Watkins hoped the crowd might top 20,000 (in the event just more than 11,000 turned up) and he too talked a good game. "If I didn't honestly believe we could win I would not bother to turn up," he said confidently.

The Welsh were always going to put up a fight in match which was also televised by the BBC and in the first half two Watkins penalties saw the home team lead 4-2 against one goal from Cronin. But the main action had been the constant aggravation shown between Beetson and his opposite number at prop, Jim Mills. Mills was a controversial character throughout his career but this World Championship was to prove his nadir. Watkins had already declared before the match that "the sheer power and ball-playing ability of [Beetson] is astonishing. He will be in direct opposition to Mills - and their duel should be a feature of the game."

Watkins was right. The pair were involved in three brawls which drew in other players and tended to draw attention away from the otherwise excellent play on show. The *Guardian* told us how superb the Kangaroos were: "The Australians certainly did back up well. Moreover, they did so with speed and assurance. They made the most, not only of their speed but of their physical strength." Eventually this strength was to tell for, after Watkins had edged Wales into a 6-2 lead with another penalty, Australian full-back Graham Eadie - who was to star in Britain with Halifax in the 1980s - received the ball on his own line and, combining with wing Schubert, famous for his long-blonde hair as well as his phenomenal ability, put John Peard of Easts under the posts.

Indeed it was Schubert who became the architect of the Welsh defeat. As Harold Mather wrote in The *Guardian*: "Prompted well, the Australian threequarters clearly were the faster set once they had settled down and, although it was teamwork which mattered it nevertheless was a pleasure to see a wing as young as the 19-year-old Schubert. He was playing in schoolboy football last year but showed good speed and took his chances so well. Without doubt he is an exciting prospect for the future." He was exciting on that day too because he scored a second-half hat-trick which virtually secured the world title for Australia and won him the man-of-the-match award. With Cronin converting two of the tries in addition to his first-half penalty, the Australians were good value for their 18-6 win.

Wales were certainly defeated by a better team that contained an outstanding pack.

Beetson was ably supported by Greg Veivers and Manly's Terry Randall and the Australian forwards were as strong on defence as they were on attack. At stand-off, Peard made the most of the possession and fed his back line well, coping with the departure of loose-forward John Quayle and scrum-half Johnny Mayes with injuries.

Welsh coach Pearce said: "They [Australia] are always looking for the ball, they do the basics well, and they're very, very fit. We are not disgraced." Watkins added that "twice when we had chances they finished up at the other end of the park and scored. But give them credit. That is what international football is all about."

Wales were beaten mainly by the strength and pace of the Australians for they were capable of matching the Kangaroos in skill, just unable to restrain the forward surges and rapid support play. Peter Banner of Featherstone at scrum-half, John Bevan and Bill Francis all played their part but, in the end, they had to concede defeat.

Sadly, the *South Wales Echo* offered little comment on the match itself, preferring to concentrate on the clashes which marred the game. Under a headline of "Brawl? this was 'mild' - Watkins" readers were treated to 10 paragraphs detailing the fighting followed by two paragraphs listing the scorers. Although Watkins insisted that "When one thinks of all the ferocity like the Newport-Pontypridd [Union] match this season such incidents as yesterday are mild when regarded in terms of people kicking each other."

The *Echo* also listed the crowd as being in the region of 20,000 which was in stark contrast to the official figure of 11,112 prompting Trevor Delaney to write: "There seemed to be thousands more in the ground and the Rugby League authorities were a little suspicious."

A crowd of 20,000 would have done wonders for the game's standing in Wales but instead most of the reports concentrated on the reasonably low turn-out and the violence of the Mills-Beetson flare-ups. Unfortunately for the sport neither of these criticisms could be dispelled when New Zealand arrived in Swansea for the last Welsh home match of the 1975 World Championship on 2 November.

Despite an exciting 25-24 victory for the Welsh, this game, played out before a tiny 2,645 crowd is remembered for one thing alone, Jim Mills's brutal trampling on Kiwi prop John Greengrass in the last minute of a very physical, bad-tempered match. Mills was dismissed by Monsieur Jameau, the French referee, but his actions were to have repercussions throughout the late seventies.

Mills was banned for life by the New Zealand RL and had to withdraw from the 1977 World Cup held in both New Zealand and Australia. Mills was also on the 1979 Lions tour to Australasia but, perhaps fortunately for the sake of diplomacy, he had to withdraw from the squad because of injury in Australia and never suffered the humiliation of being banned from playing when the Lions arrived in New Zealand.

While it is impossible to separate the match from the incident, the small crowd were treated to a close encounter. Bill Francis, playing stand-off for the Welsh had put them into the lead with two tries, both goaled by David Watkins as was a fine effort by John Bevan. A further Watkins penalty gave the Welsh a 17-14 lead at half time. Tony Coll, the Kiwi forward who won the man-of-the- match award and Philip Orchard, the right wing, had replied with tries for New Zealand with Tony Gordon kicking four goals.

Within a minute of the restart, a try by Gordon levelled the scores but David Willicombe restored the Welsh lead shortly afterwards with a Watkins-converted try. Then the game began to deteriorate into sporadic brawling as John Mantle increased the lead with a powerful try, but still the New Zealanders fought back as Wales tried desperately to hang on to their lead. A Gordon penalty reduced the gap to six points but, in the final minute, came the game's defining moment. Greengrass scored a remarkable try but, in the act of scoring, Mills committed his violent act and the Kiwi left the field (alongside the dismissed Welshman) requiring several facial stitches. Gordon converted the try but the Kiwis had no time left and the Welsh snatched a 25-24 victory.

Notwithstanding the nasty incident, the paltry crowd left the RL authorities looking despairingly at the financial implications of the 1975 tournament. Even though the Welsh finished third in the final table when the competition's last match saw them beat France in the 'home' game at Salford, it was clear that the long-winded format and global travel arrangements had cost the nations dearly - a precursor to the ill-fated World Club Championship of 1997 perhaps? Bill Fallowfield, honorary secretary of the International Board, also declared that there was no chance of Wales participating in any future competitions. The next World Cup in 1977 returned to the four nations format with Great Britain playing as a combined team, and it would be 1995 before the Welsh national team would compete in another World Cup.

It would also be three years before they played another home fixture because, although the European Championship was again revived in 1976-77, the Welsh once more played home games in England. France won the 1976-77 title defeating England 28-15 in Carcassonne and Wales 13-2 in Toulouse in what was effectively the decider after the Welsh had opened the championship on 29 January 1977 with a 6-2 win over England at Headingley. Surprisingly, the following season France lost all their games - Wales beat them 29-7 at Widnes, but lost the deciding match to England at St Helens in May 1978 by a whopping 60-13, a match which prompted Welsh team manager Ronnie Simpson to air doubts over Wales's continued existence as an RL nation.

Kangaroos' visit

It didn't auger well for the Welsh who, thanks to their permanent entry in the European Championship, were granted a tour match at Swansea against the 1978 Kangaroos. The world champions were already giving notice of their intent to be the leading international force in the game, a mantle that has stayed with them until the present day. Captained by Bob Fulton, later to be a World Cup-winning coach, the Australians would go on to take the Ashes as they beat Great Britain in the first test at Wigan 15-9, only to lose the second at Odsal 18-14 in what was to be Great Britain's last victory over Australia for 10 long years. Welshmen Jim Mills and Tony Fisher played a huge part in that victory as an ageing forward pack took the game to the tourists. The decider, however, was duly won 23-6 by Australia at Headingley and Great Britain entered an international wilderness from which they are yet to fully emerge.

Yet in the opening international fixture of the tour, on 15 October 1978, the Welsh had given the tourists a mighty scare. The match itself wasn't up to much and Wales were accused of being negative in order to keep the score low in a game marred by numerous penalties for over-vigorous play but, in the context of Australia's subsequent domination of the world game, the 8-3 defeat was a very creditable result. The tourists had lost earlier that week to Warrington, still the last club team to beat Australia in Britain, and were pleased to get away with a victory as the first test loomed.

Captain David Watkins, scorer of all Wales's points with a first-half penalty and drop goal, admitted that Wales had tried to stifle the match. "We played the game not to lose badly rather than win," he said. "We didn't realise we could have won it until it was too late."

Wales took an early lead too, with Watkins's scores and it wasn't until injury time in the first half that Welsh concentration lapsed and Tommy Raudonikis, the best Kangaroo that day by far, raced over from a quick play-the-ball. Mick Cronin converted to give Australia a 5-3 half-time lead.

The second half, though, was one of containment for the Welsh yet, had Watkins kicked three penalties - the first coming from obstruction of flying wing John Bevan by Australian full-back Graham Eadie - the result could have been very different. Watkins lamented the failure of the Welsh to use Bevan and his right-wing counterpart Clive Sullivan to greater effect and, when Bob Fulton took advantage of a tiring Welsh defence in the 76th minute from another play-the-ball, the Welsh could only ponder on what might have been. Tony Fisher went close in the dying seconds but the Australian defence held firm to secure the 8-3 victory.

Apart from the two tries the Welsh defence had been sound but as the *Guardian* reported: "They played hard and spared nothing in effort but when the time came to demonstrate their attacking flair they disappointed... Wales seemed so preoccupied with caution that they often looked incapable of snapping out of the pattern."

But the Welsh performance in keeping the Australian score low gave heart to the Great Britain management watching the game. As Raymond Fletcher, writing in the *Yorkshire Post* said: "[The Great Britain team] can at least match Wales for grit and still have enough ability to outwit Australia in the First Test." Australian forwards Greg Pierce and George Peponis both suffered injuries in a bruising encounter as did Raudonikis, Eadie and Graham Olling, who broke his nose and the British were encouraged to see how robust tactics could disrupt the tourists. The Great Britain manager Harry Womersley was impressed by the Welsh performance saying "They surprised me by going all the way. I am more confident than ever that Britain will regain the Ashes." Unfortunately his optimism was misplaced. Australia were not to play so badly again and any hope of a series victory was lost at Headingley.

Penalties marred the Swansea game though, as did the poor crowd of only 4,250. They witnessed a scrappy encounter that did little to enhance the sport's reputation in Wales. Referee Ron Campbell awarded 37 penalties as Jim Mills and Rod Reddy clashed repeatedly in bone-jarring scrum collisions. Incidentally Campbell would not allow the Australians to use sand as a goal-kicking aid even though they had been granted permission at the start of the tour. Unsurprisingly, he didn't prove popular with kicker Mick Cronin when he told him "I'm having none of that".

Trevor Skerrett, making his Welsh debut, was perhaps the only star of a pack that lost the scrums 11-9. According to The *Guardian* he made three tackles in the first minute, and kept up an astonishing rate throughout. He was to share the man-of-the-match award with Raudonikis. Eddie Cunningham of St Helens was another solid performer, this time in the Welsh threequarters, and his team-mate Bill Francis at stand-off created the few Welsh openings but still found himself out of favour with the British selectors when incumbent Englishman Roger Millward was selected for Great Britain the following week.

For Australia, Bob Fulton had a fine captain's game, often screaming at his team to organise in defence, as well as taking the ball up on numerous occasions, while Steve Rogers proved to be an elusive runner.

Sadly the game was marred further when Clive Sullivan, achieving his ambition of playing Rugby League on Welsh soil, accused Kangaroo full-back Eadie of racial abuse. Referee Campbell warned Eadie but took no further action and a disappointing match sank even further.

The crowd figure was 2,000 below the average for Swansea RUFC who played at the same venue leaving David Oxley, secretary of the RFL, to say: "It was very disappointing," although he was quick to blame the poor weather conditions earlier in the day. That fact notwithstanding, it was to be three years before the Welsh played another fixture in their home country despite continuing to play England and France each year.

Wales lost both of their other matches in 1978-79, 18-8 to France in Narbonne and 15-7 to England at Widnes as England took the European title when they beat France at Warrington. The following season, 1979-80, also saw the Welsh lose both games but their opening match of the campaign, a 21-7 reverse to the French at Naughton Park, Widnes, was cause for minor celebration as the national team played its 100th fixture. Sadly only 2,804 witnessed the event which, while providing further disappointment to a hard core of supporters of Rugby League in the principality, was a testament to the staying power of the Welsh national team, sometimes despite decades of neglect.

Only 29 of those 100 international matches had been won by the Welsh and, when they lost the remaining fixture of that season's campaign 26-9 to champions England and the two matches in 1980-81 to both England and that year's champions France, the European Championship, still no generator of supporter interest was, once again, discontinued. It seemed that the Welsh team might once more sink ignominiously out of existence with only a few stalwart expansionist dreamers lamenting its demise.

But a saviour was on hand. The end of the European competition coincided with a boom at club level in Britain. The formation of Fulham RLFC in 1980 transformed the game in this country. For the first time for many seasons new clubs and expansionist RL supporters had a role model in the astoundingly successful Londoners who won promotion in their very first season playing to large crowds in the capital.

Cardiff Blue Dragons

It was the catalyst League supporters outside the game's heartlands had been waiting long for and, buoyed by the success of Fulham, Cardiff Blue Dragons based at Ninian Park, home of the Welsh football team and Cardiff City Football Club, were admitted to the RFL for season 1981-2. Prodigal Welsh rugby son David Watkins was managing director, Welsh international John Mantle was the coach and the club, emerging from almost nothing a few months before, shocked the Rugby Union world by signing four Welsh Union internationals: Steve Fenwick, Tommy David, Paul Ringer and Brynmor Williams. It was to be a short-lived presence that began to stutter almost as soon as it was born but it proved to be the catalyst for a bout of expansionist fervour at RLHQ as the Welsh national team was reprieved to play a promotional fixture at Ninian Park against England.

This game was designed to market the new club with most of Cardiff's Union captures on show as David Watkins admitted in an article in the *South Wales Echo*. It was obvious that this time the RFL could not be criticised for not taking promotional matches to where they were required.

Under the article headed: "Beaten Wales could be a winner with youngsters" - Wales were to lose the match 20-15 - Watkins was described as "harbouring plans which are likely to cause the Rugby Union establishment infinitely more concern than the defection of the likes of Steve Fenwick, Tommy David and Paul Ringer."

Watkins said that "seeing a showpiece fixture like this must encourage youngsters to take up Rugby League. That must be our objective at Cardiff - to put down roots and bring on young players of our own." Watkins added that young players were welcome to train at Ninian Park with the Blue Dragons. Joe Lovejoy, the author of the *Echo* article added that coach-loads of schoolboys were present among the astounding 13,173 crowd (after the initial official figure was given as 8,102).

David Howes of the RFL said that the international had been played specifically to stimulate interest in the code in South Wales and, fortunately for all concerned, the match lived up to its billing. As Lovejoy noted "England, predictably, had the class, but equally predictably, Welsh commitment turned the game into a rousing contest."

Paul Fitzpatrick, writing in the *Guardian*, said: "Wales gave a highly creditable account of themselves in this first Rugby League international at Ninian Park yesterday but found that England were always out of reach."

And so it proved. At half time the scores were tied 5-5, but England broke away well against a tiring Welsh team in the second period and took an unassailable 20-7 lead before the Welsh pegged the visitors back late in the game.

For that first 40 minutes the Welsh must have felt confident of overturning their rivals as the pack, ably prompted by half-backs Danny Wilson of second division Swinton (now more famously known as the father of Manchester United footballer Ryan Giggs) and Ness Flowers of Wigan, ran and tackled with ruthless efficiency. While centres Fenwick and Steve Bayliss of St Helens were never short of ideas it was a lapse by Fenwick in the 24th minute that allowed Des Drummond in to score. George Fairbairn, the Scottish-born English full-back, had an off-day with the boot but converted Drummond's try to give England the initial lead. However, by half time Wales had bounced back with Fenwick making amends by landing two penalties and Wilson tying the scores with a 35-yard drop goal.

But after the break and for the next half hour it was all England. They should have increased their lead in the 43rd minute when John Woods of Leigh threw out a pass he would have been better advised to hold to winger Henderson Gill of Wigan who dropped the ball with the line begging. The English, though, were growing in confidence and Jeff Grayshon, Phil Lowe and Peter Gorley began to punch holes in the Welsh defence. It wasn't long before both Grayshon and Gorley had powered over for tries and, in the 63rd minute, Gill took a superb pass from Les Dyl to outstrip the Welsh cover.

With Fairbairn handing the kicking duties to Woods, two of the tries were converted and when Woods added a penalty the English lead was up to 20-7, Fenwick having landed a penalty in reply.

Yet in the final minutes Wales changed up a gear. Only Gill's superb cover tackle stopped Steve Bayliss from scoring in the corner but Wales continued to press and, a minute later, Flowers dived over to score. Fenwick, later voted man-of-the-match converted, but failed with a touchline attempt after substitute Paul Prendiville of Hull scored in the corner. Unfortunately for Wales and the appreciative crowd, time had run out with the home team still five points short of their target. It had been a rousing finale and the League authorities were impressed with the response of the public to the match. With this surprising success in mind the RFL planned to stage a tour match against the 1982 Kangaroos at Ninian Park to capitalise on the publicity of the England game, but it was played nearly 13 months later and much had happened by then.

Cardiff Blue Dragons had kicked off in front of a crowd of more than 10,000 against Salford, losing narrowly 26-21. But attendances were set to dwindle after that early high.

The writing had probably been on the wall for the Blue Dragons before the 1982 Kangaroos arrived at Ninian Park for their promotional fixture but worse was to come for Welsh Rugby League, this time on the international stage, for these Australians were the 15th Kangaroos, better known as the Invincibles. This was the team captained by Max Krilich which contained the likes of Eric Grothe, Mal Meninga, Gene Miles, Wally Lewis, Brett Kenny, Peter Sterling, Les Boyd, Wayne Pearce and Ray Price. Many of them would also find fame in club football in Britain but it is as the Invincibles that most will remember them. The squad swept undefeated through Europe, handing out a Rugby League lesson to Britain and France that is still being learnt today.

The British tests were landslide victories: 40-4 at Boothferry Park, Hull; 27-6 at Wigan and 32-8 at Headingley. Great Britain only managed to score one try against them, and France were similarly swept aside. Sadly, even though Australia only played their second string on 24 October 1982 against the Welsh, the result was never going to be in doubt.

Steve Ella was the star of the game at full-back for Australia as he notched four tries, a record for an Australian against Wales but, as far as the home nation was concerned, most of the criticism centred on the lack of pride from the players in the red jerseys. To be fair though, nothing was likely to stop Australia on that day or indeed on that tour. Their skill, fitness and professionalism was a revelation to British eyes and their 37-7 victory was no more than they deserved. It was all an ominous warning for the first test, set to be played the following week.

Ella won the man-of-the-match award, but Cardiff scrum-half Brynmor Williams - one of the few Welshmen to enhance his reputation - ran him a close second. Ella, normally a centre or stand-off, scored his tries as he joined a dominant attack by scything through from the back but Williams played a more individual role and scored Wales's only try in the second half.

David Watkins was now the Welsh coach and he readily admitted that: "We had been out-thought, outfought and outplayed. It was a fairly predictable result." Paul Fitzpatrick in the *Guardian* wrote that Wales were disappointing: "There was never much chance of a repeat of their commendable performance against the 1978 Australians when they lost by only five points."

The Australians scored two tries within the first 25 minutes - one from Ella, the other from Mark Murray - and Wales, by contrast, had missed their only opportunities when Lynn Hopkins failed to land two penalty attempts. Determined tackling had held the Australians at bay but the floodgates were prised apart before half time with further touchdowns from Ella and wing John Ribot who scored twice. Wally Lewis's two conversions left the score at 19-2 after Hopkins had finally landed a kick for the Welsh.

By the time Ella left the field with a twisted ankle in the 69th minute he had scored twice again (one converted by Lewis) and had scored enough points to beat the Welsh team single-handedly. In between his two scores Williams had notched the Welsh try when he burrowed over in the 52nd minute with Steve Fenwick converting, but the Australians finished with a flourish as Don McKinnon and Lewis scored tries which they respectively converted themselves.

The *South Wales Echo* noted that the crowd of 5,617 was a big improvement on Cardiff City's home gate but wondered, correctly in retrospect, whether the likes of Huyton and Doncaster would hold as much attraction as the scintillating Australians.

The Welsh had played five members of the Cardiff Blue Dragons which was the one encouraging sign on a dismal afternoon, but the *Guardian* pointed out that "Wales could not match Australia in any department. As far as Wales were concerned they might have been men from another planet." It was a tough lesson for the Welsh but, then again, it was a tough year for British Rugby League all round.

Return to Ebbw Vale

It was to be two years before the Welsh would play another fixture and then it was only in a one-off attempt to boost interest in the failing Bridgend club, successor to Cardiff Blue Dragons. For the first time in 73 years, on 14 October 1984, international Rugby League returned to the Eugene Cross Park, Ebbw Vale, close to the home of Bridgend Blue Dragons. Results had not been going Bridgend's way - they had failed to win a match up to the arrival of the English national team at Eugene Cross Park - and when it was learned that six of their weak team would play in the Welsh XIII (with a total of eight players from the RFL second division) and the game was to be televised, it was of little surprise that only 2,111 turned up.

The match was previewed in *Open Rugby* magazine which nonetheless hoped that the game would be a good opportunity for the sport to promote itself in the region. The article pointed out that now was the time for "the Welsh to get the utmost support from the rest of the Rugby League world." As Gordon Pritchard, captain of the new Bridgend team pointed out of recent seasons: "There has been little promotion of the game in Wales." *Open Rugby* suggested that the Wales versus England match would be one way of addressing that problem if a regular date and venue could be found for the fixture. Sadly, yet again, it turned out to be hit-and-run and pleas for a regular promotional fixture went unheeded. Indeed it would be seven more long years, following the demise of club Rugby League in Wales, before the national team would return.

The 2,000 plus who did turn out to watch the match saw it go much according to expectations although, after being 22-0 down at half time, the Welsh fought back well in the second half to register a 28-9 defeat. The star of the game was England's Garry Clark who scored a hat-trick from the left wing.

It was Clark who opened the scoring in the left corner after only three minutes prompting what Raymond Fletcher in the *Yorkshire Post* described as all the worst fears of a Welsh annihilation. His hat-trick was completed in only 19 minutes after first he intercepted Danny Wilson's floating pass with 75 yards to run and then took a simple ball from Ellery Hanley to score in the corner once more. A further try from Hanley after a 40-yard dash to the line and two conversions and a penalty from full-back Mick Burke took England out to their 22-0 lead at the break.

Fortunately for Wales the erratic Wilson at stand-off began to play a more pivotal role in the second half to enhance his reputation as either hero or villain and his runs began to break up the English defence. It was he who scored Wales's first points when, in the 46th minute, he dummied his way through the defensive line and sent Burke the wrong way with a clever shimmy before scoring under the posts. Lynn Hallett of Bridgend scored the simple conversion. Wilson, despite having a heavily strapped thigh and having been advised not to play, was selected as Wales's man-of-the-match and he led the Welsh revival from the front, ably supported by wing Phil Ford who constantly came inside looking for the ball. Wilson's injury was to see him leave the field later in the half and the Welsh momentum was halted but not before he had added a drop goal and Hallett had scored a penalty to leave Wales trailing 22-9.

So far the match had been a tough encounter although the *Yorkshire Post* praised the game for being "almost devoid of foul play", while still being a fierce contest with Welsh hooker Chris Preece of Bradford, despite losing heavily in the scrums, and England's Andy Goodway being especially dominant.

But at the death, it was the English who reasserted themselves and hooker Kevin Beardmore, winning the scrums 12-1, struck the ball well from a scrum 25 yards from the Welsh line late in the game. Burke, linking well near the scrum base, took the ball to race in under the posts and add his own conversion. England had won 28-9 but Wales had taken the second half 9-6. Paul Fitzpatrick, writing in *Open Rugby*, said "It was little wonder then that David Watkins [the Welsh coach] found much over which to enthuse." Indeed Watkins was keen to see further international matches for his Welsh team as reported in the *South Wales Echo*. It told us that Watkins was to press the RFL for a match against the French: "If we want the game to expand then we must take it down every possible avenue. I would certainly like to play France in Wales. I think we have fully justified resurrecting the Welsh team." Sadly, his calls too went unheeded.

Writing later in the year the *Shopacheck Rugby League Review Yearbook* said of this match: "This international, played in the heartland of Rugby Union, was arguably a

Wales versus England at Ebbw Vale 1984. Photo courtesy *Open Rugby*

misconceived idea that turned out better than anticipated." Watkins argued that although his selection choice was limited to many second division players, international football was vital if League was to spread its wings. The *Review* suggested that there was no point in matches with ill-matched sides even if they are internationals. However, it conceded that the Welsh had raised their game for this match but the crowd figure had shown that the public was not easily fooled.

Paul Fitzpatrick in *Open Rugby* concurred: "It is not enough to rent a decent ground, hire a well-drilled band, produce a programme, call it an international and then hope that spectators will turn up in their thousands." Yet he too admitted that "the match turned out if not quite a resounding success then an enjoyable, worthwhile exercise. Perhaps those of us who had viewed it with a degree of pessimism should have shown a little more of the faith that sustains David Watkins." As Fitzpatrick added using Watkins's words: "the people who criticise games such as this would be far better getting off their backsides and actually doing something to promote the game."

But few people were willing to contemplate further home matches for the Welsh and Watkins's many supporters were to be disappointed. As Welsh club RL disappeared with the failure of Bridgend who managed only a single win in their one season, so did the international team.

And it is quite possible that the team would still be a just a memory had it not been for the arrival of one Welshman at Widnes in January 1989. Such was Jonathan Davies's standing in the eyes of the Rugby Union media that when he signed for Doug Laughton's Cheshire-based club his first game was televised by national news bulletins, even though he was just sitting in the stands. Davies had been hailed as the saviour of Welsh Union, the man who would take it back to its glory days of the 1970s. He was the captain of his country and the media clamour and, in some quarters, hostility shown when he signed for League was enormous.

Many League followers thought - indeed hoped - that Davies might not make the grade. He was slight and his game very much a Rugby Union one involving little body strength. All the doubters were proved wrong. He went on to play a major role for Widnes, Warrington and Great Britain, culminating in a marvellous match-winning try for the Lions at Wembley in 1994 and an emotional farewell at the 1995 World Cup when he captained Wales to semi-final defeat against England at Old Trafford.

Back in 1991, following his arrival into club Rugby League, the appeal of a Welsh national team suddenly increased. More Union stars from Wales had followed their former captain into the League code, keen to play and make money from this toughest of sports. John Devereux, Allan Bateman, Paul Moriarty and David Bishop were all former Union stars suddenly making their name in League. A Welsh team was, amazingly, viable once again.

Papua New Guinea

Bearing in mind the defeat to England seven years earlier, the authorities were wary of pitching the Welsh against an established League nation. The new team needed opposition against which to prove themselves and the 1991 tour of the British Isles by Papua New Guinea offered the opportunity.

This tropical country - the only one in the world where Rugby League is the national sport - had been full members of the International Board since 1978 and had already defeated France, New Zealand and Great Britain. Their previous tours of Britain had been in 1979 when the Kumuls (a native bird of paradise) had played amateur opposition and in 1987 when they had lost a full test to Great Britain 42-0. Only the previous year though, in 1990 in Goroka, the Kumuls had stunned Great Britain by beating them 20-18 in the rarefied high-altitude atmosphere. They had proved that, on their day, they could beat the established League nations.

On their 1991 tour they were to offer a testing ground for Davies's revitalised Welsh squad at Swansea City FC's Vetch Field. The stadium had already seen the 1990 Rugby League Charity Shield match between Widnes and Wigan, a promotional pre-season match that toured various venues, this one played on the back of Jonathan Davies's signing for Widnes and more than 11,000 had turned out. The Vetch Field was therefore the most obvious venue for Wales's return.

With Welsh coach Clive Griffiths announcing a squad that was likely to entice Union supporters to the match, containing all their former idols and a huge promotional push by the RFL in Swansea in the days before the game on 27 October, a large crowd of Union supporters, disaffected with their team's performance in the Union World Cup - they had amazingly lost to Western Samoa - was predicted. And so it proved.

A crowd of 11,422 witnessed the Welsh storm to victory with a then record international winning margin of 68-0. And prodigal son Davies, with eight goals and a total of 24 individual points also set two Welsh national records. One survivor from the 1984 England international was full-back Phil Ford who picked up the man-of-the-match award with his hat-trick of tries, but the whole Welsh team played League of the highest standard. The cold certainly affected the Papuans, more used to tropical climes, but there was also no doubting the Welsh dominance both in forwards and backs, and the game of Rugby League received one of its biggest ever boosts in the principality as the Welsh press raved about their former local heroes now playing their new rugby code to the highest standard. In just a few short weeks the future of the Welsh RL team was assured for the next five years.

It was a passionate return for many of the Welsh team on a cold night (the Kumuls had spent £500 on thermal underwear), and the *South Wales Evening Post* reported that "there was hwyl in abundance. From the moment they came onto the pitch to the sound of huge cheers, Jonathan Davies's team overflowed with passion, commitment and an abundance of skill. Seldom has a lap of honour been so richly deserved."

Another local newspaper wrote: "The 13-try rout was the perfect antidote to the Union side's World Cup debacle... [answering] critics who thought they lacked the experience of the Northern code needed for the international arena." The *Western Mail* added: "If ever there was an advert for the professional code in the back yard of the Union game - this was it.

"For too long the Welsh Rugby Union... have criticised the players who sought pastures new... in the north. But had those same critics taken time to be at the Vetch Field last night, they would have seen those so called money-grabbing defectors bringing international rugby success to Wales for the first time since Paul Thorburn's Welsh [Union] team lifted the Triple Crown in 1988."

This was stunning praise indeed from what had often been an indifferent local press. But it was surely deserved for Wales scored 13 tries with Davies landing eight goals -

they were 46-0 up at half time and had already eclipsed the points record for an international match involving Wales.

The first try came after nine minutes when Wales led 2-0 from a Davies penalty as Anthony Sullivan - son of former Lions captain Clive - and Davies combined to put Ford over. The second try was from Rob Ackerman quickly followed by stand-off Jonathan Griffiths who plunged over from a Moriarty pass.

Then came the game's most thrilling try as Sullivan scooped up a poor kick by Papua's Richard Wagambie to race 60 yards down the touchline evading three defenders. Davies's first try left the PNG defence bewildered as he threaded his way over and Bateman scored shortly afterwards, picking up a pass destined for the floor. Sullivan, fed by Bishop, and Ford, from a slick Moriarty pass, both notched their second tries and Davies's conversions meant the game was over by half time.

The Welsh forwards had been expected to struggle - the transition between Union and League often being more difficult for players used to rucking and mauling - but David Young, Mark Jones and Paul Moriarty in particular were all playing with power and strength. It was a shame Moriarty had to leave the field with a dead leg but the *Guardian* told us that "Jones and Moriarty were a revelation" as props.

Wales relaxed somewhat in the second half before Ellis took advantage of slack defending to increase the lead. The next try came from Bishop, having an outstanding game despite not having played loose-forward very often and looking a little overweight, who took a pass from Ford to score and receive one of the evening's biggest cheers. Before the end, man-of-the-match Ford had notched his hat-trick, substitute Adrian Hadley had scored following a Bishop kick-ahead and Davies, showing great pace, had outflanked the Papuan defence to score the last try.

The Papuans, who were later to lose the test match to Great Britain 56-4, had thrown the ball around well but each time they had come close to the Welsh line a poor pass or a refereeing decision robbed them of a scoring opportunity. Half-back Stanley Haru and forwards James Naipo and Kes Paglipari had shown touches of individual ability but they were simply overwhelmed by a rampant Welsh team.

Davies said: "The ferocity of our forwards was tremendous... It was great to hear the hymns and arias and the fantastic reception given to us by the crowd meant a lot." The reception from the press was also remarkable. "Record win is envy of Union die-hards," was the headline in the *Evening Post* which added "Watching the Welsh team in action it was difficult to believe they had never before played together. The result augurs well for a thriving future for a Wales Rugby League team."

The *Guardian's* Paul Fitzpatrick added: "Wales's aims were twofold: to win with style and to bring some cheer back to the principality. Objectives were achieved."

But the greatest praise was offered by Graham Clutton of the *Western Mail*. He compared this Welsh RL team to the last Welsh Union side to win the Triple Crown in 1988. "Davies was an integral part of that Welsh side, as were Paul Moriarty, John Devereux and Rowland Phillips - and all looked infinitely better players, and athletes, after just three years playing the professional code. This was the important lesson learned from this - the serious relaunch of Welsh Rugby League and the Welsh folk lapped it up. Quite simply Rugby League has done to these players what the Union game failed to do... it has transformed certain individuals into world class players... players returning with a message. It was right riveting stuff."

The crowd, the performance and the amazed reaction of a stunned Welsh rugby public ensured the immediate survival of the national team and the RFL were quick to capitalise on the sudden emergence of a large number of high quality Welsh rugby players in their sport. A further match was arranged for later that season with European neighbours France returning to the principality for the first time since the pre-World Championship European competition in 1975.

Wales had won that match 21-8 and their 1990s revival continued apace on 22 March 1992 as the French were taken apart by Jonathan Davies's men. And they had the incentive too. Wales were told that, if they could defeat the French who played annual test matches against the full Great Britain side, they would be guaranteed a fixture against England later in 1992. With numerous Lions caps now in their team - including John Devereux, Jonathan Davies, Allan Bateman, Jonathan Griffiths, Anthony Sullivan, Paul Moriarty (unfortunately injured for the France game) and Mark Jones - the Welsh needed no second bidding and while France offered tougher resistance than the Kumuls, Wales always held the upper hand and recorded a 35-6 victory.

The Times wrote: "The revival of the Welsh team gained further momentum with a convincing, if hard fought, victory over the French," while *League Express* added: "In what was most definitely a tough, physical encounter, the Welshmen showed that when courage, character and commitment are required they have all three in abundance."

After a few early bad-tempered exchanges and a missed penalty attempt by French captain Gilles Dumas, Griffiths, breaking from half way, and Kevin Ellis fashioned a fourth-minute try for Devereux, converted by Jonathan Davies. Many in the crowd probably expected France to capitulate in the way the Kumuls did but sterner resistance was offered, which led to the uncharacteristic sin-binning, after much provocation from French forwards Yves Viloni and Christophe Grandjean, of Davies. The home captain dropped a goal on his return to extend his team's lead to seven points but the Welsh were finding cohesion difficult to find.

Yet David Young and Mark Jones kept the Welsh pack driving forward and, as half time approached, the Welsh were able to extend their lead. Scrum-half Ellis and stand-off Griffiths played key roles in freeing the ball for Bateman to touch down and, with Davies landing the conversion, Wales had a useful 13-0 half-time lead.

It proved to be important because the first 20 minutes of the second half were all France. Dumas led from the front with superb tactical kicking, but all the visitors had to show for their dominance were three Dumas penalties. Wales looked to be struggling, although their defence was holding firm. Then a piece of sloppy defending turned the game Wales's way once more.

Jacques Pech knocked on giving Wales the feed at a scrum 10 yards from the French line. Barry Williams heeled the ball and then seconds later crashed over himself to score. Davies goaled and Wales were able to relax and play more open football. Phil Ford scored another try for Wales, Rowland Phillips notched only his second ever RL try and, in the game's best move, Griffiths, Ian Marlow and Davies set Anthony Sullivan free to fly down the wing. As the cover came across Davies backed up well to take the scoring pass and seal a 35-6 victory, after converting two of the last three tries.

The scoreline flattered Wales somewhat and the encounter was a well-contested, if bruising, one. But yet again Wales had beaten an established International Board nation and 10,133 (twice the figure that had watched Great Britain play France only two weeks before in Hull) had turned out. By the end those supporters were calling "Bring on the English." As *The Times* wrote: "If they could hold their own in a game of that stature, then Wales could become an important player in the limited world of international rugby league." There was no disputing who the next Welsh opponents should be. "Who's next?" asked *League Express*. It was, of course, the English.

It would be eight months before they arrived but, when they did on 27 November 1992, England were to provide the newly revitalised Welsh team with their toughest assignment yet. And the job was made more difficult when captain Jonathan Davies had to undergo a hernia operation two weeks before the game and Carlisle hooker Barry Williams was forced to withdraw leaving the less-than-match-fit David Bishop to take his role, never having hooked a ball before. For England only inspirational Ellery Hanley, the Leeds loose-forward, and captain Garry Schofield survived from the previous meeting between the two nations in 1984. Phil Ford was still present for Wales, however.

The crowd of 10,243 did not enjoy this match as much as the previous games they had seen at Swansea's Vetch Field for, after a close first half, England pulled away to leave *League Express* displaying the headline "Dragon slayers". It continued: "Although England dominated for much of the game, the Welshmen certainly played their part in what was a tough bruising encounter [and] the atmosphere was electric as the Welsh fans roared on their favourites."

The crowd figure was considered to be adequate because the match was televised live on Sky TV and persistent rain had fallen all day at Swansea although, despite the conditions, the pitch held up well. The *Guardian* told us that "word was that the groundsman had put his job on the line in his efforts to get the game played."

Wales began badly by kicking out on the full and England were able to dominate possession. Lee Crooks's penalty opened the scoring and then Mike Ford provided an excellent pass for Hanley to score the first try. When Stuart Spruce, the Widnes full-back finished off a slick passing move for the second England try and Crooks scored the goal, a 12-0 lead seemed to suggest everything was going England's way.

Things got worse for Wales when right wing Gerald Cordle left the field with a broken jaw but then the home team began to claw their way back into the game. "Wales were spirited, skilful and pragmatic," said the *Guardian*. With captain David Young leading by example the Welsh began to pressure the English defence culminating in Spruce fumbling the ball as he was tackled by Allan Bateman. Jonathan Griffiths scooped up the ball to score by the posts. John Devereux landed the goal and then Mark Jones rampaged through three tackles to plunge over for a second score. Devereux failed with the kick but Kevin Ellis's drop goal brought Wales to within a point of the English.

Sadly, for Wales, the damage was done only a minute before half time. Anthony Sullivan failed to gather a Hanley grubber kick and Crooks gratefully accepted the scoring chance and added the conversion. England led 18-11.

While it took England 15 minutes of the second half to score they still dominated possession. Schofield and Ford ran the game from half-back and Richard Eyres (later to switch allegiance and play for Wales) was powerful up front allowing record-breaking wingman Martin Offiah to score twice and Paul Newlove and Schofield himself to get one each. This last score was one of the game's best as the England captain finished off a fine sweeping move. With Crooks landing only one second-half conversion the English ran out worthy 36-11 winners.

"In the end Wales were well beaten," wrote *League Express*. "The absence of captain Jonathan Davies weakened their kicking game." But the gamble of playing David Bishop at hooker worked. "'Bish' was a revelation. He brought his forwards onto the ball, produced the odd surging break, and... lasted the full eighty minutes."

For the English, Garry Schofield's attacking abilities meant that Wales were constantly on the defensive and they found Offiah very difficult to contain in the second half. Nonetheless the *Guardian* felt that, despite suffering in comparison with England, "There is every chance that Wales will defeat the French in two weeks' time in Perpignan." They did just that, but by only one point, with Devereux, Bateman and Rob Ackerman scoring tries in a 19-18 victory.

Buoyant crowds and a reasonably competitive team left the RFL feeling confident that Wales could be included on the 1993 New Zealand tour itinerary, providing the Kiwis with the opening match of their visit. More importantly, however, prolonged lobbying mounted on the back of Wales's recent success and crowd figures, some of it carried out by former Labour Party leader and Welshman, Neil Kinnock had secured the Welsh team a place in the 1995 Centenary World Cup. Initially Great Britain had been the British Isles's sole entry into the competition to be held in the UK to mark 100 years of Rugby League but with more and more nations demanding inclusion as the sport was expanding rapidly in the southern hemisphere, the British challenge in the main competition became Wales and England, with newly arrived Scotland and Ireland invited to take part in an Emerging Nations tournament.

That World Cup was to be the zenith of Welsh international competition to date and all matches played in the run up to the event were now clearly perceived and billed as warm-up games. The New Zealanders were expected to provide the Welsh with further indication of how far they had progressed.

Although New Zealand were to go on to perform disappointingly in their three tests against Great Britain, losing at Wembley 17-0 on the only occasion they have played there and then 29-12 at Wigan and 29-10 at Leeds, they were considered to be able to provide the kind of opposition the Welsh would meet in the World Cup.

The game was the tour opener on 3 October 1993 and the match report in the local newspaper was headlined "A cup booster". Wales had lost 24-19 in controversial circumstances and the report added: "The spirited display vindicated, triumphantly, the decision to allow the nation to compete in the 1995 World Cup."

This was, of course, the oldest international and the RFL had anticipated another large crowd but were disappointed with a gate of only 6,083. However, Maurice Lindsay, chief executive of the RFL, announced that the Welsh display had convinced him that another match against the French was a certainty. In a moment of lucid prediction he also described Wales as World Cup "Semi-final material".

The return of Jonathan Davies had much to do with the fine Welsh performance. His superb diagonal kicks opened up the Kiwi wings and allowed Welsh wing Gerald Cordle to have a wonderful afternoon in only his second match since he broke his jaw against England on the same field.

The opening quarter saw Daryl Halligan land an early penalty for the visitors which was soon cancelled out by two Davies penalties and a Jonathan Griffiths's drop goal before Davies's finely weighted kick into the right corner saw Cordle pounce for the first of his two tries. Davies's conversion attempt left the touch-judges in doubt but referee

John Connolly ruled it had failed leaving Wales ahead 9-2.

Two more penalties from the Halligan boot narrowed the deficit and then, after a sustained period of pressure, Quentin Pongia, the second-row Kiwi, broke clear. He passed inside to Jason Mackie who strode over at the corner. Halligan's fine kick gave New Zealand a 12-9 interval lead. That lead increased shortly afterwards when scrum-half and captain Gary Freeman sold an outrageous dummy to put Iva Ropati in the clear. Fortunately for the Welsh, Halligan missed the conversion.

But Wales were to come back strongly as first Davies kicked ahead again to allow Cordle to collect his second try and then the Welsh captain landed two more penalties to put the home team ahead by 17-16. The crowd roared their approval but the visitors scored the next vital try. Freeman and Mackie combined to put Sean Hoppe over. Halligan's goal gave the Kiwis a 5-point lead, but the final drama was still to come.

With only 11 minutes remaining Davies put up a bomb which came down behind the New Zealand posts. There was an almighty scramble and an equally almighty cheer as John Devereux pounced for possibly the match-winning score. But referee Connolly ruled Welsh substitute Adrian Hadley offside and New Zealand heaved a sigh of relief. Davies and Halligan exchanged penalties in the final seconds but Wales lost 24-19.

"We wuz robbed" said the *League Express* headline. Certainly Welsh coach Clive Griffiths was disappointed even though video evidence later proved the referee was correct. The coach's intention had been to spin the ball wider so that Wales's talented backs could benefit, but instead the game was played down the middle. Still, the forwards, especially Rowland Phillips and Mark Jones, never stopped trying despite the determined and solid Kiwi defence. Jonathan Griffiths found himself at loose-forward for the first time in his career but lived up to the task well.

New Zealand coach Howie Tamati had every reason to be relieved. "We were too impatient," he said. "Wales played with lots of fire." But his team had come through a tricky tour opener with Mackie winning the man-of-the-match award although Steven Kearney and Pongia ran him very close. The worry for the New Zealanders was that theirs was a full-strength team. If Wales could nearly beat them, the matches against Great Britain were never going to be easy, and so it proved.

Of the Welsh, however, *League Express* wrote: "Wales gave everything, and will feel encouraged to think that they have a firm foundation to build upon for a World Cup campaign in two years' time."

The next step in the build-up to that World Cup would come on 4 March 1994 when France visited the principality. Ninian Park, Cardiff was chosen for the event, hosting international Rugby League for the first time since Australia's visit in 1982.

The headlines on the day after the game would be all about Richard Webster, the Salford forward formerly from Swansea RUFC. Webster only played eight minutes of the match (and four of those were in injury time) but as Paul Rees wrote in the *South Wales Echo*: "Webster was well pleased with his work last night: a match-winning try, double international status [he had already played international Union] and extra pay for winning his League cap."

Webster bored over from close range following two quick tap penalties in the dying seconds, giving Jonathan Davies a simple kick to take Wales into a 13-12 winning lead. It was, in fact, a hollow victory, for France, the underdogs, had played well enough to win although they could feel encouraged by the near miss. Wales, however, were sent away to rethink their World Cup plans with only three full international matches remaining before the start of the competition.

Patrick Entat, the French scrum-half and one of the best players on the night opened the scoring in the 20th minute when he gathered a dropped pass from Kevin Ellis and ran from half way to score under the posts. Patrick Torreilles converted to give the French a 6-0 lead at half time.

Welsh full-back Phil Ford was having a torrid time under the high ball and Wales's handling generally let them down so it was left to the boot of Davies to notch up the points that brought them back into the game. The first came after Ellis had taken Davies's crossfield kick from an interception and Torreilles, who was subsequently sin-binned, held him down in the tackle. With 15 minutes remaining, a further two penalties had brought Wales level. Eight minutes from the end Wales snatched an unlikely lead when Davies grabbed a drop goal to make it 7-6.

Yet France looked to have sealed the victory they deserved when Jean-Marc Garcia was put into the clear by Thierry Valero for a simple try with only minutes remaining. Torreilles kicked the goal and France had a 5-point lead. However, France's 46-year run without a victory in Wales, was to continue as Webster struck at the death.

The *Echo* noted in a swipe at the poor attendance of 6,287: "Had Webster scored for Wales against France in Rugby Union, the roar would have been heard at Twickenham. With just over 6,000 at Ninian Park last night, the cheers would barely have drifted over to the Arms Park." Where, of course, Rugby League was forbidden.

"I thought I was not going to be used," said Webster. "I didn't really do a lot." But it was enough to please his coach Clive Griffiths who said he had wanted to bring Webster on earlier but never had the opportunity. "It was a dream debut for Richard but his try cannot hide the fact that it was a disappointing performance."

Perhaps the only outstanding Welsh players were Davies who played for 70 minutes with a dead leg and Rowland Phillips. The pack ploughed manfully forward but made little headway against a French defence well marshalled by Hull players Danny Divet and Entat. Divet was a stunning runner at Entat's prompting and the rest of the French pack supported well. "They deserved to win," admitted Davies honestly.

The next three games would see how well Wales had learned this lesson with the first against the toughest opposition they were likely to encounter in the World Cup competition, Australia. The 1994 Kangaroo touring team was captained by Australian legend Mal Meninga and was, perhaps, even an improvement on the teams of 1982, 1986 and 1990. Nonetheless, Australia arrived at Cardiff's Ninian Park 1-0 down in the Ashes series against Great Britain. Just like their 1990 predecessors, the Kangaroos had lost the opening match at Wembley and were under pressure to come up with the goods in Wales and in the remaining two tests.

The British coach was Ellery Hanley, making his debut in the role, and the shock of Australia's 8-4 defeat at Wembley was made doubly worse for the Kangaroos by the fact that Britain played most of the match with 12 men after captain Shaun Edwards was dismissed for a high tackle. Australia had a point to prove in Wales and they were relieved to see that the man who scored one of Rugby League's most famous tries the week before at Wembley would not be playing. Welsh captain Jonathan Davies, after notching the winning score for Britain in the first test, was injured late in the game and was not fit for the Welsh encounter with the tourists. And sadly for the Lions he did not recover in time for Britain's remaining tests as Australia once again recovered from Wembley defeat to win 38-8 at Old Trafford and 23-4 at Elland Road.

If Wales were hoping to find Australia on the defensive after their surprising first test loss they were mistaken. The Kangaroos handed out the biggest defeat for the Welsh since the team was reformed. Davies's stand-in half-back Iestyn Harris had a fine game in the 46-4 defeat but the rest of the team, missing other first-choice players Allan Bateman and Mark Jones, was outplayed. The Australians fielded a near-test strength team in appalling wet conditions and under the circumstances the crowd of 8,729 was respectable, the terrible weather no doubt restricting the turnout.

Unfortunately the game is perhaps remembered most for the horrific injury to Welsh wingman John Devereux. In the ninth minute he was met by a fierce but fair hand-off from Meninga and was left writhing on the ground in agony, his jaw broken in five places. The *South Wales Echo* feared his career was over, but a steel plate inserted into his jaw enabled him to continue playing after a long period of recovery. Only two minutes afterwards Welsh captain and prop David Young suffered a cut eye that needed 10 stitches and although no foul play was noted Welsh tempers were now running high and the match spilled over into a 15th minute brawl involving most of the players. Kevin Ellis of Wales and Australia's Paul Sironen spent time in the sin-bin but, when Phil Ford, the Welsh full-back joined them, an 11-man Wales had little chance. With key players missing, two more departing with serious injuries and two in the sin bin, Australia were able to control the match.

They already had a 6-point lead following David Furner's fifth-minute try converted by Rod Wishart and took advantage of their numerical supremacy with Steve Renouf, who had scored the World Cup-winning try against Great Britain at Wembley two years earlier, storming over for the first of his two tries, converted again by Wishart. Wishart would bag 18 points in the game with a try and seven goals but Renouf, with a powerful display, beat him to the man-of-the-match award.

By half time the match was over. Brett Mullins, Wishart and Meninga had all added converted tries to make it 30-0 and although Young heroically returned to the field at the beginning of the second half and improved Welsh concentration immeasurably, his cut reopened and he was forced to depart once more. Team manager Mike Nicholas summed up the feelings of many when he said "It was a brave thing for Young to do".

The tide was certainly slowed in the second half, helped by the sin-binning of Australian second-row David Fairleigh, but the visitors scored again before the Welsh could finally trouble the scoreboard. Substitute Greg Florimo raced in for a converted try before Welsh spirits were slightly raised by Daio Powell of Bradford Northern who, on as a substitute for Adrian Hadley, pounced on an Ellis through kick. It was to be the only Welsh score on a night when Steve Renouf and Brad Fittler rounded off the scoring to give Australia a 46-4 victory. Even more distressing for the Welsh was that Australia had only named three out of four permissible substitutes. Injuries and Fairleigh's sin-binning meant they played the second half with 12 men for most of the time.

But there were hopeful signs for a Welsh team that had never given up battling in the dreadful conditions, not least the performance of Harris.

The *Echo* also carried some praise for a team that "never gave up [even though] they were carved open at regular intervals by the sharpest attacking force in either of rugby's codes." The paper went on to praise Ellis, Young, Paul Moriarty, Jonathan Griffiths and debutant Scott Gibbs. But it was concerned that Wales had to carry too many second-rate players in order to make up the numbers, a problem that has dogged the team throughout its long history.

Welsh centre Gibbs, a recent convert to Rugby League, added: "I've seen the level to which I've got to try and aspire. They are the best team in the world and I learnt more from that match than any I've played in so far." He was confident that the experience would stand Wales in good stead for the World Cup.

European Championship

For international Rugby League in Wales the new year, 1995, was to bring the sport to the attention of the Welsh public like none before - or since. The World Cup adventure is covered in another chapter of this book, but before the competition, played in both England and Wales, got underway the European nations prepared for the October tournament by competing, yet again, for the European Championship - a regular fallback event whenever the Welsh national team was considered strong enough.

The opening game was to be against the English at Ninian Park and it was to be the last home game for the Welsh before their World Cup campaign. And it was a famous night for the prodigal sons too as, ultimately, two Jonathan Davies drop goals led Wales to victory. With the International Board allowing players to qualify to play for a country if they had a grandparent of that nationality the Welsh were able to add a forward pack of high quality to the fine back line they already possessed. Fielding five of their new Anglo-Welsh players, forwards Kelvin Skerrett, Martin Hall, Neil Cowie and Richie Eyres (who was already an England cap), plus full-back Paul Atcheson, the Welsh pack showed greater resilience than ever before.

England were without a handful of first choice players who had been sent on World Sevens duty in Australia but still carried a formidable look with Garry Schofield, Phil Clarke and Jason Robinson all in outstanding form. Robinson, Richard Russell and Paul Newlove were all injured during the course of the game and England were also without the services of centre Gary Connolly but in the early stages at least, this did not show.

Although Wales opened the scoring with Kevin Ellis taking the first of his two Davies-converted tries in the 19th minute after good work from Hall, the rest of the opening period was all England who also won the penalty count 10-5 much to Welsh coach Clive Griffiths's consternation. Debutant, and the only Asian player to yet play for England, Ikram Butt had made the mistake that led to the Ellis score but he improved as the game went on and good work by him and Schofield's fine pass sent Richard Gay over. With an earlier Deryck Fox penalty it was 6-6. A Davies goal put Wales ahead 8-6 at half time but then in the 48th minute, Atcheson, who had an otherwise superb debut, fumbled a Fox bomb under pressure from English forward Sonny Nickle and Fox pounced to put England ahead. He converted his own try and England extended their lead to 16-8 when Robinson scored in the corner.

With only half an hour left defeat looked probable but then the Welsh launched a mighty comeback spearheaded by Skerrett and man-of-the-match Kevin Ellis. *League Express* wrote of the former: "And then there was Kelvin. He wasn't quite Artie Beetson in the first State of Origin [Queensland's Beetson had run riot in the inaugural 1980 State of Origin match], but Skerrett showed from the first minute that he would be playing this game with his normal fire. The northern accents have been welcomed into the Welsh camp with no dilution of team spirit." Astoundingly Skerrett made three tackles in the first minute, equalling the feat of his uncle Trevor on his debut 17 years earlier.

And the *Guardian* waxed lyrical over Ellis too: "Playing behind the best pack Wales have had since the rebirth of the side in 1991, he revelled in the freedom. After possibly the outstanding performance of his career, he scored his second try 13 minutes from time." This was the score, set up well by Atcheson and Allan Bateman, that brought Wales right back into contention after Davies had pegged England back with a penalty. His conversion of Ellis's try made the score 16-16.

With 10 minutes remaining Rowland Phillips and Anthony Sullivan combined down the left and set up the position for Davies to attempt a drop goal. He was successful and Wales led by one. England fought back forcing Atcheson to collect a high bomb under pressure but, with the tension mounting, Davies kept his nerve to land a second drop goal with two minutes remaining and Wales were home 18-16.

It was a magnificent start to the European campaign for the Welsh. "We have made a point today," said Jonathan Davies. "Hopefully more people will watch us next time (the crowd was only 6,252). We showed a lot of character. This is a tremendous platform for the World Cup." Those who chose not to attend missed fine performances throughout the Welsh team with Phillips, Eyres and Paul Moriarty playing with vigour and Hall always a danger around the rucks.

As *Open Rugby* reported: "Wales's victory gave Rugby League in the principality its biggest boost for many years. The reaction of the Welsh team and the spectators at last proved that the country of Wales can become emotional about Rugby League. The hywl was there." *Open Rugby* also appealed for a grassroots development policy in Wales to build on the success and argued that "The days of hit and run internationals, after which officials retreat to the north of England, must be over." That plea remains unfulfilled. But for the moment the Welsh were looking for their first title since 1938.

By the time the World Cup was to come around Ellery Hanley would no longer be England coach. He was to be replaced by Phil Larder, but Hanley realised that this was no way to start the year's international campaign. Wales were now favourites to take the European title, a situation made even more likely when Hanley's side, despite having nine players withdraw to play in a Challenge Cup semi- final replay - one of the RFL's more ludicrous fixture-making decisions - managed to beat the French 19-16 at Gateshead on 15 February. This left Wales needing only a draw to take the title and they duly came up with a 22-10 victory in Carcassonne to go into the World Cup as European Champions and fourth seeds behind Australia, England and New Zealand.

The story of that World Cup campaign is told elsewhere but history has shown us that 1995 was, to date, the finest year for Welsh international Rugby League. To top a BBC poll in Wales for the nation's top sporting team as, indeed, they did that year is an achievement like no other in the world-wide history of the game. In a nation where Rugby Union has always been king, where its stars are the country's most revered figures and where the Union establishment has always attempted to undermine League development, the achievement of coach Clive Griffiths and captain Jonathan Davies and his team in bringing success and national fame to Rugby League, was nothing short of a miracle.

Chapter 10: Cardiff Blue Dragons 1981-1984

The 30 years between the demise of Cardiff RLFC as a senior team in 1951-2 and the next attempt to make Rugby League work in South Wales was, at one level, the most stable in the code's history.

From 1895 the membership of the League had been in all but constant flux. But from the early 1950s there was to be a thirty years peace, with minimal changes. Blackpool Borough's much anticipated entry into the League came in 1954-5. At the end of the same season founder members Belle Vue Rangers, one of the giants of the turn-of-the-century game under their original identity of Broughton Rangers, went under. The Rugby League concluded that debts of £1,600 and ejection from their Manchester ground made them no longer viable. Bradford Northern dropped out midway through the 1963-4 season, but returned at the start of the next season with such vigour that within just over a year they had won the Yorkshire Cup. But otherwise the same 30 clubs continued season in, season out.

More significant changes took place in the organisation and rules of the game. League experimented tentatively with a two-division structure in 1962-3 and 1963-4 - with Swinton taking both First Division titles. It then switched back to a single League for a further 10 seasons, and finally opted with greater conviction for a multilevel structure from the start of 1973-4. An equally fundamental shift occurred on the field from 1966, as the old unlimited tackle game gave way to a four-tackle limit, raised to six from 1972. Substitutes were allowed from 1964, initially only for players injured during the first half but, within a few years, for any reason at any time.

However, the really important changes took place off the field, dramatically changing the context in which the game evolved. The sport played in Wales in the late 1940s had been an unknown northern rite which had to be explained in detail to local audiences unaccustomed to League. By 1981, when the Cardiff Blue Dragons were launched, television coverage had made the game familiar to national audiences.

The impact of television

From 1965 to 1980 there had been a competition specifically designed for television - the BBC2 Floodlight Trophy, played in midweek during the first half of the season. And while television commentator Eddie Waring's idiosyncrasies infuriated many purists, impersonator Mike Yarwood's send-up of his mannerisms - replete with "up and unders", "early baths" and references to Hunslet and Whitehaven - showed how far national audiences had become aware of the game.

It was also being played more widely. In spite of advances like the formation of the London Amateur Rugby League in 1965, the amateur game stagnated badly until the formation of the British Amateur Rugby League Association in 1973. While the existence of separate, often warring, amateur and professional governing bodies has become a running sore in the 1990s, the formation of BARLA was a natural and necessary response to the way the Rugby League, preoccupied with the problems of the professional game, had let the grass roots atrophy.

Also, student Rugby League brought the game to cities and individuals who had never seen it before. The expansion of higher education in the 1960s brought in many more students whose game was League rather than Union. While the first ever student League match was emphatically cross-Pennine - Leeds beat Liverpool 32-16 in 1967 - the game spread in spite of determined resistance from Union, keen to maintain its privileged position in universities. Oxford University played their first match in 1975, were officially recognised in 1977 and played Cambridge for the first time in 1981. Oxford was also the birthplace of *Open Rugby* magazine, founded by Harry Edgar while living there in 1976. In South Wales, Wigan-born American Studies lecturer Phil Melling organised a club at Swansea University. In the late 1990s, the student game is the one level of Rugby League that can claim to be truly national. Loughborough, Cardiff Institute and Durham compete against heartland institutions like Leeds Metropolitan in the top division.

This greater national consciousness was not, however, reflected in numbers watching the game live. All spectator sports saw their crowds decline from post-war peaks - football would lose half of its paying audience between 1948 and 1981. League suffered even more grievously. Total attendances fell precipitately from the 1948-9 peak of 6.86 million, halving within a decade and dropping below 2 million in 1963-4. By the end of the 1960s they were down to 1.43 million, and the decline went on into the seventies, dipping below a million at one stage. A series of reforms - limited tackles, two divisions and the progressive introduction of Sunday play from 1967 onwards - at last reversed the trend. By the end of the 1970s, crowds were back to the levels seen at the beginning of the decade.

At the same time football clubs, squeezed by their own declining income through the turnstiles, were beginning to recognise that owning a purpose-built stadium used only once a fortnight was hardly utilising the asset to its limits. Football would be to 1980s League expansion what the greyhound tracks had been to the inter-war years. Fulham FC, confronted by just such a worry, decided that Rugby League might provide an answer and the club was accepted for the 1980-1 season.

Their first season was calculated to encourage imitators. It is best remembered for their very first game, a 24-5 demolition of Wigan, by happy chance (for Fulham anyway) available for the only time as Second Division opposition, in front of 9,554 instant converts. One symptom of unsuccessful League ventures is that their first home gate also remains their record. This was not the case with Fulham. They raised their mark to more than 12,000 for the visit of Leeds in the John Player Trophy, then to 15,013 when Wakefield Trinity visited for a Challenge Cup tie in January 1981. In the Second Division, their promotion-winning campaign proved a consistent crowd-puller. They only once fell below 5,000 and their average of 6,096 was the fourth highest in the game. It was exceeded only by a Humberside duo enjoying the most prosperous spell in their history and champions Bradford Northern, a mere handful ahead. The average Second Division crowd rose by 25 per cent, almost entirely on the back of Fulham's impact.

Welsh bid

It was always likely that a Welsh bid would follow. Here too conditions had changed. Welsh Rugby Union had less reason in the 1970s to feel threatened by League than at any time since 1895. The flow of players north had never entirely stopped - Clive Griffiths signed for Salford after a spectacular 15-minute appearance as a substitute full-back in the 1979 Wales versus England Union match while prop Glyn Shaw, one of the last coal miners to play for Wales, joined Widnes in 1977. But the serious outflow of talent halted with David Watkins (1967), Maurice Richards and Keith Jarrett (1969) and John Bevan (1973). Not until Terry Holmes joined Bradford Northern in 1985 would a high-profile player again opt to turn professional with Rugby League.

With the Welsh XV dominating the European Rugby Union game throughout the decade, top players could do well enough from the indirect benefits of celebrity without needing to take the risks of moving away, trying a new game and getting banned *sine die*. And, fine players though they were, those who had gone were scarcely missed as players of comparable talent took their place - Watkins was followed by Barry John, Bevan by J.J. Williams. If the old distrust between the codes would never fully die, the times at least minimised it.

Local economic circumstances were rather less promising. South Wales was still in the painful transition from its old heavy-industrial base. Steel and coal were still relatively important in the late 1970s and both were to suffer swingeing job cuts and national strikes. Wales suffered grievously as unemployment rocketed to over three million in the years following the election of the Margaret Thatcher Conservative government in 1979. Cardiff, cushioned by its government and service industry base, suffered less than the rest of South Wales but its 1980s boom as the western end of the information-rich M4 corridor was still some way in the future.

Cardiff City, like Fulham, were a middle-ranking Football League club - generally to be found struggling to retain Second Division status. They were owned by Kenton Utilities, a Newcastle-on-Tyne company, and chairman Bob Grogan's interest in the potential of Rugby League was stimulated by observing Fulham's progress and talking to their chairman Ernie Clay.

David Watkins

Finding the right front man for the operation was always going to be vital, and Cardiff could hardly have done better. David Watkins had unique credibility across the two codes in Wales. He was capped 24 times for Wales at Union and captain of both his country and (on one occasion) the British Lions before signing in 1967 for Salford, where he had been one of the stars of the Red Devils' best spell since the days of Lance Todd. He had coaching credentials as well after leading Great Britain to the 1977 World Cup Final, losing 13-12 to Australia at the Sydney Cricket Ground. Watkins, whose departure to Salford had been accompanied by a letter from the secretary of the Welsh Rugby Union wishing him luck in his new career, was now back in South Wales working for a finance company. He had just lost out to Ray French in the competition to succeed Eddie Waring as BBC television's voice of League.

Cardiff, together with Carlisle, were accepted by the AGM of the Rugby League in May 1981 but there was immediate proof that, while Rugby League had lacked staying power in South Wales, distrust of it had not. Watkins had been invited to a charity dinner at Cardiff Rugby Union club, but his hosts immediately withdrew the invitation.

The fear was that Watkins would use his local knowledge to plunder local Union talent - in particular young players. But in fact his interest was in players towards the end of their career. Much early speculation centred on Phil Bennett, the mercurially brilliant Llanelli outside-half who had led the 1977 British Lions in Australia.

There is little doubt that the Dragons wanted him. Watkins told Clem Thomas of *The Observer*: "I would dearly like to sign a few Rugby Union players of the calibre of Phil Bennett and Steve Fenwick who, although they have finished their careers with Wales, would give us some real credibility in Cardiff. I accept that a player like Phil Bennett, only has a couple of seasons left, could cost £25,000, but he would be worth it".

Bennett declined. But Watkins had better luck with Fenwick, a tough goal-kicking centre from Bridgend, who had been capped 32 times, the last only a few months earlier, and Tom David, a rampaging folk hero of a flanker who had been capped only four times in a decade when back-row competition was exceptionally tough but had long been recognised as a player with real League potential and had trialled once at Wigan.

David and Fenwick were, by happy chance, business partners. Their meeting with Watkins took place under comically cloak and dagger circumstances in a pub in Cowbridge, which they optimistically hoped might provide some privacy for three of the better-known faces in South Wales.

David recalled in his book *Tommy David*: "I wondered if I should say something like 'The snow is falling into the Volga tonight' which seems par for the course, but Dai sat down and spoiled my fantasy. 'Right lads', he said, 'now let's get down to business. No-one knows you're here. Right?' 'No one at all, Dai,' I said and at that moment the door opened and a bloke walked past. 'Evening Steve... Evening Tom... Evening Dai' We looked at each other. Then it happened again. Someone else. 'Evening Steve... Evening Tom.... Evening Dai'. It went on like that all night. Well after that, there was no way we *couldn't* sign, was there ?"

Fenwick, who signed for a reported £20,000, and David, whose fee was quoted at £10-15,000, were joined by a third Welsh international, Llanelli flank forward Paul Ringer who had acquired permanent notoriety (and/or martyrdom depending on your view of the incident in question) when sent off in the violent England versus Wales Union international at Twickenham in 1980. An extremely mild manner off the field belied a ferocious on-field attitude which, legend had it, had once led to his being dropped for trying too hard in his days as a student player with Leicester. Short of tempting some all-time legend such as Gareth Edwards out of retirement, there was no more effective way Watkins could have found of winning publicity for his new club.

Hardened professionals

But he recognised that his new club was equally in need of hardened League professionals, saying: "To have a chance we must recruit experienced players who know what the game is about". If they had a Welsh background, so much the better. Their first two signings epitomised what they were looking for. George Nicholls, a 35-year-old forward, had won 29 Great Britain caps - making him fourth on the all-time list at the time - and had won both the Lance Todd and Harry Sunderland trophies during his career with St Helens. When *Open Rugby* listed the 100 top players in the British game over the magazine's first 21 years - 1976-97 - Nicholls was rated 12th, ahead of such luminaries as Joe Lydon, Kevin Ward, Andy Gregory, John Joyner and Jeff Grayshon. Chris Seldon was, by contrast, a former Wales B Union cap happy to return home after a promising League career appeared to have stalled in its second season.

Fulham had based their entire squad in Widnes, whose veterans provided the core of that pioneering team, and bussed them down on matchdays. Carlisle, elected alongside Cardiff, would operate similarly although their hard core came from the Wakefield-Featherstone-Castleford triangle.

Cardiff opted from the start for a split-squad system. A dozen players trained in the north, under the supervision of club coach John Mantle, a former Newport RU colleague of Watkins who had preceded him north by a couple of years and enjoyed a hugely successful League career, appearing for St Helens in eight championship finals and three Challenge Cup finals as well as winning 13 Great Britain caps.

The other half of the squad would train under Watkins at Ninian Park, where, David recalled, the players rapidly realised Watkins - still formidably fit himself at the age of 39 - kept upping the pace in order to impress visiting reporters and television crews with the team's seriousness of purpose. One reporter, standing by himself on the Ninian Park touchline, would be told: "For Christ's sake, bugger off. He's trying to impress you".

They didn't get everybody they bid for. Talk of Widnes's formidable forward Jim Mills, who combined Welshness with an extraordinary hardman reputation and a disciplinary record to match, would ripple throughout the club's first year. But he never joined. Nor did brilliant winger Clive Sullivan, one of the numerous black Welshmen who have enriched League over the years.

But those they did sign included Welsh League players Paul Woods (Hull), Gordon Pritchard (Huddersfield), Mike Nicholas (Warrington), Peter Rowe (Huddersfield), Bob Fleay (Swinton) Frank Wilson (Salford), Adrian Barwood (Wakefield), Chris O'Brien and Ken Gwilliam (both Oldham). The non-Welsh contingent included the veteran hooker Tony Karalius, the most recent of his extensive experience being with Fulham in their first season, Rochdale prop Alan Bailey and the Leigh trio of Duncan Scott, Arthur Daley and Tony Garritty.

Like Fulham, Cardiff had the fixture planners on their side in picking the most attractive possible opening game. Salford were despatched to Ninian Park on 30 August 1981. Not only were the Red Devils David Watkins's former club, they were also unquestionably the most charismatic opposition available in that year's Second Division, one of the glamour sides of the 1970s and champions as recently as 1976. Their relegation at the end of the previous season had come as an even greater shock than Wigan's demise a year earlier. Carlisle opened their Second Division programme at Bramley, although they had been favoured two weeks earlier with a home Lancashire Cup tie against Wigan.

THE BLUE DRAGONS

CARDIFF CITY
v.
SALFORD
SUNDAY, 30th AUGUST, 1981
KICK OFF 3.00 p.m.
Official Colour Souvenir Magazine 50p

The opening day was calculated to evoke memories of Fulham's spectacular debut a year earlier. A crowd of just over 10,000 - a few hundred more than the Londoners had drawn - saw a 10-man parade of League greats including Gus and Bev Risman, Trevor Foster, Lewis Jones and Emlyn Jenkins.

The teams for this historic opening encounter at Ninian Park were:

Cardiff: Pritchard; Barwood, Fenwick, Garritty, O'Brien; Woods, Gwilliam; Bailey, Karalius, Nicholas, Daley, David, Nicholls.

Salford: Rule; Fielding, Stephenson, Whitfield, Richards; Francis, Nash; Coulman, Ashcroft, Yates, Henney, McGreal, Williams.

The one thing they didn't get was a victory, but it was a near thing. Salford led 16-4 at the interval, but a spectacular third quarter by the Blue Dragons, as the Cardiff club were nicknamed, took them into a 21-16 lead going into the final quarter of an hour. *Western Mail* columnist Mario Basini recognised the features that immediately made David as much of a folk hero at Ninian Park as he had been at Sardis Road, Pontypridd, writing that he "Immediately threatens to become the biggest attraction in his new code. Tom's bludgeoning runs, reminiscent of an angry bull who has been told that his services are no longer required by the herd, time and time again brought the crowd to its feet roaring for blood".

David started at second row, but moved forward to prop when Daley was injured: "You can imagine how I felt. I'm standing there with Tony Karalius, the hooker who was a real living legend and I turned to him and said 'Where do I put my head?' I wasn't being funny. And with that another famous international Mike Coulman, an Englishman, said 'Tom, I've been playing this game twelve years and I still don't know where to put my head". But by the end of the first season, David would have shifted permanently to the front row.

Cardiff Blue Dragons versus Salford at Ninian Park on 30 August 1981.
Photo Mike Haddon

Carwyn James

The legendary Union coach Carwyn James, reporting for the *Guardian,* recorded that the loudest roar of the entire afternoon came as David forced his way over to set up that 21-16 lead. Fenwick converted, his fourth successful kick of the game. But in the last few minutes class and experience told. Steve Nash, a world-class scrum-half, rated 19th in the *Open Rugby* 21st Anniversary list, created a try for Colin Whitfield. The final blow was administered, suitably enough, by a Welshman and a Cardiffian at that - Maurice Richards crossing for a try less popular with a Cardiff crowd than the four he had scored at the Arms Park against England at Union 12 years earlier. So Salford won 26-21.

The *Guardian* headline proclaimed a "gallant failure" while Carwyn James reported that "Cardiff were pleased to have held the likely Second Division champions to a five-point margin and the new club's management pronounced themselves pleased not only with the play of Fenwick and David, but with the crowd's general reaction".

They had every right to be pleased, even if Salford were not to be the dominant Second Division force so universally predicted. But having proclaimed the ambition of emulating Fulham, they took the comparison a little too far in their first away match. Fulham's demolition of Wigan had been followed by an anticlimactic 24-13 loss at Keighley. Cardiff too went to Keighley on their first away trip, and left even more chastened than the Londoners, going down 36-8. Mantle angrily condemned some of his players for lack of effort.

In only their second match, Cardiff displayed some of the symptoms that would dog their history. They were always prone to inexplicable sharp dips in form. Even the best Union players took time to adjust to the new game - the *Yorkshire Post*'s Ray Fletcher spoke of Fenwick looking "completely lost" until he was replaced in the 62nd minute. And lapses of discipline were to be too frequent. Woods became the first of six Cardiff sendings-off in their debut season, dismissed in the 66th minute for felling Graham Moll with a high tackle. Woods had already been warned for kneeing an opponent and compounded the sending-off by clashing with another Keighley player as he left the pitch. The dismissal, the seventh of an incident-studded career, led to a 13-match ban. Cardiff's disciplinary record was never spectacularly bad - six clubs would record more than their seven sendings-off in 1981-2, including Hull KR with 13 - but with a small squad, suspensions were invariably damaging.

Mike Nicholas was to be sent off for a stiff-armed tackle seven days later, 15 minutes from the end of Cardiff's first win, a 32-19 defeat of Hunslet. A compensation was Fenwick, nursed by the experienced Wilson as his co-centre, returning to form with a hat-trick and 17 points in all. Ringer also claimed his first League try in this match. But there was less welcome news in the gate, with only 3,401 paying customers. This was not disastrous in itself - before the season started Bob Grogan had said he was hoping for gates between 3,000 and 4,000. It would not have been realistic to expect another 10,000 crowd. But losing two thirds of them at once was still disappointing.

There were further 3,000 plus crowds for the next two games. Carlisle were beaten 12-7 in the first meeting of the League's neophytes. But it was a false indicator of what was to come over the rest of the season. The Cumbrians, built around a tough pack featuring the unmistakable billiard-ball profile of veteran Jim Thompson and try-scoring prop Mick Morgan, whose 25 scores were a record for a front-rower, lost at Ninian Park for the second time in their opening five matches. Their next defeat came in April, after 22 consecutive wins had assured them of emulating Fulham by winning promotion at the first attempt.

A slightly more realistic view of Cardiff's prospects was possible after the next home game. Halifax's Dave Callon tore massive holes in their defence and the promotion-bound Yorkshiremen ran in six tries in a 31-21 win. Watkins was determined that his team would play open, attacking rugby, but they were always prone to defensive lapses. Their eventual total of 566 points against, averaging more than 17 per game, was the highest outside the bottom four of Division 2.

They settled down just outside the promotion places, never quite consistent enough to seriously threaten the top four, but doing well enough to ensure that their hopes were not finally extinguished until six consecutive games were lost, including a double completed by fast-finishing Workington, in March and April. There were some distinguished victories - wins at Salford and Halifax avenged those early reverses at Ninian Park - but also strange lapses like a 34-19 loss at Batley, who finished 14th in the 17-team division and a 16-11 loss at Bramley. Eighth out of 17, with 35 points from 32 games, left them nine points behind fourth-placed Halifax.

However, there were conspicuous successes among the players. Fenwick took so rapidly to League that within three months of his debut, the Great Britain selectors spent half an hour discussing his claims for selection against France. He was also seriously considered for a test place against the all-conquering 1982 Australians. Gordon Pritchard declared him "the best centre I have ever played with" and he was on course to score in every match until injured at Workington seven games from the end of the season. He even attained the ambition jokily proclaimed in a match programme questionnaire of "scoring from more than 10 yards out" by going from 70 yards in the 34-5 home win at Batley. With 256 points, including 108 goals, he was one of the most prolific scorers in the Second Division.

Steve Fenwick
Photo courtesy *Open Rugby*

David, many critics suggested, would have been a certain Great Britain player if he had taken to League before the age of 32. His admirers included Great Britain manager Colin Hutton. He did win a Welsh cap, alongside Fenwick, Pritchard and Ringer, when Wales played England at Ninian Park in November, going down 20-15. But the sincerest compliment paid was in January by eventual Second Division champions Oldham. Even after a 33-15 win at Ninian Park incorporating a 25-2 half-time lead orchestrated by scrum-half Ray Ashton and a second sending-off of the season for Nicholls, they were sufficiently impressed by David to bid £30,000 for him. Cardiff refused to let him go for less than £50,000 - which would have been a record fee until the previous close-season, when Hull KR had spent £72,500 to buy George Fairbairn from Wigan.

Of the established League players the pick was the unheralded Fleay who, as the programme of his former club Swinton noted, had looked to be drifting out of League before the Cardiff club was started. Fifteen tries in 31 matches made him the clear leading scorer - Fenwick (13) was the only other man in double figures - and a resounding winner of the Man of the Season trophy.

But Watkins admitted that, in the pre-season rush to assemble a full squad in a little over three months: "We bought players we would not originally have gone for because time was not on our side". Nor was the split-squad experiment a success: "We found during the season there were suggestions that perhaps the lads in the south were getting a better deal than the northern men. This did not help knit the side together".

The tensions had been reflected as early as December, when Mantle left the club. An end of season article in the *Western Mail* spoke of "personality clashes" and Mantle declared himself unimpressed by the attitude of some players. But at the time Watkins put Mantle's departure down to the need to spend more money on players rather than backroom staff.

The move certainly sent alarming signals about the club's finances to the outside world. Paul Fitzpatrick in the *Guardian* wrote that it "Inevitably raises questions about the future of the game in South Wales. Is this attempt, like previous ones, condemned to end in failure? Cardiff hope not, but it is obviously going to be a struggle to keep the game alive here".

Certainly they must have been tempted to accept Oldham's January offer for David. At around the same time Cardiff City managing director Ron Jones was forced to issue a statement rubbishing speculation that Rugby League was in jeopardy. It was understandable that the speculation should have grown after a further precipitate fall in gates. The 3,000 plateau attained in September and October would have been acceptable - although Ninian Park, which had a capacity of 43,000, had a distinctly echoey feel with crowds of that size.

But there was a five week gap after the home defeat by Halifax, and the next Ninian Park date, 15 November, saw only 1,673 watch the 23-14 win over Huyton. Even that was not the end of the decline. The crowd fell below 1,000 for the first time when Doncaster visited after Christmas and stayed there for five of the last seven fixtures, with a nadir of just over 500 against Blackpool Borough. The one exception to the grim picture was the 6,480 who came to watch Challenge Cup holders Widnes defend their trophy in February - Cardiff fighting hard before going down 19-8 to the extra class provided by the Myler brothers. The final league position was a respectable eighth out of 17 clubs, with a league record of:

Played	Won	Drawn	Lost	For	Against	Points	Position
32	17	1	14	566	549	35	8th

From early on there had been indications that the football-type entrance prices charged by the Dragons were too high. One letter writer to the local press noted pointedly that they were twice as high as those charged by Cardiff RUFC to watch unquestionably top-class club Rugby Union. Watkins would concede at the end of the season: "I know the decision to maintain parity with the soccer section was taken for obvious reasons, but it meant Rugby League was not the 'family' day out that we had planned. It became very expensive with three or four people each paying anything from £4 to £1.80 for stand or enclosure positions. I feel we must decide whether we want 800 people in the ground paying £4 or two to three thousand paying £2".

Watkins nevertheless declared himself broadly happy with the first season. With Carlisle winning promotion, Cardiff were at this time the only new club who had not gone into the First Division. But he pointed to the way in which Fulham had dropped straight back out of the top League, and argued: "We would have had to panic buy if we had gained promotion. The side which took the field last season was not good enough to stay in the First Division. We would have come straight down if money was not paid for the top players and that would have been the death knell for the game in Cardiff."

He expressed fears for Carlisle's prospects and his forebodings were to be proved right in the subsequent season. They came extremely close to going under in mid-season and were relegated back to the Second Division with only two wins from 30 matches, never to reach the top flight again.

Watkins declared his intention of shifting progressively towards a fully Welsh-based squad. Steps were taken towards this aim in the close season as the veterans Karalius and Nicholls left and two prominent Union players - Wales B hooker Geoff Davies and the Wales and British Lions scrum-half Brynmor Williams - were signed. And the Rugby League were clearly happy with their progress, as they were admitted to full membership at the 1982 AGM, two years earlier than had originally been intended.

Second season

The second season was expected to be one of consolidation. Watkins had long been pointing to promotion as a three-year project. The results point to consolidation - 36 points this time against 35, and another mid-table eighth place. But there was reason to feel that progress had been made after a season of violently fluctuating fortunes.

The first few games had the more optimistic Dragons fans wondering if Watkins was not being a little conservative in his hopes. Batley were beaten 32-2 on opening day, and wins over Huddersfield and Rochdale Hornets, seen off by a Barwood hat-trick, followed. Cardiff ended August top of the Second Division with a 100 per cent record, and crowds were back into four figures.

It didn't last. The Dragons had 12 more games before Christmas. They won two. With typical perversity these were two of their toughest fixtures. They had lost six games in a row when they visited Swinton - who had won eight out of 11 so far - on 7 November. Pritchard and Fleay, fulfilling the 'immutable law of the ex' scored tries, Swinton could not cross Cardiff's line and the Dragons left Station Road 12-2 winners.

Five weeks and three more defeats later, including ejection from the John Player Cup at Ninian Park by a Rochdale Hornets team in the middle of a run of one win in 12 Second Division games, Cardiff went to promotion-bound Wakefield Trinity and predictably rapidly went 12 points down. Much less predictably they hit back to trail only 15-13 at the interval, and win 27-25.

But the rest of the story prior to Christmas was singularly grim, particularly at home where they lost five consecutive matches between beating Rochdale at the end of August and seeing Blackpool Borough off by a less than convincing 8-5 on 2 January. Crowds had peaked at 1,804 for the visit of Fulham on 3 October. When they were next at home again on 14 November, less than a third of that number appeared. They were rewarded by a 17-13 defeat by Huddersfield of which Watkins said: "I'm as disappointed today as I have been at any time. There have been frustrations, but you would expect a side at least to be organised on the field. Some players just aren't good enough. They follow the ball around like sheep, and we need someone to take control on the field of play".

The turnaround finally came in the New Year. Dewsbury were beaten 26-5 at Ninian Park and this was followed by a formidable effort away to promotion-chasing Salford. The Dragons led 8-0 at half time before Fleay was sent to the sin-bin, which had been introduced only three weeks earlier, for 10 minutes and they lost their grip, eventually going down only 12-8.

But the positive signs were confirmed resoundingly the following week when Cardiff went to Wigan in the preliminary round of the Challenge Cup. They did not win, but in freezing conditions held the Riversiders to a 14-4 margin - at some cost. Two players - Arthur Daley and Nigel French - suffered serious injuries while David and Fleay barely finished the match. Wigan's Graham West also had his jaw broken. Watkins, much happier than he had been three months earlier after the Huddersfield game, commented that the Dragons had matched Wigan "in the scrums, in the loose and in the tackles (and oh! were there some tackles) indeed in almost every department we were their equals".

It was perhaps predictable that this would be followed by an anticlimactic home loss to Hunslet 24-28 in front of a crowd of 521. Cardiff would need more than the odd gallant defeat to renew its early interest. But the Wigan match marked a clear upturn in their form. Swinton, evidently favourite opponents, were seen off by a club record 40-12 with David grabbing four tries. Watkins, writing in the next home programme, described it as one of the best performances in the club's short history and said he felt the three-year promotion target was back on course. The next two months suggested he was right.

Cardiff Blue Dragons 1982-3. Photo courtesy *Open Rugby*

They went down at Keighley in the following match, but then launched into a spectacular run of eight consecutive victories, scoring 202 points, that took them from the lower reaches of the Second Division to mid-table respectability. Four of those wins were admittedly against teams who would finish in the bottom four. But a double-completing 25-12 win over Wakefield Trinity, the last in the eight-match sequence, showed that they were capable of beating the best in their division. Trinity only lost five Second Division matches all season. Champions Fulham also completed a double over them and Whitehaven had an early-season win in Cumbria.

The driving force of this superb run was the spectacular form of David, now fully adjusted to the role of prop and using his bulk and pace to devastating effect close to opposition try lines. His four against Swinton came in a burst of 11 in six games.

Six more in three games close to the end of the season brought him level with Mick Morgan's previous season record for a prop of 25 tries. The Dragons and David went to London for their final match of the season, on Challenge Cup Final eve away to Second Division champions Fulham, with the prop still needing one try. Fulham's run-in had been complicated by rows with the football club, who feared that their own chase for promotion would be ruined by damage to the pitch. The Londoners were forced to seek temporary refuge at Widnes, but this final game was played at Chelsea FC.

And a highly appropriate venue it would be as well, echoing 1066 by going into League legend as 'The Battle of Stamford Bridge'. Three players - Martin Herdman and Tony Gourley of Fulham and Chris Seldon of Cardiff were sent off as the two teams staged an 80 minute bid for the League all-comers punch throwing, foul play and ungentlemanly conduct record. But the record that really mattered went, with David crossing in the first half. And the Dragons again showed their ability to upset the Second Division's powerhouses by winning 20-14.

Not everything was well with the club. Cardiff's population remained resolutely unimpressed by the late season surge, although the final home attendance of 744 to see them go down 16-10 to Bramley, who just missed promotion, was the best since October. They were clearly down to a very small and wholly inadequate hard core.

The final league record was:

Played	Won	Draw	Lost	For	Against	Points	Position
32	17	2	13	572	444	36	8th

But in on-field terms, the club's hopes had never been higher. When Bramley returned to Ninian Park again, for the first home match of the 1983-4 season, Watkins looked back on the triumphs of the second half of the previous season and said: "I feel the squad is a good one, it has the necessary skills, confidence and commitment to make the necessary drive for promotion". The important summer signing was Chris Camilleri, a former Cardiff RUFC wing, who, after joining Barrow, had been capped twice against New Zealand in 1980. A Dragons target almost from the club's foundation, he was finally signed in August 1983. There were other signs of the club's growing credibility. In the absence of any glamour clubs in the Second Division - Salford, Fulham and Wakefield Trinity had all been promoted at the end of the previous season - the fixture planners chose the Dragons to inaugurate perhaps the strangest of League's 1980s development bids, the Maidstone-based Kent Invicta club.

In front of an 1,815 crowd, they saw off Invicta 31-12. Fenwick landed seven goals and Lynn Hallett, a converted Union outside-half from Bridgend, landed the first of the record 29 drop-goals he was to kick that season. This was a good result. Invicta may have fizzled out unhappily towards the close of the season, but they won 13 of the 18 games that followed Cardiff's visit and were serious promotion contenders until March.

Optimism was tempered only by the attendance at Ninian Park. *Western Mail* correspondent Steve Bale, later one of Britain's top Union writers, said "Cardiff City Blue Dragons deserve a far better response from an apathetic public. Saturday's invigorating match, full of sparkling running and laced with seven tries, was witnessed by a paltry Ninian Park attendance of 766. In Rugby League Championship Second Division terms that isn't bad, but inside an international stadium it's a dreadful turnout in view of the splendid entertainment on view." It was, the subsequent home programme would note, "Quite frankly not nearly enough."

Even so, an inattentive fan looking at the Second Division table in mid-October could have been forgiven for thinking that the Dragons were set to fulfil the previous season's promise. Six of their first eight matches had been won, and another drawn, putting them among the early pacemakers. The trouble was that seven of the eight matches had been against teams who would finish with records of 50 per cent or less in Second Division fixtures that season.

The single exception was the visit to Hunslet on 18 September. The Dragons arrived with three wins out of three. They left having had their limitations "put into sharp focus" by a team destined to be taken to promotion by the brilliance of scrum-half Graham King - whose two tries were among 28 for the season - and the ageless skills of loose-forward John Wolford. Fenwick was out injured and Brynmor Williams only just back after a dispute with the club. Hunslet took firm control with three tries in six minutes, Woods and Barwood were sin-binned and Leeds won 40-18. Watkins commented: "Justice was paid to us for our own inconsistency and lack of commitment".

After a relative improvement in their second season, when only two players had been sent off, discipline was again emerging as a serious problem. In Fenwick's absence Watkins had appointed Paul Woods as a stand-in captain. He recognised Woods's poor

Kent Invicta versus Cardiff Blue Dragons. Bob Fleay running with the ball.
Photo courtesy *Open Rugby*

disciplinary record, but hoped: "It will serve as a spur to him and assist him in overcoming some heated situations which he tends to get into. He might be a little more discreet". The sin-binning at Hunslet came in his second game as skipper. In his first, a 21-16 victory over Carlisle, he had been sent off for tripping. Unsurprisingly, Fenwick was soon back as captain.

Even in their better results there was a sense that not all was well. Carlisle coach John Atkinson felt both sides were well short of the quality required in the First Division. Steve Bale commented of a 26-26 draw at home to Huddersfield that there were "ominous signs" of the problems which had afflicted the Dragons in the previous year's mid-season slump, pointing out that serious promotion contenders should normally deal handily with teams clearly destined for mid-table. He was similarly unconvinced by a 36-8 win at Doncaster, arguing that there were too many handling errors.

Bob Grogan

The Cardiff public clearly shared his doubts. "Frankly not enough" or not, gates stayed stuck in the 500-600 range. Worse still, the club lost one of the key supporters who had believed unequivocally in them. Bob Grogan had retired as chairman of Cardiff City due to ill-health as the season started, and died suddenly in early September. Grogan had been, as a short memorial notice in the programme noted, one of the decisive movers in starting the club. While he was chairman, Rugby League had an influential friend at court. Without him, and with the experiment showing few signs of progress, the club was that much more vulnerable. Dave Kay, summing up the unhappy conclusion of South Wales's latest abortive League venture for *Open Rugby* a couple of years after Grogan's death, was not the only person to wonder whether things might have turned out a little differently if he had lived.

Bale's forebodings were resoundingly confirmed as the wheels came off at York on 23 October. York won 50-16, a record defeat for the Dragons: "A rare hiding which they largely brought upon themselves... humiliatingly ripped apart and ended the ill-tempered proceedings with their pride and their promotion pretensions in tatters". Pritchard and Barwood were sent off, Woods and prop Alan Evans sin-binned, and the match concluded "in a semi-brawl, and it was as well that referee Kevin Allatt, who had to separate a number of men eager for a scrap, did not have to restart play". A defeat at home by Keighley, suffering one of the worst seasons in their history, in the next match did nothing to restore optimism.

The Dragons were to win only two of their next 14 Second Division matches, destroying any promotion hopes. One of those wins, with typical perversity, came against to-be-promoted Halifax, seen off 26-18 at Ninian Park just before Christmas. But that was always a frustration with the Dragons. Amid a dire run of results, they were always likely to offer a reminder of their potential by beating, or at least seriously worrying, one of the stronger sides in their division.

There was also a strong contrast with their cup form this season. As their League hopes were crashing around them, they embarked on an impressive John Player Trophy run. Coming off those disastrous performances against York and Keighley, they had every reason to regard Rochdale Hornets' visit for the first round with some apprehension. The Dragons team produced what Watkins called "the best team Rugby since its inception" - winning by a club record 41-6 as David went over for two tries.

A fortnight later Huyton came to Ninian Park for the second round, and pulled in the first four-figure gate for more than a year. Brynmor Williams produced the form which had made him a British Lion in his Union days, scoring two tries. Although David went off injured and Ringer was sent off - allowing cartoonist Dorrien to draw a cartoon about the *Ringer is Innocent* badges issued after his sending-off at Twickenham in 1980 - the Dragons went into the last eight with a 38-12 win.

Cartoon courtesy Dorrien and the *Western Mail*

The draw took them to Leigh, champions only two years earlier. Predictions that they would slide out peacefully were confounded as they took an 8-4 lead into the second half and felt they were robbed of victory by the controversial ruling out of an apparently legitimate late try by half-back Ken Gwilliam. Leigh won 12-8, but their coach Tommy Bishop was highly impressed: "Cardiff's tactics were very good. They slowed us down and played the sort of game we had planned, but never put into operation".

Bale noted that the previous season's revival had been sparked by a near-miss in the Challenge Cup at Wigan and hoped that this disappointment against high-ranking opposition might have a similar effect. He, and the Dragons' tiny following, were to be disappointed. The worst of their mid-season slump was still to come - six consecutive defeats in January and February.

Watkins still felt that he had potentially the best squad he had had in three seasons, but that his team lacked the killer touch needed to play to their full potential. They again impressed against superior opposition when Hull came to Ninian Park for a Challenge Cup tie in February. The 2,735 was the best since Widnes had arrived at the same time two years ago - although the comparison with the 6,480 attracted on that occasion was sobering. Hull eventually won 34-6, but not before the Dragons had given them a distinctly uncomfortable first half hour. Arthur Bunting was yet another visiting First Division coach to proclaim himself impressed.

Seven wins out of nine between late March and April at least restored mid-table respectability. Crowds were now on occasion dipping below 500, with a nadir of 365 for the visit of Rochdale Hornets in early April. The main successes were individual. David scored tries with the same consistency that he had the previous season. Injuries in mid-season and again at the end cost him another shot at his record mark for a prop. But he still had the satisfaction of reaching 50 tries faster than any forward in previous League history - his 50th, at Dewsbury in late March, came in his 80th appearance only two and a half years after his debut. When he scored four times against Batley a couple of weeks later, the second quartet of his career, he had scored 21 times in 23 appearances. There were nine games to follow, but he appeared in only three, adding one more try.

The Batley game saw another multiple scoring feat, with outside-half Lynn Hallett dropping four goals. Hallett, in the middle of a run that would bring him 14 single-pointers in 10 matches, overtook the previous League record of 22 in a season the following week at home to Kent Invicta and ended the season with 29. After taking over from Fenwick as the main goalkicker when the Dragons captain was injured early in the season, he reached a total of 279 points.

Another Dragon who had a satisfactory season was Chris O'Brien. His 16 tries was second only to David - his total of 30 tries in 79 appearances second, again to David who had scored 54 in 85, in the club's three-year history.

But the season ended on a flat note with consecutive defeats against Bramley, Swinton and York - whose 28-26 victory in front of 446 people on 13 May 1984 was to be the last match played by the Dragons. In spite of the creation of a stronger committee system to support Watkins in February, support for maintaining Rugby League at Ninian Park had been running out.

SLALOM LAGER
Rugby League
Championship
Division Two
Season 1983-84

CARDIFF CITY R.L.F.C.
v.
HUYTON R.L.F.C.
SUNDAY, 29th APRIL, 1984   KICK OFF 3 p.m.
At Eugene Cross Park, Ebbw Vale.

THE BLUE
DRAGONS

Admission by programme only
Adults £2.00, Juveniles and O.A.P. £1.00

A final record of 11th place out of 18, with 31 points from 34 matches, did not encourage more positive thoughts. Nor did average crowds of 581, down nearly a third on the previous season and better than only three other clubs. The aggregate attendance for the entire home Second Division programme was lower than the number who had seen the Dragons' debut against Salford less than three years earlier.

And this allowed for the best gate of the season, attracted when the Dragons played a one-off match at Eugene Cross Park, Ebbw Vale. Nothing had come of talks with Merthyr Tydfil FC earlier in the season, but the Gwent valleys showed more interest than the capital, with 1,400 turning up to see Huyton - who cannot often have been responsible for two of the three best attendances for a club during a season - beaten 34-16 with Hallett claiming 18 points. The poor form in January and February saw a fall to 11th place out of 18, two places behind new boys Kent Invicta. The club's final record was:

Played	Won	Draw	Lost	For	Against	Points	Position
34	16	1	18	710	717	33	11th

With Grogan gone, Kenton Utilities lost interest in League. Also, the Football Association of Wales were talking of developing Ninian Park as a national football stadium, but telling Cardiff City that this was not possible if it was shared with another sport. After three years losses had been considerable, the return in terms of progress very limited. It was no great surprise when, in early summer, Cardiff City FC decided to quit Rugby League.

Chapter 11: Bridgend Blue Dragons 1984-5

The early eighties bid to make League pay in Wales was not yet over. A group of businessmen bought the Cardiff Blue Dragons out of liquidation and decided to move it to Bridgend. The town is midway between the two major centres of Swansea and Cardiff, and they decided to share the Coychurch Road ground of Bridgend Town FC. The key figures were advertising executive Clive Millman, who had been on the committee set up to assist David Watkins earlier in the year at Cardiff, Barry antique dealer Laurie Tattersall, who became chairman, former black and white minstrel Bryn Williams and Eugene Caparros, an Abergavenny night club owner who lived in Bridgend.

They were accepted as League members, retaining the Dragons nickname, colours and player registrations, in early August amid optimistic noises from the new management. Millman blamed the remoteness of Cardiff City's Newcastle-based ownership for the old club's failure and argued that Bridgend should have no difficulty in attracting the 1,500-2,000 crowds set as a target: "I think Cardiff City could have averaged that if the game had been better promoted. And the feeling is that Bridgend is the ideal location for attracting people from the valleys and from Swansea."

The newcomers inevitably evoked memories of Bridgend RUFC's exile from the Brewery Field, but found the Union club in relaxed mood. Durbar Lawrie, still secretary after 35 years, said he did not see the League club as a serious threat: "At this stage we see it merely as an additional sporting venture in a continually developing town and area. It would be ungenerous of me or my club to denigrate the efforts of a very ambitious group of people who are prepared to provide the vital cash despite the calamitous record of Rugby League in Wales." He sent the Dragons a letter of good wishes before their debut against Swinton in September.

As well as a new location, the club had to find a new captain and coach. Watkins opted not to go to Bridgend, and was joined in his decision by Fenwick, David and Brynmor Williams.

The coaching was taken over, for a three month trial period, by Jeff Woods, a former Salford A team and colts player, who had made his mark in Wales as president of the students' union at Cardiff University. Following Watkins's example of the previous season, he opted for a talented player with a questionable disciplinary record as skipper, giving the job to Gordon Pritchard (his namesake Paul Woods was not available for the post this time, having picked up a 12-match ban for yet another sending off towards the end of the previous season, and had played his last match for the club). Pritchard, unhappily, would live up to the Woods precedent by getting himself sent off twice, incurring total suspensions of six matches, in his 10 appearances for Bridgend.

But Woods proclaimed himself happy with his squad, which included a link with Bridgend's Rugby League past in Welsh Students hooker Kerry Sheehy, son of former Keighley and Dewsbury player Danny, who had been among the stalwarts of the post-war Welsh League. Kerry and his brother Danny, who would also appear for Bridgend during the subsequent season, have been leading figures in Welsh League ever since - Kerry becoming Welsh development officer as the game attempted to adopt a more proactive approach to development outside the heartlands in the early 1990s.

A further link with the past was present at the opening match against Swinton on 13 September, 61-year-old Ron Durston who had been one of the stars of the post-war

Bridgend club and had played the odd game for Cardiff in 1951-2. He said: "I'll be backing them all the way and I hope that the rest of the South Wales public will give them a fair crack of the whip. I know they have some very talented players and are capable of some great Rugby... The Cardiff people didn't want to know, but I think the story in Bridgend will be a little different."

Swinton's visit

Director Laurie Tattersall had hoped for a gate of between 3,500 and 4,000 at Coychurch Road for the visit of Swinton. The gate they did get was the best for a Second Division game since the Dragons fourth ever match, nearly three years earlier. But, though Tattersall said he was satisfied, it was still some way from those optimistic hopes, at a little below 2,000.

The game too produced mixed indications. Bridgend were far from outclassed, even though they lost. *Glamorgan Gazette* reporter Ian Brown wrote that the game had made "an encouraging return to Bridgend". Coach Woods said "there were plenty of encouraging signs and we have plenty to build on" in the 28-16 defeat, highlighted by dominant scrummaging from forwards led by giant prop Alan Evans and tries from Pritchard, Camilleri and on-loan Wigan scrum-half Ness Flowers, a Welsh international.

They were not to know that, far from being a mere beginning, this was to be a high-point. Gates were to show a similar pattern to those in the opening season at Cardiff, although the numbers all too rapidly became reminiscent of those attracted by the 1951-2 Cardiff club. Just more than 1,000 attended the next home match and the next four games saw a steady drop from 780 to 532. In November, the club damaged their credibility with their supporters further by switching their first round John Player Special Trophy match with Castleford to their opponents' Wheldon Road ground. Their share of a 1,803 gate and a 42-4 defeat were the result. But the visit of the first division giants could have given the club a boost in their struggle to survive.

Bad weather and the resulting fixture schedule meant two and a half months with only a single home match, as only 275 supporters came to see Carlisle. By the time they began their post-Christmas home programme in early February, the hard core had been reached with 185, close to the average who would attend the last half dozen games.

The Cardiff Dragons had lost support hand over

fist while doing reasonably well. Given Bridgend's results they could hardly expect any better. Defeat followed defeat in apparently endless succession. Woods did his best to encourage the fans, insisting in early October that "This club is not headed for oblivion". Maybe not, but he was out before the end of the month following a series of displays variously reported as "inept" and "sorry".

He was replaced by John Warlow, who had been capped seven times for Great Britain after joining St Helens from Llanelli. He promised "we will win soon" and with the assistance of the club's northern representative Norman Graveson initiated another reminder of the post-war Cardiff club, a trawl of northern clubs seeking experienced on-loan players to reinforce his own inadequate squad.

Those so acquired included former Union internationals Glyn Shaw of Wigan and Roy Mathias of St Helens, Chris Bowman of Bramley, John Gilmore from Rochdale and Dave Vickers of Featherstone.

More permanent signings included St Helens hooker Mick Glover and goal-kicking wing Dave Alred, whose credentials included spells as a specialist kicker in American Football. But despite the new players, there was no improvement in the club's fortunes. In late December, following a second defeat by opening opponents Swinton who scored 10 tries in a 54-12 massacre, Warlow admitted: "We just haven't got the pace to compete. It's the same story every week." Since opening day, he felt, "They've got much better and we've got worse".

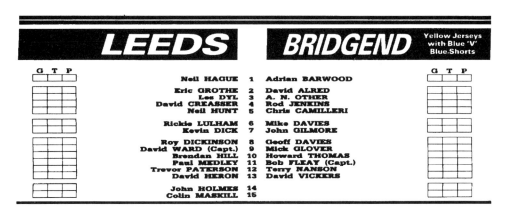

The programme team line-ups for the 68-6 cup defeat at Leeds

By the turn of the year, serious doubts were being reported over the club's future. Tattersall denied that they were in danger, but accepted that the increased cost of bringing players from the north was proving burdensome: "It's bitterly disappointing that our plans for an all-Welsh team have had to be buried. But if we are to survive we must have competent players - and they are in the north."

It is clear that the club's problems were starting to produce internal dissent - club secretary Clive Millman, in a letter to *Open Rugby* after the end of the season, would point to internal disputes without going into detail. He, Tattersall and Warlow all left in January, leaving Caparros in sole charge, although ousted coach Jeff Woods was reported to be putting together a consortium to bid for the club.

The win

Fears that the club would go through the entire season without a win were finally ended in mid-February when Sheffield Eagles, whose opening season contained only limited suggestions that they were destined to be by far the most successful of League's 1980s expansions clubs, were beaten 28-12 at Coychurch Road. David Barwood, brother of Adrian, claimed one try with others coming from Mike and Geoff Davies and former Sheffield player Dave Alred landing eight goals. This match was clearly traumatic for the Eagles. Founder and coach Gary Hetherington recalled it with horror in *The Greatest Game's* series "Most memorable matches". He said "The scenes of jubilation and euphoria at the end of the match were akin to a Challenge Cup semi-final win". The programme for the Sheffield Eagles versus St Helens Super League match at Cardiff in 1996 also recalled the "Day of Disaster". Legend has it that Hetherington compensated the 22 hardy Eagles fans who had made the trip to South Wales.

But any hopes that this presaged a serious upturn were rapidly dashed as the final few months of the season degenerated into farce. Money worries and the disillusionment of professional players meant the club became increasingly reliant on amateurs - in particular students from the South Glamorgan Institute of Higher Education. The institute has a spectacular record of producing serious rugby talent, but to ask League novices, however talented, to match professionals was too much.

A. N. Other

The end-of-season records would show that they had used 26 trialists, who made a total of 126 appearances between them. 'Trialist' was the commonest name on the scoresheet, accounting for six tries, all of them in the last couple of months.

On away trips in particular it was not uncommon for the Bridgend team to consist of two or three familiar names - Alred, Camilleri and Glover were among those who stuck it out - and the rest were A.N. Others. The programmes for the final matches at Whitehaven and Carlisle were printed with blanks where the Bridgend names should be. When the team was finally announced it had 14 A.N. Others. Visits to Fulham and Dewsbury produced similarly surreal lists, with the effect at Dewsbury compounded by a debut as substitute for the 39-year old Caparros, the oldest ever senior debutant playing his first ever game of League. Runcorn's team doctor was also recruited, although a tale about a coach driver being pressed into service may be apocryphal.

CARLISLE		BRIDGEND
1. David Smith	1.	
2. Graeme Robinson	2.	
3. Tony Binder	3.	
4. Garry Peacham	4.	
5. John Stockley	5.	
6. Kevin Pape	6.	
7. Dean Carroll	7.	
8. Colin Armstrong	8.	
9. Ian Crowther	9.	
10. Alan Hardy	10.	
11. Maurice Lucas	11.	
12. Kevan Robinson	12.	
13. Karl Portz	13.	
Subs.	Subs.	
14.	14.	
15.	15.	

The programme team line-ups
for the match at Carlisle

The final home match at Coychurch Road: Bridgend versus Doncaster 21 April 1995.
Photos: Mike Haddon

Their final league record in which they finished 20th and last, the worst for a professional club since the second world war, was:

Played	Won	Drawn	Lost	For	Against	Points	Position
28	1	0	27	258	966	2	20th

Bridgend Town FC were unsurprisingly reported to be unhappy. A tenant attracting crowds of 2,000 was one thing. When crowds were less than a tenth of that, there seemed little point. Yet the club went into the close season talking optimistically of a move to nearby Maesteg. They were included in the 1985-6 fixtures, with their opening game at Fulham on 1 September.

But the Rugby League authorities were increasingly concerned about the condition of both Bridgend and Southend (previously Kent Invicta). In August, so close to the start of the season that the article on Bridgend for the Fulham programme had already been researched and written, the League Council decided to suspend the memberships of both clubs for one year to allow them to prove that they could run viable senior clubs. Southend's results had been marginally better than Bridgend's, their crowds even worse.

It was a death sentence. Nobody appears to have doubted this or particularly worried about it. Once again the League dream had died in Wales, ironically this time at just the point when the flow of Welsh stars to the northern clubs was restarting. But this should not be taken to indicate that the likes of Terry Holmes or Rob Ackerman would have provided a lifeline. As the Welsh clubs had discovered before 1914, the best talent will want to play at the top level, irrespective of location. Bradford Northern would still have been more attractive to Terry Holmes than Cardiff or Bridgend, as would Whitehaven to Rob Ackerman. A successful Welsh club would have been a different matter, but once again it had not happened. Many observers forgivably assumed that this was the end for the game in Wales, for another 25 to 30 years at least. But in fact the next bid was only a decade away.

Chapter 12: Charity Shield and Festival

The CIS 1990 Charity Shield: Widnes 24 Wigan 8
The Vetch Field, Swansea 19 August 1990

Former Union players star

The Charity Shield was used by the Rugby League in the late 1980s and early 1990s as a development tool for the game. From the Isle of Man, it moved to Liverpool FC's Anfield ground in 1989, Swansea in 1990, then Gateshead in 1991 and 1992. Swansea has always had a fascination for Rugby League. It has seen some of the highest attendances for games in Wales and this CIS Charity Shield game drew a creditable crowd of 11,178, which was not bad considering the torrential downpour on the day.

The crowd included a preponderance of intrigued west Wales Rugby fans, and they were not to be disappointed as all the scorers were former Union stars, with former Llanelli favourite Jonathan Davies, running the show for victors Widnes. Man-of-the-Match, Davies scored three tries, curiously his first hat-trick in either code, fellow Welshman John Devereux also crossed the whitewash. Martin Offiah scored the other Widnes try with Davies kicking two goals. Perversely, all the scorers later returned to Rugby Union later in their careers, two to play in Wales.

The Wigan side had yet to reach their peak and met Widnes in their pomp. A Wigan team decimated with injuries was no match for the Chemics, though former All Black Frano Botica did manage a try and two goals for the Cherry and Whites. The attendance showed that with a serious approach a regular following could be built for Rugby League in Wales, but no one has had the long term vision, and cash, to build on the obvious interest in top quality League in the principality.

Widnes: Tait; Devereux, Currier, Davies, Offiah; Myler, D. Hulme; Ashurst, McKenzie, Grima, P. Hulme, Koloto, Holliday. Substitutes: Sorensen, Wright.
Wigan: Gilfillan; Myers, Bell, Byrne, Preston; Botica, Goulding; Skerrett, Bridge, Wane, Gildart, Platt, Betts. Substitutes: Edwards, Forshaw.

Widnes versus Wigan 1990 Charity Shield at Swansea. Photo: Mike Haddon

The 1991 Welsh Amateur Rugby League Festival

The growth of amateur and student Rugby League in Wales in the 1980s and early 1990s was apparent when the first Welsh Amateur Rugby League Festival was held in 1991. The 10-a-side tournament was held at Swansea Uplands Rugby Union club, and was contested by amateur and student Rugby League sides, and select teams often based on players from Rugby Union clubs.

Great controversy developed around the tournament over the attitude of the Welsh Rugby Union (see interview with Phil Melling in Chapter 17). Despite the "free passage" agreed between amateur Rugby League and Rugby Union in 1987, the WRU tried to undermine the tournament in different ways. Credit is due to Swansea Uplands RFC for resisting pressure put on them by the WRU to cancel the tournament. Tom Keaveney, BARLA's national secretary wrote to WRU secretary Dennis Evans, saying that his circular about the festival was "totally misleading and is obviously done with the intention of preventing your players from practising their freedom of choice". Despite all this, the tournament was a great success, with 12 teams entering. The Griffin Inn, organised by Bob Harris and including a number of Pontypridd Rugby Union players, won the trophy. They beat Bryn Rangers 20-18 after extra time in the final;. Bryn were coached by former Wales, Wigan and Cardiff Blue Dragons player Ness Flowers and included well-known Union players David Morgan of Neath and Mark Bennett of Swansea. The Plate final was won by North Gower, who beat Swansea University 18-4. Ness Flowers was voted 'Player of the Tournament'.

Maurice Oldroyd, BARLA's Chief Executive said that the festival "really was a magnificent occasion and without doubt, in my opinion, the most successful single development initiative I have had the pleasure of being involved with". And a good time was had by all.

WELSH RUGBY UNION

Headquarters: CARDIFF ARMS PARK

P.O. Box 22
Cardiff CF1 1JL
Telephone: (0222) 390111
Telegrams: Welrun, Cardiff
Telex: 498966 WRU HQ
Fax: (0222) 378472

Secretary: D. P. Evans

Our Ref:

Your Ref:

10 July 1991

To: ALL WRU CLUBS

Dear Secretary

AMATEUR RUGBY LEAGUE

You may be aware that Swansea Uplands RFC will be used for a competition with regard to the captioned sport. You should be aware that your insurance cover from the Welsh Rugby Union does not apply in this instance.

I am also seeking further advice concerning the status of Rugby Union clubs playing for a trophy donated by a professional and whether this should be accepted by an amateur Club.

I shall keep you informed of further developments.

The WRU's concern about the tournament

Chapter 13: The 1995 World Cup

The Rugby League World Cup has never quite achieved the status of its football counterpart. Not for Rugby League the metronome-like appearance of a tournament every four years, it has tended to appear on a more *ad hoc* basis.

And this is a pity really, because the tournament got off to an excellent start in 1954. The inaugural event saw a surprise final pairing as Great Britain beat France in a dramatic match in Paris, in front of more than 30,000 people. Ironically, from the point of view of Welsh Rugby League, the participation of the Great Britain side, and not separate teams representing England and Wales, was one of the factors in the demise of the Welsh international side at that time.

The five tournaments staged between 1957 and 1972 all took place over a period of three or four weeks. The first competition that saw direct Welsh interest was in 1975, when the tournament was spread over a mammoth eight months. It was played in England, Wales, France, Australia and New Zealand. Wales's best result, fondly remembered by the players who took part, was a 12-7 victory over England in Brisbane, which in effect, when the final table was drawn up, stopped the old enemy from winning the tournament.

The next three tournaments again saw Welsh players playing in the Great Britain side rather than in their own national team and so the 1995 tournament was only the second one that saw a Welsh team participating under its own flag. This competition was intended to mark 100 years of Rugby League, but originally Wales were not even included in the starting line-up, which was to be eight teams, despite their dramatically improved performances under coach Clive Griffiths and captain Jonathan Davies. Only when it was decided, after intense lobbying, to expand the tournament to 10 teams, were the Welsh included

The tournament promised much. Taking place only weeks after Rugby League's official centenary, the countries initially were divided into three groups. Two groups were based in England, one in Wales. Fiji, South Africa, Tonga and Western Samoa were competing for the first time. There was also an emerging nations tournament, including the tiny Cook Islands against the geographical might of the USA.

International exotica was coming to the Rugby League heartlands. Papua New Guinea against Tonga - at Hull; Fiji against South Africa - at Keighley. And the tournament's "Group of Death" was to be based in Wales, with the home nation, France and Western Samoa competing for one semi-final spot.

Despite inadequate publicity, limited terrestrial TV coverage by the BBC, and a ticketing system that left much to be desired, the tournament is remembered as one of the highlights of recent Rugby League history.

And for Wales, the pre-tournament signs were good. Victories over England and France earlier in 1995 had resulted in their first European Championship triumph since 1938. Some of the newer squad members had gained international experience on a tour to the USA in the summer. And the new nationality qualification rules, allowing players with Welsh grandparents to play for Wales, had given the squad new strength in depth.

Suddenly Wales's traditional strength in the backs was fortified by the Wigan front row of Kelvin Skerrett, Martin Hall and Neil Cowie. Leeds's Richie Eyres, despite having played for England against Wales in 1992, was also allowed to play for the land of his ancestors. It was not only Wales who benefited from this ruling. Similar discretion was given to Tonga and Western Samoa to include players more familiar at international level in a New Zealand jersey.

Thirteen of the Welsh squad were former Rugby Union internationals, and 11 were English-born. But nine of the players were aged 30 or older, and another two were 29. This was clearly a warning sign of the need to find younger players for the future. But for this tournament, the squad looked well-balanced and very competitive. This reflected the work that coach Clive Griffiths and team manager Mike Nicholas had done.

One unwanted distraction before the World Cup started concerned the future of Welsh captain Jonathan Davies. He was looking to return to Rugby Union with Cardiff after the lifting of the Union ban on former League players. He wanted the World Cup to be his finale to a superb six-year Rugby League career. Warrington were seeking a transfer fee for him, because he was under contract to them. It was also a first warning of how Rugby Union might start to "cherry pick" from Rugby League.

An Australian newspaper preview of the tournament saw Wales's group as set to be "the closest and most intriguing of the three groups". Dave Hadfield in *The Independent* believed that Wales "start with obvious advantages and with the mighty asset of Jonathan Davies... as captain and inspiration". He also believed that "the sheer size of their forwards is Wales's other potential trump card". Of the other two teams in the group, he said that Western Samoa had "wonderful individual talent", and that the French had an "eternal unpredictability". One weakness for the Western Samoa side was that they had not played together before as a team, although they had star individuals such as Va'aiga Tuigamala of Wigan. Coach Graham Lowe, who had played and coached at the top with Wigan and New Zealand, would have to build them into a team very quickly.

Wales coach Clive Griffiths. Photo: Peter Lush

Wales versus France

The group opener saw Wales play France at the Cardiff Blue Dragons' former home, Ninian Park. Scheduled to kick off at 8.00 pm, the kick off was delayed by a bizarre ticketing system that meant fans had to queue at a ticket office rather than buy tickets at the turnstiles. The crowd, one of the highest ever for a Rugby League game at Ninian Park, clearly inspired the Welsh team. The Rugby Union supporters present were sometimes confused by the referee's signals, mixing up the signal for the fifth tackle with that for a try, but all were certainly very enthusiastic!

The early exchanges had Wales on top but, after 24 minutes, they only had two Jonathan Davies penalties to show for their pressure producing a 4-0 lead. But then a move initiated by Davies, and involving Iestyn Harris and Allan Bateman saw Anthony Sullivan score in the corner.

Davies missed the conversion, and the Welsh then had a let off when the French hit the posts with a penalty. But two minutes from half-time, Davies gathered a loose ball after Mark Perrett tackled Thierry Valero, and Harris put Sullivan through for his second try. So Wales went in at half time with a 12-0 lead.

Seven minutes after the break, Wales consolidated their lead with Sullivan's third try. Harris gathered a kick, and charged into the French half. He passed to Martin Hall, who released the ball to John Devereux, and then to Davies, who put Sullivan in for his hat-trick.

The French briefly threatened when Torreilles scored after 54 minutes, Banquet converted for a score of 18-6. Wales then had to reorganise when Davies was taken off with mild concussion. With their inspirational captain on the way to hospital, Harris moved to stand-off. He then made the game safe for Wales with a solo try after 61 minutes. Devereux added a further try to give the Welsh a well deserved 28-6 victory.

An unexpected concern for Wales came after the game, when it was realised they had made five substitutions. There was confusion over the 'blood bin' rule, but luckily the tournament organisers decided that no action should be taken against the Welsh. Graham Thomas in the *South Wales Echo* recognised the impact of the "power-packed surges of the impressive Welsh forwards", while *League Express* reporter Andy Wilson saw Iestyn Harris as the "man-of-the-match".

French manager Tas Batieri acknowledged his team's problems, saying "We are a very amateur team with a lack of experience of professional football. Wales are big name, top line players".

The Welsh now realised that if the strong Western Samoa squad could overcome the French at Ninian Park on Thursday as expected, the clash of the group titans for a semi-final place would happen the following Sunday at Swansea's Vetch Field ground.

France versus Western Samoa

This was Western Samoa's debut in the World Cup. But to class them in the same lowly status as the other debutantes - often keen but naive, would be a major mistake. Virtually every player was with a major English, Australian or New Zealand club. And any side with Halifax's John Schuster and Wigan's Tuigamala in the backs was a serious

Anthony Sullivan: hat-trick hero against France. Photo: Graham Clay & *League Express*

proposition. In the forwards, St Helens's star Apollo Perelini could not even make the starting line up.

Western Samoa came fresh to the game, while France were still recovering from their beating by Wales three days before. Despite this, the French took the lead after two minutes, Didier Cabestany and Karl Jaavou setting up Pierre Chamorin to score. Freddie Banquet missed the conversion. After this brief French lead, the rest of the half was one-way traffic.

A Willie Poching drive saw Tony Tatupu score, and Schuster's conversion gave Western Samoa the lead. By half-time, it was 26-4, with Schuster having kicked five goals from five attempts.

The Western Samoan pressure continued in the second half, and they were leading 50-4 before Cabestany scored for the French eight minutes from time. A final Western Samoa try - their tenth - with Schuster's eighth goal - gave the Samoans a 56-10 victory.

Only 2,173 people attended the game. Although this was described as "sparse" in *League Express*, and "a few dozen" by Simon Barnes in *The Times*, it was not a bad attendance given that more than 10,000 had been at the same ground to watch home favourites Wales only three days before.

Graham Lowe said his team had prepared with "a few beers, touch rugby and a sing song". But the *Daily Telegraph's* John Whalley recognised their qualities: "Samoa looked a very good side, full of enterprising runners, while some of their handling was a delight to watch".

Would this be enough to beat Wales at Swansea on Sunday? A full house was expected at the Vetch Field for the game that would decide the "group of death".

Wales versus Western Samoa

For Welsh Rugby Union fans, the name "Western Samoa" was a bitterly familiar one. One of the lowest points of Welsh Rugby Union in recent years had been Wales's defeat by the Western Samoans in the 1991 Rugby Union World Cup. Could the Rugby League team avenge this defeat, and win a semi-final place against England, who had won their group, at Old Trafford?

The Western Samoan side certainly brought great national pride to the game, combined with enormous strength and skill. Kevin Mitchell's preview in *The Observer* described the "uninhibited menace and joy" with which they "trampled on the egos and bewildered bodies of France". Coach Graham Lowe said that "they play with a flair that many clubs spend hours trying to develop and they've got the size that people spend thousands of dollars in the gym trying to reproduce". But Welsh coach Clive Griffiths was confident, saying "I think we've got the firepower to match these fellows".

Hundreds were locked out of the Vetch Field, as the kick was delayed (again) by 15 minutes. A 15,385 crowd were joined by record viewing figures on Welsh TV channel S4C. And even the weather was good - not always the case for big Rugby League occasions in Wales.

The tone was set almost immediately, with Kelvin Skerrett clashing with the Western Samoan forwards - and winning the penalty from English referee Russell Smith. The Welsh were powering forward and Scott Quinnell, on his international home debut, was held up on the line. Tea Ropati was sin-binned for holding down, but Jonathan Davies missed the resulting penalty.

However, shortly afterwards Wales took the lead. From a scrum after the Western Samoans had been forced into touch, Kevin Ellis passed to Iestyn Harris, who scored under the posts. Davies converted - six minutes gone and 6-0 to Wales.

A further penalty miss by Davies followed. Quinnell was again stopped on the line. But then the Western Samoans were suddenly back in the game. Sam Panapa fed Via Matautia, who beat two defenders, dummied around Iestyn Harris and scored under the posts. Schuster converted, and with 18 minutes gone it was 6-6.

Although Davies had missed a couple of penalties, it was his superb kick through that restored Wales's lead. Kicking on the first tackle from the scrum caught the Western Samoan defence flat-footed, and Anthony Sullivan sped through to score in the corner. Davies converted, 22 minutes gone, 12-6 to Wales.

A 50-metre penalty from Schuster bought the Samoans back to 12-8. Any club ties were forgotten as Tuigamala flattened his Wigan colleague Martin Hall, and it was all very tight. A couple of minutes later, Davies restored Wales's six point lead with a penalty to make it 14-8. Then just on half time, a Schuster penalty bought the gap back to four points, and Wales went in 14-10 ahead.

The second half opened with Davies narrowly missing with a penalty five yards into the Samoan half. And Russell Smith's tolerant refereeing continued of what was becoming a fierce contest, when a punch-up involving Matautia and Moriarty on the Welsh line resulted in a penalty to Wales, but no other action being taken.

Davies consolidated Wales's lead with a drop-goal after 49 minutes, stretching the lead to 15-10. Perhaps the turning point came when the inspirational and talismanic figure of Rowland Phillips came on for the battered Moriarty, who slumped in the dugout. His running began to cause panic in the Samoan ranks, and their indiscipline was shown again when Des Maea was sin-binned for a high tackle on Bateman. Davies kicked the penalty, and with 58 minutes gone, 17-10 to Wales. The Samoans, temporarily down to 12 men, now needed two scores to take the lead.

The battle continued as both sides came close to scoring. Adrian Hadley was caught by Panapa on the line, when it looked certain he would score. Skerrett came back on from the substitutes' bench, and was soon tackled high by Tuigamala. As Wales were camped on the Western Samoa line, Harris dropped a goal to stretch the Welsh lead further. 18-10 with five minutes left. "Land of my fathers" rang out from the terraces.

As the Samoans tired at the end of what Christopher Irvine in *The Times* called a "brutally compelling" contest, Kevin Ellis sealed the victory with a try from a Rowland Phillips pass to give the Welsh a 22-10 victory and the semi-final place.

Scott Quinnell won the 'man-of-the-match" award, but Iestyn Harris was again superb for Wales at full-back. Kevin Ellis acknowledged the inspirational atmosphere, saying "When the going got tough, the crowd got behind us. Hearing "Bread of Heaven" and the anthem sung like that was unbelievable".

Dave Hadfield in *The Independent* said the match was "the fiercest if far from the fanciest" of the World Cup, and recognised Kelvin Skerrett's role in "waging war from prop, and the rest of the pack following his lead".

The celebrations at the end were long and passionate. Pride had been restored to Welsh sport by its Rugby League team. And the old enemy, England, awaited them at Old Trafford the following Saturday.

England versus Wales

The motorways from the valleys to Old Trafford were filled with cars and coaches bringing the Welsh supporters to the semi-final. Many were wearing Welsh Rugby League replica shirts, showing the impact the team had made. Ken Jones in *The Independent* described the "groundswell of enthusiasm" that had overcome "deep prejudice" against Rugby League in Wales.

The impact the team had made was spreading. In the *South Wales Evening Post*, former Wales and Great Britain Rugby Union international Clem Thomas suggested that if a Welsh team was chosen from players of both codes, every position would be filled by Rugby League players. Apparently, even former Welsh Rugby Union skipper Cliff Morgan agreed!

And if Wales lost, the semi-final would be Jonathan Davies's international finale, and as it turned out his final Rugby League match. Mike Nicholas, the Wales team manager, said he was "right up there with the best of them" of players who had gone north. Davies himself said that "the spirit in our squad is greater than any I have known in Union or League". He said that people had been stopping the players in the street and wishing them luck. Six years before, when he had left Welsh Rugby Union to join Widnes, he was not sure he would be welcome back home.

Memories of the World Cup: Pennants proudly on display in Clive Griffiths's office at London Welsh RUFC. Photo: Peter Lush

John Devereux and Scott Gibbs passed fitness tests to take their places in the Welsh team. England fielded four Wigan players, and three former ones now playing for clubs in Australia or New Zealand. Gary Connolly was unfit, and Bobby Goulding continued at scrum-half for the injured Shaun Edwards.

The sides had met twice before in the World Cup, in the marathon 1975 tournament. Wales's famous victory at Brisbane in June was avenged by a 22-16 England victory at Warrington in front of 5,034 fans. More than 30,000 would fill Old Trafford, the crowd restricted by the redevelopment work at the stadium, for this battle for a Wembley final place. Between 7,000 and 10,000 had made the journey from South Wales.

A Davies penalty gave Wales the lead after 16 minutes, quickly equalised by one from Andy Farrell. Then, after a Jason Robinson run had taken England to the half-way line, a move between Farrell and Phil Clarke gave Paul Newlove the chance to score in the corner. 6-2 to England.

Another Davies penalty bought Wales closer at 6-4. Then Kris Radlinski launched a bomb, it bounced back to him, he slipped the ball to Goulding who scored a drop goal, to make it 7-4 to England after 34 minutes.

Just before half time, a Farrell pass put Tony Smith through, and he put Dennis Betts in to score. Farrell missed the conversion, so at half time, England led 11-4.

Two minutes after the break, Paul Moriarty was sin-binned. England's numerical advantage immediately came into play. Goulding's cross-field kicking had already been a key feature of England's play in the tournament. A minute after the sin-binning, the tactic worked again. Offiah caught the ball unchallenged and touched down to score. Was he offside? The officials didn't think so. 15-4 to England.

Fifteen minutes later, Offiah ran onto another Goulding kick. This time video replays showed that he appeared to 'bounce' the ball instead of making a clean touchdown. But this was before the 'video replay' was available to the officials, and they gave the try. It was now 19-4.

Rowland Phillips then came on for Skerrett, and quickly scored to raise Welsh hopes. Tackled by Nick Pinkney, he played the ball to himself, and crashed over. Davies converted, and Wales had pulled back to 19-10 with 14 minutes left.

With three minutes to go, Anthony Sullivan broke away and sped down the touchline, only for Radlinski to catch him and tackle him into touch. It was a key moment. Wales's last chance had gone, and a final England try by Phil Clarke, converted by Bobby Goulding gave England a 25-10 victory, and the prized place at Wembley. Jonathan Davies wiped away a tear at the end of the game, as the Welsh team left the pitch to an ovation from both sets of fans.

As Peter Corrigan said in the *Independent on Sunday*, "the Welsh team... has done so much to give this World Cup a touch of extra magic and drama". In the *Observer*, Eddie Butler said that Iestyn Harris was "again outstanding" at full-back, and that Anthony Sullivan "ran with an unrewarded spirit and strength".

Graham Thomas in the *South Wales Echo* said that the Wales Rugby League side had "won nothing but pride and new admirers", and compared them with the Rugby Union team's experience in their World Cup in South Africa, when they were "humbled and humiliated".

The team's outstanding achievements were recognised when they won the BBC Wales Sports Team of the Year award for 1995. Presenter Alan Wilkins described them as "the team that captured the hearts and minds of the Welsh public". Surely now Rugby League would build on this success, and make a breakthrough at club level in Wales.

Chapter 14: South Wales RLFC 1996

It may seem strange to those who do not understand the Welsh love of rugby, but the biggest viewing figures in proportion to regional population for Rugby League on Sky satellite television are not in the north of England but in South Wales.

As preceding chapters have shown, the area is potentially fruitful ground for professional Rugby League. On the back of its rising popularity thanks to Sky TV's coverage, and the 1995 World Cup, came the birth of South Wales RLFC. The World Cup had seen a full house at Swansea's Vetch Field for Wales versus Western Samoa, a crowd of more than 10,000 for Wales versus France in Cardiff but also more than 2,000 for the midweek France versus Western Samoa clash, played only three days after Wales had played in the same stadium. In fact, the response of the Welsh public to the Wales games took everyone from the ticketing agency to the game's administrators by surprise.

Thus the potential support for the South Wales club was the army of between 7,000 and 10,000 Welsh supporters who travelled from the principality to Old Trafford for the World Cup semi-final against the old enemy, England. If this number of rugby lovers was prepared to travel to see a game 150 miles away, how many would turn up to see competitive Rugby League in South Wales? The Welsh Rugby League team had won the BBC Wales *Sports Team of the Year* award for their World Cup exploits. Accepting the award, captain Jonathan Davies (ironically by then back in Rugby Union with Cardiff) said that "The RFL should build on the progress that was made last year [1995]".

The response of the hierarchy was predictably slow and cautious. Despite the creation of the new Rupert Murdoch-backed Super League venture and its 'European' tag, the idea that Wales was another country in Europe was slow to dawn. The initial announcement from the RFL at the birth of Super League in April 1995, did suggest a club from Wales would be part of Super League. But when the dust settled, the brave new Rugby League world in South Wales would have to live with the initial idea of a Second (in reality third) Division side. Super League status would come, the club was told, when they had established themselves in the lower flight. It was Wales national team manager Mike Nicholas's initiative and hard work in getting the club off the ground that saw South Wales accepted as League members in February 1996, just six weeks before the new season.

In some ways the idea for a two stage development was not a bad one. The club could gather its resources, build up a base, gain good publicity and then the following season burst ready into the big time. But this plan was to fail, not least because the wild enthusiasm of the World Cup period was allowed to dribble away and a new professional Rugby Union revolution was about to muddy the best laid plans of the club and the RFL.

As with all Rugby League developments, the first and last worry was money, after all the sport is professional and books have to be balanced. The main problem for South Wales was that, although the Rugby League Council members were happy with the £87 million bestowed on them by Rupert Murdoch's News Corporation at the launch of Super League, they did not necessarily wish to share it with a new club from Wales, until they had proved themselves worthy of funding. Wasn't it enough that London had been given preference over other clubs to join the Super League, and that there was already one new club from foreign parts in Paris St Germain?

The new boys not only would have to start at the bottom initially but also did not even ask for a share of the Murdoch millions. Incredibly (but not suprisingly), the existing clubs had shared this among themselves and had not left enough for developing the game in other areas, despite the almost claustrophobic clutter of clubs along the M62 corridor in Yorkshire and Lancashire. Therefore the seeds for the future development of any new Super League club were already in doubt. Even if not asking for financial support probably helped gain acceptance, it limited the South Wales club's activities.

In December, Mike Nicholas had moved from his Warrington home to set up a base in Cardiff. He won the support of a number of businessmen to back the new South Wales venture, including locals Bob Phillips and Jeff Taylor and northerner Joe Cassidy.

The club clearly had to be built from the bottom up. The first priority for Nicholas was to tempt the Welsh national coach Clive Griffiths back to South Wales. By mid-March he had succeeded, also employing Danny Sheehy as assistant coach. Clive Griffiths, capped by Wales at both codes, and a Rugby League coach of high standing was a very significant signing for the new club. Danny Sheehy was manager of the Welsh Students team, and one of the key people in amateur Rugby League in Wales.

Union reaction

The Welsh Rugby Union response was mixed. Whereas both Second Division Aberavon and First Division giants Cardiff were happy to ground share with the new League minnows, because this brought them valuable income in the new Union professional era, the question of sharing players, which had been considered now that Union was openly professional, was a different matter.

Surprisingly, it was the Welsh ex-League players who were the biggest opponents of the South Wales club. Stuart Gallacher of Llanelli and Terry Holmes of Cardiff, were hostile to co-operating with the new boys. This posed a problem for the club, because they had hoped that with the new era of professional Union there would be a cross-over of players, especially with the dawn of Super League seeing a switch to summer Rugby League which meant the codes' seasons were no longer concurrent.

Both Pontypridd and Swansea put a block on their players training with the new outfit and there was in fact a *de facto* wall built between the codes with only a few clubs like Aberavon and Glamorgan Wanderers breaching it. Mike Nicholas even went as far as seeking legal advice on the question of restraint of trade. Clive Griffiths said in an interview in *League Express*: "Rugby League is used to having its back against the wall in Wales. It's been that way since 1895. What the people who still can't come to terms with League must realise is that it has survived that dark age and simply won't go away. I keep asking myself what are they afraid of ?"

The players

So, despite a number of well-known Union players being interested, and some training with the club, they mainly withdrew under pressure from their clubs. Some of these Union players had played Rugby League for the Welsh Students side coached by Clive Griffiths. So, the club was left to rely on former Welsh student players, Welsh amateurs, old pros on loan from the north plus a handful of Welsh RU trialists, it was definitely a theme of "something old, something new, something borrowed, something hywl".

That is not to say that the players South Wales were able to assemble did not have potential - there were the old stagers, such as Hugh Waddell, whose previous experience included playing for Leeds and Great Britain. Hugh travelled down from Cumbria where he had been playing in the BARLA National Conference for Egremont. Another signing with international credentials was Andy Currier from Warrington. Mike Riley came on loan from St Helens and Australian Andrew Lippiatt strengthened the pack.

Two of the most successful players in the side were ironically not these established Rugby League internationals, but players like Ioan Bebb a Welsh Union Under-21 international, and former Student Rugby League international, who finished as the club's top goal scorer with 45, and Shaun Marshall, who had Rugby Union experience with Ebbw Vale and Newbridge, and finished as joint top try scorer on 14 with Currier.

Dual home grounds

It is a maxim in business that location, location and location are the keys to success. This is just as true in sport, and therefore the choice of South Wales's home stadium was of crucial importance. To avoid the parochialism that besets the region of South Wales, as with the north, the team was named the formless and geographically neutral 'South Wales'. The decision to go for dual home grounds, Aberavon RUFC's Talbot Athletic Ground and Cardiff RUFC's Arms Park, was an attempt to break out of the old west (Swansea) versus the east (Cardiff) Welsh dichotomy. The ground at Cardiff, next door to the national stadium, and in the city centre, with a capacity of 15,000, was a potential venue for Super League. The obvious downside to this plan was that there would not be the local attachment that occurs when a team represents a town or city. The club would also to play one game at the Morfa Stadium in Swansea, arranged at very short notice

The first game

The first game for the fledgling South Wales side was against fallen Humberside giants Hull Kingston Rovers. In terms of the Second Division (in practice the Third Division if Super League was taken into account), this was the hardest test possible. Hull KR were in fact in the top flight only two seasons previously and only fell into the lower division because of the Super League shake-up. Championship winners in 1923 and 1925, Division 1 champions as recently as 1984-5, and Challenge Cup winners in 1980, few clubs have a greater pedigree.

Even this side contained a current international in Papua New Guinea's Stanley Gene, and it also had former Kiwi test prop Sam Stewart, and former Great Britain winger Paul Eastwood. Hull KR was still a prominent Rugby League name and proved to be a draw.

The game was played on 31 March 1996 at the home of Aberavon RUFC ground, coincidentally Mike Nicholas's home ground in his Rugby Union days. A crowd of 1,800 turned up, maybe more out of curiosity than anything else. Not only was the national anthem played, but the home team was decked out in the Welsh national shirts, and had a bevy of cheerleaders.

The home side for this historic encounter was (with their previous club in brackets): Ioan Bebb (Cardiff Sea Eagles ARL); Ian Perryment (London Crusaders), Andy Currier

(Warrington), Mike Riley (St Helens), Sean Marshall (Newbridge RU); Dai Rees (Cross Keys RU), James Churcher (Llanishen RU); Barry Pickton (Llandovery RU), Byron Lloyd (Caerphilly RU), Hugh Waddell (Carlisle RL), Matthew Taylor (Pontypool RU), Andrew Lippiatt (Perth Western Reds RL), David Williams (Warrington). Substitutes: Mike Jarman (Aberavon RU), James Alvis (Pontypridd RU).

Hull KR lined up as: Mike Fletcher; Paul Eastwood, John Okul, Rob D'Arcy, Gary Brown; Gary Atkins, Stanley Gene; Paul Scott, Sean Hoe, Craig Hardy, Chris Harrison, Paul Fletcher, Sam Stewart. Substitutes: Mike Crane, Neil Wardrobe.

As might be expected with a starting side that contained seven players who had not played professional Rugby League before, South Wales struggled against the best side in the division. Hull KR crossed the line with monotonous regularity and only a classy try by Dai Rees, in which he side-stepped past four visitors, gave the home side any encouragement in the first half. Unfortunately, the second half continued in the same vein and, despite a try from substitute James Alvis, the Welshmen were taught a heavy rugby lesson, the Humbersiders running out winners by 70-8.

Such is the uneven nature of British Rugby League, even in the Second Division, that the new club had an ideal test a week later against perennial strugglers, the newly named Prescot Panthers. Prescot, previously called Highfield had, unlike South Wales, not been trying to establish the game for seven days, but for seven decades having played at several venues mainly between Wigan and Liverpool, with one exotic season's excursion as London Highfield. The South Wales side made eight changes from the first game and drew Prescot's third highest crowd of the season, 477, to their Hope St home.

What a difference a week makes. With a large portion of the squad based in the area, this was as much a home game as one in the principality was. The game started with a sweeping 60-yard first minute try by Currier and further tries followed from Marshall, a rare score from Waddell, and Ian Perryment and the visitors were up 18-10 at half time. South Wales held on well in the second half and a try by debutant John McAtee clinched a 24-22 win. Having survived their 'political' problems with Rugby Union, the club then ran into difficulties with BARLA, the British amateur League administrators. Three trialist players had to withdraw at very short notice from the Easter Monday match with Bramley, because BARLA had refused them permission to play.

South Wales versus Bramley on 8 April 1996 at the Morfa Stadium, Swansea.
Photo: Mike Haddon

Phil Melling's report in *Super League Week* described this as "Another example of the bigotry and narrow-mindedness which is so characteristic of Rugby League at its worst". Despite this, South Wales beat their Yorkshire opponents 22-18.

Development was also being prioritised, with Wales Rugby League development officer Kerry Sheehy recognising the influence of Sky television's coverage on school students. This was creating a demand for playing the game, and 100 schools were now involved. Neil Kelly, a recruit from amateur club Woolston, became another development officer, employed by the South Wales club.

Player recruitment was also progressing. Gerald Cordle reappeared in his native country after his fine career with Bradford Northern. Another Welsh international on loan with an eye to a possible Super League place was Paul Moriarty. His presence, with that of former Great Britain prop John Fieldhouse, strengthened the pack and added much needed League experience. These players alone had far more glamour than the run-of-the-mill players normally found in the lower reaches of professional Rugby League.

And there was an unusual recruit to the ranks too in Gerald Williams, who arrived at the club via South Africa and Australia. Williams had played for South Africa in the games against Australia, Fiji and England in the previous Rugby League World Cup. Nick Jenkins returned to his ancestral homeland after playing for Perth Western Reds and the Western Australian regional side. It was, then, a great tribute to both Clive Griffiths and the South Wales management that they were able to put together such a squad considering the difficulties of both the BARLA dispute and the restrictions and swaggering cheque books of the Welsh Union sides.

But the whole season still had an experimental air about it. The club's A team had beaten august opponents Bath Rugby Union club in a practice match for Bath's famous cross-code clash with mighty Wigan. This showed the difference between the two games as much as the actual Wigan versus Bath clashes at Maine Road, Manchester and Twickenham.

In June, South Wales jumped at the opportunity to play a curtain raiser at a Super League game between Sheffield Eagles and St Helens that was to be played at Cardiff RUFC. This was both a bold and helpful gesture from the Eagles who could not use their own ground because of an athletics meeting. It was certainly a trial run for future South Wales Super League games.

South Wales RLFC 1996. Photo: Andy Howard

Despite hopes of a gate of more than 10,000 the crowd of 6,708 was viewed in most circles as a success and the 1,200 or so who had turned up at the start of the South Wales versus Carlisle game saw a feast of flowing rugby.

Carlisle were looking to strengthen their bid for a promotion spot but were knocked out of their stride by hard running and good handling. Ioan Bebb had a field day collecting 16 points in a 37-18 win over the Cumbrians. By the end of June, the side had a respectable record of seven wins from 14 games. The improvement was shown with a 44-6 win at strugglers Bramley. The home game on Easter Monday against the same opponents had been won by only four points.

Super League bid

While the team was improving on the pitch, only small crowds were coming to the matches. After the Super League game, only around 300 attended each of the next two home games. It was now very clear that Super League was the only way forward in South Wales.

With some prominent Welsh players already being signed by Rugby Union clubs, the future of the Welsh national team was also in jeopardy if a Super League place was not secured. And a decision was needed quickly.

Positive news had come for the club in May, when they announced that a £500,000 sponsorship was available if they were accepted into Super League.

In June, the RFL Board of Directors agreed to support the club's Super League bid, but told the club's directors that they would have to match the News Corporation funding they would receive as Super League members. The Rugby League Council would consider their application on 3 July.

This meeting, which lasted eight hours, delayed the decision for two weeks, with concerns over the financial backing, a home venue and player strength. On the key area of finance, the club had a major backer, with a banker's letter to support the bid. Cardiff RUFC were keen for South Wales to play there. The playing squad would only be finalised when Super League acceptance was agreed - the club could not expect top quality players to sign until this was in place.

Mike Nicholas pointed out that if the club was not accepted, an "M62 Super League" was a possibility. Prophetic words when you consider that 10 out of 12 teams are from the M62 corridor for Super League in 1998.

South Wales versus Barrow at Cardiff RUFC on 7 July 1996. Photo: Peter Lush

Two weeks later, the reconvened Rugby League Council accepted the club for membership. Now the task of building a Super League squad for 1997 could begin.

Back on the pitch, one of the team's greatest achievements was a fine away victory at promotion-chasing Hunslet. Two tries by Perryment and one from Mike Riley plus three goals by Bebb and two drop goals from John Doherty and one from Anthony Hatton sealed a 21-14 triumph at the South Leeds Stadium. The result effectively ended Hunslet's promotion bid, leaving the Yorkshire side in third place.

The season came to an inauspicious end with a courageous 16-26 defeat at promoted Swinton and a final 6-58 drubbing away at Carlisle with the last South Wales try being scored by Andy Currier and a conversion by Bebb. Sixth place was a worthy achievement given everything the club had been through in the season. The progress on the pitch was shown by three players, Ian Perryment, Mike Riley and John Doherty being mentioned in *Open Rugby's* focus on star players in Division Two.

The team's final record was:

Played	Won	Draw	Lost	For	Against	Points	Position
22	12	0	10	528	548	24	6th

The Welshmen finished in a creditable position just off the promotion fringes, despite the large turnover of players, which saw 42 make appearances. However, the reluctance of the South Wales public to watch Second Division Rugby League in large numbers showed clearly that only Super League was viable.

First Division

Then came dreadful news. At the beginning of September, the RFL Board of Directors refused a final endorsement of the club's Super League place. Suddenly they were not happy with the club's financial position. Apparently the £1 million guarantee of support was not enough.

A couple of days later, a special meeting of the Rugby League clubs decided to place the club in the First Division for 1997. In reality, this was a non-starter. Having seen Super League each week on Sky television, the Welsh public were not going to watch Dewsbury and Whitehaven any more than they had come to the Second Division fare offered in 1996.

Given the dire financial position of many of the clubs already in the RFL, and the strategic importance of South Wales for Rugby League, the decision was a severe blow to the development of the game.

Once again, the existing clubs seemed to put their own interests first, rather than share the Super League money with a new Super League club. Maurice Lindsay, the chief executive of the RFL said that he and chairman Sir Rodney Walker had been "desperate" to get South Wales into Super League, but had not been able to get the clubs to agree.

Within three weeks, the South Wales club's board had considered their position, and decided that a Division 1 place was not a viable option, and the club was closed down. Their major backer subsequently moved to another Super League club. The Super League dream for 1997 was over.

Postscript

Although there were reports that Clive Griffiths would be given the task of preparing a South Wales Super League entry for 1998, nothing came of it. He went on the tour to New Zealand and Papua New Guinea with the Great Britain squad, and then did some Rugby Union coaching with Treorchy. Having failed to secure a Super League coaching position, one of the best British Rugby League coaches joined London Welsh RUFC in May 1997.

In 1997, the Rugby League recruited a new development officer, and set up an Academy team in Cardiff. While these moves, and the securing of a £10,000 sponsorship for 1997-8, are positive ones, without a senior club to link up with, much of the young talent produced will probably be lost to Rugby League.

In 1997 and at the beginning of 1998, there was speculation about a Super League team being set up in Swansea. With new franchises possibly available for 1999, maybe the game will finally have a top-division, top-quality side in Wales.

But probably the best opportunity in the game's history, to build on the 1995 World Cup success, had been missed. How many of the game's top Welsh stars will be playing Rugby League by 1999, and where will the Welsh basis for a side come from then? The Welsh public will not accept 13 Australians and northerners playing in red jerseys claiming to be a South Wales side. To have credibility, the basis of the team must be Welsh, and it is that opportunity which has been lost.

And as a final blow, it seems, at the time of writing, that Wales will not be included in the next World Cup whenever it is played. From a semi-final to not being allowed to compete. When will Rugby League ever learn?

**RUGBY LEAGUE
DEVELOPMENT OFFICER
(SOUTH WALES)**

As part of its highly regarded development programme, the Rugby Football League is seeking to appoint a suitably qualified, highly motivated individual to the post of Rugby League Development Officer for South Wales.

Responsible to The Rugby Football League's Development Executive, the successful applicant will be based in Cardiff and will be expected to work closely with Cardiff County Council, the Sports Council for Wales and other local authorities in South Wales.

His/her main objective will be to increase participation at junior level within local schools, and to establish a schools and junior Rugby League structure to support and complement the South Wales Schools U16 Premiership squad and the proposed Cardiff Rugby League Academy.

Applicants should possess a sound knowledge of Rugby League at all levels and preferably hold an appropriate coaching qualification under the British Rugby League Coaching Scheme. You should also hold a current, clean driving licence.

**CARDIFF RUGBY LEAGUE ACADEMY
GENERAL MANAGER/HEAD COACH**

To capitalise on the success of its highly regarded development programme, The Rugby Football League, in conjunction with Cardiff County Council and Rugby League Wales Ltd, is to form the Cardiff Rugby League Academy, an elite squad of players in the 16-19 age group who will participate in the game's premier youth competition, the Rugby Football League Academy.

To lead this ambitious project the Cardiff Rugby League Academy is looking to appoint a General Manager/Head Coach.

Based in Cardiff, the successful applicant will work under the guidance and direction of a Board of Management to establish the Cardiff Rugby League Academy. Responsible for the day-to-day management of the Cardiff Rugby League Academy, he/she will have a proven track record in rugby coaching with relevant experience within this age group, and hold an appropriate coaching qualification (at least equivalent to Level 3 of the British Rugby League Coaching Scheme).

A determined self-starter with first-class communication skills, he/she will be expected to work in conjunction with The Rugby Football League's full time Rugby League Development Officer for South Wales, and to reside in the Cardiff area or be prepared to relocate at own expense. He/she will be a car owner and hold a full, clean driving licence.

A competitive salary is on offer for a unique opportunity in Rugby League football.

Further information and a job description can be obtained from Thomas P. O'Donovan, Development Executive, The Rugby Football League - Tel: 0113 232 9111.

Applications for both of these posts should be made by way of a full CV and covering letter to:

The Chief Executive
The Rugby Football League
Red Hall
Red Hall Lane
Leeds LS17 8NB

For both the above posts the closing date for applications is Friday, 14th March, 1997 and it is intended that interviews will take place in Cardiff on Wednesday, 26th March, 1997.

Chapter 15: The 1996 international matches

The postscript to the 1995 successes of the Welsh national team makes for uneasy reading. Wales competed in just one more European Championship, in 1996. Despite the loss of five prominent players to Rugby Union, Wales started their campaign with an excellent 34-14 win at Carcassonne against France. An Iestyn Harris hat-trick, other tries from Paul Atcheson, Richard Webster and Gareth Davies, with Harris adding five goals, gave the Welsh a convincing win.

Their home game was against England at Cardiff on 26 June 1996. The professional arm of Rugby League, thanks to the Super League revolution, had moved to playing in summer and, astoundingly, the Cardiff game was scheduled for the same evening as football's European Championship Wembley semi-final between England and Germany.

It was to be the Welsh national team's last international match to the present (April 1998). There are many reasons that can be attributed to the rapid demise of the squad after achieving such heady heights only the year before, not least the failure of the RFL to give the South Wales club team a place in Super League as they had done under the banner of European expansion when they promoted London Broncos and Paris into the Super League shortly after the RFL signed the big money deal with News International to form the new competition.

However, there are probably two other key factors which have seen the Welsh national team placed on the backburner since 1996. The first was the decision of Rugby Union's International Board to allow professionalism. Many Union commentators had for a long time suggested that professionalism in their sport would mark the end for Rugby League. They figured League's *raison d'être* would be removed. But they also failed to realise that League was not just professional Rugby Union. It was a totally different sport and the majority of people who play it choose to do so, whether at professional or amateur level, because they prefer it to other sports. League was never under threat from a professionalised Rugby Union.

However, those players from Wales who came north to earn a living from playing Rugby League had been brought up playing Union. It is almost certain they would not have taken League contracts had payment been openly available for playing Union, clearly a less physically demanding game, in their own country. Once their League contracts had expired they were far more likely to return to the sport of their youth. And this, to some extent, is what happened, with Jonathan Davies, Scott Gibbs and Scott Quinnell leading the exodus. Notably, however, born-and-bred Welsh League players such as Anthony Sullivan and Iestyn Harris chose to remain in Rugby League, giving further opposition to the lie that Rugby League was unnecessary once Union went professional. Nonetheless the reduction in numbers of former Welsh Union players playing League has certainly reduced the quality and availability of players able to form a Welsh League team.

But such a team would certainly be viable, even without the missing Union stars, were it not for the Super League war which stymied international competition. When News International paid its money into Rugby League in 1995 with the attendant stipulations of summer competition, merged clubs and franchises, it never figured it would not be able to buy the global game. A 'global vision' was one of their new catch-phrases, but the game's new backers did not bank on the Australian Rugby League not buying into their plans. Money was poured down the drain in Australia on endless courtroom battles between the factions fighting for control of the sport and any international future the game might have had, following on from the astounding success of the 1995 World Cup competition, was lost. With one eye on Australia, the British RFL lost sight of the global expansion factor and international competition was put back on the shelf.

Wales and Welsh players are still a major part of Rugby League and a national team is still viable but, now that all is resolved in Australia and there is talk of reviving World and European competition for national teams, only time will tell whether the Welsh squad figures in those plans.

Thus the Welsh team's swansong came and went in the 1996 European Championship competition. Both England and Wales had beaten the French in early June and the English came to Cardiff on the 26th, in what was the deciding match.

England coach Phil Larder was keeping faith with the squad that beat the French, including Martin Offiah, Shaun Edwards and Gary Connolly. Captain Andy Farrell of Wigan had a thigh injury but was able to start the game and he predicted in *Super League Week* that England were expecting "a tough examination in Cardiff. Playing in their capital always seems to give the Welsh boys a lift."

That feeling was echoed by Welsh full-back Paul Atcheson who, according to *Super League Week* had "discovered the secret to Welsh passion and courage."

"Our coach Clive Griffiths made it quite clear to us all in training," said Atcheson. "Just look at your chest. There we can see the three feathers of the Welsh crest. Then we know just why we are there and what we have to do."

It is an attitude that has sustained the Welsh national team through long periods of adversity and gives a clue as to why it has survived both on and off for 90 years. Unfortunately, for the Welsh, Atcheson's call to arms failed to bring the championship home to Wales. It was England's night in European Rugby League, even though their football counterparts lost on penalties to Germany in their European Championship, as the visitors came home 26-12 to the good.

Wales had injury worries before the game too which forced coach Clive Griffiths to leave out Anthony Sullivan with a dead leg and replace him with Castleford's Diccon Edwards who was a Welsh A Union international only playing his first season of Rugby League. Griffiths was already alarmed at the rate his players were returning to Union saying in a *League Express* interview: "It was bad enough losing Jonathan Davies after the World Cup, but since then Kevin Ellis, Jonathan Griffiths, Adrian Hadley, David Young and Scott Quinnell have all signed up with Union clubs." Griffiths called for the South Wales club team to receive more support to attract Welsh youngsters to League. He insisted that there was massive interest in the South Wales team and RL in general from young players but his call fell on deaf ears, for the following season the club would not even exist. "If Wales can win the European Championship again... it will be the biggest boost of all," he added. "When England come to Cardiff it should be like Australia's State of Origin."

And, for the 5,425 who tore themselves away from the football on TV, it proved to be so, for one night anyway. England won but Wales were resilient as always. It was only the inspiration of England scrum-half Bobby Goulding, on as a substitute for Sheffield hooker Johnny Lawless, that saw England through in the final quarter.

"England coach Phil Larder asked for a tough match from Wales and that's just what he got," announced *Super League Week*. "This was real international Rugby League with commitment and passion as well as a dash of drama.

"In the end, the match hung on two men, England's Bobby Goulding and Wales's mercurial stand-off Iestyn Harris. Goulding's 14 points - five goals and a try - earned him the man-of-the-match award [and] until he arrived on the pitch England were flat, lacking in inspiration and penetration."

Harris, voted man-of-the-series, was almost as influential although he finished on the losing side. England had great difficulty in containing him but in the end the burden of responsibility proved too much.

As *The Times* said: "Phil Larder [the English coach] got the competitive encounter deemed necessary... but it was neither the convincing nor inspiring European triumph that he wanted to see." Wales were very reluctant to relinquish their title and it wasn't until the final quarter that England secured victory.

Wales's centre Allan Bateman had flown from Australia where he was playing with Cronulla Sharks to play in the international and he was instrumental in the fine first-half performance of the Welsh. His tackling denied England repeatedly, allowing Wales to take the early lead. Harris took the English defence wide before slipping an inside pass to loose-forward Chris Morley who scored by the posts. Harris converted and with Lawless leaving the field injured it seemed that things were not going England's way.

But the introduction of Goulding provided the spark for the visitors. His penalty clawed back points for England and then, after having one try already disallowed by the newly introduced video referee, Jason Robinson set up the position from which Paul Broadbent dummied to send Chris Joynt over from close range. Goulding's conversion left England fortuitously ahead at half time.

With the second half only eight minutes old, Goulding again provided the inspiration to stretch England's lead. He took the ball from dummy half, shot between Cunningham and Mark Perrett and scored under the posts, before converting his own try. But Wales were not finished. Only two minutes later Harris put Atcheson in the clear to feed wingman Jason Critchley of Keighley. His try and Harris's conversion left Wales trailing by only two, 14-12.

It was as close as Wales got. As the effort involved in stopping a powerful English attack took its toll, gaps began to appear in the Welsh defence, although it took until the 67th minute for England to score. Gary Connolly finally broke free of Bateman and fed Shaun Edwards who ran 40 yards to score by the posts and make Goulding's goal kick a simple one. With four minutes remaining England's victory was complete when Steve Prescott, the English full-back, showed electrifying pace to speed past Harris and outpace the defence for a 60-yard score. Goulding's conversion gave him 14 points in all and the English a 26-12 win.

For England, in addition to the splendid Goulding, Robinson, Prescott and Broadbent all had good games but in all honesty the team failed to perform to its best. Coach Larder said "We were disappointed with our performance but we got more commitment from the Welsh than we did against France. English captain Farrell admitted that his debut as skipper was not the one he had hoped for: Obviously we are pleased with the win, but we didn't play to our strengths," he said.

Clive Griffiths had mixed emotions. It was a stout Welsh performance but he was disappointed to lose. "England will know they have been in a game," he said. "And it took individual brilliance to beat us. My players rose to the occasion well, even though many had only recently come out of reserve team football. They mixed it with the best."

And Harris, of whom the *Daily Telegraph* wrote: "In Iestyn Harris [Wales] have the player of the series", commented: "It just didn't happen for us, but we have proved that Welsh Rugby League has a future if we can be guaranteed a fast track into Super League." If only...

Of the match and its significance in the sporting calendar, the following week's editorial in *Super League Week* had much to say. "The attentions of sports enthusiasts were at Wembley Stadium. The [Rugby League] international also deserved a full stadium and it deserved a big TV audience. To schedule the game on the same night as the Euro 96 semi-finals was an obvious folly. The success of Wales... is wholly dependent on the ability of the administrators."

And that, of course, includes providing fixtures in which Welsh players can compete for their country. With the departure of the RFL's chief executive Maurice Lindsay at the beginning of 1998, the whole debate over a meaningful international calendar has been raised once again. His successor, Neil Tunnicliffe, is apparently committed to healing international relations with the newly reformed and merged National Rugby League of Australia (a result of the ending of the spilt between Super League and the Australian Rugby League in that country) and Tunnicliffe is also very keen to see a five nations European Championship involving the two new League nations of Scotland and Ireland in addition to England, France and, of course, Wales. At the time of writing, plans are being made for this tournament to take place. There is certainly hope once more that Wales can be part of a meaningful international competition. The last 90 years have proved that ability is there in abundance and the 1995 World Cup confirmed that the Welsh public will turn out if the competition is one that can capture their imagination.

But, to return to Ninian Park in 1996, Wales had competed well in their last fixture to date, although a Welsh Academy side is now competing in 1998. Indeed the match was a microcosm of much that had occurred in their preceding 90 years as an international Rugby League nation: a sterling performance against the odds and against opponents who had a bigger reputation. Pride and passion, and a lot of basic rugby know-how, were still the major hallmarks of one of Rugby League's two oldest international teams. A fitting postscript, perhaps, to a long history that has seen equal measures of success and failure and a story that has, no doubt, many more chapters still waiting to be written.

Part five:

Players and people

Chapter 16: An All-Time Great Wales team

The editors of this book originally suggested that I compile about a dozen profiles of the greatest Welsh players in Rugby League history. I did not think much to that proposal. It was not my idea of a lot of fun. How would I choose them? They would probably all be backs. I would certainly offend lots of people and it was not worth the endless arguments. I suggested it would be more fun to select an all-time best Wales XIII. Not exactly original, admittedly, but 13 is more than 12 and when four substitutes are added, it would mean that fewer folk would be outraged.

Because I have studied the subject - Welsh Rugby League players, that is - and published books and articles on it, some people think that I must have Welsh blood in me. Not a drop. Pure Yorkshire, not remotely Welsh. I do have a very Welsh wife, Myfanwy, but for this chapter she is an absolute irrelevance. She comes from Aberystwyth, her first language is Welsh and she is about as interested in Rugby League as I am in flower-arranging. Besides, I had been a Leaguie for nearly 20 years before I met the woman.

She does have one claim to fame, however, as she was one of the 1,168 lost souls who witnessed Halifax's historic defeat by Cawoods one dismal afternoon at Thrum Hall in October 1977. For political reasons - in other words, to avoid doing something even more distasteful - she has been to four and a bit Rugby League matches. There were no Welshmen on the pitch on that melancholy occasion although, given the huge number of expatriate Welsh rugby players in the Halifax area, there were doubtless some looking on, disbelieving, horror-stricken.

Thrum Hall

No, I think my interest in Welsh players was kick-started by my earliest experiences as a spectating child at Thrum Hall. They began in 1956 just as the great Halifax team of that era was beginning to disintegrate. There were Welshmen everywhere in the team - internationals like Tuss Griffiths, Arthur Daniels and Dai Bevan in the backs and 1954 World Cup hero John Thorley and fiery Les Pearce in the pack. That quintet was on the way out but two newer Welshmen filled my thoughts, drew my total admiration. Garfield Owen and Johnny Freeman were the bee's knees, the Celtic gods' gift to Rugby League, simply the best, better than all the rest. Owen, ex-Newport, capped half a dozen times at full-back by Wales at Union, was signed in a blaze of publicity live on 'Sportsview', a totally unprecedented event. I have never seen a better goal-kicker (Frano who?) or punter of the ball and his catching of the ball was beyond belief. His tackling, low, surgical and classical, was a thing of beauty. What is more, he had the temper of a saint.

Then there was Johnny. Johnny Freeman, only one Johnny Freeman. He was Halifax's answer to Billy Boston with whom he had gone to school at South Church Street in Cardiff. Johnny was one of Tiger Bay's own along with his cousin, Joe Erskine, heavyweight boxing champion of Great Britain and Shirley Bassey, all pals together. As a winger Johnny could show every other winger a clean pair of heels. In 1958 he was rated as the world's best winger by *Rugby League Gazette* and there you all were thinking *Open Rugby* invented the world ratings concept. There is nothing new under the sun. Then just as he was getting ready to pack his bags for the 1958 Lions Tour having scored 109 tries in 91 matches for 'Fax, he suffered a diabolical injury at Batley which crocked him for a year. He was never quite the same again. At his peak he was pure dynamite.

Johnny and Garfield set all the standards for this particular awe-struck kid. Johnny scored all the tries, ran faster than anyone, continually brought the stand down at Thrum Hall. Garfield landed all the goals, out-punted all the greats, kicked and tackled the opposition out of the game... and neither of them ever got a test cap. It was an absolute scandal.

It wasn't just Johnny and Garfield, however. Those Welshmen were everywhere. I soon learned that Billy Boston was as awe-inspiring as they said he was and as for that Lewis Jones? How could anyone do that? He really did mesmerise the ball into floating in thin air until one of his minions picked the crucial time to pluck it down and shatter the defence. Hell, he could do anything. There was dashing Glyn Moses, different altogether from Garfield as a full-back, at St Helens, his terrifying brother Dai at Salford, the irrepressible Tommy Harris at The Boulevard, Ray bloody Price at Warrington, who had done for Halifax far too often, flying Malcolm Davies at Leigh and Oldham had half a pack full in Don Vines, Charlie Winslade and brainy Bryn Goldswain. They were only the tip of the ice berg. The game was crawling with Welshmen.

It always had been too. Hundreds upon hundreds had abandoned the valleys for Lancashire and Yorkshire. They had been trekking north to play rugby before the words Northern Union had even entered the language. At Halifax up to the 1970s only a handful of occasions had seen the blue and whites take the field without a Welshman in the side. Sometimes they were in the majority and the history of the club was littered with famous Welsh names. It was the same with many other clubs. The Welsh were a huge presence and influence, the scale of their northward migration never having been fully appreciated by historians or myopic anti-Rugby Unionists.

Rugby Union

There is a trend prevalent today which denigrates Rugby Union players who convert to Rugby League. The knockers say they are a waste of space, a waste of time and a waste of money. Well, of course, some are. However, as the overwhelming majority of ex-Union converts down the century have been Welsh, perhaps the critics should look closely at the records of Welsh players in the game. They would find that Rugby League has had a more than adequate return on its Welsh investments.

The selection of a best-ever Welsh XIII represents a search through an absolute treasure house of wonderfully gifted players. It is as well to set some of the ground rules before the off. Firstly, all the players selected would be assumed to be at the peak of their powers. Secondly, as I am nowhere near old enough to have seen the majority of them play, the selections are based on the individual player's status relating to the records and folklore of the sport and, more especially, on the esteem in which they were held within their own playing eras. Finally, this team is being selected on the basis that it would be playing Rugby League as a game which involved the old specialisms.

That means it would be a game played at close quarters, in which hookers were hookers and scrum-halves actually came into contact with other scrum-halves. It would be a game in which scrummaging was esteemed as an essential part of the proceedings and referees did not cravenly peer across the top of the scrummage signalling the non-possession-getting side to stay onside and ignoring all the accepted age-old conventions.

It would be a game in which forwards actually expended energy, ingenuity and desperation to obtain the ball. It would also be a game where there was more than today's solitary game plan of five drives and a kick, mystically wrapped-up in coaching mumbo-jumbo. It would be a game which allowed different teams to develop entirely disparate styles and which allowed a situation in which the better footballing team did not necessarily win. It would also be a game which embraced players of all shapes and sizes.

Invariably all-time best teams are logged from full-back to loose-forward so, just to be awkward, this one will turn that procedure on its head. Rugby League matches are generally won upfront by the forwards so the front-row appears the logical place to start.

Prop forwards

The natural evolution of forwards is to metamorphosise from loose-forward to second-row to front-row. The process very seldom works in reverse. That is why it is very difficult for Rugby Union props to thrive in Rugby League. If a Union back-row forward comes into League and finds he is not quick enough, he can move forward into the front-row. If he comes into League as a prop and is too slow, there is simply nowhere else for him to be accommodated. Even so Wales has produced some outstanding props.

Among those who immediately come into consideration is Frank Whitcombe, invariably recalled as the heaviest man, at 18 stones in 1949, to have played in a Wembley Challenge Cup Final. He was not, of course, always that size. A Cardiffian, Frank took the unusual route of coming into League via the Army to Broughton Rangers in 1936, before making his name with the redoubtable Bradford Northern team of the 1940s. With Whitcombe on the open side a hooker was scarcely necessary and for such a big man he was renowned for nimbleness of foot.

Rivalling Whitcombe would be W.A. (Billy) Williams, ex-Crumlin RU, skipper of Salford in the early 1930s and a Lion in 1928 and 1932; Elwyn Gwyther, ex-Llanelli, who, from the long-lamented Belle Vue Rangers club, won tour honours in 1950; and the former Neath man, John Thorley, athletic and mobile yet strong in the tight, who starred in the formidable Halifax pack of the 1950s.

The prop forward positions in this all-time Wales XIII, however, would be filled by the legendary **Jim Mills** and mighty **Joe Thompson**, a pair from vastly different eras and of markedly contrasting temperaments. Mills, much the bigger man, would operate on the open side.

No one who saw him play, let alone anyone who ever played against the man, could forget Big Jim Mills. In the folklore of the game Jim is either a bogeyman or a hero, but usually the former, depending on whether he was playing against your team or for it. On your side or on the opposition's, he was, however, a one-man entertainment/enragement package. At 6 feet 4 inches and 17 stones in his pomp, Jim Mills was one of the biggest men to have played the game, and he was assuredly no shrinking violet. His disciplinary record - 20 dismissals (15 in Britain, five in Australia) and the distinction of being the only man to have been sent off twice in Welsh internationals - is an eloquent indication of the way he played the game. Hard and frequently not fair. He lived by the sword and he was often wounded by the sword. His reputation always went before him and he undoubtedly took a lot of rubbish from real and aspiring hard men. He seemed to take and give with equanimity and at least it was usually done in the open.

There was more to Jim Mills than a natural talent as an enforcer, nevertheless. He could play football too, particularly as he got older. It was not an easy road to immortality for Mills, however. A native of Aberdare, he played Union for Wales Youth and for the first XV at Cardiff before being enticed to Halifax for £3,000 in 1964, having just turned 20. Jim was a big, willing but raw second-rower at that stage. He learned plenty from his stay at Halifax, who were champions in 1965, but he could not command a first team place. Transferred to glamour club Salford in 1968 for £4,000, his career stalled. After only five games he was sold on to Bradford Northern for only £2,750. By now he had settled at open-side prop and things began to happen for him. Wales capped him in 1969 and in 1970 he was selected for the Australasian tour. He promptly passed up the tour and signed a three-year contract for North Sydney.

Three seasons in Australian Rugby League were not especially fruitful but on signing for Widnes in 1972, aged 28, his career blossomed. In the eight remaining years of his career, which included a brief spell at Workington, Mills played in 14 major finals, including three at Wembley. He also embarked on a Great Britain career which brought him six test caps and took him on Lions tours in 1974 and 1979. Widnes certainly saw the best of Jim Mills. He remained a fearsome physical force. But instead of fighting a one-man battle with all and sundry before dying with the ball, he developed a capacity for standing in the tackle, drawing the attention of several defenders and still slipping away balls which released Widnes's match-winners.

Jim Mills was literally one of the game's larger than life characters. Even after finishing playing, he proved himself unique by becoming the only Welsh ex-test prop to become chairman of a professional Rugby League club, his adopted Widnes.

Joe Thompson was an entirely different kettle of fish from Jim Mills. He spent his entire career with Leeds; he was sent off only once, playing for the 1932 Lions at Newcastle, New South Wales, and only the referee ever knew why. He was six inches shorter than Mills and at most weighed 15 stones. Unlike Mills he had no junior pedigree in Union, having taken up the game in his late teens with Abercarn because he could not get a game of football locally. He was a natural and quickly graduated to Cross Keys where he helped them to win the unofficial Welsh Championship in his only full season, 1921-22. On 20 January 1923, a month past his 20th birthday, Joe was in the Welsh pack at Twickenham. Wales lost the game, Joe had his front teeth kicked in and within three weeks he had turned professional, for Leeds.

Joe was actually born in England, at Hambrook in Gloucestershire on 22 December 1902 but he grew up Welsh in Cross Keys. Like many other Welsh players he was down the pit by the time he was 13 and he hated it. He had no hesitation at all in accepting Leeds's £300 and never regretted trading in a pitman's life for a career in maintaining trams at Headingley tram sheds.

I had the pleasure of interviewing Joe Thompson at his home overlooking Kirkstall Abbey in 1983, not long before his death. He was 80 and he looked like he was made out of granite. He was built like a rock even then. He must have been truly formidable in his playing days. Certainly all the written and anecdotal evidence on Joe Thompson indicates that he was not to be messed about and yet he was not at all noted for belligerence. He simply got on with the game and left the crazy stuff to the crazy.

On joining Leeds his rise was meteoric. His 16th game brought him a Challenge Cup winners' medal as Leeds stuffed Hull 28-3 in the 1923 final at Wakefield. Joe kicked five goals. In 1932 he earned a second winners' medal, this time as captain as Leeds defeated Swinton 11-8 at Central Park, Wigan. His four penalty goals kicked between the eighth and 20th minutes were the platform on which Leeds gained their victory. Joe Thompson was, in truth, one of the game's great goal-kickers. He had an immense range, despite taking a short run, and in his time held or broke most of the Leeds kicking records, his first-class career record producing 921 goals in 462 games. From 1921-22 until the outbreak of the Second World War the incomparable Jim Sullivan headed the goal-kicking lists in all but two seasons -1927-28 and 1929-30 - when Joe usurped his title with 106 and 111 goals respectively.

While Joe Thompson's sharp-shooting enhanced his reputation, he was a superb all-round forward. He was a model of consistency who rarely had a sub-par game. He tackled tirelessly, scrummaged remorselessly, foraged hard and led by example. His crowning glory, however, was his masterful dribbling, possibly a legacy of his football background. Although dribbling is a long lost art, it was once a prime form of attack. Joe Thompson exploited it to the full for the simple reason that he knew anyone dribbling the ball proficiently could never be tackled.

At the very top level Joe Thompson was in his element. He won eight caps for Wales, captaining them at Wembley against Australia in 1930, five for Other Nationalities and a dozen in Great Britain test matches. His value to the national side is reflected in his extraordinary achievement of being selected for three Lions tours in 1924, 1928 and 1932. That alone is sufficient reason to include him in this sublime XIII.

Hooker

Traditionally it has been the hooking role which has been the most difficult to fill for Rugby Union converts and relatively few Welshmen have made it to the very top in League. In pre-Second World War days, when hooking really did mean trying every which way to get the ball and failure to do so meant relegation to the reserves, Wales had its finest crop of Rugby League number nines. It was probably no coincidence that Wales won the European Championship for three consecutive seasons from 1935-36 when they had Bert Day (Salford), Con Murphy (Acton & Willesden, Streatham & Mitcham, Leeds), Mel Meek (Halifax) and Jim Regan (Huddersfield) vying for the position.

However, when it comes to the crunch it is a three-cornered fight for the privilege of packing down between Mills and Thompson. Les White (ex Pontyclun RU and Pontypridd RL) had been a master-hooker for Hunslet in the 1920s and 1930s, had won seven test caps and toured Australasia in 1932. He was a brilliant ball winner in the days when 80 scrums in a game was the norm. Rivalling White from a much later era was Tony Fisher of Bradford Northern, Leeds and Castleford, capped 11 times by Great Britain (1970-78) and 16 times by Wales. Fisher may not have been the best ball winner in the game but he got his share, was a workaholic in defence and physically and psychologically would have traumatised Attila the Hun, had he decided to take up rugby.

Outranking even White and Fisher, however, would be **Tommy "Bomber" Harris** who came north from Newbridge to Hull in the 1949-50 season and played 444 games for the Airlie Birds before retiring in 1962, having established himself as one of the game's all-time great hookers. With 25 test caps (1954-60) Tommy Harris is the most capped British test hooker, and unless the game's legislators restore competitive scrummaging to Rugby League, will always remain so.

In pure hooking terms there have certainly been more proficient ball-getters than Tommy but he was good enough in that department to hold his own. In the loose, however, he had a massive advantage over his rivals. He was basically perpetual motion and operated like a third half-back. In that respect his size - 5 feet 7½ inches and around 12 stone 10 pounds - was an advantage. He was quick, alert, a super support player, adept at dummy-half and the very devil as a defender. It helped, of course, that he played in one of the greatest club packs in history but he would have been sensational anywhere.

Tommy Harris represents my own first televisual memory. It was Tommy, in glorious black and white, who absolutely dominated the screen in BBC's coverage of the 1960 Challenge Cup Final between Hull and Wakefield Trinity. There was this little chap in black and white irregular hoops constantly breaking up the middle of the pitch, in what seemed like a one-man war against a superior force. Trinity would always eventually bury him but he just kept resurrecting himself and coming back for more. There seemed to be something strange about Tommy in that game, even to me as a young boy. He almost seemed demented. It was only later that we discovered he was concussed and played a large part of the game blind in one eye. Yet his performance, even in a crushing record 5-38 defeat, was as magnificent as any given by any hooker in the history of the game. It won him the Lance Todd Trophy.

Second-row

Second-row is a position for which there is a plethora of prime candidates. It is a terrible shame to be unable to accommodate such luminaries as Doug Phillips, Charlie Winslade, George Parsons, John Warlow and the great John Mantle from post-war days. Pre-war days produced equally fine men in the shape of Dai Rees, Norm Fender, Norman Pugh, Edgar Morgan and Jack Beames, to name but a few.

One name that simply could not be omitted is **Trevor Foster.** For an ideal model of a second-rower there is no need to look further than Trevor John French Foster, born in Newport in 1916, the son of a rugby-playing professional soldier-turned-publican. Trevor turned professional with Bradford Northern for £400 in 1938. It was probably the best £400 the club ever spent for Trevor gave 17 years exemplary playing service and has remained with the club in one capacity or other for nigh on 60 years. He was arguably the best non-capped player Wales has ever lost to Rugby League.

Trevor Foster won only three test caps for Great Britain although he did tour with the Lions in 1946 and tallied 16 Welsh caps between 1939 and 1951. He was unfortunate enough to be from that generation whose professional sporting careers were blighted by Hitler's imbecility. The war probably robbed him of two tours and 20 caps but in other ways enriched his career as a rugby player. With the wartime dispensation for League men to play Union, Trevor played with and against the greats of both codes for the duration. In so doing he came to be regarded almost universally as the finest second-row, many said the finest forward, period, of his generation in either code.

His reputation was built on his supreme running and handling skills; he could make play and his support work enhanced the playmaking of others. Temperamentally Trevor

Trevor Foster (right) captaining Wales against England at Wigan in 1950. Ernie Ward is the England captain. Photo courtesy Robert Gate

was a paragon, always playing the game in the right spirit, never resorting to the unworthy. Apart from excelling in all the departments expected of a forward, Trevor was a voracious try-scorer. No other Welsh forward in history has scored as many as the 140 tries Trevor Foster claimed in his first-class career of 462 games. Against Wakefield Trinity in 1948 he scored six, and had one disallowed, a truly amazing performance as Bradford only scored eight tries in a 28-16 win. This feat constitutes another record for a Welsh forward, Bill Sandham (Hull KR and ex-Neath) being the only other to bag six back in 1913.

During the 1940s Bradford Northern won everything. They had a wonderful team but, perhaps uniquely, it had a dual leadership which dovetailed perfectly. Ernest Ward, all class and calmness in the centre, was its skipper but up front, where games are shaped, Trevor Foster was the driving force.

Partnering Trevor Foster in the second-row would be **Colin Dixon,** a man who always played the game for all he was worth. Get-stuck-in could have been Colin's middle name for he was a veritable whirlwind. On his greatest days Colin Dixon drew all eyes - constantly in the thick of the action, fearlessly confronting the most damaging of runners with a no-nonsense approach to tackling and then exploding into breathtaking attack. He could batter through the most steadfast defence and once through he had the pace to hold off chasers over 50, 60, even 70 yards. It is hard to imagine a more thrilling sight on a rugby pitch than Colin Dixon in full flight. Wise men got out of his way.

Colin scored even more tries - 177 - than Foster but a good many were scored from the centre position. That is where he began his professional career as partner to Johnny Freeman as a 17-year-old in 1961. Halifax had signed him on a three year contract worth £1,000 and clearly picked up a bargain. From the beginning it was evident that he had what it took. He was big, brave and boisterous. His partnership with Freeman was successful from the off but no one who knew about these things doubted that he would eventually end up in the pack. By the time he was 20 he made the transition to second-row although he often reverted to the centre when necessary.

Halifax versus Doncaster 1961. Johnny Freeman breaks down the wing supported by Colin Dixon. Only the fear of accusations of bias prevented Robert Gate from including Freeman in his Welsh team. Not even accusations of bias could keep Dixon out of the XIII.
Photo courtesy Robert Gate

He helped Halifax to the Championship in 1965 and by 1968 he was the hottest property in the game. He was captain of Halifax and had been capped by Wales and Great Britain, when Salford signed him for a world record fee. He was to be the leading light in the Red Devils' pack for a dozen seasons, seasons in which big-spending Salford became the glamour team of the sport. Colin continued to lead from the front. You could never mistake him, this son of Tiger Bay, he was the eye of the storm and he was black and in those days black forwards were almost unknown.

He certainly caught the eyes of the international selectors. His career in international football lasted a staggering 18 years (1963-81). It encompassed 14 test caps, 15 Welsh caps, a Lions tour in 1974, a Welsh World Championship tour in 1975 and membership of Great Britain's World Cup-winning squad in France in 1972. By the time his career came to an end with Hull KR in 1981 he had rattled up 738 first-class appearances, a record surpassed by only five men in the history of the game. With a record like that, how could anyone leave Colin Dixon out of this side?

Loose-forward

Scanning the possibilities for the loose-forward position conjures up figures such as Eddie Watkins, Alec Givvons, Bryn Goldswain and Kel Coslett. Watkins, formerly of Cardiff and capped eight times at Union before the war, skippered Wigan at Wembley in 1946 and to Championship Final victory over Huddersfield in the same year. His career was ruined by the war, however. Alec Givvons, ex-Cross Keys, was the first black forward to win international status at Rugby League, winning half a dozen caps (1936-39) while with Oldham. His versatility - he was an outstanding half-back too - like that of St Helens' Kel Coslett, a full-back-turned-loose-forward-turned-prop of the 1960s and 1970s, probably cost him more honours. Goldswain, the catalyst on which the spell-binding Oldham team of the 1950s was formed, won 16 Welsh caps (1947-53) but, like all those mentioned, never quite made it into the Great Britain test XIII.

One man who did and who claims the number 13 jersey in this all-time best Welsh team is **Ike Owens.** Owens hailed from Pontycymmer and played for his village XV at 16 before graduating to Maesteg and Aberavon. After gaining Glamorgan county honours and winning Welsh trials, the Second World War conspired to deprive him of a full Wales RU cap. But he did win selection for Wales in wartime services internationals against England on several occasions. He had a distinguished career in the RAF as a parachutist and it was while serving in the North of England that he threw in his lot with Leeds in 1943.

Within 18 months, after very few League games, he won the first of his dozen caps (1945-49) for Wales and in 1946 was selected for the Australasian tour with Gus Risman's 'Indomitables'. Although not particularly big at 5 feet 11 inches and around 13 stone 8 pounds, Ike was an absolute sensation on tour. It is unlikely any other British loose-forward ever got such consistent rave reviews from the Australian press. R.B. Noble, writing in 1950, shocked that Ike had ruled himself out of that year's tour, said, "I don't think you people back home have ever realised just how well Ike did play in Australia during the 1946 tour. It was wonderful the way he made our boys run helter-skelter - always to the wrong places. His marvellous football sense produced innumerable tries."

Ike Owens's trade marks were his superb handling, his tremendous acceleration and his capacity for running amok in loose play. Add to that a dreadnought defence and an image of a truly exceptional talent emerges. Ike played in all four tests on the 1946 tour but never donned a test jersey again.

After captaining Leeds to Wembley in 1947 his value went through the ceiling. In 1948 Castleford paid out a world record fee of £2,750 to Leeds for his services and, when things did not gel at Wheldon Road, Huddersfield grabbed him for the same fee a few months later. No matter that he was already past his 30th birthday. The Fartowners already had Dave Valentine at loose-forward and preferred to play Ike in the second-row. It was with Huddersfield that Ike won his biggest domestic honour when they defeated Warrington 13-12 at Maine Road in the classic Championship Final of 1949.

With a back row comprising Foster, Dixon and Owens, spare a thought for the poor wretches condemned to eternally chasing shadows in defence and having the wind knocked out of them in attack.

Moving to the selection of backs presents even more crises of conscience than picking the forwards. Wales has always been a bigger provider of backs for Rugby League than forwards, quite clearly because the transition from Rugby Union for forwards is so much more difficult.

Scrum-half

The most difficult back position for a Rugby Union player to adapt to in League has traditionally been scrum-half. Even so, there have been some exceptionally fine Welsh converts at number seven. Five particularly stand out. The four who do not quite make it are Tommy Grey (Huddersfield and ex-Swansea), who in 1911-12 became the first Welshman to score 200 points in a League season; little Billy Watkins (Salford and ex-Cross Keys), a 1936 Lion, holder of seven test caps and hub of the sublime Salford team of the 1930s; and Dai Jenkins (capped 1938-48) and Billy Banks (capped 1949-53) who

Johnny Rogers. Photo courtesy Robert Gate.

both won 17 caps for Wales at League, the national record for the position.

All, however, are eclipsed by **Johnny Rogers,** a shining light in Huddersfield's glorious 'Team of all the talents' of the period prior to and after the First World War. He was the classic scrum-half - 5 feet 4 inches, 10 and a bit stones and greased lightning. It was that speed, particularly off the mark and over the vital first 10 yards that set him apart. Harold Wagstaff, his skipper at Fartown, described him as "the best attacking half of all" while Billy Batten, Wagstaff's fellow Hall of Famer, dreaded playing against Johnny "who's so fast that he's through before you know where you are."

Johnny had played for Bridgend and Cardiff before joining Huddersfield for £100 on 1 March 1913, by which time the Fartowners were already the game's supreme team. Johnny actually succeeded Tommy Grey as scrum-half to form a devastating half-back pairing with his compatriot Jim Davies. Johnny quickly established himself in the Welsh team and in 1914 and 1920 was a British Lion. In 1920 and in the 1921 home Ashes series, Rogers joined up with Jonty Parkin to form what many old-time rugby fans described as the greatest half-back pairing the game would ever see. The partnership would be renewed when Johnny moved to Wakefield Trinity for £300 in January 1925. It did not particularly matter which of the two played scrum-half because both also excelled at stand-off. They do not make scrum-halves like Johnny Rogers, or Tommy Grey, or Billy Banks, or Jonty Parkin, or Alex Murphy any more. If they did, they would stick them in a scrum and call them hookers. Criminal.

Stand-off

It is also criminal that only one stand-off can be picked in this team and the truth is that the selection has been decided by a mental toss of a many-sided coin. Johnny Rogers's stand-off partner at Huddersfield, Jim Davies, was certainly one of the all-time greats. This ex-Swansea RU man, was one of the masterminds of Huddersfield's all talents team and it was his manoeuvring with Harold Wagstaff which gave birth to the run-around moves that have brought variety to the game, but which were dubbed scientific obstruction at the time of their development. Contemporary with Davies was the great Johnny Thomas of Wigan. Thomas, from Maesteg, served Wigan from 1904 to 1920 and captained both Wales and Great Britain. A great kicker, he also had the temperament for big occasions.

Swinton's diminutive Billo Rees (ex-Glanamman) and Salford's auburn-haired Emlyn Jenkins (ex-Cardiff) were the two finest stand-offs of the interwar years. Both went on Lions tours - Rees in 1928, Jenkins in 1936 - and both were mainsprings for their clubs, which were among the most successful in history. Then again, were either of those genii nearly as devastating on attack as Wigan's George Bennett, scorer of 101 tries in 232 games (1930-37)? Bennett, the first black Welsh international, was a native of Newport but played for Risca and arrived at Wigan via Weston-Super-Mare RU.

Two truly brilliant men who might have claimed this all-time stand-off spot had their careers ruined by the Second World War. Willie (W.T.H.) Davies is still regarded as one of Union's greatest fly-halves for his classical displays with Swansea and Wales. After signing for Bradford Northern in 1939, there were many League fans who were prepared to call him the greatest stand-off in their game. Willie served Northern, Wales and Great Britain nobly for 11 years. At least Willie survived the war. Oliver Morris did not; he was killed in Italy. If he had lived, he might have become the stand-off of all stand-offs. Compared to Johnny Rogers, Oliver was a pygmy. He barely weighed nine stones. He played for Pontypridd RU before joining Hunslet in 1937 and subsequently transferred to Leeds, for whom he scored 44 tries and 33 goals in only 61 games.

In the end the selection goes to **Dickie Williams.** Like Oliver Morris, Dickie Williams played for Leeds (1944-1953) and Hunslet (1954-56). Born in Mountain Ash, Dickie Williams was a Welsh Schools cap in 1939 but played his senior Rugby Union, albeit briefly, with Bristol. Eddie Waring, who knew what he was doing, signed him for Leeds on a seven year contract. Dickie was not your usual Welsh signing. He had a BSc degree from London University and he played classical piano. He was, however, a natural for League.

Ginger-haired and boyish-looking, Williams was another in the classical League half-back mould - 5 feet 6 inches and 10 stone 7 pounds, just right for the job of carving through granite defences on bewildering solo runs or of releasing flying three-quarters. He could tackle too - bravely, low. He had that touch of the spectacular about him and the crowds adored him. He had whatever it took. Some said he was a bit too individualistic, some preferred another marvellous contemporary Welsh stand-off, the tough as old boots Ray Price of Belle Vue Rangers, Warrington and St Helens fame, who had originally made his name with Abertillery RU. It did not matter what the detractors said. The records say it all - 13 caps for Wales (1947-53), five of which were as captain; a dozen Great Britain caps (1948-54); a first Lions tour in 1950; a second in 1954 as captain; 97 tries in 329 senior games and an unblemished reputation for sportsmanship.

Wingers

The choice for wingers is just flabbergasting. It is obvious that no one in their right mind could leave out **Billy Boston** but what about the other winger? Unsurprisingly the top 10

Welsh Great Britain Lions: Dickie Williams, Trevor Foster, Jim Mills, Billy Boston and John Mantle. Photo: Photogenic - D.J. Williams

Welsh try scorers in Rugby League history are all wingers - Boston, Johnny Ring, Clive Sullivan, Maurice Richards, Alan Edwards, Johnny Freeman, Arthur Daniels, Stuart Llewellyn, Roy Mathias and Jack Morley. Setting those aside, there are other superb wingers who might claim the vacant spot. Arthur Bassett, John Bevan, Phil Ford, Frank Evans, Frank Wilson and the magnificent Roy Francis are just some of the names which come to mind. In the final analysis another mental toss-up between Johnny Ring, scorer of 415 tries (1922-23), and **Clive Sullivan** came down in favour of the latter, the Humberside legend.

Boston - 'Bouncing Billy', 'Billy B' - was a total one-off, one of those once-seen-never-forgotten players, one of those you'd-never-believe-it-if-you-hadn't-seen-it-with-your-own-eyes characters. For anyone not old enough to have seen Billy Boston, it is probably impossible to convey the frisson which took hold of the onlookers as he bumped and barged through a barrage of tacklers and left a trail of bruised and battered bodies in his wake... and that was only in his second incarnation after he put weight on after starting his career as a perfect athletic specimen of a winger whose original attributes had been speed, swerve and the natural instinct of a predatory try-scorer.

Billy joined Wigan in 1953 while still serving in the Royal Signals. By the time he had retired in 1970 he had scored 571 tries, second only to Brian Bevan in the history of the game. On figures alone, then, it is impossible to leave Boston out of any all-time great team, never mind the Welsh one. Figures cannot convey the excitement that Boston generated, however, and certainly no one in the modern game comes anywhere remotely near to Billy in that respect. In fact, daft though it sounds, they would probably have to ban Billy from the modern game. It would not be fair. Imagine the damage he would do under present conditions. In his time Boston was confronted with opponents who were

Clive Sullivan running with the ball against France 1972. Photo courtesy Robert Gate.

three or five yards away at the ruck, who were used to tackling both properly and with malice. They could not stop him then. What chance would they have today with a ten-metre rule and tackling a lost art?

Like Billy, a Butetown boy, Clive Sullivan was a Cardiffian, from Splott. Like Billy he was black but physically the two were entirely disparate. Robust could have been Billy's middle name. Clive suffered terribly from leg problems as a child and in his playing career, and underwent surgery frequently. He was tallish at 5 feet 11 inches but not heavy at 12 and a half stones. He had tremendous upper body strength for one so light but his spindly, glistening legs hardly seemed designed by the same maker. The whole amounted to a flying machine, however.

Clive's career took in a massive 639 games between 1961 and 1984 and he played for Hull, Hull KR, Oldham and Doncaster. His try tally of 406 was nine fewer than Johnny Ring's and took twice as long to gather. But Sully played in an era when wingers had a harder time than Johnny Ring and Ring had the advantage of playing for a consistently brilliant Wigan back line. Clive never had the luxury of playing with such talented colleagues. Although Clive was a beautifully balanced and graceful sprinter, capable of tearing past opposing wingers on the outside and going the length of the field if necessary, he was much more than just a running winger. He was also a brave defender who eschewed the idea of staying rooted on the wing. He could be found tackling almost anywhere on the field and he defied convention by becoming a great captain from that most unsuitable position. His greatest triumph was undoubtedly his leadership of Great Britain's World Cup-winning squad in France in 1972 although on Humberside they would probably regard his unprecedented achieving of cult status with both Hull and Rovers as more of a miracle.

Centres

One of the centres to feed Boston and Sullivan should perhaps be Bert Jenkins. A native of Troedyrhiw, who made his name with Mountain Ash, Jenkins joined Wigan in 1904 and did not vacate the centre spot at Central Park until 1920. His career in first-class Northern Union took in 451 games and 218 tries and he was the complete practitioner of orthodox and unselfish centre play. He was the only man to play in all Wales's internationals from 1908 to 1914 and was Great Britain's first captain in an Ashes test.

Equally successful was Roy Francis, yet another outstanding black Welshman, who did for unorthodoxy what Jenkins did for orthodoxy. Francis made his name as a wing at Barrow and Warrington after signing first for Wigan as a boy wonder in 1936 but later became an outstanding centre with Hull. Three other contenders, all of whom played at some stage for Leeds, would be Jim Bacon, Mel Rosser and Gareth Price.

The choices, however, must be **Lewis Jones** and **Gus Risman**. The two presented an identical problem - where, not whether, to play them? Both could just as well have been selected at full-back or stand-off. Both played international League in all three positions whilst Jones also played test football on the wing.

Risman, another Cardiffian from Tiger Bay, came north to Salford in 1929 aged 17. His fee amounted to £77 and kept him out of the clutches of both Cardiff RU and Tottenham Hotspur. At 20 he was a Welsh international and went on to play eighteen times for Wales (1931-45). In view of his versatility it is surprising that all his Welsh caps were won as a centre, often as partner to his Salford wing, Alan Edwards. At the highest levels Gus was certainly one of the most successful players the game has seen. He toured Australasia as a Lion three times - in 1932, 1936 and 1946, the latter as captain. He played in five Ashes-winning series and captained Great Britain in nine of his seventeen tests (1932-46). By the time he ended his career at Salford in 1946, having rattled up 2,007 points in 427 games for the club, he was already 35.

He then launched another equally successful career with the fledgling Workington Town club which did not end until 1954 and took in another 301 games and 1,533 points. He skippered both Salford and Town to Challenge Cup victories at Wembley and to Championships.

By the time he finally did call it a day, after a brief spell at Batley in 1954, his career record of 25 years stood at 873 games, 232 tries, 1,678 goals and 4,052 points. Impressive though the bare figures are, they do not remotely convey what an impressive performer Gus was, nor how sportsmanly he conducted himself. He had all the attributes - he was big and strong but would employ science and subtlety when more appropriate. He was a master kicker and a fine tackler and he was a born leader. In 1988 he was an automatic entrant to the Rugby League Hall of Fame, along with fellow Welshmen, Billy Boston and Jim Sullivan. No recommendation could be higher.

Alongside Gus in the centre would be Lewis Jones, 'the Golden Boy'. Jones, a native of Gorseinon, followed a very different route to Rugby League from Risman. By the time he was 20 he had played in three different positions in seven Welsh RU internationals. By the time he joined Leeds from Llanelli in 1952 he had won 10 caps and had starred, aged only 19, for the British Isles on the 1950 tour of Australasia. Leeds had to fork out £6,000 for Lewis - £1,000 more than any club had ever paid for any player, League or Union.

In the end Lewis Jones was a bargain. He lit up the game. Genius was the term most often and most aptly applied to him. Many who saw him will swear that they will never see a player with as sublime an instinct for attack and invention. He had all the recognised talents and some more that had until then been unknown. He was a master of

Lewis Jones. Photo courtesy Robert Gate

the unpredictable, always willing to take risks. Well, at least they would be risks if performed by mere mortals. They just looked natural when Lewis was involved. He was quick off the mark, had a homing instinct for the smallest of openings, had a magician's hands and could kick the opposition to death. It was he who developed the hanging pass but his greatest glory was blazing acceleration, a weapon that debilitates even the deadliest of tacklers. Jones was a match-winner *par excellence*. In bald figures he played 429 first-class matches and scored 158 tries, 1,449 goals and 3,372 points before he went to Australia to player-coach Wentworthville in 1964. His greatest triumph was probably to lead Leeds to their first ever Championship in 1961. Apart from that, he set a record for a Lion on tour with 278 points in 1954, which included a British test record of 10 goals and 20 points against the Aussies at Brisbane. In the domestic season of 1956-57 he piled up an all-time record of 496 points. It was his misfortune to play test rugby for only three years (1954-57), scoring 147 points in 15 tests before, it is rumoured, the autocratic Rugby League secretary Bill Fallowfield, in infinite folly, decided that he ought to be able to tackle better. It takes all sorts.

Full-back

Full-back? Jim Sullivan. End of discussion. It is not that Wales has not provided Rugby League with dozens of splendid full-backs from the year dot onwards. It is just that every full-back in the game will always have the giant shadow of Sullivan hanging over them and Sullivan achieved so much over such a long period that it is scarcely credible that anyone will ever match him.

Jim Sullivan had great predecessors in the game - Dickie Thomas (Oldham), Dai Jim

Jim Sullivan (on left) playing for Wigan. Photo courtesy Robert Gate.

Smith (Salford), Chick Jenkins (Ebbw Vale), Frank 'Bucket' Young (Leeds) and, best of all, his immediate predecessor for Wigan and Wales, Gwyn Thomas, who finished his career with Huddersfield's wonder team after the First World War before leaving for America in 1923 where he became a top executive with Pepsi Cola. Contemporary with 'Peerless Jim' in the inter-war years were such stalwart Welsh full-backs as Tommy 'Guardsman' Rees (Oldham), Dick Davies (Halifax), Tommy Scourfield (Huddersfield) and George Lewis (St Helens), all of whom would have had a stack of caps in any other era. The post-war years threw up other tremendous full-backs in Joe Jones (Wigan and Barrow), Jack Evans (Hunslet), Glyn Moses and Kel Coslett (St Helens), Terry Price (Bradford Northern), David Watkins (Salford) and the Halifax trio of Tuss Griffiths, Garfield Owen and Ronnie James, to mention but some.

Sullivan, probably the youngest Barbarian in history, left his native Cardiff for Wigan in 1921 for a signing fee of £750, a prodigious amount for a basically untried boy who had not yet reached 18. For the next quarter of a century he was the towering figure in Rugby League, his existence a vehicle for creating and shattering records. There is no doubt that he was truly charismatic. Not only was he the best in his position but he was an inspirational leader, who in retirement became a master-coach. Physically he was a big, heavy man. His crowning glory was, of course, his cannonball kicking. His career total of 2,867 goals is almost 300 greater than his nearest challenger, Neil Fox, while no one in history can match his appearances tally of 928. Those two statistics alone set him apart and statistics cannot itemise his crunching tackling, immaculate fielding and perfect positioning, nor, more is the pity, can they portray a persona which clearly captivated all who beheld him.

On the bench

Finally, the four substitutes. At this elite level any substitute should be able to fill a variety of positions and to turn a game. Four who fit the job description are **Danny**

Hurcombe, **David Watkins**, **Ben Gronow** and **John Mantle**.

Hurcombe, former captain of Talywain, whose greatest days were spent with Wigan between 1919 and 1926, was only a small chap at 5 feet 7 inches and 10 stone 9 pounds but he was chocabloc full of confidence and could perform brilliantly anywhere in the backs. A Lion in 1920 and 1924, he also captained both Wales and Other Nationalities. Both Johnny Ring and Jim Sullivan admitted that they had learned more from Hurcombe than any other man.

Sharing the back substitutes role might not suit either Hurcombe or David Watkins. Both were aggressive for their size and would want to be on the pitch from the off. Watkins, a veritable wizard of a stand-off for Wales at Union, found the conversion to League something of a problem on joining Salford from Newport in 1967 but by the time he retired aged 40 a decade and a half on, he had become a legend in his adopted code. His ability to play devastatingly at centre and full-back and to kick record numbers of goals made him an out and out match-winner.

Ben Gronow began his career playing full-back for Bridgend, was the first man to kick off in a Union international at Twickenham (Wales versus England) in 1910 and, before Jim Sullivan arrived on the scene, was regarded as the most remarkable goalkicker the Northern Union had seen. Another member of the Huddersfield 'Team of all the talents', Gronow was a big man for his time at over 6 feet and over 16 stones at his peak. Apart from his phenomenal kicking which allowed him to set Northern Union records of 140 goals in 1914-15 and 148 goals in 1919-20, Gronow was a fearsome tackler, skilful dribbler and amazingly long passer of the ball. A double Lion (1920 and 1924), he could play anywhere in the pack.

John Mantle. Photo courtesy *Open Rugby*

John Mantle, too, was an outstanding all-round forward, although, unlike Gronow, he never played hooker and hardly ever put boot to ball. Mantle joined St Helens from Newport in 1964, having been capped by Wales twice at Union. Saints gained one of the greatest forwards to have left Wales. He was a tower of strength at loose-forward, second-row and prop in a career which stretched to 1982 and embraced seven clubs after leaving St Helens in 1976. Like Colin Dixon, his great contemporary, his early career was marked by tremendous running and an athletic, all-action style. Latterly with diminished speed and in spite of an amputated finger, he made the transition to a ball-playing prop. On retiring he had played in 596 games, a record for a Welsh forward in Rugby League.

And now argue among yourselves as to whether this is the best team Wales has produced over the last century:

1 JIM SULLIVAN

2 BILLY BOSTON   3 LEWIS JONES   4 GUS RISMAN 5 CLIVE SULLIVAN

6 DICKIE WILLIAMS   7 JOHNNY ROGERS

13 IKE OWENS

12 TREVOR FOSTER   11 COLIN DIXON

8 JIM MILLS   9 TOMMY HARRIS   10 JOE THOMPSON

Substitutes:

14 DANNY HURCOMBE

15 DAVID WATKINS

16 BEN GRONOW

17 JOHN MANTLE

Chapter 17: Interviews

All the interviews below are verbatim. Explanatory notes have been added for clarity where necessary.

Trevor Foster

Trevor Foster has given a lifetime's service to Rugby League. Apart from his feats as a player, when he was capped by Wales and Great Britain, he was involved in forming the new Bradford Northern club in 1964, served the club as a coach and director and is currently their timekeeper. He was also the Rugby League's chief coach for a time.

Moving from South Wales to sign for Bradford Northern

I signed in September 1938, when I was playing Rugby Union for Newport. I had never been north before. I had been approached to sign for Wigan, but I was not interested. I was playing my first season for Newport, and my one idea - as with any young boy in South Wales - was to play Rugby Union for Wales.

Wigan's approach came halfway through the season before. We were playing Cardiff at Rodney Parade. After the match, two men came either side of me, wearing big coats and homburg hats. They said they were from Wigan, and came home with me. We lived at the Church House, a public house my father ran. By the way, William Henry Davies was born there.

I felt uncomfortable with this approach. They put £200 on the table, but it felt like they were trying to kidnap me. I had no desire to leave Newport.

Also, Mr Hornby from Bradford Northern had written to me. He said he had seen me play, and was interested in signing me for Bradford. This seemed a nicer approach. He came to Newport's last match that season, and saw my mum and dad.

It was a good offer - £400. He said to think about it. Despite playing wing forward, I had finished the season as Newport's leading try scorer with a dozen tries.

In the summer there was another letter saying that Bradford Northern wanted to sign me, and would guarantee me a job in Bradford.

By this time I had played for Monmouthshire, and for Captain Crawshay's Welsh XV, a select team who toured Devon and Cornwall. All the other players in that select team were full internationals.

My parents said it was up to me. I trained on a Thursday, and I knew the people from Bradford were waiting for me at home. I was downhearted when I saw the big Buick outside the door. I walked into the bar, and said to my mum that I was not going. She said I had to do the proper thing and tell them.

Mr Hornby was there, and when I said I was not going, he went red, white, blue and green. He had come all the way from Yorkshire. But there was only one thing I was interested in, and that was a Welsh cap. He said I could go and buy half a dozen with their money.

Then my elder sister came in, and said that I could play for Newport and break my leg and have nothing. I understood and picked up the pen and signed. It was the greatest thing I ever did.

In the end I did win Welsh caps in Rugby League and was captain of the side. I also played for the Wales Rugby Union side during the war.

We drove in the car on a Monday through Halifax, which looked pretty awful, with the factories, very dour. I was nervous about the whole thing. Then we arrived at Odsal, and it looked a colossal place.

There were a couple of other Welsh players at Bradford Northern then - Charlie Freeman, and Desmond Case, who had signed from Cross Keys. Many came later, such as Billy Davies from Swansea, who was signed after the Second World War.

Debut for Bradford Northern

I was kept back for a couple of weeks by Dai Rees, the team manager. Then I played my first match at Odsal against Hull, at loose-forward. I was completely lost, with the difference between the play-the-ball rule and the rucking that I was used to in Rugby Union. But once I got used to the game, the space the five-yard rule gave me as a running forward suited me.

From then I was always in the first team. After the war, we had a marvellous run, going to Wembley three times, in 1947, 1948 and 1949. I met the Queen earlier this year when I received Maundy Money from her. I said I had met her mum and dad at the 1948 Cup Final.

Playing for Wales

I played 16 times for the Wales Rugby League side, and was captain six times. We played both in Wales and in the north. My first cap was in December 1939 in a wartime international against England at Odsal. Jim Sullivan captained the team and Gus Risman also played. Jim Sullivan's pre-match talk was inspirational. Also in the team was Alex Givvons, who played for Oldham. We had been at school together.

Gus Risman gave me a pass, and I scored under the posts. My father, who was blind by then from an accident, was listening on the radio, and was so excited he jumped up and knocked the table over! And we beat England.

Rugby during the war

During the war I was allowed to play for the Wales Rugby Union team. This included great players such as Haydn Tanner and Bledwyn Williams. We beat the English Rugby Union team. The war saw some magnificent matches. In 1943 and 1944, the British Army played Ireland, with Jackie Kyle playing for Ireland and Gus Risman for the British Army.

I also played in the Rugby Union versus Rugby League matches, played under Union rules, which the Rugby League team won. For the first game, in January 1943, there were five Welsh internationals in the Rugby League team. We won 18-11 at Headingley. Robin Prescott and Bob Weighill, who were at different times secretary of the RFU, played in these matches.

The standing of players who had gone over to Rugby League was shown by Gus Risman being chosen as captain of the Welsh team in the first wartime services international at Swansea. This was a wonderful tribute to a Rugby League player, especially when the team was full of Rugby Union internationals.

In the 1944-5 season, I was posted to Egypt as a Staff-Sergeant Instructor in the Army Physical Training Corps, based in Cairo. I played Rugby Union for the Welsh Rugby Services XV against the English Services XV, and against the South African Services XV. Both games were at the El Alamein Cairo Sports club, before large crowds. I captained the Welsh team to victory in both games.

The 1946 Great Britain Rugby League tour to Australia

This was the first tour after the war and we left Britain at the end of April. Gus Risman captained the side, and there were 11 Welsh players in the squad. We went on the HMS Indomitable, through the Suez Canal. It took 28 days to get there. We docked in Fremantle, and were met by the Australian press who had come 2,600 miles from the east coast to see us. We played a trial game there, and then crossed Australia by train to Sydney. Hundreds of people greeted us in Sydney. Someone came up to me, and said he had had a pint of beer in my dad's pub 20 years before!

Our first major match was against New South Wales, with a crowd of over 50,000 people. We were the only Great Britain side to be unbeaten in a test series in Australia, winning two and drawing one. However, we did lose to some of the club sides.

I remember people queuing overnight to be sure to get into the test matches. They were titanic struggles. You had to fight for every yard on the pitch, but we were given wonderful hospitality off it, and food parcels to send home. *[Britain still had rationing]*. Then we went to New Zealand, and lost to them at Carlaw Park, in the worst conditions I ever played in.

Trevor Foster scoring a try in a charity game at Headingley in 1966, for former British Lions against the British Lions. Photo courtesy *Open Rugby*

The Welsh team after the war

The Welsh Rugby League team was always well received in South Wales. After the war we played a couple of games in front of crowds of around 30,000 at the St Helen's ground in Swansea. We were received with great pride. At one game the Mayor of Swansea said that we were representing our country. Many of us were still in our forces uniforms.

They were great games. Cliff Morgan told me that he saw them as a schoolboy, and could name the whole team. Those matches, with the flow of the ball and the skills, impressed him.

There will always be a relationship between the Welsh people and Rugby League. Throughout the history of Rugby League, Welsh players have graced the game. When I was young, the local paper in Newport had a column about how the Welsh players in Rugby League were getting on. There was an affinity there.

The Welsh team stopped playing in the early 1950s. But in the 1970s, the team was resurrected, and I was happy to be involved, giving support in the background. I have been time-keeper for the Welsh team. The 1995 games in the World Cup at Swansea and Old Trafford were very memorable.

The team also did well in the European Championship, and Mike Nicholas and Clive Griffiths established the South Wales club. But then the Rugby League seemed to think there shouldn't be a place for their club, or a Wales national team, which was a tremendous blow.

The future for Rugby League in Wales

The 1995 World Cup, and the people that go from Wales to the Challenge Cup Final show that the inclination and desire to support Rugby League is there. But it must be with top class players, a team people want to see like the 1995 World Cup games in Wales which got good crowds.

At least there is a Wales development officer to build junior teams, and now there seems to be a chance of a club team starting again. But there should be a Wales national team as well. There should not be a World Cup without a Welsh side. I am optimistic that the professional game will be established in Wales again.

October 1997

Clive Griffiths

Clive Griffiths was central to the revival of the Welsh international side in the 1990s. He also coached the Welsh Students team and in 1996, became coach of the South Wales RLFC. An international in both codes, and one of the best Rugby League coaches of the modern era, he returned to Rugby Union with London Welsh in 1997.

Starting in Rugby Union

I started playing at Gowerton Grammar School, at full-back. I was then selected for the Welsh Secondary Schools team. I was invited to train at Llanelli, and joined them. My first game, when I was still in the sixth form, was against Bath. This was a traditional fixture which we played for the "Rag Doll". Bath at that time were not in Llanelli's league, so it was a good game to start in. We won by 50 points and I nearly scored.

I had also played for Penclawdd RFC, a club in the West Wales League and won a championship medal with them.

In 1972, I went to Cardiff College (now UWIC). I had three fantastic years there. I played for British Colleges, the Public School Wanderers, and for Llanelli in two cup finals. At a representative level, I played for West Wales against Argentina, Wales B , Wales and the Barbarians.

I continued at this level until 1979. I had had an offer from St Helens to 'go north' after I had played for the Wales B side. But I wanted that full Union cap, to make my dream come true. After I had got my cap, against England at Cardiff, they asked again and this time I couldn't refuse.

It was a big decision to take, but I had to treat it as a business-like decision. In one way it was heartbreaking, as I had worked so hard to win a Welsh cap. But my future in Rugby Union was unsure. There was nothing guaranteed. I could be the next Welsh full-back, but then all of a sudden St Helens came in for me again. They are a very famous club, and I thought their style of football would suit me.

I received the world record fee, at that time, to switch codes. So you can see the dilemma I was in! The decision was made, but there were some tears as I left. People don't see that. They see you as a mercenary, a bad boy for going to the dreaded game of Rugby League. That's how it was then. I broke my arm in my second game for St Helens and went back to Llanelli to watch a game. I was not very welcome in the committee box, but I've been back since, and now that's water under the bridge. Everything is fine with them now.

I had qualified as a PE teacher, and was involved in coaching at that time. I had always been interested in coaching.

Going north

So I went to St Helens. It was not an easy start, it would have been better to have played in the A team for a few matches. I signed on the Thursday, and we played Widnes on the Sunday. I had not even had a run out with the team. *[Widnes were the Challenge Cup holders at the time].*

Roy Mathias took me out onto his front lawn on the Saturday morning to teach me how to 'play-the-ball'. As we were doing this, he stepped on my hand! "Surely that's not allowed", I said, but it was a warning of the pressure I could expect. That was my first coaching in Rugby League.

It was a shock to go to a Rugby League club that I didn't find to be as 'professionally' organised as Llanelli. I was being paid more than in Rugby Union, but I didn't find the training as professional as Llanelli. Tom Hudson was at Llanelli, and Carwyn James was a big influence on me. I also learnt a great deal from Norman Gale. This is not to be disrespectful to Eric Ashton, *[the St Helens coach]* but it was still a shock.

I was going through the learning process of Rugby League. But I broke my arm in my second game. That first season was a catalogue of injuries. I would recover, play, then get injured again. I was not an injury-prone player, but the physical nature of Rugby League involves harder collisions. I had pulls and strains, would work hard to recover, but the whole season seemed to be stop-start. When I had a good run going, I enjoyed the game, and my play started to improve.

Was it a big change to move to the north?

I still live in St Helens. The odd person has no time for you, but the people of St Helens, Lancastrians, are very similar to the people of South Wales and that helped us to settle in. I like living there, and have many friends there. It would be a big wrench to leave. It was a new experience playing at different venues - Castleford, Featherstone, Hull, Hull KR - the fans would bawl and shout at you.

From 1979 until 1984 I played at St Helens. My big regret is that I had a bad injury before the start of the 1984-5 season, when I tore my hamstring during pre-season training, and missed the first part of the season. This was when Mal Meninga played for the Saints. Sean Day was one of many players who benefited from playing with Mal Meninga. It was the highlight of his career, and should have been one of mine.

After my injury, I could not get back into the team, so I went on loan to Salford, who were in the Second Division. After the loan spell, I signed full-time for them, and we were promoted from the Second Division. I scored 302 points in 1984-5 at Salford.

We had a good run, but then the coach, Kevin Ashcroft, felt he needed a change because the defence was vulnerable, so he changed both wingers. It gets to the stage when you know it is time to finish. You think "What am I doing here?" This happened to me on a wet March night, when I was playing for the reserves. So I finished at the end of that season, even though a couple of offers came my way.

I had played seven seasons of Rugby League. It was a rocky path, with its ups and downs, but I wouldn't have swapped it for anything. Rugby League toughens you up mentally and physically.

I had developed my coaching in Rugby League. In 1982, I attended a level 3 course, and have been involved in Rugby League coaching ever since. I am still an honorary staff coach with the Rugby League Coaching Scheme.

Turning to coaching

I went back to St Helens, joining the coaching staff as fitness and skills coach. Alex

Murphy was manager, and Dave Chisnall and I were the track suit coaches.

This was a good start, working with those players. Of course I had played with some of them. I stayed there for two years as a coach, with my role expanded from my original brief of fitness and skills.

Then I went to Warrington, working with Tony Barrow, and then as assistant coach to Brian Johnson. I finished there as director of coaching. I have now worked full-time in coaching for four years.

Involvement in Welsh Rugby League

In 1987, I coached the Welsh Students team in a one-off match at St Helens. I stayed with them until 1993, although I officially retired after the 1992 World Cup, when we lost in the semi-final at Parramatta. I helped Danny Sheehy in 1993, when we won the European Championship. In fact, we ruled Europe for three years.

In 1991, the Welsh national team was reborn, with a tremendous win against Papua New Guinea at the Vetch Field. The side was mainly former Rugby Union players, mainly internationals. We had very few players who had not come from Union and were qualified for Wales. Ian Marlow was one, and Anthony Sullivan was another.

After the Papua New Guinea game, we beat France 35-6, and in two games had not conceded a try. We soldiered on with limited resources, and did quite well.

I think, on reflection, we played England too early. We were missing Jonathan Davies, who was injured, and only had 24 players to choose from. We didn't have the firepower against them, and lost 11-36, which was still a respectable result.

The crowds in Wales were fantastic. The support we had was so encouraging. It was a motivation for everyone. The lowest crowd was in Cardiff, 5,000 to 6,000. That was on a bad weather night. At the Vetch in Swansea we were always well supported.

Our team was reinforced when we persuaded the Rugby League to change the rules on players qualified to play for us. In 1994, we had played Australia, after the first test match against Great Britain at Wembley. Allan Bateman and Jonathan Davies were injured and could not play. Then John Devereux and David Young were injured and had to be substituted. We were beaten 46-4, our heaviest defeat in my time. We wrote to Maurice Lindsay, asking for a change in the rules, allowing players with Welsh grandparents to play for us. The change meant we could play the Wigan front row, Paul Atcheson, Richie Eyres and others. It worked for us, we now had a side balanced with the Rugby Union converts, and the players whose roots were in Rugby League.

In 1995, we won the European Championship for the first time in 57 years. England had a good side, but we beat them in Cardiff. In Carcassonne, we played France, it was horrible, like a wet night in Maesteg. We won there, and won the trophy. It was a very proud achievement.

The 1995 World Cup

The match against Western Samoa was fantastic. The ground was absolutely full, bursting at the seams. People were locked out. It was the biggest audience ever for S4C, beating *Pobol-Y-Cwm [the Welsh Coronation Street]*. The team stayed on the field for 20 minutes at the end of the match, such was the support.

Then we went to Old Trafford for the semi-final. We took between 5,000 and 7,000 supporters with us. This following was very special, and I will always remember it. It was very emotional for me as it was also Jonathan Davies's final game for us.

This side had caught the imagination of the Welsh public. In 1996, we did well in the Fiji Nines tournament, winning the Super League Trophy, and then in June ran England close, only losing in the final few minutes. By then, Jonathan Davies had gone back to Rugby Union, as had Scott Gibbs and Scott Quinnell.

The players had done Wales proud. I am still (in theory) the Wales Rugby League coach, until Red Hall write to me and tell me otherwise.

We still have a squad that is mainly Super League players, even though many of the Rugby Union converts have returned to Union or retired. It is very disappointing that we were omitted from the *[now cancelled]* 1998 World Cup, given what we achieved in 1995. Rugby League needs as many countries as it can get to be involved.

My involvement with the Wales side was a fantastic six years. I think I speak for all the boys when I say that we enjoyed every minute. We need to stick with it. People forget that we were not in the 1995 World Cup originally. Becoming European Champions and reaching the semi-final was a nice way to prove people wrong.

1996 South Wales RLFC

Following the success of the Wales team in the World Cup, it was decided to start the South Wales club side. Mike Nicholas was the driving force. He moved to Cardiff to get the club going.

We got a good side together, and finished in a creditable position in the league. But the aim was to get fast-tracked to Super League for 1997. We met the Rugby League Council, who agreed to this, and then did a U-turn, saying that our business plan was not acceptable. Paul Thompson, now with the Sheffield Eagles, was behind us financially.

There was no better time to start a Super League team. When we brought a Super League match down to Cardiff, Sheffield Eagles versus St Helens, it was well attended. We had played Carlisle as the first match, with Mini Rugby League beforehand involving Cardiff Schools and Pilkington Recs ARLFC (from St Helens) under-9s. The whole day was good entertainment. And we finished fifth in the league. The venture did not get the support from the game that it deserved.

The South Wales board did not believe that the offer of fast-tracking to the First Division was viable. Only Super League would work. Again, there was an enormous sense of disappointment. People lost their jobs, and the club folded.

We had signed players like Paul Moriarty, who would have been in a Super League side. We would have needed to strengthen the side, but in every game we were competitive. Would we have been worse than Paris or Oldham in 1997? We would have aimed to establish a creditable side.

Working at London Welsh

After South Wales folded, I went on the 1996 tour with the Great Britain team as assistant coach. When I came back, there was another attempt to get South Wales going again. But that fell through, although a side was entered in the Academy competition.

So this left me without a job. While in Cardiff, I had done some Rugby Union coaching at Treorchy. This became public knowledge, and I had offers from Rugby Union clubs. I also applied for the Halifax and Castleford positions, but was unsuccessful. So in many ways it was inevitable that I would return to Rugby Union.

I came close to joining the Ulster provincial team, but then Kelvin Bryon, the chairman of London Welsh phoned, asking me to come for talks. I accepted the position. I have now been here for six months. I am bringing in some of the things I learnt in Rugby League to a new set-up. We won the Team of the Month and the Coach of the Month awards for September and October (1997), which was a great honour for the club. We've made a good start, but people will judge us by our position at the end of April, not the end of October.

Time will tell if I go back to Rugby League. I can't make people give me a job. It was disappointing for us all - when we saw what could be achieved.

The future for Rugby League in Wales

To my mind, it must be a European Super League. The game must expand outside the M62 corridor. I try to look at it positively and objectively, but it is demoralising to look at what has happened to the game in Wales. People from outside don't know what we have gone through, and the work that has been put in.

Wales is a rugby nation. With quality and success, people will support you. The players are competitive, and there is very little else to watch in the summer months.

For a club to be successful, it must have sound finance, and attract the best players. I hope it comes. It needs support from the top, both physical and financial. We can't compete against other sports if we are being restricted from within our own sport. And it needs patience, a new team will not beat Wigan immediately.

We constantly put resources into other areas, but can't establish a team in Wales. Yet Wales are at least the fifth strongest Rugby League nation as it stands today.

November 1997

John Mantle

John Mantle played for Wales at both codes, and represented Great Britain at Rugby League. He also coached the Cardiff Blue Dragons during their first season, and is now Secretary to the Welsh Rugby League Players Association.

Rugby Union

I started playing Rugby Union at grammar school, and was selected for the Welsh Secondary Schools side in 1959-60. In 1959, I had a trial at football for Wolverhampton Wanderers. I played six games and had an interview with Stan Cullis, who asked me to turn professional. I said not at the moment, because I was doing my A levels, and wanted to get some qualifications. He said I was wise, as it was a precarious living. But I had an open invitation to return.

I was also Welsh Triple Jump champion at under-15, under-17 and under-19 levels, and fourth in Great Britain at under-19. I also played cricket at county level while at school. But rugby was becoming the biggest sport for me.

I then went to Loughborough, and played for Loughborough College. I was there from 1961 to 1964, and got into the first team straight away. I also played club rugby for Bargoed. We played all the top Welsh clubs and, in my third year, I captained the side. We were Universities Athletic Union champions in my second and third years. In my third year, I played for Newport in the holidays, and was selected for a Welsh trial.

I then played against England at Twickenham, at blindside wing-forward. Despite a lot of criticism of the Welsh selectors, we drew 6-6. The week before, I had stubbed my toe playing for Loughborough against Ebbw Vale, and was in agony. I really shouldn't have played, but I had a local anaesthetic, and borrowed some soft leather boots. The night after the game I really suffered, but it was worthwhile.

In my third year, we won the Middlesex Sevens in front of 60,000 people at Twickenham. I had already been picked by Wales to tour South Africa, and there was a rule that you should not play after being selected. But I wanted to play in the Sevens, so my "defence" was that one of our players had not turned up. Fortunately the Welsh officials accepted this "excuse", so I did go on tour.

I played in the test match, which we lost. Their side included Doug Hopwood at number 8, Jamie Engelbrecht and Frik Du Preez. We won the other games on tour, and it was a good tour for me, because I had replaced Alan Pask as the Welsh number 8.

In the summer of 1964, I got a teaching job at Chepstow. Newport made a good start to the season. The side included David Watkins, Brian Price and Bob Prosser, who later followed me to St Helens.

Going north

I was starting to attract attention from the Rugby League clubs in the north. The first time I met the chairman of St Helens, it was in secret. Even speaking to a Rugby League scout could lead to suspension. We met in a country lane outside Newport, but I didn't sign then.

Ten weeks later, they came to my house, and my mind was made up. I had always fancied playing Rugby League. I had heard about the game from a lad from St Helens at college. We agreed the financial side of the move, but it was with the proviso of me getting a teaching job. I had an interview with the director of education, and then it was signed and sealed.

On 21 December 1964 I signed for St Helens. You never forget certain dates. I had only seen a few games of Rugby League on television, but it appealed to me. Scoring tries was a big part of my game, and I was on the way to breaking the Newport try scoring record for a back-row forward. I had scored nine or 10 already that season.

It was a big change. I knew some people in the north, and had been a few times, but I had not seen Rugby League in real life. It was not just a financial move, it was a way to help my parents who had put me through college, combined with a desire to make it in Rugby League.

My only slight regret was that I had not toured with the Rugby Union British Lions. But I did tour with the Rugby League British Lions, which was a partial compensation.

Rugby League career

I played for 12 seasons, appearing in 19 finals. I played at Wembley three times, when we won the Challenge Cup in 1966, 1972 and 1976; and in end of season Championship, BBC2 Floodlit Trophy and Lancashire Cup finals. I played 435 games for St Helens.

My debut for Saints had been on Boxing Day 1964, for the A team against Wigan. I had never had any Rugby League training. Steve Llewellyn took me into a corridor and showed me how to play-the-ball. The game went well, I scored two 75 yard tries, and we won by 30 points in front of a big crowd.

My next game was in the first team. I was nursed along. I was fortunate that I came north to go to a good team. But I had faith in my ability to learn the game.

After 10 years at St Helens, I had a testimonial season in 1974-5. That was the only season in my time that we did not win anything. But the testimonial was still a record amount for that time.

I played for Great Britain 13 times, and turned down two tours to Australia because of injury. I missed the 1968 World Cup because I was having two cartilages taken out of my knee. I knew my leg wouldn't last on the hard pitches out there. I played for the Wales Rugby League side 16 times, including three as captain.

After St Helens won the Cup and the Premiership Final in 1976, I moved to Salford. Eric Ashton had become coach at St Helens, and wanted to make some changes. I had been involved in David Watkins signing for Salford in 1967, and stayed there for a year, playing 36 out of 37 games. But I felt the team had lost their cutting edge - the chairman Brian Snape would give winning money even if we had lost, but played well!

Basil Lowe had been secretary at St Helens for most of my time there. He had then become chairman at Leigh, and was interested in me joining them as player-coach. I spent 18 months there, and in my first season we won the Division 2 championship in style. The following season, we had got a few points, but had had a lean run. They had not spent money on the team, and we lacked strength in depth. So they decided to change the coach.

We had a board meeting, and were discussing one of the players, Paul Grimes. I wanted him to change from second row to prop, because I felt he could develop as a

Great Britain player in that position. But he was staying away, so Stan Roberts, the chairman of Leigh, asked me to phone him. I refused.

I went home, and as I got in, the chairman phoned me and said they had decided to change the coach. They were notorious for this, changing coaches almost every year. They paid up my contract.

Wigan came in for me, because Vince Karalius was looking for an experienced forward. Wakefield were also interested, but I decided to go to Barrow. Steve Tickle, who was working with me, was playing there. I enjoyed my time at Barrow, we had some good young players. Bill Oxley (a club director) told me that the local press wanted me to become coach, and Frank Foster (the Barrow coach) saw his position threatened, and made things uncomfortable for me.

So I moved to Keighley. That was really the end of my playing career, although I played a few games for Oldham, helping out in an injury crisis. I remember playing in their A team with a raw youngster called Andy Goodway! After my time at Cardiff, I did some coaching at Blackpool Borough, and played my last game in March 1982 for Blackpool.

Playing for Wales

I always enjoyed playing for the Wales Rugby League team. People could see what they had missed from the players who had gone north. People there like their rugby - Union or League - and we were always well supported.

The 1975 World Championship was the highlight. We had a great team spirit, and I enjoyed playing in Australia and New Zealand.

Cardiff Blue Dragons

David Watkins rang me to ask if I was interested in becoming their coach. I met their chairman, Bob Grogan, who outlined what was available to spend on players.

I did the training and organising, and tried to gel the two halves of the squad *[one was based in Wales, the other in the north of England]* together. For a home game, the northern-based players and me would travel down on the Saturday morning, have a training session on Saturday afternoon, and then stay in a hotel before the game on Sunday.

From Rugby League, the club had recruited old pros, such as George Nicholls and Tony Karalius.

Of the players who came from Rugby Union, Tommy David was a natural for Rugby League. If he had come earlier, he would have been a sensation. Steve Fenwick was a good player - what he lacked in pace he made up for in speed of thought. Paul Ringer brought with him a 'hard man' tag from Rugby Union, and found it more difficult in Rugby League.

But after a few months, Bob Grogan said to me that the club couldn't afford to pay me and David Watkins, because he was losing money on every home game. So David took sole responsibility for playing affairs. Bob wanted me to carry on solely in a playing role, but I didn't want to play - I was 40 then! The Welsh papers were very hostile, and gave us minimal coverage compared to Rugby Union. I think this was a deliberate ploy.

Welsh Rugby League Players Association

I took over as secretary two years ago from David Watkins. The committee asked me to become secretary. We need to get the younger players involved - a lot of our members are players from the 1940s and 1950s. We have a get together a couple of times a year, and a dinner once a year. This year (1997) it was at Salford, and Ray French spoke. Last year we had the dinner in Llanelli, and in 1995 at Huddersfield. Cliff Morgan was our speaker, with 400 people there. Cliff loved the Rugby League game.

There is a lot of enthusiasm for the association. Jim Mills is the chairman, Roy Mathias is the treasurer and Trevor Foster is president. Brian Butler, Kel Coslett, Billy Boston, Les Pearce and John Thorley are on the committee.

It's nice to speak to people I played against from the past, even if I did batter them on occasions! There is always plenty of talking, laughing and drinking. I hope the more recent players become involved. Iestyn Harris came to the dinner this year and enjoyed it. I hope he will encourage more current players to come to future meetings.

Apart from my involvement with the Players' Association, I also coach a local under-7s side, which keeps me fit. Neil Holding coaches the under-8s.

Future for Rugby League in Wales

Professionalism in Rugby Union has taken players such as Scott Gibbs, Allan Bateman and Scott Quinnell from us. I don't know if their Rugby Union clubs would allow them to play for a Wales Rugby League side. Rugby Union has become more entertaining at the top level since professionalism. You could see the influence of Phil Larder in the England performance against New Zealand in 1997. Running at angles - we were doing that years ago at St Helens. Phil Larder was at Loughborough with me by the way.

I hope there is a future, but I am not optimistic.

December 1997

Phil Melling

Phil Melling started student Rugby League in Wales by setting up the first club at Swansea University in 1978. He also managed the Welsh Student team and was involved in developing the amateur game in Wales. He wrote Man of Amman, *a biography of Welsh Rugby League player Dai Davies, and has written plays about Rugby League. He teaches American Studies at Swansea University.*

What is your background in Rugby League?

I come from Wigan. All my family followed Rugby League. My father had watched Wigan since World War One. His heroes were Danny Hurcombe and Jim Sullivan. We lived in Dicconson Street, half a mile from Central Park, which was a focal point for the town.

I grew up in the 1950s and went to school with Derek Birchall, a talented coach for schools Rugby League. Derek coached Shaun Edwards and Andy Gregory. Both of us idolised Billy Boston. Everyone did. There were crowds of 30 to 40 thousand at Central Park in the 1950s. I remember playing St Helens, one Good Friday. There were nearly 50,000 in the ground. David Vose and I stood on a toilet wall on the Douglas side for two hours before the game. Everyone in Wigan was immersed in Rugby League. Football was not very strong, although Wigan Athletic was a reasonable team. Rugby Union was purely social, and Orrell was an up-and-coming village side.

Welsh players had always starred for Wigan. The most famous was Jim Sullivan. Graham Thomas, my uncle, was looked after by Jim Sullivan after his father was killed in the war. In Wigan, Sullivan is still regarded as the greatest of players.

How did you get involved in starting Rugby League in Wales?

In 1978 I got a job in American Studies at Swansea University. I saw Rugby League as a means of self-preservation. The first thing I wanted to do was find out who had played Rugby League. I contacted the old players who had gone north and moved back here after they finished. I started to look for Ted Ward and this led me to Dai Davies, a wonderful character. I wrote about him in *Man of Amman*. In 1979 I organised a month-long photographic exhibition at the Swansea Museum on Rugby League, and we contacted some old League players through that. It generated exposure for the game in the papers.

After I came to Swansea I decided to have a crack at starting Rugby League in Wales. I put posters up at the university and got a good response. In January 1979 we played Reading and Oxford. We had a very good side and were unbeaten for the first two or three years.

None of the students had played before. In *Open Rugby* in 1982 Phil Larder wrote an article about what we were doing and was very complimentary. Shame he's gone. We benefited from the cliquishness of Rugby Union and its ritualised laddishness. A lot of our players weren't into pretend machismo and off the field bravado, so they played Rugby League and proved themselves on the field. The usual routine.

When we started our club there was trouble. The director of the University Sports

Centre, Stan Addicott, was the coach of Swansea Rugby Union Club.

It's hard to imagine now, but people like Stan Addicott had no understanding of Rugby League as an amateur sport. I can't stress that enough. Rugby League was seen as exotic and professional. Rugby Union coaches simply did not believe there were hundreds of amateur teams in the north. This took a long time to sink in. Players were banned from Rugby Union within the university and by the Welsh Rugby Union. It was commonly thought we were on a mission to professionalise student Rugby Union. Players were regularly sent warning letters. It was a strangely amusing period.

In the early days there was pressure both from Rugby Union and from people within the university. I remember being told I would get no further in my career at Swansea if I carried on with Rugby League. I'm not trying to sound melodramatic. This did happen. I was taken aside and told that senior people in professorial and administrative positions in the college were saying I should stop straightaway. It may have been a bluff, but it was also meant as a warning.

I was also given a dressing down by Stan Addicott who said I was enticing his players away from Rugby Union. Of course, we had no money and no kit. We were lent an old Great Britain kit, and it was said that "proved we were professional". It was in tatters. It was so old the white had turned pink!

A lot of people were paranoid but looking back it's not surprising. I would probably have been the same. Rugby League had no meaning as an amateur sport in Wales. Even so, the worst thing the Union could have done was stop the students playing Rugby League. It got us a lot of attention and won us friends.

When there was trouble the students felt important. They became honorary northerners. They showed a lot of loyalty and we had reasonable backing from the Student Rugby League. David Chambers helped and Maurice Oldroyd of BARLA sent teams down. Wigan St Patricks and Dewsbury Celtic visited regularly. They were fantastic and very understanding. I can't speak highly enough about those teams. Their attitude was exemplary. They were a credit to the sport.

How did Student and amateur Rugby League then develop?

We got to the final of the Universities Athletic Union trophy in 1983, and lost 15-5 to Liverpool University at Widnes. We had been in three semi-finals before that and, in the late 1980s, got to the final against Loughborough at St Helens. Given our geographical limitations we always did well.

I was asked to become involved elsewhere so in the mid-1980s we started a Welsh League. This included open age and student clubs. I must confess, I always felt uneasy about putting teams from the universities against open age teams. Things could easily go wrong and did. If the students were winning against an inexperienced amateur team then invariably the nasty stuff crept in. We didn't have independent referees, often a local lad who was not experienced. Discipline was hard to maintain.

I also felt that students were a special category, and played best against other students. At Swansea University our bread and butter were the student competitions. In South Wales in the 1980s we had 10 to 12 teams in different stages of development. There was a mixture of student and open age club sides. Jeff Woods was involved at Cardiff University. We had teams at Maesteg and in the Rhondda Valley at

215

Porth with the inimitable Fred Patrick. North Wales came later.

Throughout this period we needed the support of a development officer. Had the right person been appointed a lot of the students could have gone on to great things in the game. As it was, some of them drifted back into Rugby Union. Others went on to play Rugby Union for Wales, like Rob Appleyard.

I was the Welsh Student team manager in the mid-1980s. In 1984 we beat England at Bridgend. In the late 1980s, the team reappeared, with Clive Griffiths as coach. Martyn Sadler was the chair of the Student Rugby League and recommended him. Later we brought in Danny Sheehy from Aberavon. Together we made a great team.

That side had a lot of success. In 1989 we beat the French Students in Paris. It was the first time France had lost at home in 20 years. We were European Champions five years running. In 1992 we got to the semi-final of the Student World Cup in Australia. We played the Australians at Gosforth, 60 miles up the coast from Sydney and lost, predictably! We weren't slaughtered though and gave them a good game.

In 1990 I was manager of the British Students in France. We played in Apt and drew with the French team. All in all it was a great experience. As manager of Wales I was involved in all aspects of team work and preparation. The work was often unglamorous, but we all pitched in and complemented each other. Clive Griffiths was intense and committed. He is without doubt the best coach I have come across: demanding, thorough and intelligent. Rugby League should be ashamed of the way it has treated him. It is scandalous that Clive is not coaching in Super League. I'm afraid we'll live to regret it. But that's Rugby League for you. We remain highly suspicious of people with flair and, sadly, we tend to view them as a threat.

Danny and Kerry Sheehy also worked with us. They had formed the Aberavon team in 1983. They were equally committed and a credit to Rugby League. Danny took on the Welsh Students senior coaching role in 1992 when Clive went to Warrington. My last game in charge was in December 1992, when we beat the French in Perpignan.

I had been involved for 15 years and it was time to move on. It was becoming quite stressful at that period. I was putting more time into Student Rugby League than my own job. It was supposed to be voluntary but I had a huge budget and was responsible for international sides, club sides, the whole thing. I was also refereeing games. The work needed to be done by a development officer. Rugby League was getting it for nothing plus the services of Sharon Hansard, the American Studies secretary. God knows how much we cost the university in time, man hours, phone calls and stamps.

Throughout the 1980s I wrote to the Rugby League, asking them to invest long-term in Wales. They had a wonderful opportunity but the hierarchy were slow and timid. To be fair, David Oxley was supportive, but I suspect he was on his own. Other people didn't give a damn about whether Rugby League developed in Wales or not. We had had a professional side, the Cardiff Blue Dragons, but that fizzled out when the side moved to Bridgend. The failure of the professional game traumatised Rugby League and left a deep scar. Senior administrators privately believed that Wales was a place that should play Rugby Union. They were desperately slow to respond to our initiatives. In 1994, Kerry Sheehy became the development officer, but by then it was 10 years too late.

In the 1980s we found people with money who sponsored us and paid for our strip. With Clive Griffiths involved, doors opened. Clive had been a Rugby Union international and was teaching at Cowley Grammar School. Danny Sheehy was a manager at British

Steel. We had a 'professional' base outside of the sport, which gave us a gloss. I think that confused our friends in the north, never mind the Rugby Union. They didn't know what to make of us. We gained something of a maverick reputation.

If only Rugby League could have seized the opportunity that existed in the 1980s. By then we had conquered much of the bigotry, and we had a big future. Clive and I fought as a team, whatever our private disagreements. We used our intelligence and never came second, whoever was the enemy: the Rugby Union or the English Students Rugby League.

My happiest times in Rugby League were with Swansea and the Welsh Students team. We had no right to beat the English Students as consistently as we did in the late 1980s and early 1990s. But they couldn't get near us and it always narked them. We were very committed. Our planning, organisation and coaching were first rate.

Cardiff Blue Dragons and Bridgend

I was not as involved as Danny or Kerry Sheehy at Bridgend, but I know that some of the Cardiff professional players were very committed to helping develop student and amateur Rugby League. They coached amateur clubs. Bob Fleay, who worked as a prison officer, would come from Cardiff to referee our games at Swansea.

Some of the players who were signed, such as Tommy David and Steve Fenwick, were not immersed in Rugby League and you always felt they would go back to Union. Others had played in the north and returned home. They knew as much about Rugby League as anyone and, like Gordon Pritchard and Bob Fleay, helped develop the game.

A great example was Ness Flowers. He had returned to Wales and wanted to put something back into the game. He came to the university as a mature student, and played for the Blue Dragons, and then Swansea University.

Ness was involved in the amateur and student game for years and started his own team, in between breeding pit bulls terriers! He also did commentaries for Welsh radio on the Wembley Cup Finals.

When Ness was playing student Rugby League there was still a ban in place that stopped amateur Rugby League players from playing Rugby Union. This exploded in 1991, when we organised a nine-a-side Rugby League tournament at Swansea Uplands Rugby Union Club. We aimed to provide a festival of rugby over a weekend, in mid-summer. We invited teams from all over Wales.

We sent out circulars, put an advert in the *Western Mail*, and got around 50 responses - mainly from Rugby Union teams, including Ammanford, Amman Valley and Pontypridd. A few Rugby League clubs came, like Eccles.

The Welsh Rugby Union responded by saying that anyone who played in the tournament would be 'professionalised', because former professionals such as Ness were playing. As a result we lost a lot of our entries. Correspondence from Dennis Evans (the Welsh RU Secretary) was also sent to every Rugby Union club in Wales about this competition. One circular had us as the first item, a higher priority than the Welsh tour to South Africa. That is how much they regarded Rugby League as a threat. Swansea Uplands was threatened by the WRU that funding for new floodlights would not be approved if the tournament went ahead. To their eternal credit they did not back down.

We bought a trophy for the tournament and called it the Jonathan Davies Trophy.

The Welsh RU then sent out a another circular that said anyone who even "touched" the trophy would be "professionalised" and automatically banned from Rugby Union. This got a lot of newspaper coverage. Jonathan's mother heard about the fuss, and wrote to the papers saying that the Welsh RU were slandering her son.

We changed the name of the trophy to the Dennis Evans trophy, but he never got the joke. The tournament went well and we had a great weekend. The whole affair proved to me that major organisations like the WRU, with their reputation for being tough and inscrutable, were brittle and neurotic. We in Rugby League need not be scared of them.

GIVE AMATEUR RUGBY LEAGUE A TRY

FIRST EVER NATIONAL

10-A-SIDE AMATEUR RUGBY LEAGUE COMPETITION

FOR TEAMS IN WALES ·

at

SWANSEA UPLANDS RUGBY FOOTBALL CLUB

SATURDAY, AUGUST 10th

Winners to receive the Jonathan Davies Trophy

Utilising the free gangway between the two codes at amateur level, your amateur status will not be infringed.

No previous experience required. `"` ɔams welcome. Coaching available to any side requiring assistance.

Teams already entered from WREXHAM, CARDIFF, SWANSEA, ABERAVON and COLWYN BAY

For further information and application forms contact Dr. Phil Melling or Sharon on **SWANSEA (0792) 295305** (daytime) or **(0792) 465358** (evening)

In the early days the Cardiff Blue Dragons had a lot of goodwill, but some of the players they signed were a mistake. There was little financial investment and many of the players were clearly at the end of their careers. There was a persistent lack of discipline with a lot of sendings off. I don't think the club was promoted well. I actually think they could have done better in West Wales, but there were financial and political reasons for being based in Cardiff.

For professional Rugby League to succeed in Wales you need a quality product. The players at Cardiff did their best, but in my opinion they lacked pace. They couldn't compete at the highest level although, that said, I think the northern referees did them very few favours. The famous game at Leigh when they lost the match through a dreadful decision which cost them a John Player Trophy semi-final place was a case in point. Later, at Bridgend, they had a good team spirit and involved the amateur players, but they weren't strong enough and once the novelty wore off they didn't have the players or the money to continue. Some of the best student players at that time went on to Rugby Union as there were no professional clubs in Wales after the end of 1985-86. In 1984, the Welsh Student team had defeated England at Bridgend, with around 2,000 people there. That game gave Clive Millman the idea of moving the Blue Dragons to Bridgend.

South Wales 1996

Clive Griffiths did his best on the field, but there was very little promotion of the club off the field. They needed more financial backing but even Rugby Union is struggling these days for sponsors. You can't do it on the cheap. You need a quality product, and the support will come.

The Future

If only Rugby League had the organisational and administrative flair to match the athletic skills of the players. With the exception of odd individuals like David Oxley we have never had the people with the intellectual skill and composure of the Rugby Union. At critical times in our history we have just backed off and waved the white flag - not just here but all over the world. In the 1950s we could have established the game in Italy, and that opportunity was missed. In France we have failed to develop the game to its full potential. We can't blame anyone but ourselves for that.

We now try to build in Ireland and Scotland from a very small base. I don't begrudge that but there is still an incredible pedigree for the game in Wales. In the amateur ranks we have a 20-year history of real achievement.

Things have improved since the mid 1990s and we now have a development officer and a youth coach. The game is strong at the under-19 level and people like Mark Isherwood (the development officer) are doing a great job. In Wales we have continued to show the potential that still exists. Could anyone better the game against Western Samoa in the 1995 World Cup? A Super League team building on that would have produced great openings for all concerned. Once again, we dithered when we should have seized the day.

I took a break in 1993 after 15 years involvement with Student Rugby League. I would have been happy to play another role but I am not sure the Rugby League knew what to do with me. I was a writer with an academic background who didn't fit the mould. I have written books and plays about Rugby League and that's been fun. In 1985, my Rugby League play *The Day of the African* was put on at the George Orwell Heritage Centre in Wigan, and caused some controversy in the town. At present I am writing an article on Billy Boston for the University of Wales press, and I have just completed a novel about the game.

December 1997

Jim Mills

Jim Mills was one of the best Welsh Rugby League forwards of the modern era, although his considerable skills were sometimes forgotten because of his disciplinary record. He was a key member of the great Widnes side of the 1970s, and was capped by Wales and Great Britain. Since retiring he has stayed involved in the game at Widnes, including seven years as club chairman. He also was Wales's team manager from 1991 to 1993.

Rugby Union

I first played Rugby Union when I was 12 years old. One of my teachers, Sid Judd, who was a Welsh international and British Lion talked me into playing. I played for Cardiff schoolboys, and then for Cardiff's Youth side. From there I progressed to the Welsh Youth side, which I captained once.

In club rugby, I made my debut for the Cardiff first XV at 17, against London Welsh at Cardiff Arms Park. Before I went north, in October 1964, when I was coming up to my 20th birthday, I had played in all the first team games that season. My last match for Cardiff was against Aberavon.

Going north

I joined Halifax, on Colin Dixon's recommendation. We had played in the Cardiff Youth side together, and he had gone north when he was 17. I took time to settle. I was homesick, and living in digs. I missed my mother's cooking. But I settled down and became a regular at Halifax. Colin Dixon encouraged me to stick at it.

The game was very different. In Rugby Union forwards had to release the ball. In Rugby League you could run the length of the field and score. Rugby League was much faster, and the tackling was tougher.

Rugby League

In 1968, I joined Salford. I only stayed there for a short time. David Watkins was playing for them then and Griff Jenkins was the coach. There were personal reasons why I left and I was deciding whether to go back to Wales when Harry Womersley, the chairman of Bradford Northern, resurrected my career.

He signed me for Bradford Northern and gave me a fresh start. Welshmen Berwyn Jones, Terry Price, Tony Fisher and Les Thomas were all there, so I felt at home. Things turned for me from that point.

I was selected for the Welsh Rugby League side, and started to play well. In 1970, I was selected for the Great Britain tour to Australia and New Zealand but I withdrew from that side to join North Sydney.

I was offered a good contract. Roy Francis was their coach. He was on holiday in Britain when he signed me. They needed a prop, so I got a two-and-a-half year contract.

The game in Australia was faster, with the firmer grounds. We did not have any great success, and were usually in the bottom half of the table. But I enjoyed my time in

Australia. I made some good friends there. Merv Hicks (formerly of St Helens and Warrington) and Graham Williams (formerly Swinton) were there. Mal Reilly and Phil Lowe were both playing in Australia then. There were also a few other British players, such as David Bolton, Tommy Bishop and the South African Len Killeen.

Widnes

In November 1972, I came back into British Rugby League with Widnes. Vince Karalius *[the Widnes coach]* came to see me in Cardiff. I had approaches from three clubs - Wigan, Bradford Northern and Widnes.

Vince Karalius was very persuasive. He said the club would become great, and he wanted me to join them. It was the best thing I could have done, because he was developing a great side.

In 1974, I was selected for the British Lions to tour Australia. I played for the Wales Rugby League side again, and won a lot of honours with Widnes at club level. We went to Wembley on three occasions, winning two of them. I scored the winning try against Warrington in 1975. We won four Lancashire cups, the John Player Trophy, and the Championship, in the 1970s and early 1980s.

Vince Karalius was a great motivator. I can be lazy, so he was very good for me.

Wales Rugby League team

I first played for Wales when I was with Bradford Northern. In 1975, Wales were in the World Championship. I went to Australia and New Zealand with the Welsh side. We beat England in the 'battle of Brisbane'. We did well although we did not have that many players to pick from - only about 30. Our coach was Les Pearce, from Skewen near Neath. He was a great character, and good to be with. Ronnie Simpson was our (English) team manager. It was my most enjoyable tour of Australia. The camaraderie was tremendous. We would have died for one another.

We got a tremendous reception when we played in Wales. They locked the gates at the St Helen's ground in Swansea when we played France in 1975. In Swansea we always got good gates, especially against New Zealand and Australia.

Jim Mills (white shirt) in action for Widnes against Warrington. Photo courtesy Robert Gate

Then in 1975, I was sent off in the World Championship match at Swansea against New Zealand for stamping on John Greengrass. I'm not proud of that incident, but there were mitigating circumstances. I was suspended for six months. The New Zealanders banned me for life, although the Australian RL didn't ban me. I appealed, and the British ban was extended to 12 months! So I took the Rugby League to court. The six months ban was restored and, because half of it was in the close season, so that wasn't too bad.

In 1978 we had a very close match with Australia. They fed the ball into the second row, which wasn't allowed then. The referee let them get away with it, and they scored, which was the turning point in the match. I was so upset. Ray Price was laughing about the decision, so I belted him. Fortunately, no one noticed. It was a terrible decision. I didn't speak to that referee for a year!

For Wales when I was playing, Colin Dixon was a great all round player and John Mantle was a wonderful forward. Other great players from that time were David Watkins, John Bevan, Clive Sullivan, Roy Mathias, Terry Price and Kel Coslett.

When my long ban finished, I went to Workington for 12 months. Tom Mitchell talked me into going there. They were trying for promotion. We were promoted, and into the final of the Lancashire Cup against Widnes [Widnes won 16-11]. Tom agreed that after 12 months I could go back to Widnes, where Frank Myler was now the coach.

I was selected for the World Cup tour in Australia and New Zealand in 1977, but had to withdraw through injury.

I had more success with Widnes, with a Championship and another Wembley appearance. I was selected for the 1979 tour to Australia, with Eric Ashton as the coach. Dougie Laughton was the captain. But by now I was 35, and my knees were knocked about. I came home from the tour with a knee injury. Dougie Laughton, Roger Millward, Steve Nash, and Tommy Martyn all returned home with injuries.

When I returned from the tour, I carried on the next season. We played Bradford Northern at Widnes, and the ligaments snapped in my knee. I had an operation the next day, and the surgeon said I shouldn't play again. I was 36, so I took the surgeon's advice. I had had a good run, and done everything I wanted.

After retiring, I set up a nightclub business in Widnes which I am still involved in. I also became a member of the Widnes club committee. I didn't have enough time for coaching. Eventually I became chairman of Widnes, which I did for seven years. In my first year we won the John Player Trophy and I also led the side out at Wembley against Wigan.

Of course, one of the most significant events during my time as chairman was signing Jonathan Davies. His mother-in-law lives in Trimsaran, near Llanelli. We met him and his wife there, late at night, so no one would see us. We were going to Burry Port, to see John Warlow, but he was not there. We were keeping a low profile, because we were signing Jonathan the next day in Swansea.

We stopped in Llanelli for a drink. Behind the bar was Norman Gale. He had been hooker for the Welsh Rugby Union side, so he recognised us. We denied we were signing any players. He said his son played for Llanelli. I asked if he was anything to do with the Llanelli club, and he said "I'm the chairman". We drank up quickly, and left. I would have liked to have seen his face the next day when we had signed Jonathan, Llanelli's biggest star. We also got Paul Moriarty and John Devereux from South Wales.

I called my father before we signed Jonathan, saying we were after him. He's a

Rugby Union fan, and said "That'll be the day". I won't say what he called me when Jonathan joined us.

When the new Super League structure came in, things turned sour. I was very disappointed that Widnes were not involved in the Super League. We were not relegated, but the Rugby League decided the bottom four would go down, not the bottom two, so we lost our place.

After seven years I felt it was time for a change. But I am still on the board, and am chairman of football.

One of the highlights is the brand new stadium we have. It is one of the best stadiums, but we are not in Super League, and it will be difficult to get back to the top.

Managing the Welsh Rugby League team

When the team was starting again in 1991, I was asked to be the manager by the Rugby League. We had been promised that if we beat Papua New Guinea and France, we would be put in the World Cup, which we did. But they didn't put us in. I rang Maurice Lindsay, saying that I didn't agree with this, so I resigned in protest. After a lot of pressure from different groups, the decision was reversed. That was very satisfying.

It was very nice to be involved with the team. They were a great set of lads, with some great players.

The role of the team manager is covering all the administrative duties - organising training grounds, making sure everyone is on the bus, players' problems, speaking to the media, and arranging meals.

Clive Griffiths did an excellent job as coach. He put in 100 per cent, and got the best out of the players. We had a good mix of the former Rugby Union players, such as Jonathan Davies, David Bishop and Kevin Ellis. Players such as Gerald Cordle and Phil Ford added Rugby League experience. It was a well-balanced side, but with a few injuries, we could be struggling.

Mike Nicholas took over from me as team manager. We had played together, and I had been sent off at St Helens in a John Player Trophy final after a clash with Mike!

Future for Rugby League in Wales

They have the Wales Academy side, and my son has been training with them. We must develop the game at the grassroots. Rugby Union still has a strong hold, with support from the big companies.

We must have a top class side there, with the big teams from the north coming down to play. Otherwise it is very difficult to build. Cardiff, when they signed Steve Fenwick and Tommy David, had a good go, but the crowds dropped off. The new summer season has advantages, but there are also clashes with holidays.

People will always support the international team, especially to see their old Rugby Union heroes playing.

January 1998

Glyn Moses

Glyn Moses went north to join Salford. He returned to Wales and briefly played for Cardiff in 1951-2. Jim Sullivan resurrected Glyn's Rugby League career by signing him for St Helens in 1952. He went on to play for St Helens for seven years, win nine Great Britain caps and twice tour Australia.

Rugby Union

I played Rugby Union at school, and then for the local boys club. I captained the Glamorgan Boys Club team, and played for a local senior side. At the age of 14 I went to work in the pits. I was glad of anything that would get me away from there. When I was 18 I joined Maesteg. That was in 1947.

Going north

I had an offer from Batley, but I signed for Salford. I was at the cinema, and a message was given out for me to go home. When I got there, Cyril Braund, the Salford manager was there. My brother was already playing for Salford. So I signed for them for £600, which was a lot of money at that time. I went up to Salford, and my brother didn't know I was coming. "What are you doing here?" he said when I saw him.

I found the game was very different from Rugby Union. There was not so much kicking. The players were fitter, and there was more training. At that age coming north was a big upheaval. It was a big new world compared to South Wales. I was living near Manchester and there were no mountains like South Wales. It was industrial and smoky.

Once my brother and I were at home for a wedding, and went to watch Maesteg. The secretary asked us to leave. It was very petty - Rugby Union was a bit aloof then.

Playing for Salford

I wasn't well known from Rugby Union, so I was not a target for the other teams like some of the players who went north were. I played one and a half seasons at Salford, at full-back. I wanted a transfer, and they would not agree. So I said I would pack the game in and I went back to South Wales, to work in the mines again. But this time I was not working at the coal face.

Playing for Cardiff in 1951

The 1951-2 Cardiff team competing in the RFL were allowed to sign players who had gone back to South Wales. I was quite fit. I worked as a miner, and used to go to the gym at the Boys Club. I also went running in the mountains. But after four games, Salford stopped me playing because they wanted a transfer fee. I had to catch two buses to get to the stadium, which was 20 miles away from where I lived. It was a greyhound stadium and, sadly, there were very few supporters. The Cardiff Rugby Union side was strong at that time, and got big crowds. Ted Ward had gone back to South Wales, and he also signed. He had played with the great Wigan sides after the war and was very experienced. He was a prolific goalkicker. Bernard McNally played in the pack.

Joining St Helens

In December 1952, Jim Sullivan, who was coach at St Helens, asked me to come up. I played a game, and then they signed me from Salford for £600. At St Helens everything seemed to click for me. When I joined, I didn't get losing money until we got to Wembley, when we played Huddersfield. I settled in St Helens and had no intention of returning to South Wales again.

Jim Sullivan was great as a coach. He was a man's man, and had been through it all. He knew everything about the game. St Helens had seven Welsh players then.

I played for the Wales Rugby League side in 1953, and then played for Great Britain. I played a trial for the 1954 tour, and reports said I was unlucky not to be picked. I then won my first cap in 1955-6 and was selected for the squad for the 1957 World Cup in Australia.

On the way back from the World Cup, we played three exhibition games in South Africa against France. We played in Johannesburg, East London and Durban. They were good games and well contested - nothing "friendly"! The games went down well, but it was strong Rugby Union territory. Of course Saints signed Tom Van Vollenhoven from South African Rugby Union. I played in his first game in 1957.

In 1958, I was selected for the Australia tour again. My club colleague Alan Prescott was captain. Eric Fraser was the other full-back and moved ahead of me on the tour, and played in the test matches. I hurt my leg in Perth and came home on crutches.

The 1958-9 season was my last in the game. I knew my knee wasn't right, and so I retired at the end of the season. I didn't get involved in coaching, but I still watch St Helens. The club look after their old players very well.

Future for Rugby League in Wales

I think it will be very hard. It is still strong Rugby Union territory. But we need to get a foothold. It is no good going to Wales with a second class side. I would like to see the game take off there.

January 1998

Mike Nicholas

Mike Nicholas was one of six Aberavon players to go north in the early 1970s. He was a key part of the great Warrington side of the 1970s, and was capped by Wales. He played briefly for Cardiff Blue Dragons before retiring in 1981. He went on to be the Wales team manager from 1993 to 1996, and set up and ran the South Wales club in the second division in 1996.

Rugby Union

I was playing for Aberavon in 1972, and had been selected for Crawshays XV on a pre-season tour, with players such as J.P.R. Williams, Phil Bennett and John Dawes. This was generally seen as a step towards a Welsh cap. I had also played for the Irish Wolfhounds in the final of the Centenary Sevens tournament at Neath.

Aberavon had already lost a number of well-known players to Rugby League. Kel Coslett had gone in 1962, and Jim Evans, although he didn't make it in Rugby League. In 1968, Bobby Wanbon had joined St Helens and later moved to Warrington. In 1971, Frank Reynolds had signed for Warrington and Bob Fleay joined Swinton. In August 1972, Dennis Curling and Clive Jones played in a trial at Warrington and signed. Ray Wilkins joined Workington. Aberavon were decimated more than any Union club at the time. It was to their credit they reached two Welsh Cup Finals in 1974 and 1975.

In 1972, I had been approached by Dennis Maddocks, a Warrington scout. He arranged a clandestine meeting at a phone box in an out-of-the-way area so I could talk to Alex Murphy.

I wanted a new challenge, but there was also the omnipresent need to win a Welsh cap. I knew that if I joined Rugby League, I would be burning my bridges with Rugby Union. It was very unsatisfactory that people had the power to stop you playing Union if you had played Rugby League. It was a civil rights issue. Rugby Union (at that time) was the only sport without a professional arm where you could exploit your skills.

I had previously been approached by St Helens and Featherstone. I was phoned by Featherstone, but when they found out I was only 5 feet 9 inches and 13 stone, they put the phone down! Two years later I lined up against Featherstone at Wembley and scored the winning try against them.

So in the summer of 1972, I was selected to play for Public School Wanderers in the Border Sevens. We beat Melrose in the final. I was with John Thomas, from Amman United, and to break the journey on the way home, we decided to stop at Warrington to watch them play Wigan. We could also see our friends who had joined them from Aberavon.

I was very impressed with the set up at Warrington, with a good clubhouse and a big crowd for the match.

After the match I went to the dressing rooms, and bumped into the scout who had tried to sign me for Warrington. He was very surprised to see me, and said "stay there", while he went to get Alex Murphy, Warrington's manager. "This is the one I told you about" he said, and Alex persuaded me to stay, and play in a trial match for the A team. John Thomas went home by train the next day.

So I played against Barrow for the A team. The crowd were shouting "Sign him up".

I signed for Warrington after the game, and was paid £5,000 in two parts.

I then phoned my mother, and told her what I had done. There was a stunned silence. My girlfriend was not very pleased either. But I was over 25, and if I had left it much longer, I may have jeopardised my chance of playing Rugby League. My parents were very supportive throughout my career.

I went home to sort things out before moving north and went to watch Aberavon against Pontypridd on the Monday evening, and stood on the terraces. I had my cheque in my pocket. After the match, I was in the clubhouse, and was approached by the secretary, Brian Tashara with a letter. I said: "I thought you were going to ask me to leave," and he said "That's what I am doing". He had taught me at school and later told me it was one of the worst things he had ever had to do. But the Aberavon chairman was in line to be chairman of the Welsh Rugby Union in a couple of years, and there were senior people from the WRU there, so they couldn't tolerate me being in the clubhouse. It was a long time before I would go back in the clubhouse - if I was at home, I would watch the match from the terraces. I had supported the club as a child, as well as playing for them, so it was a big break.

I had a good job as a chief safety officer for a petrochemical company. They were moving to the Gulf and if I hadn't signed for Warrington, I may have gone with them. But I'm not sure - rugby was my life then.

Going north

I made my first team debut against Barrow. We won easily, but I was tackled by Frankie Jones, their scrum-half, and wrenched my knee ligaments. Before that, in three or four seasons, I only missed one game. Now I was out for two or three weeks.

I found Rugby League to be a very tough game. I was sent off twice that season. On Boxing Day, in the local derby with Leigh, when I was the last one into a brawl and against Widnes on Good Friday.

I had been punched by one of their forwards - welcome to Rugby League - and taken off injured. But Alex Murphy sent me back on, and soon I punched the man who hit me, broke his nose and walked off before I was sent off. This was on national television and the next day I was back in Aberavon, watching the match against London Welsh from the terraces, with my mates joking about it.

There was a very tough physical side to the game then. A high tackle was above the eyebrows. Part of the theatre of Rugby League then was the battles between the 'enforcers' for different teams. We had a very good run that season. We were knocked out of the John Player Trophy by Huddersfield, but then only lost one league match before February. We lost in the Challenge Cup to Featherstone in the third round. My lack of Rugby League experience was shown up by Steve Nash, and Frank Reynolds and I collided as Mel Mason scored the winning try. That was a big disappointment.

The next season, 1973-4, we won virtually everything. In 1973, we signed John Bevan, a high-profile Union signing. He showed his value with 200 tries in 300 matches.

In 1974, I was picked for the Great Britain Lions tour, but in the Challenge Cup Final I fractured my jaw. I carried on playing, and scored the winning try. But I also injured my knee, cruciate ligaments, and was out for eight months. So I had to withdraw from the tour.

In 1975, Warrington lost in the finals of the Floodlit Trophy and the Challenge Cup. But between 1972 and 1981 we were in 14 major finals. When Alex Murphy left, in 1978 it was the end of an era.

We had some fierce battles with Widnes. My clashes with Jim Mills are mentioned in the Widnes Hall of Fame. A real David and Goliath scenario! But we were great friends off the field.

In 1978, I captained Warrington when we beat the Australians *[the last British club side to do so]*. Bobby Fulton *[now Australia's coach]* was playing for them. That match is folklore in Warrington. I had been out injured for five weeks with a broken thumb, and did not even expect to play.

I was always a tough player. In sendings off, I'm up there with the all-time greats - 15 in all. Once I was at the Disciplinary Committee with a 'full house' - three yellows and two reds!

My time at Warrington ended on a sour note. I had not been in the first team, and felt that the coach was only interested in the first team players. I was only six months away from a benefit year when they said I could leave on a free transfer. There was a new regime - Ossie Davies, the chairman when I signed, had gone.

Cardiff Blue Dragons

This was at the time the Cardiff Blue Dragons were starting up. So I thought I could play for them, and maybe move back to Wales. Looking back, I should have retired when I left Warrington. I tried to help, but only played four games and got sent off in one of them. I was injured, and it took a long time to clear up. So I drifted out of the game. Financially, I was never really compensated for what I had lost by leaving Warrington, and missing out on a benefit year.

We could have beaten Salford in Cardiff's first game. But the crowds dwindled to 1,500. The club had invested a lot in the big name Rugby Union players, who were at the end of their careers. But Tommy David was a great success.

With hindsight, I should have stayed in the game as a coach, but I was building up a business at the time and was very occupied with that.

Wales Rugby League team

There has always been a positive welcome for the team in Wales. There is a sneaking respect and admiration for the guys who have gone up north. When we played France at Swansea in 1975, there was a 20,000 crowd and they opened the gates, it was so big.

I played in the 1975 World Championship. The Great Britain side was split into England and Wales. Half the tournament was in Australia, so we went there for six weeks. We had a good side. Some were veterans at that stage, but we were still formidable. We beat England in Brisbane and stopped them winning the tournament. Then we had to double back to Sydney and play Australia at the SCG four days later. We lost 30-13, and they went onto win the tournament

I was fortunate to be given the chance to manage the Welsh team in 1993. Jim Mills had resigned, and to follow him was something special. I worked well with Clive Griffiths and we built a good side.

The qualification rules were relaxed, so people could play through having Welsh grandparents. That was controversial, but players came to us, we never approached anyone. So suddenly we had the Wigan front row.

I enjoyed that period immensely. Working with Jonathan Davies was very good. I knew him because I looked after him when he came up to play for Widnes. His family stayed with me for four months.

A team manager looks after the organisation off the field. All the players' needs have to be catered for - kit, hotels, etc., with a responsibility for discipline overall.

The only time we were heavily beaten was by Australia in 1994, when John Devereux and David Young were badly injured. John had a compound fracture of the jaw following a tackle by Mal Meninga. It was nothing illegal - two juggernauts collided - but it was one of the worst injuries I witnessed on a rugby field. David had 15 stitches in a gaping head wound, and went back on - a very brave act. Iestyn Harris made his debut as a 17-year-old, our man-of-the-match, and completely unfazed by the occasion.

In the 1995 World Cup, I thought we were slightly hard done by at Old Trafford. Two of their tries were dubious. But the Western Samoa game had taken a lot out of us. Iestyn Harris really blossomed in the World Cup. He became a star in Wales. Clive Griffiths had worked with him at Warrington and bought him through. What a talent. What a great lad. Born in Oldham of Welsh parents and granddad Norman Harris who played for Oldham. Welsh through and through.

There was amazing support for us. Welsh rugby had been starved of success, and people got behind a successful team. S4C got record viewing figures for the Western Samoa match at Vetch Field. That was a special night, an epic battle, with ferocity and intensity. The Rugby Union guys couldn't get over the level of contact in the game.

It was this experience that made me want to start a Super League team in Wales. I saw there was a window of opportunity, and decided to capitalise on it.

South Wales 1996

When Rugby Union became professional, I realised we could lose players to them. We needed a Super League presence in South Wales to keep the players, and build on the support for the national team. When Super League was launched, they wanted to have teams in various areas.

We needed to force the issue. It was worth a gamble to get a presence at any level. It was not possible to get a Super League team up and running, but we could enter Division 2, and then aim for Super League status the following year.

I took a big gamble and moved back to Wales, and set up an office. Bob Phillips and Doug Francis backed us. Without Bob nothing would have happened. He was a tremendous help. We would not have got off the floor without him.

But for four months nothing happened. We were trying to attract investors. A month before the season, I met Jeff Taylor, a former Pontypool Rugby Union player. He is a successful businessman, and his family wanted him to get involved in something as a hobby. His involvement, with Bob Phillips, convinced Maurice Lindsay that we were viable. Joe Cassidy, a friend of mine and Rugby League nut, contributed an immense amount of time and money as well.

Clive Griffiths came in as coach. We had our first match against Hull KR at

Aberavon, and got nearly 2,000 people. But we were having problems getting a team on the field. There was no help from most Rugby Union clubs, who stopped their players coming. Union players Appleyard and Hurcombe were both interested. We used student players, and players we had signed from Second Division clubs.

From that start (losing 8-70 to Hull KR), we turned the team around, which is down to Clive Griffiths. We went over budget though! We finished in a respectable position. Neil Kelly came down from Woolston to work as a development officer and player. He was the best half-back in the amateur game, but he dislocated his shoulder after two matches. If he had played a full season, we may have finished close to second place.

Cardiff and Aberavon Union clubs welcomed us. David Thomas, the Aberavon chairman welcomed us with open arms and with tremendous encouragement. Peter Thomas, the chairman at Cardiff, charged us virtually a peppercorn rent because he could see the long-term possibilities for us. It was our idea to bring a Super League game to Cardiff, and we approached Gary Hetherington and David Howes for the Sheffield versus St Helens match. Despite clashes with other sports, we still had a reasonable crowd. It allowed the Welsh public to see Super League live.

We were still up against Rugby Union bigotry in some quarters. However, the Treorchy club, a very progressive Welsh Division 1 side with similar aspirations supported us more than any other club through their management team.

But we needed to be in Super League to get the correct funding and to build a high profile. I feel that the existing clubs didn't want to dilute the funding by admitting another club. We had the financial backing we required from Paul Thompson, the Sanderson Electronic magnate, and I think it was a shock to the Rugby League that we got that support. We had also started to build support from local businesses in Cardiff. Also, Doug Francis from Cardiff City Council and Alan Rogers, the MP for the Rhondda, were very supportive. Clive and I made a presentation to the All Party Rugby League group of MPs at Westminster.

We were initially put into Super League providing we produced a suitable backer. This we did by introducing Paul Thompson to the game. We were then pulled out of Super League and offered a First Division place. This allowed Paul Thompson to get involved at Sheffield, enabling Gary Hetherington to be released to revive an ailing Leeds outfit. Talk about politics and the kiss of death!

Mike Nicholas. Photo: Peter Lush

A place in Division 1, even with the £250,000 we were promised, was never going to be viable for us. It had to be Super League or nothing. I think a golden opportunity was missed. I feel terribly let down by the game. We were so close, and had worked so hard. It is tragic really.

I didn't take wages from the club. I lost money on the whole project, but it was a labour of love. The support from my wife Jennifer, and our children, Christopher, Evie and Morgan was also very important. Without Jennifer's support, it wouldn't have happened. She was pregnant when we moved to Wales, and rented a 10-bedroom house so we could accommodate some of the players.

I must give a special mention to three people without whose help life would have been very difficult. Paul Cooper (Carlysle Finance), Steve Dew (general manager Brannigan's Bar) and Phil Myles (Hi-Motive) were all a tower of strength and remain friends to this day. Last but not least I must mention Tim Dines (regional manager Trusthouse Forte) who, like the aforementioned, was behind me all the way.

Future for Rugby League in Wales

Sky television are saying to the Rugby League that they must expand the game. If it can't happen in Wales, where can it happen? It must work in Wales.

I hope Rugby League has a future in Wales. But I am a little bit cynical. We have missed a fantastic opportunity, but I hope the problems can be overcome.

I see the game becoming more involved with big investors. The people who have run the game as a hobby for the last 100 years need to step aside for the professional, big business style of management, so the game can be run properly.

On a personal level, my involvement with the game now is advising Greenalls on their activities in rugby. I enjoy it, and it keeps me involved. They own a third of Warrington RLFC, and see their future involvement in the game growing.

December 1997

George Nicholls

George Nicholls was one of the best forwards of the 1970s, winning every honour in the game. He played for Cardiff Blue Dragons in their first season.

Rugby League career

Widnes was my first club. From there I moved to St Helens, where I spent most of my career. I played in two Wembley finals for Saints. I played in 40 internationals, 29 for Great Britain and 11 for England. I also played at Wembley for Great Britain against Australia in 1973. I am the only player to have won the Lance Todd, Harry Sunderland and Man of Steel trophies.

Joining Cardiff Blue Dragons

In 1981 I was coming to the end of my career with St Helens. David Watkins asked if I would be interested in joining Cardiff, to give some experience to his team. I knew David from touring with him, and was pleased when he asked me to captain the side. He also signed other experienced players from the north to help bring on the Rugby Union players. From the north, Tony Karalius, Paul Woods and Mike Nicholas all joined as well. I enjoyed my time there. For the Salford match, we had more than 10,000 there. That was a really good start. But we were always up against Rugby Union.

The players signed from Rugby Union

Tommy David and Steve Fenwick adapted well, and could have played Rugby League at any time. Their positional play was very good. Paul Ringer took a bit longer to adapt. He was very enthusiastic and chased the ball everywhere. I think forwards always find it more difficult to change codes. In Union, forwards don't run with the ball, they are more involved in rucks and line outs. In League they must carry the ball more.

The split squad system

We operated with two squads - one based in the north and one in South Wales. We trained two or three times a week in the north. For a home match, we would travel down on the Saturday morning, meet the South Wales group after lunch, and have a joint training session to work on moves. Bob Fleay, Chris O'Brien and Chris Seldon had all moved back to Wales, and they all joined as well. The supporters there were really warm towards the game and us. In the social club after the games, they liked talking to us, even an Englishman playing in Wales!

After that season, Salford approached me and asked me to play a season with them, to provide experience for their pack. But I had enjoyed my time playing in Wales with the Cardiff Blue Dragons.

January 1998

Danny and Kerry Sheehy

Danny and Kerry Sheehy have been mainstays of amateur Rugby League in Wales since 1982. Danny now manages the Welsh Students team, and was assistant coach at South Wales RLFC in 1996. Kerry was development officer for Wales for two years.

Getting involved in Rugby League

K: I had read in the *Western Mail* about a club being formed at Swansea University. I trained at Swansea RUFC as a young player with Stan Addicott. He was also the Swansea University RU coach. He told the Swansea University players that the players who played Rugby League would be banned from Union. I wondered - why is it wrong to play Rugby League? There was something not quite right about Rugby Union. I have always felt we were right to do what we wanted to do.

I was a student at Cardiff University in 1981. I saw a poster a chap from Irlam had put up about forming a Rugby League club. I met him, and helped him organise the club. I became captain, but it was always a struggle to get players. Danny became involved to help out. It went on from there. I wanted to carry on playing, but there was no opportunity after college.

D: My first involvement was the Cardiff University team but I remember watching the game on television. Our father had played for Dewsbury and Keighley after the war, and our cousin, Bobby Wanbon had signed for St Helens in 1968. I was playing at Aberavon in 1971-2, when five players in close succession joined Warrington.

K: So we formed Aberavon ARLFC in August 1982. This didn't seem to be a problem. I bought the kit from my grant. But then we had no one to play. So Danny wrote to people. He wrote to the Rugby League, who referred us to BARLA. Then we contacted the Southern Amateur League. The first season, we just played friendlies.

Aberavon ARLFC

D: I had written to David Oxley and then we contacted Tom Keaveney at BARLA. They sent out a circular saying we were looking for fixtures. Our first two fixtures were against Irlam Hornets and Peckham. We lost both, by 12 points to Irlam, and 14 to Peckham. We had no coaching or training, but most of the players had played Rugby Union before. We were both playing for local Union clubs at the time. We had good players, but lacked experience. We got a fixture with Underbank Rangers in the new year. I was in Bradford, shopping, and I saw a car with their club sticker in the window. So I put a note under the windscreen wiper, saying if you fancy a trip to Wales, give me a ring. A month later their secretary phoned. Apparently it was Neil Fox's car! He was their coach at the time.

K: Those Underbank fixtures continued for several years. One match in Wales and the next year in the north.

D: In the first season, we played 18 games. We played Swansea University, Cardiff University twice, and Peckham. The rest were good quality northern opposition.

K: Joining the Southern ARL was beyond anything we'd thought of - the costs, the standard of play. The idea came after we had played in a seven-a-side tournament at Milton Keynes. We played in that league for two years, and it was great. It was a good standard, the opposition teams were reliable, and we became more confident because we were playing every week. We could always raise a side and would take a coach of supporters to London as well.

D: We didn't win the league, but teams always had to beat us to win it. Long away trips every other week were the problem. We always had a team, but not always the strongest.

K: Those were good trips, and good rugby. It was an adventure. It did not have the problem that has bedevilled us ever since - you could be confident that the opposition would turn up.

We decided to leave the London ARL *[which had changed its name from the Southern ARL]* and joined the new Midlands and South Wales League (MASWARLA). It was a lower standard, and the visiting teams were less reliable. Distances were shorter, and it cost less, but it became unreliable. This made it difficult to promote the club locally. The quality of players between the top and the bottom of the league was vastly different but we always fulfilled our fixtures.

D: We played Wolverhampton, and won 120-0. We beat Hemel Hempstead 77-0 in their early days. Look what they've done since then.

K: It became difficult to fund the club, and raise a team. We started to realise that the priority should be to promote the game in Wales.

D: In 1983-4, we had helped form the Welsh League. Bob Fleay was the chairman, Jeff Wood the secretary and Phil Melling was treasurer. Apart from Aberavon, there were teams from Cardiff, Maesteg, South Glamorgan Institute, Cardiff University and Swansea University. So we played in two leagues.

The Welsh League has a rather chequered history. At one time there were three teams in Cardiff. But the unreliability put people off. But we were still playing and enjoying it at that time and were prepared to do whatever it took to make it succeed.

K: That was the motive. We did aim at the beginning to develop the game.

D: In the early days, some of our players were playing Rugby Union at Aberavon. They did not want their names in the paper, so we changed their names in the reports. Dai Joseph was the first one to stand up to this, and was featured in the paper as playing both codes. I was still playing Rugby Union when we started the Aberavon club. I felt that sometimes BARLA were subservient to Rugby Union at that time. There are still some League people who felt there was something "morally superior" about amateurism.

K: Once I had played the game, in the first 10 minutes, I made my mind up that all I wanted to do was play Rugby League. It didn't worry me about being banned.

We worked hard for the game, but it didn't seem like work because we enjoyed it. But it was difficult to convince some of the other players that it would last. Some wanted to keep in with Rugby Union.

Playing for Bridgend Blue Dragons

K: We were fans of the Cardiff Blue Dragons.

D: I played in John Bevan's testimonial against Warrington.

K: Then the Blue Dragons moved to Bridgend. There was a student international at the soccer ground before the Blue Dragons moved there. They asked me and Danny to go and play for them. I played half a season, and then let it go. I was running the Aberavon team, going training two or three times a week, and playing for Bridgend. It was difficult to do it all. And after Christmas, it was clear that Bridgend didn't have the money to survive, so I devoted all my time to Aberavon.

D: I stayed until the end. I was enjoying playing at a relatively high standard. It was better than first class Rugby Union. I was still club secretary for Aberavon, and doing some coaching.

K: Aberavon depended on us. But I was proud of having been a professional player.

D: That's exactly what I felt. We were losing every week, but some of the games were close. We travelled away with what was often almost an amateur team. Some of the South Glamorgan Institute players played. Bob Fleay never played at the very top of the game, but he was truly a professional.

K: We played Batley, and Carl Gibson scored five tries. I was doing the tackle count. Apart from Bob, the top tackler was Geoff Davies with 11. Bob had 38. At Leeds, we had an amateur winger marking Eric Grothe. Both the Barwoods tackled him, and bounced off him. He ran through Paul Thomas to score.

D: I remember Mike Davies who had joined Cardiff from a local amateur side. He played for Bridgend. He was special - pace, a side-step, and he could tackle. He played for Wales against England at Ebbw Vale in 1984, marking Schofield and Hanley and was equal to the task. He was injured in a seven-a-side tournament and had to retire.

Continuing with Aberavon

K: When Maurice Lindsay started to work for the Rugby League, Tom Donovan moved there from BARLA. We weren't pleased with BARLA, so the Welsh Amateur League went to the Rugby League. We didn't agree with BARLA's position on ex-professionals. We changed the name to the Welsh Rugby League. The game should be open.

D: We did not feel that BARLA could help us. We didn't want money, if we played games, the club would run itself. We asked them to encourage amateur clubs to come to Wales to play us. If every amateur club came once, they would only come each once every 20 years! Their clubs are all organised in leagues, which gave them an inward looking view. They had no fixture secretaries - so it was hard for us to arrange friendly fixtures. We wanted opposition, not money. BARLA didn't seem to understand this.

When BARLA did send out a circular, we would get some phone calls, but no one wanted to come to Wales. They expected us, the developing team, to do the travelling and bear the cost.

K: Many wanted to come to Wales at Easter, but not at other times. Having teams in leagues with odd numbers, so teams had a week off, would have helped. But BARLA and the leagues were unreceptive to any such idea.

D: BARLA said that any team could postpone one league fixture to play a team from a development area. But they never told the clubs. We could have developed a league in Wales with some support but the clubs were never quite strong enough. We could always get players, but needed administrators. In 1995, we switched to summer, and had the Sunshine League. The first season was great, with some good quality players.

Development Officer

K: From 1991, Wales had played some international matches, and then before we played New Zealand it was announced that we would not be in the World Cup - it would just be a Great Britain side. I had a letter in the *Rugby Leaguer* saying the Welsh press would rubbish the New Zealand game because of this. Anyway, I went to meet Maurice Lindsay, with Clive Griffiths.

We explained why it was so important we were in the World Cup. But what about after the World Cup? It was then they decided to have a development officer. He also told us that Wales would be in the World Cup. We believed that the money from the international matches should be used to develop the game in Wales. The money would disappear up the M5 and M6 otherwise, giving the impression of a "raid" on Wales.

D: Wales has a strong identity. The game here had to be run by Welsh people. It can't be people coming down from Leeds to run it here. Otherwise it would be seen as something the English were trying to impose on us. You can't get an impression of how to promote the game in Wales from two nights at the Marriott Hotel in Cardiff.

K: The development officer post was advertised and I applied for it. But it went to Mark Isherwood. He was a good choice, very enthusiastic, but he didn't stay that long. So then it was offered to me. My main work was trying to establish Little League in schools. That was the main thrust. And, against Tom O'Donovan's advice, I was trying to push the Sunshine League forward. Also, I was trying to encourage secondary schools to play. It was mainly in Cardiff, but some people also helped in Port Talbot and west Wales.

There were 12 teams in Cardiff that would play in Little League tournaments. I felt it was important to **sell it** to the teachers, so they would carry on. I tried to work out what is in it for the teacher. I would **sell it** to the teachers, as a qualification if they came on a six week coaching courses, and play a team in Little League for one season. They could put the qualification on their CV. The RFL seemed to want to give it away - it is worth more than that.

I developed a timetable of work. I would visit six schools, probably get four involved, and work with them for half a term. Then those children would go to the comprehensive schools, and I would try to make the game available to them there. It was a good time, because Wales were European Champions, and the World Cup was on. I will never forget that night in Swansea for the Western Samoa game.

I finished as development officer in the summer of 1996. I had had problems as there were two separate councils covering the area - Cardiff and South Glamorgan, and I couldn't get the administrative support I needed. That has been resolved now the councils have merged. Now the Rugby League development officer is part of the Sports Development Unit.

South Wales RLFC and the Welsh Students

D: I first met Clive Griffiths in 1990, and we had become friends. Clive had worked with Phil Melling with the Welsh Students side for the 1989 Students World Cup. I worked with Phil and Clive on the organisation for the Swansea Upland festival in 1991.

Clive needed an assistant coach based in Wales to prepare for the 1992 World Cup. I had been through the Coaching Scheme to Level 3 (I have done Level 4 since then). Bev Risman, who was Director of Student Rugby League at that time, asked me to a meeting in Aberavon with Phil and Clive. Clive asked me to be assistant coach for the Welsh Students team, and I was the third member of the management team for the 1992 World Cup in Australia.

After that tournament, Clive had too many commitments in the professional game to carry on, so I became the coach. We keep in touch. When the South Wales club was set up in 1996, I assumed that Clive would get the job. I had written to Mike Nicholas saying that I would like to be involved with the club. Clive offered me the post of assistant coach. I worked with the squad based in South Wales when the training was split. Some players were based in the north, some in South Wales. The second session of the week would be a joint one.

I was quite nervous about working with very well-established professional players. I was confident in my ability, but how would they take instructions from me? In fact, it was no problem. Those players, who had done it at Super League level, were truly professional. It isn't always as easy working with students. I was disappointed to only finish ninth in the 1996 Student World Cup, but I am sure we will do better next time.

Future for Rugby League in Wales

K: A Welsh Academy team is being set up, and the Cardiff Academy side and under-16s are doing well. The amateur game is dead at the moment, but it will come back in the future, as players come through from the youth and student sides.
D: I see the Aberavon club as dormant at the moment. It will come back in the future, possibly at under-16 level in the near future.

Danny Sheehy (senior)

Danny Sheehy (senior) first played Rugby Union for Aberavon. He then played Rugby League for Leeds during the war and in 1947 joined Dewsbury. On returning to Wales, he played for Aberavon in the Welsh League and for Cardiff in 1951-2.

Rugby Union origins

In 1937-8, I started playing Rugby Union for Aberavon. I played until I was called up in 1939. During the war I was stationed in Preston. A friend of mine, Dennis Madden, was playing for Leeds Rugby League club. He asked me to go to Leeds with him and try Rugby League. I was first aware of Rugby League in 1937. I saw Salford play in 1937-8, and liked the game very much. I remember when Salford played Halifax at Wembley in 1939.

So I played during the war for Leeds and Dewsbury. Eddie Waring was Dewsbury's manager during the war. He did everything, from running the team to taking the money at the gate.

My Commanding Officer was from Leeds, so he was happy for me to play for them. I also played Rugby Union during the war - for the battalion team and for Preston Grasshoppers. Then I went to France in the invasion and came home in 1946, and started playing for Aberavon again. They may have known I had played Rugby League during the war, but it was not a problem for me.

Going north

I played in the centre, so I found it a lot easier to adapt to Rugby League than forwards did. I joined Dewsbury in January 1947. They had sent a scout down to see me. He asked me if I wanted to go and play a game. They were eager to sign me. I knew the game, and I still prefer to watch Rugby League than Union.

I found it easy to settle in the north. People were very friendly. They were similar to the people in South Wales. I got £700 as a signing on fee from Dewsbury.

Playing for Dewsbury and Keighley

I met my wife at a dance when I had only played a couple of games. She had been at the match with her father. She came to every game after that.

The rivalry between Dewsbury and Batley was very strong. My wife's father was a Batley supporter. The old Dewsbury ground had a bigger slope than Batley. Our full-back could kick using the slope, because the opposing wingers couldn't deal with it.

Things went well at Dewsbury, and we were successful. W.T. Davies was at the club then. He had played in the centre, and then switched to outside-half when I signed. He was a good player, a Welsh Rugby League international. We got on well off the field as well. We used to coach in local schools.

I knew Eddie Waring then. This was before he was famous when he got on television. Then, after the war, he was a sports reporter on the local paper.

We won the Yorkshire League, and were runners-up in the Championship. I broke my leg in the semi-final when we beat Widnes. The final was at Maine Road, and my leg was in plaster. We lost to Wigan

I had a disagreement with Dewsbury in 1948, and told them I wouldn't play for them anymore. For a while I didn't go near the club, but then Keighley approached the club and I signed for them.

Keighley looked after the players' wives and families, and took them on a bus to away games. I think they were the only team that did that. I played there for a couple of years, but then I was 31, and intending to get married. I wanted a better paid job. I was a joiner, but my father worked on the docks in Port Talbot. He got me a job as a docker and I earned more than my joiner pay and Rugby League pay combined. Being a docker was hard work, but well paid.

I have relatives in Dewsbury, and still visit them

Returning to South Wales

Randall Lewis, who had played for Swinton, and a couple of others were starting a Rugby League side in Aberavon. So I played for them. We didn't get big gates in the Welsh League, and didn't have good grounds to play on. They couldn't really pay the players. In 1950, Warrington won the Challenge Cup, and a Welsh League side played them in Cwmavon. They beat us by 40 or 50 points. I scored an interception try from the half-way line. A team of international players played us at Llanelli, and beat us easily. Another time, a Welsh League side played at Wigan. They beat us easily, but I scored against them. Cec Mountford was playing outside-half for them, and he told the other players not to chase me.

The Welsh League standard was quite poor. Llanelli had a few former northern players, and they were the best side. They had two front-row forwards who had played in the north, and none of the other players could hold them in open play. However, Ystradgynlais had a fair side, even though it was only a small place.

Playing for Cardiff in 1951-2

In 1951-2, Cardiff were playing in the Rugby League. My former club Keighley wouldn't give me permission to play for them, but they were overruled. Bill Fallowfield (the general secretary of the Rugby League) wrote to me and to Cardiff saying that I could play for Cardiff. I didn't play that many games for them.

Other RL involvement after that

I coached the Aberavon team when I stopped playing. I did that for three years. For many years I never missed the Challenge Cup final on television. I didn't encourage my sons to play Rugby League. They played Rugby Union at school and I went to watch their matches, and go training when they were very young. I encouraged them to think about Rugby League, but they chose it themselves.

February 1998

Bobby Wanbon

Bobby Wanbon played Rugby Union for Aberavon and Wales. In 1968, he went north to join St Helens, and that year was capped by Wales at Rugby League, the same year he had won Welsh international honours at Union. He went on to play for the very successful Warrington side of the 1970s.

Rugby Union

I was playing at Aberavon, and was selected to play for Wales against England at Twickenham in February 1968 at number 8. David Nash was the Welsh coach, the first coach we had. It was the first time there was squad training.

We had a planned move from the training. I was at the back of the scrum. I was meant to let the ball out for Gareth Edwards to try a drop goal. But the ball didn't reach him. I stood up, the ball was on the floor so I picked it up again, went blindside and scored a try. It was our first try in an 11-11 draw. But because the move had gone wrong, I was dropped. So the next week I signed for St Helens.

Going north

I had been approached before to play Rugby League. I had been to Leeds for a weekend, and to Huddersfield. I played for West Wales against the All Blacks, who included Colin Meads, and a Rugby League scout came to the dressing room after the match to see me.

By 1968, I needed a new challenge. Some of my family had moved up north. I settled in quite easily. I had watched Rugby League on television. I always admired Roger Millward. I knew it was a harder game than Rugby Union - it was more of a physical confrontation. I played one A team game, and everyone seemed to be having a dig at me. But I didn't find it difficult to adapt to Rugby League.

Rugby League

I played for St Helens from 1968 to 1971, and then joined Warrington. At St Helens we had won the Championship, then I played in two Wembley finals with Warrington, winning one and losing one. In 1973-4, we won all the cups, the Challenge Cup, Players No.6, Premiership and Captain Morgan Trophy. There were five players from Aberavon in the Warrington team, three in the pack and two backs. I started my Rugby League career in the second-row, and then switched to prop when I got older. I retired in 1978. I never got involved in coaching or that side of the game. I settled in the north, and married a girl from Warrington. I am part of a Rugby League family. My uncle is Danny Sheehy who signed for Dewsbury after the war. He also played for Aberavon's Rugby League team but I never saw him play. His sons, Danny and Kerry are involved in Rugby League in South Wales.

Playing for Wales at Rugby League

In 1968, the Wales Rugby League team started up again, and in November 1968, I was selected for the team in its first match. We beat England 24-17 at Salford. So I was one of a select band of players to win a cap at both codes in the same year.

When we went back to Wales to play international matches, we always got a good response from the spectators there. We usually got good crowds. I won seven Welsh caps in Rugby League, and played in the 1975 World Championship. That was a great squad of players. We beat England at Brisbane - it was a battle from the beginning, and the referee was weak. I lost half a stone in that game, it was so humid.

Four days later, we had to play Australia in Sydney. We had no chance to recover mentally or physically from the Brisbane game. But that was a fantastic tour.

I remember when we won in the last minute against France at Perpignan. The crowd attacked the referee, and we were locked in the changing rooms for two hours after the match finished.

The best players I ever played with were Jim Mills, Kel Coslett, Mike Nicholas, David Watkins and Colin Dixon.

January 1998

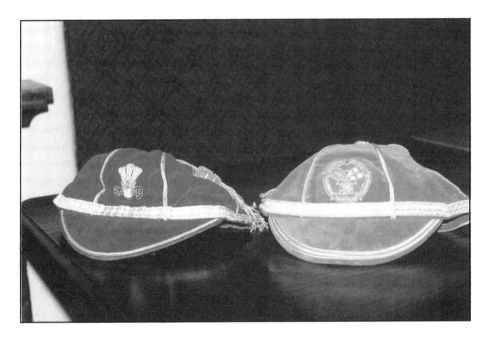

Dual international in the same year - Bobby Wanbon's caps for Wales. Photo: Peter Lush

David Watkins

David Watkins is one of the greatest players from both codes in the modern era. He went north in 1967, joining Salford. He was managing director of the Cardiff Blue Dragons from 1981 to 1984, and is currently chairman of Newport RUFC.

Rugby Union origins

I come from a coal mining village in Blaina. My father was a miner and didn't read and write well until he was in his 20s. For the first few years, we lived in a mining village. I saw little of my father - he was always working to provide for his children.

I played football as a child, and cricket and athletics in the summer. That's all there was then - no snooker or golf.

I didn't play Rugby Union until I was 15. I had trials at school level, and set my goal to be a career in Rugby Union. I wanted to captain my country at Cardiff Arms Park. When I left school I played for a youth club side, and won six under-18 caps for the Wales Youth side.

My father realised he had a talented youngster, and always supported me, as did my grandfather who accompanied me to all my games.

In 1960, I had my first offer to go north. My brother found me in the village, and said come home quickly, there are three people at home with funny accents. As I came home, I saw a Mark 10 Jaguar parked outside our door. It was bigger than the bus that took me to school!

They were three directors of St Helens - Joe Pickavance, Basil Lowe and Geoff Sutcliffe. They outlined the virtues of Rugby League, how they could offer me a job and education. My father was wary of this and after two hours turned them down.

So Joe Pickavance went to get a briefcase. He put it on the kitchen table and opened it. There was £5,000 in cash. My father said "Where do we sign - we'll all come for that!". But I didn't go - my aim was to captain Wales at Cardiff Arms Park.

At that time, if you were approached by a Rugby League scout, you had to be careful not to be seen with him. You could be banned if you were seen with a Rugby League scout.

As a Rugby Union player, it meant everything to me to play for Wales. It was the ultimate achievement.

I went on the 1966 Lions tour. I was at the top of my game, and felt I could go forward for ever. Then I was left out of the Wales side, when I had expected to be captain. Barry John took my place. It showed me I was not indispensable. Different selectors had different ideas, and I was dropped, which was a shock.

For two internationals, Wales didn't play well, so I was bought back, as captain. I played with Gareth Edwards, and was his first partner. In my opinion, he was the greatest rugby player in the northern hemisphere.

But I realised I could be dropped again. The following season, I went to Ireland on tour with the Wolfhounds, who included most of the 1966 Lions team. Then Newport were invited to a seven-a-side tournament in Manchester. But because the club did not play on Sundays, we played as a David Watkins Seven, and I came back from Ireland to play in the tournament.

In the tournament, I was spotted by Brian Snape, who was rebuilding Salford at that time. He put a bid in for me, but I was working for the Midland Bank, and was not convinced about moving.

He continued to ring me, with the offer going up. First £8,000, then £10,000 and finally £16,000 - tax free. The bank were happy to arrange a transfer to Manchester, so it was too good an offer to refuse.

Going north

I was 25 when I went to Salford. Their usual gate was around 3,000. There were 14,000 to see me on the first Friday I played. There were three groups - some to see a Rugby Union international make his League debut, the doubters, and the inquisitive.

I had no coaching, no prior knowledge of Rugby League before making my debut. It was the toughest, hardest most "violent" game I had ever played.

The signing on fee *[a world record at that time]* didn't help. On Boxing Day 1967, I had my nose broken by Kevin Ashcroft. I complained to the referee, and was told I was being paid enough to look after myself. That fee hung round my neck for years. I rarely retaliated, but I learnt to get to grips with the game.

I was scoring spectacular tries, and the Salford supporters never lost faith in me. I became part of them. We got to Wembley in 1969, but we lost in a poor game. I was overawed by the occasion.

Rugby League was tougher and harder than Rugby Union. League teams took a pride in their performance and even the lesser sides made it hard for you. But class would usually tell in the end.

Brian Snape was an entrepreneur. He had a huge vision for the club. He wanted to build it up, get better players and better facilities.

We played on Friday nights and a lot of Manchester United and Manchester City fans would come and watch. We signed Keith Fielding, the England Rugby Union winger, Mike Coulman at prop-forward, and Maurice Richards, a British Lion and Welsh Rugby Union international. Colin Dixon, another Welsh player came from Halifax, and Eric Prescott and Paul Charlton were signed, so we had a team of stars. That team were capable of so much, playing open hard rugby.

Despite the quality of the team, we never got back to Wembley, which has always been a disappointment for me.

Playing Rugby League

I started playing at stand-off. Cliff Evans came from St Helens in 1970 to be our coach. He gave me a lot of help, working with me and could draw out what potential you had as a player.

He suggested I move from stand-off to play in the centre. I reluctantly made my debut in this position against Whitehaven and scored three tries. Tackling was not the best part of my game, but defensively I eventually became as good as anyone. I learnt how to get to people quickly.

This helped me get into the Great Britain side. I won my first cap at St Helens against France in 1971. I came on as a sub for Billy Benyon, a St Helens favourite, and was booed onto the pitch on my international debut!

In 1970-71 season, I was asked to become Salford's goalkicker. I had never been a regular kicker in Rugby Union and had only kicked goals in emergencies. But this started another aspect to my career - as a goalkicker. I broke the Salford record for a season and, in 1973-4, broke the world record. I scored in 92 consecutive games.

I went on the 1974 tour to Australia and New Zealand. I was also player coach of the Great Britain side in 1977. We lost the World Cup final 13-12, but it was a successful tour.

I retired in 1978-9, but was tempted back to play for Swinton. They had said they would invest in the team, but it didn't really happen. And at 37, I was finding the game physically too demanding.

Playing for the Wales Rugby League team

Playing for the Wales Rugby League team was important for me. In the Great Britain side there were a number of Welsh players, and in 1967-8 it was decided to relaunch the Wales side. At the beginning we were short of players and personalities, but by the early 1970s we had a quality side - Maurice Richards, Jim Mills, Ken Coslett, Roy Mathias, John Mantle, Stuart Gallagher, Mike Nicholas and John Bevan. It was built around former Rugby Union internationals.

We played France in Swansea, and had a crowd of 20,000, and a resounding win. There was a lot of optimism about the side, so we were able to enter the 1975 World Championship, rather than playing with England as Great Britain. We played in Australia, and beat England at Brisbane, which cost England the Championship.

David Watkins in his playing days. Photo courtesy *Open Rugby*

We always got a good reception when we played in Wales. We had the personalities in the team, and people wanted to see the "legendary" players who had gone over to Rugby League.

To the real sportsmen, we were accepted. Their approach was - they're playing for Wales, let's give them a cheer.

Unfortunately, as this generation of players finished, players with less genuine Welsh connections were included in the team and, in my opinion, it lost its validity.

Cardiff Blue Dragons

I had got involved with media work when I retired, presenting *Scrumdown* on television in the Lancashire and Yorkshire areas.

In 1980-81, Bob Grogan had bought Cardiff City FC. He was an entrepreneur of the John Hall type. He was trying to revitalise the club, and wondered why they had this pitch that was only being used once a fortnight.

Fulham RLFC had started at Craven Cottage, and made a big impact. Bob knew Ernie Clay [*who was Chairman of Fulham FC when the Rugby League team was launched*], and wanted to try the same idea in South Wales.

He approached me to be managing director. As well as my Rugby League background, I had been involved in business and had developed some business acumen. John Mantle became the coach.

The squad was split, with some players based in the north and some in South Wales. We brought in some veteran players, such as George Nicholls, Arthur Daley and Tony Karalius, to help us. From Welsh Rugby Union, we recruited Tommy David, Steve Fenwick (the most capped Welsh centre) and Paul Ringer. They joined with some Rugby League players who had prematurely retired to return to South Wales, such as Bob Fleay, Chris O'Brien and Gordon Pritchard. So I felt we had a squad that could cope with the Second Division.

Salford were the opponents for our first game at Ninian Park. More than 10,000 attended, but we narrowly lost the game. We had to keep costs under control, but we were not as successful as we wanted, and found ourselves in mid table. Against Widnes in the Cup, we had a crowd of nearly 9,000. That showed that if we could give the Welsh public a successful side, it would work.

The Welsh Rugby Union were very critical. They said that anyone seen training with us would be treated as professionals, and banned from Rugby Union. Therefore, young players would not risk a try-out with us, because they could be banned. That's how it was at that time. But today, they still face some of the same problems we did.

We also had a struggle against the media, who were more interested in our finances than the game itself. But we had a hard core of 1,000 who loved the game and our team. They kept us going.

It was very expensive to run the team, with training in two camps, and bringing players down from the north for home games. For a team to succeed, it must be based in South Wales, with the players living here.

There were lots of rumours about well-known Rugby Union players joining us. It was an opportunity for some at the end of their Rugby Union careers, but they also had the fear of not making it in Rugby League. It is a hard game. Also there were players just below international level who were interested, but could not come and train because of their fear of being found out by the Welsh Rugby Union.

If there had been the open passage between the codes that there is now, the Blue Dragons would have been viable.

After a few months, I became coach as well, because John Mantle was released for financial reasons. In the second season, in a crisis, I played three games, because I thought my experience would help the younger players. One of our best results was beating Second Division champions Fulham at Stamford Bridge at the end of the season.

We were given very little encouragement from the Rugby League, and some clubs complained about the expense of travelling to South Wales once or twice a year.

Sadly, Bob Grogan died during the second season, and for me that marked the start of the end of the Blue Dragons. His business partners were more concerned about their company and not interested in sport.

I did not want to work with the people who bought the club when it moved to Bridgend, so I finished my association with it then.

Rugby activity since the Blue Dragons

I did some more media work on Radio 2. Then I got involved in a pressure group to try to develop Newport RUFC. I felt I owed the club something. I subsequently became chairman, which I still am. We have stopped the downward decline and kept the club in the First Division. But I do have fears for the future of Welsh Rugby Union.

The two codes now face the same problems. Both face the problems of full-time professionalism, television and high player salaries.

The future for Rugby League in Wales

There are opportunities for Rugby League in Wales if it is organised on a proper basis. It needs an office in South Wales, and development officers. It needs to get into the schools and colleges with good coaching.

A club here would need proper funding, good training and discipline for its players. But it must also have a sound structure and business plan. It might be slow to start, but if it was a quality team, it would grow. A new club would have to establish its credibility. Sport nowadays must be run as a business.

The national side has been successful, and well supported, especially in the World Cup at Cardiff and Swansea in 1995. Rugby League is an incredible sport, and would win over the youngsters to watch it.

November 1997

Part Six:

Statistics and records

Wales international matches 1908-1996

Date	Opponents	Score	Venue	Crowd
1 Jan, 1908	New Zealand	9- 8	Aberdare	15-20,000

T: D.J. Thomas, D. Jones, Francis

20 Apr, 1908	England	35-18	Tonypandy	12-15,000

T: Treharne 2, B. Jenkins 2, D.J. Thomas, Ruddick, Burgham.
G: J. Thomas 7

28 Dec, 1908	England	7-31	Broughton	4,000

T: D.J. Thomas. *G:* J. Thomas 2

4 Dec, 1909	England	13-19	Wakefield	4,000

T: W.T. Davies, Francis, Foley. *G:* Young 2

9 Apr, 1910	England	39-18	Ebbw Vale	4,000

T: W.J. Williams 3, T. Jenkins 2, Llewellyn 2, B. Jenkins, J. Thomas.
G: Young 3, J. Thomas 3

10 Dec, 1910	England	13-39	Coventry	4-5,000

T: Llewellyn, Foley, D.B. Davies. *G:* Gronow 2

1 Apr, 1911	England	8-27	Ebbw Vale	4,000

T: B. Jenkins, Llewellyn. *G:* J. Thomas

7 Oct, 1911	Australia	20-28	Ebbw Vale	7,000

T: W.T. Davies 4. *G:* J. Thomas 4

20 Jan, 1912	England	5-31	Oldham	8,000

T: W.T. Davies. *G:* G. Thomas

15 Feb, 1913	England	16-40	Plymouth	7-8,000

T .T.J. Williams, D.B. Davies, E. Jones, Chilcott. *G:* J. Thomas 2

14 Feb, 1914	England	12-16	St Helens	10,000

T: F. Williams 2, Francis, Coldrick

19 Jan, 1921	England	9-35	Leeds	13,000

T: B. Williams. *G:* Gronow 3

10 Dec, 1921	Australia	16-21	Pontypridd	11,000

T: Rogers, Howley. *G:* Gronow 4, Sullivan

11 Dec, 1922	England	7-12	Herne Hill	3,000

T: Morgan. *G:* Sullivan 2

7 Feb, 1923	England	13- 2	Wigan	17,000

T: Hurcombe 2, Brown. *G:* Sullivan 2

1 Oct, 1923	England	11-18	Huddersfield	11,066

T: Hurcombe 2, H.R. Rees. *G:* Thompson

7 Feb, 1925	England	22-27	Workington	14,000

T: F. Evans 2, Ring 2, Thompson, Howley. *G:* Sullivan 2

30 Sep, 1925	England	14-18	Wigan	12,000

T: D. Rees, Ring, Howley, F. Evans. *G:* Sullivan

| 12 Apr, 1926 | England | 22-30 | Pontypridd | 23,000 |

T: Morgan, Fowler, Sullivan, Bacon, F. Evans, Rosser. *G:* Sullivan 2

| 4 Dec, 1926 | New Zealand | 34-8 | Pontypridd | 18,000 |

T: F. Evans 3, Gore 2, Caswell, Hurcombe, Sullivan. *G:* Sullivan 4, Rhodes

| 6 Apr, 1927 | England | 8-11 | Broughton | 6,000 |

T: Bacon, Ring. *G:* Sullivan

| 11 Jan, 1928 | England | 12-20 | Wigan | 12,000 |

T: G. Parker, Gore. *G:* Sullivan 3

| 14 Nov, 1928 | England | 15-39 | Cardiff | 10,000 |

T: Ring, D.M. Jenkins, Maidment. *G:* Sullivan 3

| 18 Jan, 1930 | Australia | 10-26 | Wembley | 16,000 |

T: Ray, Rosser. *G:* Sullivan 2

| 18 Mar, 1931 | England | 18-23 | Huddersfield | 6,000 |

T: Risman, Rosser, Thompson, G. Parker. *G:* Sullivan 3

| 27 Jan, 1932 | England | 2-19 | Salford | 8,000 |

G: Sullivan

| 30 Nov, 1932 | England | 13-14 | Leeds | 4,000 |

T: Morley, White, Rosser. *G:* Sullivan 2

| 30 Dec, 1933 | Australia | 19-51 | Wembley | 10,000 |

T: Isaac, Morley, Fender. *G:* Sullivan 5

| 1 Jan, 1935 | France | 11-18 | Bordeaux | 15,000 |

T: Morley. *G:* Sullivan 4

| 10 Apr, 1935 | England | 11-24 | Liverpool | 7,100 |

T: G. Davies, Orchard, Griffiths. *G:* I. Davies

| 23 Nov, 1935 | France | 41- 7 | Llanelli | 25,000 |

T: Risman 2, Isaac 2, Morley 2, Griffiths 2, W. Watkins, A. Edwards, Madden. *G:* Sullivan 3, Risman

| 1 Feb, 1936 | England | 17-14 | Hull KR | 17,000 |

T: Bennett 2, Madden. *G:* Sullivan 4

| 7 Nov, 1936 | England | 3-2 | Pontypridd | 12,000 |

T: A. Edwards

| 6 Dec, 1936 | France | 9-3 | Paris | 17,000 |

T: Madden, Gummer, Risman

| 29 Jan, 1938 | England | 7-6 | Bradford | 8,637 |

T: C. Evans. *G:* Sullivan 2

| 2 Apr, 1938 | France | 18-2 | Llanelli | 20,000 |

T: Case, Sullivan, Madden, A. Edwards. *G:* Sullivan 3

| 5 Nov, 1938 | England | 17- 9 | Llanelli | 17,000 |

T: Case, Risman, A. Edwards. *G:* Sullivan 3, Risman

| 16 Apr, 1939 | France | 10-16 | Bordeaux | 25,000 |

T: H. Thomas, G. Williams. *G:* Sullivan 2

23 Dec, 1939	England	16- 3	Bradford	15,275
	T: Foster, W.T.H. Davies. *G:* Sullivan 5			
9 Nov, 1940	England	5-8	Oldham	5,000
	T: Foster. *G:* J. Jones			
18 Oct, 1941	England	9-9	Bradford	4,339
	T: A. Edwards. *G:* Risman 3			
27 Feb, 1943	England	9-15	Wigan	17,000
	T: J. Jones. *G:* A. Davies 3			
26 Feb, 1944	England	9-9	Wigan	16,028
	T: A. Edwards 2, J. Jones			
10 Mar, 1945	England	8-18	Wigan	23,500
	T: Edwards 2. *G:* Powell			
24 Nov, 1945	England	11-3	Swansea	30,000
	T: G. Price 2, I. Owens. *G:* Risman			
24 Mar, 1946	France	7-19	Bordeaux	Not known
	T: Foster. *G:* Ward, Foster			
12 Oct, 1946	England	13-10	Swinton	20,213
	T: Lloyd, W.T. Davies, Francis. *G:* W.T. Davies			
16 Nov, 1946	England	5-19	Swansea	25,000
	T: D. Jenkins. *G:* W.T. Davies			
18 Jan, 1947	France	5-14	Marseilles	24,500
	T: Gwyther. *G:* W.T. Davies			
12 Apr, 1947	France	17-15	Swansea	20,000
	T: Walters, N. Harris, R. Williams. *G:* W.T. Davies			
20 Sep, 1947	England	10-8	Wigan	27,000
	T: L.M. Thomas 2. *G:* Ward 2			
18 Oct, 1947	New Zealand	20-28	Swansea	18,283
	T: I. Owens, Ward, Lloyd, R. Williams. *G:* Ward 4			
23 Nov, 1947	France	21-29	Bordeaux	26,500
	T: Goldswain, Walters, N. Harris, W.R.T. Jones, L.M. Thomas. *G:* Ward 3			
6 Dec, 1947	England	7-18	Swansea	10,000
	T: Foster. *G:* Ward 2			
20 Mar, 1948	France	12-20	Swansea	6,500
	T: G. Price, Foster. *G:* Ward 3			
22 Sep, 1948	England	5-11	Wigan	12,637
	T: Mahoney. *G:* Ward			
23 Oct, 1948	France	9-12	Swansea	12,032
	T: Howes. *G:* Ward 3			
20 Nov, 1948	Australia	5-12	Swansea	9,224
	T: G. Price. *G:* Ward			

| 5 Feb, 1949 | England | 14-10 | Swansea | 9,553 |

T: Daniels, D. Phillips. *G:* Ward 4

| 10 Apr, 1949 | France | 0-11 | Marseilles | 25-30,000 |

| 22 Oct, 1949 | Other Nationalities 5-6 | | Abertillery | 2,000 |

T: J. Davies. *G:* J. Davies

| 12 Nov, 1949 | France | 16- 8 | Swansea | 4,749 |

T: Gwyther, L. Williams, Daniels, W.G. Morgan. *G:* R. Morgan 2

| 1 Mar, 1950 | England | 6-11 | Wigan | 27,500 |

T: Daniels, R. Williams

| 14 Oct, 1950 | England | 4-22 | Abertillery | 8,000 |

G: Goldswain 2

| 31 Mar, 1951 | Other Nationalities 21-27 | | Swansea | 5,000 |

T: Cook 2, Ford, James, Gullick. *G:* J. Evans 3

| 15 Apr, 1951 | France | 13-28 | Marseilles | 18,000 |

T: Gullick, L. Williams, Cook. *G:* J. Evans 2

| 19 Sep, 1951 | England | 11-35 | St. Helens | 20,918 |

T: Daniels, L. Williams, Lambert. *G:* Harrison

| 1 Dec, 1951 | Other Nationalities 11-22 | | Abertillery | 3,386 |

T: Hunt, R. Williams, L. Williams. *G:* Ward

| 7 Dec, 1951 | New Zealand | 3-15 | Bradford | 8,568 |

T: Gullick

| 6 Apr, 1952 | France | 12-20 | Bordeaux | 15,678 |

T: Daniels, R. Price. *G:* R. Price, Banks, Goldswain

| 17 Sep, 1952 | England | 8-19 | Wigan | 13,503 |

T: Lambert, R. Price. *G:* Goldswain

| 25 Oct. 1952 | France | 22-16 | Leeds | 10,380 |

T: Banks, T. Harris, Daniels, Gullick. *G:* J. Evans 5

| 15 Apr, 1953 | Other Nationalities 18-16 | | Warrington | 8,449 |

T: T. Harris, Parsons, N. Harris, L Williams. *G:* J. Evans 3

| 16 Sep, 1953 | England | 5-24 | St Helens | 19,357 |

T: Daniels. *G:* J Evans

| 7 Oct, 1953 | Other Nationalities 5-30 | | Bradford | 14,646 |

T: R. Williams. *G:* J. Evans

| 13 Dec, 1953 | France | 22-23 | Marseilles | 25,000 |

T: Daniels 2, M. Davies, R. Price. *G:* L. Jones 5

Wales played no full international matches 1954-1967

| 7 Nov, 1968 | England | 24-17 | Salford | 6,002 |

T: Sullivan, Watkins, Rees, Dixon. *G:* T. Price 6

| 9 Mar, 1969 | France | 13-17 | Paris | 6,189 |

T: Lewis 2, T. Price. *G:* T. Price, Watkins

| 18 Oct, 1969 | England | 23-40 | Leeds | 8,373 |

T: Dixon, D. Jones, Rowe, Sullivan, Morgan. *G:* T. Price 4

| 23 Oct, 1969 | France | 2-8 | Salford | 5,610 |

G: Coslett

| 25 Jan, 1970 | France | 15-11 | Perpignan | 11,000 |

T: Sullivan 2, T. Price. *G:* T. Price 3

| 24 Feb, 1970 | England | 7-26 | Leeds | 9,393 |

T: Jarrett. *G:* Ferguson 2

| 16 Feb, 1975 | France | 21-8 | Swansea | 15,000 |

T: Bevan 2, Mills, Mathias. *G:* Coslett 4. *DG:* Watkins

| 25 Feb, 1975 | England | 8-12 | Salford | 8,494 |

T: Watkins 2. *G:* Watkins, Coslett. *DG:* Watkins

| 2 Mar, 1975* | France | 7-14 | Toulouse | 7,563 |

T: Wilson. *G:* Coslett 2

| 10 Jun, 1975* | England | 12-7 | Brisbane | 6,000 |

T: Sullivan, Treasure. *G:* Watkins 3

| 14 Jun, 1975* | Australia | 13-30 | Sydney | 25,386 |

T: Fisher. *G:* Watkins 5

| 28 Jun, 1975* | New Zealand | 8-13 | Auckland | 18,000 |

T: Mills, Francis. *G:* Watkins

| 20 Sep, 1975* | England | 16-22 | Warrington | 5,034 |

T: Banner, Coslett. *G:* Watkins 5

| 19 Oct, 1975* | Australia | 6-18 | Swansea | 11,112 |

G: Watkins 3

| 2 Nov, 1975* | New Zealand | 25-24 | Swansea | 2,645 |

T: Francis 2, Mantle, Bevan, Willicombe. *G:* Watkins 5

| 6 Nov, 1975* | France | 23-2 | Salford | 2,247 |

T: Willicombe, Bevan, Francis, Banner, Gregory. *G:* Watkins 4

| 29 Jan, 1977 | England | 6-2 | Leeds | 6,472 |

T: Cunningham. *G:* Woods. *DG:* Rowe

| 20 Feb, 1977 | France | 2-13 | Toulouse | 5,827 |

G: Woods

| 15 Jan, 1978 | France | 29-7 | Widnes | 9,502 |

T: Mills, Mathias, Sullivan, Cunningham, Francis. *G:* Woods 7

| 28 May, 1978 | England | 13-60 | St Helens | 9,759 |

T: James, Sullivan, Willicombe. *G:* Watkins, Woods

| 15 Oct, 1978 | Australia | 3-8 | Swansea | 4,250 |

G: Watkins. *DG:* Watkins

| 4 Feb, 1979 | France | 8-15 | Narbonne | 13,728 |

T: Rowe. *G:* Watkins 2. *DG:* Watkins

| 16 Mar, 1979 | England | 7-15 | Widnes | 5,099 |

T: Box. *G:* Box 2

| 26 Jan, 1980 | France | 7-21 | Widnes | 2,804 |

T: Bevan. *G:* Diamond 2

| 29 Feb, 1980 | England | 9-26 | Hull KR | 7,557 |

T: Juliff. *G:* Woods 3

| 31 Jan, 1981 | France | 5-23 | Narbonne | 4,120 |

T: Parry. *G:* D. Wilson

| 18 Mar, 1981 | England | 4-17 | Hull KR | 4,786 |

G: Rule 2

| 8 Nov, 1981 | England | 15-20 | Cardiff | 13,173 |

T: Flowers, Prendiville. *G:* Fenwick 4. *DG:* D. Wilson

| 24 Oct, 1982 | Australia | 7-37 | Cardiff | 5,617 |

T: D.B. Williams. *G:* Fenwick, Hopkins

| 14 Oct, 1984 | England | 9-28 | Ebbw Vale | 2,111 |

T: D. Wilson. *G:* Hallett 2. *DG:* D. Wilson

| 27 Oct, 1991 | Papua New Guinea 68-0 | | Swansea | 11,422 |

T: Ford 3, J. Davies 2, Sullivan 2, Bateman, Griffiths, Ellis, Hadley, Ackerman, Bishop. *G:* J. Davies 8

| 22 Mar, 1992 | France | 35-6 | Swansea | 10,133 |

T: B. Williams, J. Davies, Bateman, Ford, Devereux, Phillips *G:* J. Davies 5. *DG:* J. Davies

| 27 Nov, 1992 | England | 11-36 | Swansea | 10,243 |

T: Griffiths, M. Jones. *G:* Devereux. *DG:* Ellis

| 13 Dec, 1992 | France | 19-18 | Perpignan | 3,700 |

T: Devereux, Bateman, Ackerman. *G:* Pearce 3. *DG:* Pearce

| 3 Oct, 1993 | New Zealand | 19-24 | Swansea | 6,083 |

T: Cordle 2. *G:* J. Davies 5. *DG:* Griffiths.

| 4 Mar, 1994 | France | 13-12 | Cardiff | 6,287 |

T: Webster. *G:* J. Davies 4. *DG:* J. Davies.

| 30 Oct, 1994 | Australia | 4-46 | Cardiff | 8,729 |

T: Powell

| 1 Feb, 1995 | England | 18-16 | Cardiff | 6,232 |

T: Ellis 2. *G:* J. Davies 4. *DG:* J. Davies 2

| 4 Mar, 1995 | France | 22-10 | Carcassonne | 6,000 |

T: Bateman 2, Atcheson, Harris. *G:* J. Davies 3

| 9 Oct, 1995+ | France | 28-6 | Cardiff | 10,250 |

T: Sullivan 3, Harris, Devereux. *G:* J. Davies 3, Harris

| 15 Oct, 1995+ | Western Samoa 22-10 | | Swansea | 15,385 |

T: Ellis, Sullivan, Harris. *G:* J. Davies 4. *DG:* Harris, J. Davies

| 21 Oct, 1995+ | England | 10-25 | Old Trafford | 30,042 |

T: Phillips. *G:* J. Davies 3

| 5 Jun, 1996 | France | 34-14 | Carcassonne | 4,382 |

T: Harris 3, Atcheson, Webster, J. Davies. *G:* Harris 5

26 Jun, 1996   England   12-26   Cardiff   5,425
T: Morley, Critchley. *G:* Harris 2

* World Championship +World Cup

Wales's leading individual performances in international matches

Most caps
   26 Jim Sullivan (Wigan) 1921-39
   20 Roy Mathias (St Helens) 1975-81
   19 Bill Francis (Wigan, St Helens, Oldham) 1975-80
   18 Alan Edwards (Salford, Bradford Northern) 1935-48
   18 Gus Risman (Salford) 1931-45

Most tries - career
   9   Arthur Daniels (Halifax) 1949-53
   9   Alan Edwards (Salford, Bradford Northern) 1935-48
   7   Frank Evans (Swinton) 1921-28
   7   Clive Sullivan (Hull, Hull KR) 1968-79
   6   Will (W.T.) Davies (Batley, Halifax) 1909-12
   6   Iestyn Harris (Warrington) 1994-96
   6   Anthony Sullivan (St Helens) 1991-96

Most goals - career
   60 Jim Sullivan (Wigan) 1921-39
   44 Jonathan Davies (Widnes, Warrington) 1991-96
   36 David Watkins (Salford) 1968-79
   25 Ted Ward (Wigan, Cardiff) 1946-51
   19 Johnny Thomas (Wigan) 1908-14

Most points - career
  129 Jim Sullivan (Wigan) 1921-39
   99 Jonathan Davies (Widnes, Warrington) 1991-96
   74 David Watkins (Salford) 1968-79
   53 Ted Ward (Wigan, Cardiff) 1946-51
   41 Iestyn Harris (Warrington) 1994-96
   41 Johnny Thomas (Wigan) 1908-14

Most tries - match
4	Will (W.T.) Davies v Australia	at Ebbw Vale	7 Oct, 1911
3	Billy (W.J.) Williams v England	at Ebbw Vale	9 Apr, 1910
3	Frank Evans v New Zealand	at Pontypridd	4 Dec, 1926
3	Phil Ford v Papua New Guinea	at Swansea	27 Oct, 1991
3	Anthony Sullivan v France	at Cardiff	9 Oct, 1995
3	Iestyn Harris v France	at Carcassonne	5 Jun, 1996

Most goals - match

8	Jonathan Davies v Papua New Guinea	at Swansea	27 Oct, 1991
7	Johnny Thomas v England	at Tonypandy	20 Apr, 1908
7	Paul Woods v France	at Widnes	15 Jan, 1978
6	Terry Price v England	at Salford	7 Nov, 1968
6	Jonathan Davies v France	at Swansea	22 Mar, 1992
6	Jonathan Davies v England	at Cardiff	1 Feb, 1995

Most points - match

24	Jonathan Davies v Papua New Guinea	at Swansea	27 Oct, 1991
22	Iestyn Harris v France	at Carcassonne	5 June, 1996
15	Jonathan Davies v France	at Swansea	22 Mar, 1992
14	Johnny Thomas v England	at Tonypandy	20 Apr, 1908
14	Paul Woods v France	at Widnes	15 Jan, 1978

Wales Students World Cup Results

1989:

Wales 48 Holland 10
Wales 10 New Zealand 28
Wales 4 France 18

1992:

Wales 20 Fiji 18
Wales 7 Western Samoa 6
Wales 38 Ireland 10
Quarter-final: Wales 57 Fiji 20
Semi-final: Wales 7 Australia 35

1996:

Wales 4 Australia 50
Wales 8 Russia 12
Wales 28 South Africa 30
Plate semi-final: Wales 42 USA 18
Plate final: Wales 20 Ireland 12

Wales 9th out of 12 in the final standings

Club results

All matches listed are League matches, unless shown otherwise:
(i): Challenge Cup   (ii): John Player Trophy   (iii): Tour match   (w): Welsh League
Not all Welsh League results are included. We believe some matches were not played. All the
League matches in the 1980s and 1990s were in the second division.

Ebbw Vale 1907-08

7.9.07	A	Keighley	3-26
14.9.07	H	Salford	0-29
21.9.07	A	Oldham	5-26
28.9.07	H	Bramley	11-13
3.10.07	A	Dewsbury	0-12
12.10.07	H	Merthyr Tydfil	2-0
19.10.07	H	Swinton	10-2
26.10.07	A	Hull	2-22
2.11.07	A	Barrow	2-3
9.11.07	A	Warrington	0-16
16.11.07	A	St Helens	11-11
7.12.07	A	Leeds	7-18
9.12.07	H	Hull	3-0
21.12.07	H	Hull KR	3-5
26.12.07	A	Merthyr Tydfil	2-14
28.12.07	H	Leeds	9-2
11.1.08	A	Salford	2-15
18.1.08	H	Halifax	8-33
25.1.08	H	Dewsbury	14-5
1.2.08	H	N. Zealand (iii)	2-3
8.2.08	H	Barrow	5-10
15.2.08	H	St Helens	3-5
24.2.08	A	Swinton	0-13
25.2.08	A	Halifax	11-15
7.3.08	A	Broughton R	4-20
21.3.08	A	Warrington	9-40
25.3.08	H	Oldham	0-16
28.3.08	A	Bramley	5-5
4.4.08	H	Broughton R	5-10
11.4.08	A	Hull K.R.	4-30
18.4.08	H	Keighley	13-10

Ebbw Vale 1908-09

5.9.08	A	Hunslet	3-21
7.9.08	H	Wigan	5-36
12.9.08	H	Mid-Rhondda	15-7
26.9.08	H	Hunslet	3-10
3.10.08	A	Barry	12-3
10.10.08	H	Bramley	29-14
12.10.08	H	Warrington	10-10
17.10.08	H	Barry	37-0
24.10.08	A	Mid-Rhondda (w)	9-0
31.10.08	H	Rochdale H	11-3

7.11.08	A	Treherbert	3-2
14.11.08	H	Aberdare	23-5
21.11.08	A	Mid-Rhondda	7-2
28.11.08	H	Treherbert	16-2
5.12.08	A	Hull KR	5-18
12.12.08	A	Merthyr Tydfil	2-12
19.12.08	A	Rochdale H	0-13
26.12.08	H	Merthyr Tydfil	0-4
2.1.09	A	Warrington	3-11
9.1.09	H	Hull KR	15-9
18.1.09	H	Australia (iii)	8-9
30.1.09	A	Bramley	8-3
6.2.09	A	Aberdare	19-5
8.2.09	H	Salford	6-20
13.2.09	A	Wigan	3-40
20.2.09	H	Treherbert (w)	18-5
27.2.09	A	Beverley (i)	2-7
17.3.09	A	Salford	14-19
27.3.09	H	Aberdare (w)	30-5
1.4.09	A	Merthyr T (w)	3-0
3.4.09	H	Mid-Rhondda (w)	16-0
10.4.09	H	Barry (w)	38-0
12.4.09	H	Merthyr T (w)	19-2
17.4.09	A	Treherbert (w)	2-9
1.5.09	H	Welsh Lge XIII	20-0

Ebbw Vale 1909-10

18.9.09	A	Broughton R	8-15
20.9.09	H	Treherbert	11-0
25.9.09	H	Wakefield T	0-10
2.10.09	H	Widnes	2-5
4.10.09	H	Oldham	5-13
9.10.09	A	Bradford N	3-7
16.10.09	H	Batley	6-2
23.10.09	A	Leeds	13-25
30.10.09	A	Merthyr T	8-8
6.11.09	A	Treherbert	10-3
20.11.09	H	Merthyr T	11-5
11.12.09	H	Hunslet	8-3
13.12.09	H	Leigh	6-0
18.12.09	A	Widnes	3-0
26.12.09	A	Merthyr T (w)	6-3
3.1.10	A	Oldham	8-30
8.1.10	A	Warrington	5-16
15.1.10	H	Treherbert (w)	11-0

Date		Opponent	Score
12.2.10	A	Hunslet	10-11
14.2.10	A	Batley	0-0
19.2.10	H	Bradford N	8-0
26.2.10	A	Merthyr T (i)	12-7
12.3.10	A	Huddersfield (i)	8-3
19.3.10	A	Salford (i)	2-8
25.3.10	A	Leigh	3-8
26.3.10	A	Wakefield T	0-28
28.3.10	H	Leeds	8-11
6.4.10	H	Warrington	0-3
16.4.10	H	Broughton R	20-8
18.4.10	H	Merthyr T (w)	29-5

Ebbw Vale 1910-11

Date		Opponent	Score
3.9.10	A	Huddersfield	3-21
10.9.10	H	Dewsbury	3-6
17.9.10	A	Hull	0-41
24.9.10	H	Rochdale H	16-7
1.10.10	A	Oldham	10-18
8.10.10	A	Wigan	3-16
15.10.10	H	Runcorn	14-3
22.10.10	H	Swinton	8-2
29.10.10	A	Bramley	8-10
5.11.10	H	Hunslet	15-6
12.11.10	A	Coventry	8-6
19.11.10	H	Halifax	6-0
26.11.10	A	York	3-13
3.12.10	H	Wigan	3-8
10.12.10	H	Bramley	19-5
17.12.10	A	Runcorn	0-3
26.12.10	H	Merthyr Tydfil	25-3
27.12.10	A	Merthyr Tydfil	0-2
31.12.10	A	Widnes	0-19
7.1.11	H	Hull	2-6
14.1.11	A	Rochdale H	0-20
21.1.11	H	Coventry	10-11
28.1.11	A	Swinton	2-5
4.2.11	H	Huddersfield	0-8
18.2.11	A	Batley (i)	2-7
25.2.11	A	Hunslet	2-14
11.3.11	A	Dewsbury	2-18
1.4.11	A	Halifax	0-5
8.4.11	H	Widnes	2-10
15.4.11	H	Oldham	0-5
18.4.11	H	York	14-6

Ebbw Vale 1911-12

Date		Opponent	Score
2.9.11	H	Huddersfield	10-27
9.9.11	A	Hunslet	5-33
11.9.11	A	Leeds	7-34
16.9.11	H	Broughton R	2-4
23.9.11	A	Swinton	8-11
30.9.11	H	Wakefield T	3-3
14.10.11	A	Wigan	0-36
21.10.11	H	Hull	0-0
4.11.11	A	York	5-16
11.11.11	H	St Helens	2-0
18.11.11	H	Dewsbury	2-12
25.11.11	A	Warrington	10-18
2.12.11	H	Halifax	3-27
9.12.11	A	Wakefield T	3-18
16.12.11	H	Warrington	8-8
23.12.11	A	Dewsbury	3-38
30.12.11	A	Huddersfield	5-24
6.1.12	H	Hunslet	0-8
13.1.12	A	St Helens	0-34
27.1.12	H	Swinton	22-5
10.2.12	H	Widnes	3-6
17.2.12	A	Halifax (i)	2-10
24.2.12	A	Broughton R	5-43
9.3.12	H	Leeds	0-5
13.3.12	H	Wigan	6-5
16.3.12	A	Widnes	4-14
23.3.12	H	Hull KR	3-13
28.3.12	A	Hull	14-37
8.4.12	A	Halifax	3-11
9.4.12	A	Hull KR	15-30
20.4.12	H	York	17-0

Merthyr Tydfil 1907-08

Date		Opponent	Score
7.9.07	H	Oldham	6-25
14.9.07	A	Wakefield T	8-35
21.9.07	H	Batley	4-5
28.9.07	A	York	9-17
5.10.07	H	Broughton R	10-14
12.10.07	A	Ebbw Vale	0-2
19.10.07	A	Wigan	3-44
26.10.07	H	Bradford N	6-8
2.11.07	H	N.Zealand (iii)	9-27
9.11.07	A	Runcorn	0-19
16.11.07	H	Runcorn	15-13
23.11.07	A	Rochdale H	0-8
30.11.07	A	Huddersfield	8-8
7.12.07	A	Batley	6-13
21.12.07	H	Widnes	11-5
26.12.07	H	Ebbw Vale	14-2
18.1.08	H	Huddersfield	16-7
25.1.08	A	Oldham	0-20
27.1.08	H	Hunslet	13-9
1.2.08	H	York	12-2
8.2.08	A	Hull KR	7-35
15.2.08	A	Broughton R	3-25

Date	H/A	Opponent	Score
22.2.08	H	Wakefield T	16-2
29.2.08	A	Beverley (i)	15-3
7.3.08	H	Rochdale H	6-11
14.3.08	H	Whitehaven (i)	33-5
21.3.08	A	Bradford N	0-13
23.3.08	A	Hunslet	3-5
28.3.08	A	Leigh (i)	2-8
4.4.08	A	Widnes	0-9
11.4.08	H	Wigan	3-13
13.4.08	H	Hull KR	3-8
17.4.08	A	Leigh	8-17
30.4.08	H	Leigh	39-6

Merthyr Tydfil 1908-09

Date	H/A	Opponent	Score
12.9.08	A	Batley	7-18
19.9.08	H	Barrow	15-12
26.9.08	H	Mid-Rhondda	6-5
3.10.08	A	Huddersfield	5-35
10.10.08	H	Warrington	12-28
17.10.08	A	Mid-Rhondda	3-7
24.10.08	H	Aberdare	24-3
31.10.08	A	Warrington	0-5
7.11.08	H	Barry	21-7
14.11.08	H	Treherbert	9-2
21.11.08	H	Huddersfield	3-3
28.11.08	A	Aberdare	12-9
12.12.08	H	Ebbw Vale	12-2
19.12.08	A	Barrow	9-5
26.12.08	A	Ebbw Vale	4-0
2.1.09	H	Aberdare (w)	24-0
9.1.09	A	Barry	27-2
30.1.09	A	Barry (w)	16-0
13.2.09	A	Treherbert	10-0
27.2.09	H	Australia (iii)	15-13
13.3.09	A	Treherbert	3-13
27.3.09	H	Barry	11-8
1.4.09	H	Ebbw Vale (w)	0-3
3.4.09	H	Batley	5-13
10.4.09	H	Treherbert (w)	19-7
12.4.09	A	Ebbw Vale (w)	2-19
17.4.09	H	Mid-Rhondda (w)	3-10
24.4.09	A	Mid-Rhondda (w)	2-5
Unknown	A	Aberdare (w)	21-5

Merthyr Tydfil 1909-10

Date	H/A	Opponent	Score
4.9.09	H	Hull	0-4
11.9.09	A	Halifax	8-22
25.9.09	A	Treherbert *	7-3
2.10.09	A	Swinton	7-14
9.10.09	H	Wigan	6-25
16.10.09	H	Runcorn	5-13
18.10.09	H	Batley	2-17
23.10.09	A	Rochdale H	0-6
30.10.09	H	Ebbw Vale	8-8
6.11.09	A	Dewsbury	7-9
13.11.09	A	Warrington	0-56
20.11.09	A	Ebbw Vale	5-11
27.11.09	H	Halifax	3-5
4.12.09	A	Bramley	5-8
26.12.09	H	Ebbw Vale (w)	3-6
1.1.10	H	Treherbert (w)	24-0
8.1.10	H	Dewsbury	3-9
5.2.10	A	Wigan	0-67
12.2.10	A	Treherbert *	7-5
26.2.10	H	Ebbw Vale (i)	7-12
5.3.10	A	Hull	0-29
19.3.10	A	Runcorn	8-33
28.3.10	H	Swinton	2-4
7.4.10	H	Warrington	13-6
16.4.10	H	Rochdale H	4-5

* Some records show the match on 12.2.10 as the NRL match, and the match on 25.9.09 as the Welsh League match, others vice versa.

Merthyr Tydfil 1910-11

Date	H/A	Opponent	Score
3.9.10	A	Salford	2-34
10.9.10	H	Leigh	3-13
17.9.10	A	Wakefield T	10-23
24.9.10	H	St Helens	6-17
1.10.10	A	Warrington	3-19
8.10.10	A	Hull KR	13-70
15.10.10	H	Barrow	5-0
22.10.10	H	Bradford N	5-3
29.10.10	A	Leeds	0-19
5.11.10	H	Batley	9-10
12.11.10	A	St Helens	3-13
19.11.10	H	Coventry	4-9
3.12.10	H	Salford	7-2
10.12.10	H	Keighley	10-3
17.12.10	A	Barrow	0-57
26.12.10	A	Ebbw Vale	3-25
27.12.10	H	Ebbw Vale	2-0
31.12.10	A	Coventry (i)	3-18

Aberdare 1908-09

Date	H/A	Opponent	Score
5.9.08	H	Wigan	0-56
19.9.08	A	St Helens	13-46
26.9.08	A	Treherbert	0-8
3.10.08	H	Treherbert	5-13
10.10.08	A	Barry	5-13
17.10.08	H	Wakefield T	0-26

24.10.08	A	Merthyr Tydfil	3-24
31.10.08	H	Treherbert (w)	20-5
7.11.08	A	Mid-Rhondda	2-12
9.11.08	H	Australia (iii)	10-37
14.11.08	A	Ebbw Vale	5-23
21.11.08	H	Barry	43-5
28.11.08	H	Merthyr Tydfil	9-12
5.12.08	A	York	13-36
12.12.08	A	Barry (i)	5-9
19.12.08	H	Mid-Rhondda	3-8
2.1.09	A	Merthyr T (w)	0-24
23.1.09	A	Wigan	5-49
30.1.09	A	Treherbert	15-3
6.2.09	H	Ebbw Vale	5-19
13.2.09	A	Barry (w)	19-2
20.2.09	H	York	5-16
13.3.09	H	St Helens *	18-40
20.3.09	A	Mid-Rhondda (w)	0-9
27.3.09	A	Ebbw Vale (w)	5-30
8.4.09	H	Mid-Rhondda (w)	0-14
Unknown	H	Merthyr T (w)	5-21

* Played at Merthyr

Barry 1908-9

5.9.08	H	Treherbert	6-3
12.9.08	A	Keighley	0-31
19.9.08	H	Leeds	3-17
3.10.08	H	Ebbw Vale	3-12
10.10.08	H	Aberdare	13-5
17.10.08	A	Ebbw Vale	0-37
24.10.08	A	Widnes	6-31
31.10.08	H	Oldham	0-54
7.11.08	A	Merthyr Tydfil	7-21
14.11.08	H	Mid-Rhondda	5-6
21.11.08	A	Aberdare	5-43
28.11.08	H	Keighley	3-23
5.12.08	A	Treherbert	5-11
12.12.08	H	Aberdare(i)	9-5
26.12.08	A	Mid Rhondda (i)	0-2
1.1.09	A	Oldham	0-46
9.1.09	H	Merthyr Tydfil*	2-27
23.2.09	A	Mid Rhondda	6-16
30.1.09	H	Merthyr T (w)	0-16
6.2.09	H	Mid-Rhondda (w)	3-11
13.2.09	H	Aberdare (w)	2-19
20.2.09	H	Widnes	12-6
27.2.09	A	Treherbert (w)	7-7
20.3.09	A	Leeds	0-56
27.3.09	A	Merthyr T (w)	8-11
10.4.09	A	Ebbw Vale (w)	0-38

* Played at Merthyr

Mid-Rhondda 1908-9

5.9.08	H	Bradford N	5-15
12.9.08	A	Ebbw Vale	7-15
19.9.08	H	Treherbert	3-5
26.9.08	A	Merthyr Tydfil	5-6
3.10.08	H	Australia (iii)	6-20
10.10.08	A	Swinton	7-23
17.10.08	H	Merthyr Tydfil	7-3
24.10.08	H	Ebbw Vale (w)	0-9
31.10.08	A	Bradford N	8-29
7.11.08	H	Aberdare	12-2
14.11.08	A	Barry	6-5
21.11.08	H	Ebbw Vale	2-7
28.11.08	A	Hull	6-36
12.12.08	H	Treherbert (i)	8-7
19.12.08	A	Aberdare	8-3
26.12.08	H	Barry (i)	2-0
2.1.09	A	Treherbert	0-0
23.1.09	H	Barry	16-6
30.1.09	H	Broughton R	0-6
6.2.09	A	Barry (w)	11-3
13.2.09	H	Swinton	7-16
20.2.09	H	Hull	7-15
27.2.09	A	Hunslet (i)	5-25
20.3.27	H	Aberdare (w)	9-0
24.3.09	A	Broughton R	5-22
27.3.09	A	Treherbert (w)	15-7
3.4.09	A	Ebbw Vale (w)	0-16
8.4.09	A	Aberdare (w)	14-0
17.4.09	A	Merthyr T (w)	10-3
24.4.09	H	Merthyr T (w)	5-2
26.4.09	H	Treherbert (w)	6-8

Treherbert 1908-09

5.9.08	A	Barry	3-6
12.9.08	H	Halifax	6-29
19.9.08	A	Mid-Rhondda	5-3
26.9.08	H	Aberdare	8-0
3.10.08	A	Aberdare	13-5
10.10.08	H	Runcorn	2-15
24.10.08	H	Leigh	6-14
31.10.08	A	Aberdare (w)	5-20
7.11.08	H	Ebbw Vale	2-3
14.11.08	A	Merthyr Tydfil	2-9
21.11.08	A	Halifax	5-23
28.11.08	A	Ebbw Vale	2-16
5.12.08	H	Barry	11-5
12.12.08	A	Mid-Rhondda (i)	7-8
17.12.08	H	Australia (iii)	3-6
19.12.08	H	Dewsbury	2-15
2.1.09	H	Mid-Rhondda	0-0

9.1.09	A	Leigh	6-11
23.1.09	A	Runcorn	8-24
30.1.09	H	Aberdare	15-3
6.2.09	A	Dewsbury	0-25
13.2.09	H	Merthyr Tydfil	0-10
20.2.09	A	Ebbw Vale (w)	5-18
27.2.09	H	Barry (w)	7-7
13.3.09	H	Merthyr T (w)	13-3
27.3.09	H	Mid-Rhondda (w)	7-15
10.4.09	A	Merthyr T (w)	7-19
17.4.09	H	Ebbw Vale(w)	9-2
26.4.09	A	Mid Rhondda (w)	8-6

25.9.09	H	Merthyr T *	3-7
2.10.09	H	Oldham	3-26
9.10.09	A	St Helens	12-36
23.10.09	A	Keighley	3-20
6.11.09	H	Ebbw Vale	3-10
18.11.09	H	Salford	2-19
20.11.09	H	Huddersfield	3-27
27.11.09	H	Keighley	3-6
22.1.10	A	Huddersfield	0-50
1.1.10	A	Merthyr T (w)	0-24
12.2.10	H	Merthyr T *	5-7
9.4.10	A	Oldham	13-54

* Some records show the match on 12.2.10 as the NRL match, and the match on 25.9.09 as the Welsh League match, others vice versa.

Treherbert 1909-10

11.9.09	H	Hull KR	10-22
20.9.09	A	Ebbw Vale	0-11

Pontypridd 1926-27

4.9.26	H	Oldham	15-33
11.9.26	H	Swinton	5-28
18.9.26	A	Salford	7-20
25.9.26	H	Leigh	3-11
2.10.26	A	St Helens	13-35
9.10.26	H	Widnes	17-15
16.10.26	A	Wigan	15-23
23.10.26	A	Swinton	3-20
30.10.26	H	Leeds	7-8
6.11.26	H	Rochdale H	11-10
13.11.26	A	Wigan Highfield	0-0
20.11.26	H	Wigan Highfield	10-3
27.11.26	A	Barrow	3-8
11.12.26	H	St Helens Recs	0-5
18.12.26	A	Broughton R	5-8
25.12.26	H	N. Zealand (iii)	8-17
27.12.26	A	Leigh	3-12
1.1.27	H	Barrow	9-3
8.1.27	A	St Helens Recs	6-13
15.1.27	H	Warrington	8-13
22.1.27	H	Wigan	5-13
5.2.27	A	Widnes	5-6

12.2.27	A	Widnes (i)	2-23
17.2.27	A	Hull	0-26
19.2.27	H	Hull	18-8
5.3.27	A	Rochdale H	0-16
12.3.27	H	Salford	13-5
19.3.27	A	Batley	7-16
26.3.27	H	St Helens	5-10
9.4.27	A	Leeds	6-27
16.4.27	A	Warrington	8-21
18.4.27	H	Broughton R	3-17
23.4.27	H	Batley	10-8
25.4.27	A	Oldham	3-6

Pontypridd 1927-28

27.8.27	A	Leigh	0-17
3.9.27	H	Bradford N	8-11
10.9.27	A	Wigan Highfield	7-20
17.9.27	H	Rochdale H	5-14
24.9.27	A	Castleford	6-26
1.10.27	A	St Helens Recs	0-40
8.10.27	H	Barrow	13-7
22.10.27	H	Oldham	5-14

Cardiff 1951-52

18.8.51	A	Hull KR	13-39
22.8.51	H	Widnes	10-27
25.8.51	H	Hull	10-31
29.8.51	A	Wigan	5-72
8.9.51	H	Barrow	13-66
14.9.51	A	Doncaster	10-17
15.9.51	A	Hunslet	15-40
22.9.51	H	Bradford N	12-52
29.9.51	A	Workington T	8-30

6.10.51	A	Belle Vue R	14-25
13.10.51	H	Castleford	5-26
20.10.51	H	Wakefield T	8-31
27.10.51	H	York	12-6
3.11.51	A	Leigh	15-22
10.11.51	H	Leigh	16-19
17.11.51	A	Widnes	5-30
24.11.51	H	Workington T	8-18
1.12.51	A	Castleford	8-16
12.12.51	H	N. Zealand (iii)	10-18

15.12.51	H	Hull KR	7-10	23.2.52	H	Rochdale H	8-4
22.12.51	A	Barrow	0-32	8.3.52	A	Rochdale H	5-16
25.12.51	A	Liverpool	11-0	22.3.52	H	Liverpool	18-5
26.12.51	H	Swinton	6-18	29.3.52	A	Swinton	5-38
29.12.51	H	Belle Vue R	8-27	5.4.52	H	Doncaster	5-21
5.1.52	H	Hull	3-23	12.4.52	A	Bramley	2-33
12.1.52	A	Bradford N	5-38	14.4.52	A	York	12-31
19.1.52	H	Hunslet	3-39	15.4.52	H	Bramley *	19-16
26.1.52	A	Wakefield T	24-47	26.4.52	H	Wigan **	14-59
9.2.52	H	Dewsbury (i)	7-7				
16.2.52	A	Dewsbury (i)	0-16				

* At Headingley
** At Maindy Stadium, Cardiff

Cardiff Blue Dragons 1981-82

30.8.81	H	Salford	21-26	29.8.82	H	Rochdale	15-10
6.9.81	A	Keighley	6-38	12.9.82	A	Hunslet	17-17
13.9.81	H	Hunslet	32-19	19.9.82	H	Whitehaven	1-20
20.9.81	A	Huyton	25-4	26.9.82	A	York	13-20
27.9.81	H	Carlisle	12-7	3.10.82	H	Salford	18-28
4.10.81	A	Doncaster	19-12	10.10.82	H	Fulham	10-15
11.10.81	H	Halifax	21-31	17.10.82	A	Batley	16-20
18.10.81	A	Carlisle (ii)	7-14	31.10.82	A	Huyton	8-15
23.10.81	A	Salford	17-14	7.11.82	A	Swinton	12-2
15.11.81	H	Huyton	23-14	14.11.82	H	Huddersfield	13-17
22.11.81	A	Huddersfield	11-9	21.11.82	A	Whitehaven	8-15
29.11.81	H	Bramley	17-12	5.12.82	H	Rochdale (ii)	7-11
6.12.81	A	Batley	19-34	12.12.82	A	Wakefield	27-25
3.1.82	H	Rochdale H	15-11	2.1.83	H	Blackpool	8-5
24.1.82	H	Doncaster	14-12	9.1.83	A	Bramley	8-31
31.1.82	H	Oldham	15-33	16.1.83	H	Dewsbury	26-5
7.2.82	A	Oldham	7-10	23.1.83	A	Salford	8-12
14.2.82	H	Widnes (i)	8-19	30.1.83	A	Wigan (i)	4-14
21.2.82	A	Rochdale H	12-12	6.2.83	H	Hunslet	24-28
28.2.82	H	Dewsbury	26-4	20.2.83	H	Swinton	40-12
7.3.82	H	Keighley	13-15	6.3.83	A	Keighley	12-20
14.3.82	H	Batley	34-5	13.3.83	H	York	33-14
21.3.82	A	Halifax	22-10	16.3.83	A	Doncaster	33-10
26.3.82	A	Swinton	14-21	20.3.83	H	Huyton	30-5
28.3.82	H	Workington T	20-35	27.3.83	A	Dewsbury	15-6
4.4.82	A	Dewsbury	5-18	3.4.83	H	Doncaster	25-11
9.4.82	A	Carlisle	21-33	10.4.83	A	Blackpool	9-4
11.4.82	A	Workington T	8-36	17.4.83	H	Keighley	32-11
16.4.82	A	Hunslet	10-13	20.4.83	A	Wakefield	25-12
18.4.82	H	Blackpool B	32-6	24.4.83	A	Rochdale	17-17
24.4.82	A	Blackpool B	18-8	26.4.83	H	Bramley	10-16
25.4.82	A	Bramley	11-16	6.5.83	A	Fulham	20-14
3.5.82	H	Huddersfield	22-19				
9.5.82	H	Swinton	22-14				

Cardiff Blue Dragons 1983-84

21.8.83	A	Kent Invicta	31-12
27.8.83	H	Bramley	27-10

Cardiff Blue Dragons 1982-83

22.8.82	H	Batley	32-2	10.9.83	H	Carlisle	21-16
25.8.82	A	Huddersfield	7-5	18.9.83	A	Hunslet	18-40
				24.9.83	H	Huddersfield	26-26

2.10.83	A	Doncaster	36-8	26.2.84	A	Blackpool B	25-32
9.10.83	H	Dewsbury	26-14	4.3.84	H	Blackpool B	19-18
16.10.83	A	Huyton	23-18	11.3.84	H	Workington T	20-22
23.10.83	A	York	16-50	18.3.84	A	Halifax	20-22
30.10.83	H	Keighley	6-11	25.3.84	A	Dewsbury	16-12
6.11.83	H	Rochdale (ii)	41-6	6.4.84	H	Rochdale	27-5
13.11.83	A	Batley	15-21	8.4.84	H	Batley	40-16
20.11.83	H	Huyton (ii)	38-12	11.4.84	H	Kent Invicta	21-12
27.11.83	A	Leigh (ii)	8-12	15.4.84	A	Carlisle	10-14
4.12.83	H	Swinton	12-25	20.4.84	H	Doncaster	32-21
18.12.83	H	Halifax	26-18	23.4.84	A	Workington T	30-38
1.1.84	A	Rochdale	4-7	24.4.84	A	Keighley	30-6
8.1.84	H	Barrow	14-26	29.4.84	H	Huyton *	34-16
15.1.84	A	Huddersfield	10-14	2.5.84	A	Bramley	20-25
22.1.84	H	Hunslet	6-34	7.5.84	A	Swinton	16-44
12.2.84	H	Hull (i)	6-34	13.5.84	H	York	26-28
19.2.84	A	Barrow	7-36	* At Ebbw Vale			

Bridgend Blue Dragons 1984-85

9.9.84	H	Swinton	16-28	3.2.85	H	Keighley	15-38
23.9.84	H	Dewsbury	13-23	24.2.85	H	Sheffield E	28-12
30.984	A	Salford	18-64	3.3.85	A	Keighley	4-40
7.10.84	H	Rochdale H	1-22	8.3.85	A	Fulham	8-23
21.10.84	H	Mansfield M	9-35	10.3.85	H	Runcorn H	8-28
28.10.84	A	Sheffield E	10-26	17.3.85	A	Doncaster	6-38
4.11.84	H	Salford	17-38	24.3.85	H	Batley	9-14
11.11.84	H	Whitehaven	10-32	27.3.85	A	Dewsbury	3-48
18.1184	H	Castleford (ii) *	4-42	31.3.85	A	Mansfield M	18-48
25.11.84	A	Runcorn H	0-28	5.4.85	A	Rochdale H	0-58
2.12.84	A	Blackpool B	10-43	8.4.85	H	Fulham	8-32
9.12.84	H	Carlisle	0-28	14.4.85	H	Blackpool B	17-42
16.12.84	A	Swinton	12-54	21.4.85	H	Doncaster	10-28
20.1.85	A	Batley	0-32	26.4.85	A	Whitehaven	2-52
27.1.85	A	Leeds (i)	6-68	28.4.85	A	Carlisle	6-12
				* At Castleford			

South Wales 1996

31.3.96	H	Hull KR *	8-70	7.7.96	H	Barrow **	48-16
5.4.96	A	Prescot	24-22	14.7.96	A	Doncaster	18-24
8.4.96	H	Bramley ***	22-18	21.7.96	H	Leigh **	30-22
12.4.96	A	Barrow	4-16	28.7.96	A	Chorley	18-16
21.4.96	H	Doncaster *	12-22	4.8.96	H	York **	20-16
5.5.96	A	Leigh	23-20	11.8.96	A	Hunslet	21-14
12.5.96	H	Chorley *	58-0	18.8.96	A	Swinton	16-26
17.5.96	A	York	26-54	25.8.96	A	Carlisle	6-58
26.5.96	H	Hunslet *	19-26	* At Aberavon RUFC			
2.6.96	H	Swinton **	8-26	** At Cardiff RUFC			
8.6.96	H	Carlisle ** x	37-18	*** At Morfa Stadium, Swansea.			
16.6.96	A	Hull KR	16-40	x Played before Sheffield versus St Helens			
23.6.96	H	Prescot **	50-18	Super League match.			
30.6.96	A	Bramley	44-6				

Club top scorers

(Welsh League matches are not included)

Ebbw Vale

1907-08   *T:* T. Davies 9. *G:* Carpenter 7, T. Davies 7.
1908-09   *T:* Llewellyn 19, Higgins 6. *G:* D. Davies 11.
1909-10   *T:* Llewellyn 13, Smith 5. *G:* D. Davies 15.
1910-11   *T:* Llewellyn 22, Burgham 4, Roberts 4.   *G:* Roberts 10.
1911-12   *T:* Llewellyn 13, Cox 4, Jenkins 4. *G:* Davies 17.

Merthyr Tydfil

1907-08   *T:* Cowmeadow 12, D.B. Davies 11, Rees 10. *G:* S. James 14.
1908-09   *T:* Cowmeadow 14, Smith 5, S. James 5, D.B. Davies 5.   *G:* S. James 19.
1909-10   *T:* Harris 3, D.J. Rees 3. *G:* T. Thomas 8.
1910-11   *T:* P. Thomas 4, Lewis 3. *G:* S. James 14.

Aberdare

1908-09   *T:* Loosemore 5, Whittle 5. *G:* D.J. Rees 23.

Barry

1908-09   *T:* Roberts 5, Chick 4, Kirby 3.   *G:* Dow 4.

Mid-Rhondda

1908-09   *T:* J.N. Jones 5, Matthews 5, P. Griffiths 4. *G:* E.D. Rees 8.

Treherbert

1908-09   *T:* Edwards 6. *G:* Fitzgerald 15.
1909-10   *T:* Francis 6. *G:* Fitzgerald 5.

Pontypridd

1926-27   *T:* Loveluck 10, Rhodes 5, Fairfax 5. *G:* Shea 18, Mills 10.
1927-28   *T:* Loveluck 3, Kay 3. *G:* Mills 3.

Cardiff

1951-52   *T:* McNally 8, Douglas 5, Rosser 5, Russell 5.   *G:* Ward 34, Russell 19.

Cardiff Blue Dragons

1981-82   *T:* Fleay 15, Fenwick 13. *G:* Fenwick 108. *DG:* Hallett 3.
1982-83   *T:* David 26, Barwood 12. *G:* Fenwick 109. *DG:* Hallett 8.
1983-84   *T:* David 22, O'Brien 16. *G:* Hallett 111. *DG:* Hallett 29.

Bridgend Blue Dragons

1984-85   *T:* Camilleri 4, G. Davies 3. *G:* Alred 43. *DG:* Alred 5.

South Wales

1996   *T:* Marshall 15, Currier 14. *G:* Bebb 45. *DG:* Hatton 4.

Glamorgan and Monmouthshire County Championship 1927-1931

	Opponents	Score	Venue	Crowd
26 Sep, 1927	Yorkshire	12-20	Hunslet	Unknown
	T: Ring, Flynn. *G:* Sullivan 3			
15 Oct, 1927	Cumberland	12-18	Pontypridd	Unknown
	T: Ring, Maidment. *G:* Sullivan 3			
12 Nov, 1927	Lancashire	12- 7	Pontypridd	Unknown
	T: Ring, Parker. *G:* Sullivan 3			
20 Oct, 1928	Cumberland	5-15	Whitehaven	5,200
	T: Sullivan. *G:* Sullivan			
8 Dec, 1928	Lancashire	10-25	Leigh	8,000
	T: Ring, Walker. *G:* Sullivan 2			
15 Apr, 1929	Yorkshire	17-22	Cardiff	10,000
	T: Ring, Sullivan, White. *G:* Sullivan 4			
11 Dec, 1929	Australia	9-39	Cardiff	2,500
	T: Rosser. *G:* Sullivan 3			
21 Dec, 1929	Cumberland	6-14	Cardiff	Unknown
	T: W.A. Williams, Evans			
27 Feb, 1930	Yorkshire	13- 6	Hunslet	2,000
	T: Rosser, Ring, White. *G:* Sullivan 2			
12 Apr, 1930	Lancashire	3-29	Warrington	9,000
	T: E. Williams.			
22 Nov, 1930	Lancashire	14-10	Salford	4,000
	T: Maidment, Risman. *G:* Sullivan 4.			
21 Mar, 1931	Cumberland	19-12	Whitehaven	5,000
	T: Jenkins 2, Lloyd. *G:* Sullivan 5			
15 Apr, 1931	Yorkshire	12-33	Halifax	1,500
	T: Risman, Thompson. *G:* Sullivan 3			

Most goals	Jim Sullivan 33
Most tries	Johnny Ring 6
Most points	Jim Sullivan 72
Most appearances	Jim Sullivan 12

Played 13 Won 4 Lost 9 For 144 Against 250

Bibliography:

Brian Clarke	Murphy's Law
Ken Dalby	Nothing but the Best
Trevor Delaney (ed)	Code 13 (No.9) and others
Trevor Delaney	The Grounds of Rugby League
	The International Grounds of Rugby League
Robert Gate	An Illustrated History: Rugby League
	Gone North Volumes I & II
	The Struggle for the Ashes II
Ron Gethin	Merthyr RFC Centenary Year Brochure
Gareth Harris &	
Alan Evans	Pontypridd RFC The Early Years
John M. Jenkins, Duncan	
Price & Timothy Auty	Who's who of Welsh International Rugby Players
Lewis Jones	
& J.R. Jones	King of Rugger
Joe Latus	Hard road to the Top: The Clive Sullivan Story
Keith Macklin	The Story of Rugby League
Phil Melling	Man of Amman
Geoffrey Moorhouse	A People's Game: The Official History of Rugby League
Tony Pocock	Stones Bitter Rugby League Yearbook
Pontypridd Historical	
Centre	Sport in Pontypridd
Gus Risman	Rugby Renegade
Irvin Saxton	History of Rugby League (various volumes)
David Smith	
& Gareth Williams	Fields of Praise
David Watkins	
& Brian Dobbs	The David Watkins Story
David Watkins &	
David Parry-Jones (ed)	David Watkins: An Autobiography
Gareth Williams (ed)	1905 and all that
Graham Williams	The Code War
Jack Winstanley	The Billy Boston Story

Magazines and newspapers

Athletic News
Glamorgan County Times
League Express
Merthyr Express
Open Rugby
Pontypridd Observer
Rugby Leaguer
Rugby League Gazette
Super League Week
Western Mail

**IF YOU ENJOYED "TRIES IN THE VALLEYS", YOU WILL
CERTAINLY ENJOY THE TWO VOLUMES OF
"GONE NORTH: WELSHMEN IN RUGBY LEAGUE" BY ROBERT GATE**

Volume 1 contains, amongst others, profiles of Wattie Davies, Jim Sullivan, Roy Francis, Trevor Foster, Tommy Harris, Billy Boston, Colin Dixon, Kel Coslett, Jim Mills and John Mantle. Price £6.50

Volume 2 contains, amongst others, profiles of Ben Gronow, Johnny Rogers, Joe Thompson, Gus Risman, Lewis Jones, David Watkins, Garfield Owen, Clive Sullivan, John Bevan and Maurice Richards. Price £9.99

Both volumes are well illustrated and contain substantial statistics sections. Volumes 1 and 2 are available individually (post free) or can be ordered as a pair for £13.50 (post free).

Also available: "The Struggle For The Ashes II" - the history of Anglo-Australian test matches 1908 to date. A record of every Ashes test match, profusely illustrated. Price £12.99 (post free)

All the above titles are available from:
Robert Gate, Mount Pleasant Cottage, Ripponden Bank, Ripponden, Sowerby Bridge HX6 4JL
Tel: 01422-823074

Please make cheques payable to R.E. Gate

SPECIAL OFFER:
All three books for £20 (post free)

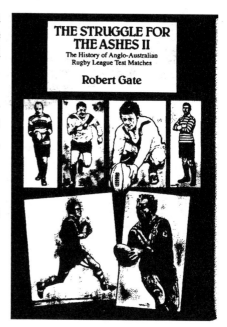

THE STRUGGLE FOR THE ASHES II
The History of Anglo-Australian Rugby League Test Matches
Robert Gate

PUBLISHER'S SALE
The International Grounds of Rugby League: £5.95 (was £15.95)
Rugby Disunion - Broken Time: £2.95 (was £12.95)
Code 13 Journals: 1 & 3: £1.00 each, 7 - 9 and 11 - 17 80p each.

All prices include p & p (UK only)

Order from: Trevor Delaney, 6, Elmwood Terrace, Keighley BD22 7DP
                  Tel: 01535-215550

Cheques payable to T.R. Delaney

Don't miss out on

Rugby League's
Biggest Selling Quality
Weekly Newspapers

RUGBY
League Express

Every Monday

Every Friday

Subscriptions: UK rates: £25 for 20 issues, £40 for 40 issues, £55 for 60 issues
Please state which newspaper you would like to receive.
To receive both publications simply multiply the cost by two.
Send subscription orders with cheque - payable to "League Publications Ltd" - to:
League Publications Ltd., Wellington House, Briggate, Brighouse, West Yorkshire, HD6 1DN
Tel: 01484 401895 Fax: 01484 401995
Email: leaguex@legend.co.uk

SUBSCRIBE TO

Guarantee your copy of **OPEN RUGBY** by post every month. It's the easy way to ensure you don't miss any of the Rugby League action **OPEN RUGBY** style.

Our subscription rates (for 12 consecutive issues) are:

Within the U.K	£29.00
Europe(Airmail)	£36.00
Zone I (Airmail) Africa,	
Americas, Middle East	£47.00
Zone 2 Asia, Australasia:	
(Airmail)	£49.00
(Surface mail)	£34.00

Apply to:
OPEN RUGBY
Munro House
York Street
Leeds LS9 8AP

Credit Card orders charged in Sterling.

Call: 0113-245-1560
Fax: 0113-242-6255

Cheques payable to **OPEN RUGBY**.

To book your subscription, write clearly your name and full address, and tell us which issue (number and/or date) you wish your subscription to start with. Subscriptions can be back-dated to include previous issues.

Credit card payments by VISA, ACCESS and MASTERCARD accepted. When ordering by post or fax using a credit card, write clearly the number of your card and expiry date, plus your name and signature.

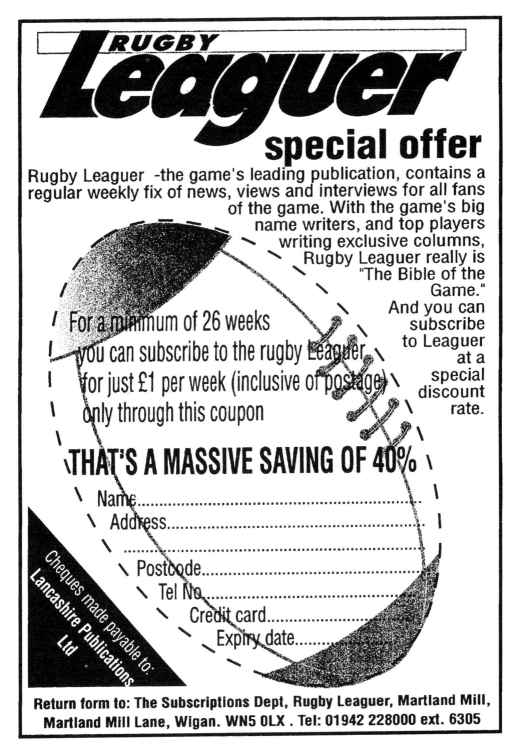

RUGBY Leaguer

special offer

Rugby Leaguer -the game's leading publication, contains a regular weekly fix of news, views and interviews for all fans of the game. With the game's big name writers, and top players writing exclusive columns, Rugby Leaguer really is "The Bible of the Game." And you can subscribe to Leaguer at a special discount rate.

For a minimum of 26 weeks you can subscribe to the rugby Leaguer for just £1 per week (inclusive of postage) only through this coupon

THAT'S A MASSIVE SAVING OF 40%

Name...

Address...

....

Postcode..

Tel No..

Credit card...

Expiry date...

Cheques made payable to: Lancashire Publications Ltd

Return form to: The Subscriptions Dept, Rugby Leaguer, Martland Mill, Martland Mill Lane, Wigan. WN5 0LX . Tel: 01942 228000 ext. 6305

Sports Books from London League Publications Ltd

The Sin Bin

A new collection of Rugby League cartoons and
humour. Caricatures of leading people in the game
... the Adventures of Mo ... The Flatcappers... Bath v Wigan
... Life Down South ... and much more. **Price: £5.95.**
Published in October 1996.

Touch and Go
A History of Professional Rugby League in London

From the clubs in the 1930s to the London Broncos. Includes all the
international matches played in London, and the first Wembley Cup Final.
. Many photos and illustrations, and comprehensive statistics.
Published August 1995. 380 pages for just £9.00.
SPECIAL OFFER: £5.00 ONLY.

From Arundel to Zimbabwe
**A Cricket Followers' Guide to British and
International Cricket Grounds**

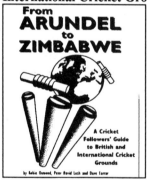

Detailed information about all British First class grounds, and
international test grounds. Over 30 photos, local maps and
descriptions of grounds.
Cost: £6.50. Published in April 1997.

BOXING SHADOWS:
1,500 BOXING QUIZ QUESTIONS
Test your boxing knowledge! Questions for all levels of
knowledge. Written by boxing quiz specialist Ralph Oates.
Published in September 1997 at £6.95. **SPECIAL OFFER:**
£6.50 post free.

To order any of the above books, make cheques payable to:
London League Publications Ltd, and send to: London League
Publications Ltd, PO Box 10441, London E14 0SB. Special
offers for readers of this book: All books post free. **Order all
four books for only £20.00**

THE SPECIALIST SPORTS BOOKSHOP

Europe's Leading Sports Bookshop
with branches in London & Manchester

Stocking rugby league books, magazines, & videos
from all over the world

WE ARE THE RUGBY LEAGUE SPECIALISTS

We have a worldwide mail order service
and now

WE'RE ON THE WEB

You can order direct from the largest fully searchable
database of rugby league books & videos in Europe

to find out more just visit us at

www.sportspages.co.uk

or

call in at

**BARTON SQUARE
ST ANN'S SQUARE
MANCHESTER M2 7HA**

**TEL: 0161 832 8530
FAX: 0161 832 9391**

**CAXTON WALK
94-96 CHARING CROSS ROAD
LONDON WC2H 0JG**

**TEL: 0171 240 9604
FAX: 0171 836 0104**

**OPENING HOURS
LONDON
9.30AM - 7.00PM
MONDAY-SATURDAY**

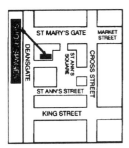

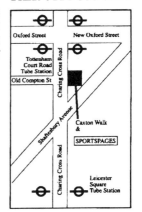

**OPENING HOURS
MANCHESTER
9.30AM - 6.00PM
MONDAY -SATURDAY**

IF YOU LOVE SPORT YOU'LL LOVE SPORTSPAGES

'EYUP OLD COCK!

- Have you ever felt frustrated because you don't feel represented as a supporter of Rugby League?
- Do you have a point of view you'd like to make but don't feel that there's anywhere for you to make it?
- Do you want to be consulted about how Super League is run?
- Are you tired of being labelled a flatcapped whippet fancier by the press, just because you like Rugby League?
- Do you want to receive TGG!, the world's best Rugby League fanzine, before anyone else?

Maybe you do.
So maybe you ought to join the R.L.S.A. now, and become part of the only national RL Supporters Association in the UK.

OUR AGENDA
- to democratically represent the views of members ·
- to campaign for supporters' opinions to he heard at all levels in the game
- to encourage friendship between supporters of all clubs and countries
- to work for the promotion and development of Rugby League

For more information please write to :

The Rugby League Supporters' Association
5 Wesley Street, Cutsyke, Castleford,
West Yorkshire WFIO 5HQ

Six years experience of working for supporters

LONDON CALLING!

To know what's going on with the London Broncos and the game in the south, you need to read London Calling!
Subscribe to the game's longest running club fanzine:

5 issues: £5.00
10 issues: £9.00
15 issues: £13.00

Send your subscription to:
London League Publications Ltd
P.O. Box 10441
London E14 0SB
(Cheques payable to London Calling!)